INDIAN PATHS - VILLAGES
- COLONIAL FORTS.

INDIAN VILLAGES.
COLONIAL FORTS.
INDIAN PATHS.
MILITARY ROADS.

Cumberland County, Pennsylvania Quarter Session Dockets 1750-1785

Diane E. Greene, AG
Accredited Genealogist
(Eastern States)

CLEARFIELD

Printed for
Clearfield Company, Inc. by
Genealogical Publishing Co., Inc.
Baltimore, Maryland
2000

Reprinted for
Clearfield Company, Inc. by
Genealogical Publishing Co., Inc.
Baltimore, Maryland
2001

International Standard Book Number: 0-8063-4965-4
Made in the United States of America

Contents

Preface

While on a research trip I discovered extracts of Cumberland County, Pennsylvania Quarter Session Dockets at the Coyle Free Library, 102 North Main Street, Chambersburg, PA. They are in a brown envelope, R 974.844 Fr.

"John G. Orr 1925," handwritten on the first page of the typewritten extracts. He described his work as follows: "The following pages contain certain copies and extracts made from the records of the Court of Quarter Sessions of Cumberland County as they relate to transactions affecting the territory outside of its present bounds." Cumberland County, Pennsylvania, was created from Lancaster County in 1750 and became the parent county of Bedford (created 1771), Mifflin (created 1789) and Perry (created 1820) counties.

When I began to index these records, I quickly discovered that Mr. Orr only extracted those concerning present-day Franklin County. Using Orr's extracts as a basis, I added additional "missing" information from a microfilm of the original records at the Family History Library in Salt Lake City, utah (film #1011065).

In July 1750, the county seat of Cumberland, was Shippensburg, and court cases included indictments for carrying spirits and liquor to the Indians, assault and battery, larceny, forgery, and extortion. Unfortunately, details inferred about some cases is very vague. In the 1770s, Carlisle was the county seat, and the court saw a variety of misdemeanors and felonies including horse thefts, bastardy, fornication, and trespass. Township officers were listed, as were cases dealing with tavern licenses, petitions for new roads, and jurors.

The reader is warned to check all variant spellings when using the index, as the microfilm was sometimes difficult to read. Also, Docket 5, labeled(1772-1776), actually covers records through 1785.

Quarter Session Docket 1 1750-1761

Page 1

At Shippenburg, Cumberland County, 24 July 1750, before Samuel Smith and his brethren keepers of the peace. The sheriff returned the following persons sworn in grand jury; William Magaw, John Petter, John Mitchell, John Davison, __ Dunning, John Holidey, J. Lindsay, Adam Hoop, James Forsyth, Thomas Bro__, George Brown, John Reynolds, Robert Harris, Thomas Urie, Charles Murray, James Brown, Robert Meck.

Domus Rex vs. Bridget Hagan
Larceny. Not guilty, defendant submits to Court, ordered that Bridget Hagan restore the sum of 6 pounds, 17 shillings and six pence unto Jacob Long, the owner and make fine to the Governor in the like sum, pay the cost of prosecution, 15 lashes on her bare back at the public whipping post, stand committed until the fines and fees are paid.

Domus Rex vs. James Woods
Assault and battery. Fined __ and be committed till the fine and penalty are paid.

Domus Rex vs. Robert Wilson
Keeping a public house without license.

Page 2

At Shippensburg, 22 January 1751, before Samuel Smith and his associate justices. The sheriff, John Potter Esq., returned the following persons for the Grand Inquest; Daniel Williams, William Chosena, John Forsyth, Patrick Juss (?), Thomas Poe, Anthony Thompson, Robert McCoy, William Sewry, William Crofts, Alexander Miller, Henry Pauling, Giles Shenker, Joseph Culberson, John Mushett, Oliver Wallis, Nathaniel Wilson.

Page 3

Joseph Neillson vs James Brown
That Jos. Neilson be of good behavour and observe and keep all the laws of this province relating to Indian __ during the __ of his licence.

Domus Rex vs John McCallister
Indictment for carry of liquor to Indians. Defendant pleads guilty.

Domus Rex vs Joseph Neillson
Assault and battery.

Domus Rex vs Samuel Moorehead
Indictment for carrying spirits and liquor to the Indians.

Page 4
The King vs Alexander Roddye
Alexr. Roddy in £100, conditioned the defendant appear at sessions July 1750.

The King vs William White, Richd. Rankin, David Heidleston
W. White in £100, Richard Rankin in £100, David Heidleston in £100,
conditioned that the defendant appear at this sessions July 1750.

The King vs James Murray, John Scott, Henry Gass, John Lelaugh, George
Cowan
Jointly & severally each in £100.

The King vs John Erwyn, George Cohoon
Each in £100, that the defendant appeared sessions, defendant made default.

Page 5
The King vs George Galloway, Wm. Galloway
Each in £100, that defendant appear at this session, July term 1750. Defendant
being solemnly called made default.

The King vs Abraham Slack, James Blair, Moses Moor, Arthur Dunlap,
Alexandr. McCareby, David Lewis, Adam McCarby, Felix Doyle.
Jointly & severally tenant each in £100, conditioned that the defendant appear
at this sessions July term 1750. Defendant being solemnly called made default,
except Arthur Dunlap, Alexander McCarly and Felix Doyle who are cont. on
their recognizance till next term.

The King vs John Watson, Nichos. DeLong, Samuel Perry, John Charlton
jointly each in 100, conditioned that the defendants appear at session.
Defendants being solemnly called made default.

Page 6
Hermanus Alrichs Esqr produced to the Court a __ under the hand of the
Honrable James Hamilton Esqr. appointing him the said Hermanus Clerk of the
Peace. The same was read and allowed and ordered to be recorded.

Page 7
At Shippensburg, 23 October, before Samuel Smith and his associate justices.
The sheriff John Petter returns the following list of grand jurors; William
McGaw, James Silver, Henry Johnston, John Mitchell, Charles McGill,
Matthew Patton, Robert Barnet, Alexander Culbertson, Robert Miller, John
Carr, John Winter, William Dunwoody, John Smith, John Nesbit, William
Parker, Robert Patrick.

The King vs Thos. Urie
Assault.

The King vs John Mushet
Indictment for selling liquor with [out] licence.
Defendant being charged submits to the Court.

Page 8
The King vs Saml. Saunders
The Defendant appearing according to his recognizance and no prosecution
being exhibited him as charged on matter of Mr. Cross of Council for the
defendant, he is discharged from his recognizance.

Page 9
The King vs Adam Masaker, William Patrick
Jointly each £50, that the defendant appear at this session and that he shall
behave himself to his Majesties subjects during that time.

The King vs William Karr, John Erwyn
Jointly each £100, that William Karr appear at this session. Defendant being
solemnly called made default.

The King vs Abraham Erwin, John Erwin, Nathaniel Willson, Joseph Mitchell,
conditioned that Abraham Erwin appear at this session. Defendant being
solemnly called made default.

The King vs Mary Ramage, William Karr
Jointly each £100, condition that Mary Ramage appear at this session.
Defendant being solemnly called made default.

Page 10
The King vs James Boyd
Condition that James Boyd appear at this Session

Page 11
At Shippensburgh, 27 January 1750, before Saml. Smith and his associates
Justices. The Sheriff, John Potter returns following grand inquest; Daniel
Williams, Wm. Chisno_ (?), John Forsyth, Patrick Jack, Thomas Poe, Anthony
Thompson, Robert McCoy, Wm. Lawry, Wm. Cross, Alexander Miller, Henry
Pousling (?), Giles Shankse (?), John Marshall, Joseph Culberson, Oliver
Wallis, Nathanl. Wilson.

4   Cumberland County, PA Quarter Session Court Dockets

The King vs James Gabbie.(?)
Forgery. Saith he is not guilty. Jury; John Rogers, James Lindsay, David Scott,
Thos. Barr, Joseph M__, Henry Johnson, Andrew Finley, James Norris, Wm.
Barr, __, Wm. Rankin, Wm. Ramsay, Wm. Moore, Wm. Mc C__, James
Chambers, Chas. McGill, Jam. Culberson and Robt. __, being elected, tried and
sworn do say that James Gabbis is not guilty.

The King vs Josiah Ramago (?)
Forgery.

Page 12
The King vs Abraham Irwyn
Forgery.

The King vs Wm. Graham
Extortion.
Wm. Graham £200, for his appearance at next sessions. Chas. McGill £200

The King vs Patrick Slavon(?)
Larceny. Saith he is guilty. Adjudged that he receive 21 lashes well laid on
upon his bare back at the public whipping post between the hours of 11 and 12
oclock tomorrow morning and that he make restitution to Wm. McCord of the
sum of 10 pounds 16 shillings by him stolen from said McCord, make fine to
the Court in the like sum, stand committed till fine and fees are paid.

Page 13
At Shippensburg, 23 April, before Samuel Smith, and his associate justices.
The sheriff John Potter Esq., returns the following panel of grand jurors; James
McIntire, Joseph Clerk, Tobias Hendricks, Ezekial Dunning, William
McDowell, Phillip Davis, Allen Killough, Charles Campbell, Robert Newell,
William Gamble, Joseph Mitchell, James Wilson.

The King vs Saml. Park
Felony.

The King vs James Butler Bland
Felony. Saith he is not guilty. Jury; John McCallister, David Scott, James __,
James Dysert, Archibald Mahan, John Finley, James Tate, John McClure,
Nathaniel Wilson, James Blair, William Rankin, and George Denny. Do say
that James Butler Bland is guilty. Ordered that the said James Butler Bland
shall receive 21 lashes on his bare back at the publick whipping post tomorrow.

Page 14
[cont] between 9 & 12, pay the sum adjudged by the Court to George Cowan in
satisfaction of his damages occurred by his taking and stealing George Cowan's
mare, fined 8 pounds and be committed till fine and fees be paid.

The King vs Nehemiah Steven
Suspicion of the murder of Benj. Moore. Nehemiah Steven £100, on condition
that he appears at the next court. James Crawford & Archibald Douglass £100,
for appearance of Nehemiah Steven at said next Court.

Page 15- blank

Page 16
At Carlisle, 23 July 1752, before Samuel Smith, and his associates justices.
The Sheriff John Potter made return of the following list of grand jurors; John
Mitchell, foreman, William Arstron, John Denison, Archibald McCallister,
John Calhoun, John McClure, John McBride, William Campbell, Thomas
Rankin, Benjamin Wallace, James Chambers, Andrew Miller, Arthur Foster,
John McClue, John Davis, Ezekiel Dunning, David Scotte.

The King vs Bridgett Gullory
Assault. Robt. Gullory £100, for the appearance of Bridgett Gullory his wife at
next Court.

Robert Kirkpatrick, Joshua Drummond, William Laughlin
Discharged on paying her fees.

Page 17
The King vs Dennis Lochell
Assault. Dennis Lochell £50, for his appearance at next court. Robert Gullory
£50, for the appearance of Dennis Lochell at next court.

Robt. Kirkpatrick, Joshua Drummond, Wm. Laughlin, discharged on paying
fees

The King vs Hugh McIlhenny
Assault.

The King vs Thos. Brown & Wm. Cross, overseers of the highways
For neglect of duty. Thos. Brown pleads not guilty. Defendant retracts his plea
and submits to the Court.

Page 18 22 October 1752
The sheriff Ezekiel Dunning returns the following list of grand jurors; John
McCormick, James McConnel, Samuel Fisher, James Carouthers, William Orr,
James Silver, William Parkinson, Samuel Wilson, Robert Brovard, William
Patten, Charles McGill, James Sharron, James Irvine, John Craighead, Thomas
Bairde, William Ferguson.

The King vs Fardarach O'Gallocher
Indictment for selling liquor without license. Saith he is not guilty. Jury; John Mitchel, Thomas Urie, John Reynolds, Thomas Brown, James Harris, James Henderson, Robert Campbell, Thomas McKenny, William Grimes, William Trindle, Hugh Mahool (?), and James Carnahan say that the said Fardarach O'Gallaher is guilty. Adjudged Fardarach O'Gallochor make fine to Governor of 5 pounds and be committed till fine and fees are paid.

Page 19
The King vs Robt. Gullory
Selling liquor with license. Process awarded.

The King vs Charles Murry
Assault. Saith he is not guilty, now the defendant comes into Court retracts his plea, not being willing to contend with the King, protests his innocence, prays to be admitted to a small fine. Adjudged that he make fine to the Governor of 6 shilling, and six pence and be committed till fine and fees are paid.

The King vs Chas. Murry
Assault.

Page 20
At Carlisle, 21 January, before Samuel Smith and his associate justices. The sheriff Ezekiel Dunning returned the following list of grand jurors; John Hoge, foreman, John Davison, Jonathan Holmes, John Davis, Andrew Craig, William Dunbar, James Blair, James Moore, Adam Hayes, Thomas Locquart, Andrew Miller, John McClure, Robert Walker, James Crawford, Arthur Foster, Samuel Lamb, Adam Hoop.

The King vs Wm. Chosnay (?)
Indictment for stealing 7 hogs. Saith he is not guilty. Jury; James Sharp, Thomas Barnett, Wm. Dilwood, Saml. Culbertson, Robt. McIlhinny, Edward Crawford, James Chambers, Charles Morrow, John Reynolds, Joseph Cruneleton, Patrick McCl__, and Robt. McConnell do say that the said Wm Chosney is not guilty of the larceny whereof he stands indicted, but that the property of the said Hoggs are in William Carruthos. (?)

Page 21
The King vs Edward Welsh
Felony. Says he is guilty. Adjudged he receive 21 lashes well laid on his bare back at the publick whipping post tomorrow morning between the hours of 11 & 12 o clock, that he make restitution to Wm. Anderson of 18 pounds 14 shillings, that he make fine to the Governor in the like sum and stand committed until fine and fees be paid. Test. Wm. Anderson Robt. Denny

The King vs Patrick Allen
Felony. Saith he is guilty, judged he receive 21 lashes well laid on his bare
back at the publick whipping post tomorrow morning between the hours of 11
& 12 o'clock. That he make restitution to Wm. Maxwell Esqr in the sum of 2
pounds 12 shillings and 6 pence that he make fines to the Governor in the like
sum and stand committed until fine and fees be paid. Test. Wm. Maxwell

Page 22
At Carlisle, 21 April, before Samuel Smith Esq., and his associate justices. The
sheriff Ezekiel Dunning returns the following grand jurors; James Lindsay,
foreman, Thomas Beare. Charles Mgill, John Patterson, Archibald McAllister,
Jonathan Hoge, John Mushet, David Scott, William Morton, Patrick Jack.
James Wilson, Thomas Rankin, Andrew Armstrong. James Biggon, William
Scott, James Cruncleton, John Mitchell.

King vs John McKinney
Indictment for stealing horse, saith he is guilty, receive 21 lashes well laid on
his bare back at the public whipping post tomorrow morning between the hours
of 11 and 12 oclock, that he make restitution of the goods stolen, the value of 8
pounds, pay fine to the Governor of the like sum, and he stand committed until
the fines and fees are paid.

Page 23- blank

Page 24
At Carlisle, 21July 1753, before Samuel Smith Esq., and his associate justices.
The sheriff Ezekiel Dunning returns the following list of grand jurors; John
Calhoun, William Thompson, James Jack, Joseph Dane, Arthur Foster, James
Dunning, Alick McBride. William McCrosby, Robert Elliot, William
Ferguson, Samuel Fisher, Robert McDonald.

The King vs Peter Walker
Indictment for assaulting Robert Chambers, says he is guilty. Adjudged he
make fine to Governor of 10 pounds, stand committed until fine & fees are
paid. Test. Jno. Finley, Jno. Forsyth

Page 25
The King vs Anthony Groasia (?)
Larceny. Says he is guilty. Anthony Grassia receive 5 lashes well laid on at the
publick whipping post between the hours of 2 & 6 this afternoon, that he make
restitution to Archibald McCurdy in the sum of 50 shillings the value of the
goods stolen, that he make fine to the Governor in the like sum and stand
committed until fine and fees are paid.

The King vs James Read
Indictment for assaulting Agnes Hendricks. Test. Tobias Hendricks, Robt. Frotter, Isaac Hendricks

The King vs James Read
Indictment for assaulting Tobias Hendricks. Test. Tobias Hendricks, Robt. Trotter, Isaac Hendricks

Page 26
At Carlisle, 22 October 1753, before Samuel Smith Esq., and his associates. The sheriff Ezekiel Dunning returns the following grand jurors; Daniel Williams, John Mitchell, James Young, William Ferguson, John Semple, John Robb, John McClure, William Armstrong, William Trindle, John Dickey, William Ross, George Armstrong, David Wilson, John Ryers, Alexander Sanderson, James Senderson.

Upon the motion of George Ross for the prosecutors of the Crown, Abram Slack was committed to the custody of the sheriff to be kept until he give bail for the sum of £100 each for his appearance at the next session and not to depart etc., to answer such things as shall be judged against him and his settling on land unpurchased from the Indians and without warrant and bill be otherwise legally discharged.

Page 27
The King vs Wm. Hays
Felony. Saith that he is guilty. It is ordered that he receive 21 lashes well laid on upon his bare back at the publick whipping post between the hours of 3 & 4 oclock this afternoon. That he make restitution to Margt. Clarke the sum of 7 pounds 10 shillings and 10 pence by him stolen from sd. Margt. Clark. That he make fine to the Governor in the like sum and stand committed till fine and fees are paid.

The King vs Saml. Fisher
Indictment for threatening of Wm. Allison.
Saml. Fisher £200, Jno. McCormack £50, on the condition that he appear at the next Court of General Quarter Sessions.

The King vs Saml. Fisher
Saml. Fisher £100, Thos. Willson £50, on condition that he appear the next Court.

Page 28
The King vs Wm. Allison
Assault and Battery. And now the Defendant saith that being unwilling to contend with our Sovereign Lord the King submits to the Court and prays to be admitted to a small fine. Test. Saml. Fisher, Andw. McFarlan

Page 29

At Carlisle, 17 April, before Samuel Smith Esq., and his associates. The sheriff Ezekiel Dunning returns the following list of grand jurors; William Parker, foreman, Stephen Folk, John McClure, George Brown, Andrew McCartire. William Campbell, Samuel Wilson, Robert Campbell, Arthur Foster, James Kilgore, William Riddle, Noah Coaply, John Robb, Joseph Davis, Joseph Rennels.

The King vs. James Branden
Sur indictment for selling liquor and keeping a public without license.

The King vs John McCallister
For selling liquor and keeping a publick house without license.

Page 30

County of Cumberland, 24 July. The sheriff Ezekiel Dunning returns the following list of grand jurors; John McClure, James Byers, Samuel Parker, Charles McGill, John Patterson, James Wilson, Joseph Spears, James Gordon, John Rennells, James Moore, Francis McGuire, John McDaniels, Robert Campbell, John McBride, William McCosky, Patrick McLean, John Ramsey, William White.

Page 31

The King vs Samuel Robison
Indictment for carrying spirituous liquors to the Indians. Test. Andrew Wenbur (?), Williams Sills, Michl. Teaff (?), Danl. Lanray, James Dunning

The King vs Arthur Donoly
Indictment for carrying spirituous liquors to the Indians out of the inhabited part of this province. Test. Andw. Monlour, William Sills, Michl. Toaff Danl. Lawrey, James Dunnin

The King vs Thomas Murrer
Indictment for carrying spirituous liquors to the Indians, out of the inhabited part of this province. Test. Wm. Montour, William Sills, Mich. Teaff, Danl. Lowrey, James Dunning

The King vs Thos. Smith
Indictment for carrying spirituous liquors to the Indians, out of inhabited part of this province. Test. Andw. Montour, William Sills, Micl. Teaff, Dan Lowry

Page 32

The King vs James Moore
Indictment for carrying spirituous liquors to the Indians our of inhabited part of this province. Test. Andw. Montour, William Sills, Michl. Teeaff, James Dunning, Danl. Lawrey

The King vs William Kelly
Indictment for carrying spirituous liquors to the Indians.

The King vs John McCollem
Indictment for carrying spirituous liquors to the Indians.

The King vs James Rearty (?)
Indictment for carrying spirituous liquors to the Indians.

The King vs Thos. McClallen
Indictment for carrying spirituous liquors to the Indians.

The King vs James Black
Indictment for carrying spirituous liquor to the Indians.

Page 33
The King vs Adam Hoop
Indictment for carrying spirituous liquor to the Indians.

The King vs James Robeson
Indictment for carrying spirituous liquor to the Indians.

The King vs John Anderson
Indictment for carrying spirituous liquor to the Indians.

The King vs James Hess
Indictment for carrying spirituous liquor to the Indians.

The King vs Patrick Lafferty
Indictment for carrying spirituous Liquor to the Indians.

Page 34
23 October 1754, before Samuel Smith Esq., and his associate justices. The sheriff Ezelial Dunning Returns the following list of grand jurors; William Trunnell, forman, David Kennedy, Alexander Sirog, Daniel Williams, Joseph Cook, John Mitchell, James Bigger, William Lemon, Joseph McFarran, Robert Eddy, Samuel Weire, James McConnol.

The King vs William Armstrong & William Campble
Indictment for neglecting the highway.

The King vs Samuel Rippy
For keeping publick house without license.

The King vs Adam Hoop
For keeping a publick house without license.

Page 35
The King vs Eliz McGave (?)
For keeping tavern without license.

The same vs William Anderson
For keeping tavern without license.

The King vs Adam Dickey
For assault & battery.

The King vs Jno. Nickolson
For assault & battery.

The King vs Martin & Nulson
For not cleaning & repairing the roads.

Page 36
The King vs James Dunnng
For keeping publick house with license.

The King vs James Silver
For keeping a publick house without license.

The King vs Tobias Hendricks
For keeping publick house without license.

The King vs Robt. Erwin
For keeping publick House without license.

Page 37
The King vs Mary Reynolds
For keeping publick house without license.

The King vs Jane Pipper
For keeping publick house without license.

The King vs James Brandon
For keeping publick house without license.

The King vs Henry Pawling
For keeping publick house without license.

The King vs Arthur Buchanan
For keeping publick house without license.

Page 38- blank

Page 39
23 October 1755, before Samuel Smith, Esq., and his associates. The sheriff John Petter returns the following list of grand jurors; William Ferguson, John Mishett, Joseph Rarron, Matthew Neiler, James Kilgore, Thomas Rankin, Robert Cruncleton, Henry Statts, John McCall, Barnaby Hughs, Henry Quigley, William White, Thomas Calvert (affirmed), George Wood, Anthony Thompson.

The King vs John Patterson
Assault & battery. Defendant pleads not guilty.

The King vs Samuel Nicholas
Felony. Defendant pleads not guilty.

The King vs Anthony Thompson
Anthony Thompson £ 50, Joseph M. Tarvin (?) £50, on condition to appear at next session to give evidence

Page 40
James Brown £25, William Campbell £25, for James Brown appear at next Court to give evidence against Anthony Thompson.

John Paterson £50, Andrew McIntyre £40, William McCoserive (?) £40, for John Patterson appear at next session to answer bill of indictment against him and abide the judgment of the court and not depart in the mean time to keep the peace & be of good behaviour.

The King vs James Moor
Defendant retracted their plea protesting their innocence, submits to the court and pray to be admitted to a small fine, fined six pence.

Page 41
The King vs Robert Murray

The King vs Anthony Morison

The Same vs Fran. Erwin

Page 42
The King vs James Murray

The Same vs John Erwin

The King vs John Murray

The Same vs John Carrithers

Page 43
The King vs James Adams

The King vs John Wall
January 1755, John Wall £50, William Adams £50, Thomas Adams £25,
Joseph McClinlock £25, for the appearance of John Wall & William Adams at
our next court.

The King vs Thomas Adams

The Same vs Alexander Murray
James Robert Thomas & Wm. Adams paid the King all __ his fees & also Mr.
Alrick

The Same vs Robert Adams

Page 44
The King vs William Hamilton

The King vs William Adams
January term 1755, William Adams £50, John Wall £50, Thomas Adams £25,
Joseph McClinlock £25, for the appearance of William Adams and John Wall
at our next Court.

The King vs Robert Adams
January 1755, Robert Adams £50, Thomas Adams £50, Thomas Adams Senior
£25, on condition that Robert & Thomas Adams appear next court.

Page 45
At Carlisle, 21 January 1755, before Samuel Smith, and his associates. The
sheriff John Potter the following list of grand jurors; Francis Foreman,
Jonathan Holmes, William Armstrong, William Armstrong, Jr., Robert Cars,
George Armstrong, James Beatty, Hugh Laird, James Crawford, Robert
Rosenborough, William Harkness, Peter Tittle, Arthur Foster, Walter Denny,
Samuel Rippey.

The King vs William Read
Fornication. Defendant pleads not guilty. William Read £100, Nathaniel Smith
£50, James Brandon £50. Nathaniel Smith & James Brandon have in
discharged of their bail delivered the body of Wm. Read to the __. John Read
£50, James Read £50, John Read, Jr. £50. Acknowledged the 15th day of April
1755. The defendant on his recognizance being called has made default.

Page 46
The King vs Hester Endlow
Defendant not guilty. Robert McCinhinny (?) £50, Robert Gibson £50,
Abraham Enlowe £50, on condition that Hester Endlow appear at court.

The King vs Samuel Nicholson
Felony. Jury; Tobias Hendricks, Jonathan Hog, James Carather, John McClure,
Bishop David Hog, Alexander Paterson, William Graham, John Robb, John
Dickey, John McKnight, John McWuire, & John Chambers who are their oaths
& say that Saml. Nicholson is guilty. The Court adjudge that the said
Nicholson shall receive 21 lashes on his bare back well laid on at the publick
whipping post tomorrow morning between the hours of 12 & 1 o clock, that he
make fine to the Governor, fined10 pounds.

Page 47- blank

Page 48
At Carlisle on 22 April, before Samuel Smith and his associates. John Potter
returned the following list of grand jurors; Henry Pawling, John McCowan,
William Willson, James Willson, Charles Campbell, John Wright, James
Carmanghen, Thomas Roo (?), John Mushel, Alexander Miller, James Erwin,
Robert Campbell, James McCormack, Thomas Brown, James Crawford, James
Jack.

The King vs Hugh Cramer
Assault & battery.

Page 49
The King vs Robert Gullery
Assault & battery.

The King vs the same
Assault & battery.

The King vs William Reed
Fornication. William Reed £100, Samuel Lamb 5 £0, James Reed £50

The King vs Wm. Reed
Fornication. Wm Reed £100, Saml. Lamb £50, James Reed £50

Page 50
At Carlisle, 23 October 1756, before Samuel Smith Esq. John Potter returned
list of grand jurors; James Patterson, William Miller, Paul Pierce, Charles
Patterson, James Reed, John Lusk, Thomas Holt, James Spear, Samuel White,
John Wallace, John Rule, James Jack, John Haston, Robert Newell, Samuel
Perry, James McClean, William Blythe.

The King vs Wm. Read, James Read, Samuel Lamb, Rowland Judge Riotously assembly. William & James Read plead not guilty. Saml. Lamb & Rowland Judge plead not guilty, The King will not further prosecute.

The King vs Wm. Read, Jas. Read, Saml. Lamb, Rowland Judge, James Starkpole (?) Riotously assembly. Wm Read £100, Jas. Read £100, Saml. Lamb £100, Rowland Judge £100, James Starkpole £100

Page 51
The King vs Thomas Urey
Indictment for keeping publick house without license.

Page 52
At Carlisle, 20 April 1757, before Saml. Smith and his associates.

The King vs Mary Dyson
Bastardy. Defendant pleads guilty , fined 5 pounds besides costs.

The Same vs Marg & Elinor Finley
Discharged by court on payment of fees.

The Same vs John __uell & Robt. Finley
Defendants are discharged by the Court on payment of their fees.

Page 53
The King vs Orven McGuire
Basterdy. James Magil £50, Roger Hollan (?) 50, Stephen Ferney £50 Defendant pleads not guilty. Mary Dyson £25

The same vs Mary White
Felony.

The Same vs Sarah Clark
Felony. Defendant sent to York County, being committed there.

The same v Nichalas Snider
Trespass. Plea not guilty. January session 1758. Jury; John Newman, Robert Erwin, Thomas Lockhart, John Holmes, John Kinhead, Robert Reynolds, William Harkness (?), John Anderson, William Mc__, Robert Urie, David McCurdy, William Carr. Is guilty of the trespass and the said Nicholas is fined 5 shillings by the Court & ordered that he stand committed until fine are paid. Nicholas Snider £50, Peter Snider £40, John Harman £40, for the appearance of Nicholas Snider at the next Court, abide by the judgement of the court & not depart and in the mean time to keep the peace.

16 Cumberland County, PA Quarter Session Court Dockets

Page 54
The King vs Marg White
Felony. Plea guilty. Fined according to act of assembly, ordered to receive 5 lashes on her bare back at the publick whipping post on Friday the 22nd April 1752, committed till fine and the fees are paid.

The King vs the Same
Felony. The same judgement & only that she receive __ lashes.

Page 55- blank

Page 56
At Carlisle, 19 July 1757, before Saml. Smith & his associates.

The King vs James Foley

Page 57
At Carlisle, 18 October 1757, before Francis West and his associate justices.

The King vs Elizabeth Ross
Indicted for keeping a tippling house. Pleads guilty. Fined 5 pounds for the Governor, costs of prosecution & stand committed until fine & fees are paid.

The King vs George Armstrong
Assault & battery on James Young the defendant came into Court & protesting his innocence saith he is unwilling to contend with out Sovereign Lord the King and submits to the Court praying to be admitted to a small fine. Fine sixpence with costs of prosecution & that he give bail for his good behaviour __ next Court in the sum of 25 pounds.

The King vs James Stackpole
For keeping a tippling house. James Stackpole £50, James McGile £25, for the appearance of James Stackpole at next session.

Page 58
The King vs Felix Doyle
Indictment for keeping a tippling house. Defendant being called appeared not.

The Same vs James Elder
Indictment for keeping a tippling house. Defendant being called appeared not.

The Same vs Arthur Buchannan
Indictment for keeping a tippling house. Defendant being called appeared not.

The same vs Patrick _inlon
Indictment for keeping a tippling house. Defendant being called appeared not.

Page 59
The King vs Dennis Swaney
Indictment for keeping a tippling house. Defendant being called appeared not.

Page 60
At Carlisle, 24 January 1758, before Francis West and his associates. The sheriff William Parker returned the following list of grand jurors; John Smith, James Young, William Chosney, John Miller, John Montgomery, Jonathan Holmes, David Wilson, William Armstrong, Ezekiel Smith, Robert Callonder, John Graig, John Davis, William Whity, John Lusk, Daniel McAllister, William Ferguson, John Dunning, Patrick McCloan.

The King vs Isaac Steel
Assault & battery upon William Christy. Isaac Steel being charged & __ upon to answer being unwilling to contend with the King submits & prays to be admitted to a small fine and is thereupon fined by the Court one shilling.

Page 61
The King vs Jane Cristy
Assault & battery on Isaac Steel. Jane Christy being charged & called to answer & submit & pray to be admitted to a small fine and is fined sixpence.

The King vs John Hastings
Assault & battery on Saml. Stephens. Defendant unwilling to contend with the King & praying to be admitted to a small fine, fined by the Court one shilling.

The King vs Wm. Smiley
Felony.

The King vs Wm. Smiley
Felony.

Page 62
At Carlisle, 18 April 1758, before Francis West, and his associates.

Page 63
At Carlisle on the 18 July, before Francis West and his associates.

The King vs James James Sanpile (?)
The Court accepts of James Sompile (?) own appearance & his own bail for his appearance next General Quarter Session therefore he is bound to the King.

Page 64
At Carlisle 18 July 1758, before Francis West and his associates.

Page 65
The King vs William McGossoth (?)
Assault. Wm. McGoffock £40, Richd. Nicholson £25

The King vs Barnaby Hanly
Felony.
Barnabas Hanley £40, James Wakly £20, conditioned on former recognizance

The King vs Simon Collins
Andrew McIntire, Saml. Stevens, John Hastings, Pat. Kinslow, called, forfeited

Page 66
The King vs Simon Collins
Called, forfeited.

The King vs Simon Collins
Called, forfeited.

The King vs James Barclay
Fornication
Called, forfeited.

Page 67
The King vs Bridget Guthery
Assault & battery.

Page 68
At Carlisle, 24 October 1758, before William Smith, John Byers, Davis Wilson, and James Carothers, Esq., justices of the Court. The sheriff William Parker Esq., returned the grand jurors; Ezeliel Smith, John Graig, Robert Guthery, John Patterson, Robert Gibson, Samuel Wilson, James Kenny, John Hastings, William Graham, John Anderson, Richard Nicholson, James Weakly, William Russell, Walter Dunning, John Fleming.

Mary Buchanan charged to give evidence to the Grand Jury.

Jonathan Holmes, constable of Middleton Township fines 20 shillings for non-attendance.

Page 69
The King vs Wm. McGoffolk (?)
Assault.

The King vs Barnaby Hanly
Felony.

The King vs Bridget Guthery
Battery.

Page 70
The King vs Adam Hoops
Assault & battery on Mary Buchanan.

The King vs Adams Hoops
Trespass on sd goods of Mary Buchanan.

Page 71
At Carlisle, 23 January 1759, before John Armstrong, Herman Aldricks, John McKnight, justices of the said Court.

The sheriff William Parker returned the following persons were sworn on the Grand Inquest; John McCormiak [no other names of grand jury recorded.]

Page 72
The King vs Eliza (?) Jack
Felony. Eliza (?) Jack £100, Thomas Beard £100

Page 73
At Carlisle, 27 April 1759, before Francis West and his associates. The sheriff William Parker returned list of grand jurors; Tobias Hendricks, James Weakley, John Craighead, Hugh McKool, John Trindle, David Cricklow, Adam Hois, Roger Walton, William Armstrong, Robert Robb, Francis Arwin, Samuel Thompson, Francis McGuire, James Moore, Roland McDonald.

The King vs Archibald McClane
Archibald McClane £50, Robert Callender

The King vs James Kelly
James Kelly £50, George McCord £50, Robert Little £50, William Riddle £50

Page 74
The King vs Simon Collings
Simon Collings £50, Patrick Winslow £50

The King vs Alexander Walker

Page 75
The King vs John Feild
Assault & battery.

The King vs Ralph Whittsitt (?)
Keeping publick house without license.

The King vs Elizabeth Jack
Felony. Defendant pleads not guilty. Elizabeth Jack £150, Thomas Beard £100, Samuel Holliday £100, conditioned that Elizabeth Jack appear next Court to answer to a bill of indictment & not to depart.

The King vs Samuel White
Assault & battery. The Defendant arraigned pleads not guilty. July Session 1760 and now the defendant comes to Court and retracts his plea aforesaid and protesting his innocense __ to the Court and prays to __ to a small fine it therefore __ [too faint to read].

Page 76
The King vs James Kelly
Felony. Defendant being arraigned pleads not guilty. Oct 1759 Jury; Robert Gibson, William Thompson, James Alcorn (?), John Greg, James Hunter, John McCurdy, Robert Campbell, John _unter, W__ Brown, John Chapman, John __. Saml Thompson, say that he is not guilty.

The King vs John Armstrong, John Little, John Scott, Robert Stuart, Robert Logan, Thomas Champlain, Michael Coleman, Alexander Leith, Thomas Brandon, Samuel McCracken, Samuel Gealy, Cooper Miller, Abraham Millson
Riot. The defendants being severally called appear not. The King will not further prosecute.

Page 77
The King vs Adam Hoops
Riot.

Page 78
The King vs Alexander Walker
Felony. Defendant says he is not guilty. Jury; William Thompson, Thomas Butler, John Stewart, Alexander McClintock, Robert Irwin, William Caruthers, Robert McDowell, Joseph Cruncleton, John Pinkead, Robert Mc Whinney, Robert Guthery, Robert Little say that the defendant is guilty. It is considered by the Court here that the money in the said indictment mentioned be returned or the value thereof, that the defendant pay a fine of one pound 12 shillings and six pence to his Honour the Governour and be whipped with 15 lashes __ and that he whipped on the 15 day of May next.

The King vs Adam Hoops
Assault & battery. The defendant appears protests his innocence unwilling to contend with our Sovereign Lord the King and submits to this Court.
Defendant fined six pence and to stand committed until fines and fees paid.

The King vs John Armstrong
Riot.

Page 79
The King vs John Miller & Arch. McCallister
Defendant submits to this Court & pray to be admitted to a small fine. The
Court adjudge the defendant each make fine in the sum of 5 shillings.

The King vs Edward Murphy

The King vs Wm Road
Riot.

Page 80
The King vs Jos. Armstrong
Riot. Our Sovereign Lord the King will not further prosecute.

The King vs John Armstrong
Riot. Our Sovereign Lord the King will not further prosecute.

Page 81
The King vs James McGill
Tippling House. Jas McGill £20, Robert Campbell £20

Page 82- blank

Page 83
At Carlisle, 22 January 1760, before John Armstrong, Francis West, and James
Akdricks justices. The sheriff Ezekiel Smith returned the following list of
grand jurors; David McGaw, John Dunning, Samuel Sample, James Robb,
John Sample, David Bell, William Flemon, James Young, James Allison, Jr.,
William Randles, Robert Newery, James Randles, George Moody, John Jack.

Our Sovereign King vs Anthony Thompson
Anth. Thompson £1000, Jas Potter £500, conditioned that Anthony Thompson
appear at next Court and answer such as shall be objected against him.

Page 84
The King vs John Creighton
Assault & battery. Defendant being unwilling to contend with our Sovereign
the King protests his Innocence and submits to the Court. It is considered by
the Court that defendant make fine to the King of six pence, pay the cost of
prosecution and stand committed till fine and fees be paid.

The King vs Robert Gullery
Assault & battery. Robt. Gullery £50, Christopher Brannon £35, for the
appearance of the said Gullery at the next Court & to answer to such __ & in
meantime keep the peace & be of good behavior towards all his Majesties
subjects, especially toward Mary Burni (?), Mary Henilow (?) And Eleanor

McGurk(?). Defendant not willing to contend with the King submits himself to the Court. Fined 5 shillings, pay the cost of prosecution, stand committed till fine & fees paid.

The King vs Robert Gullery, Jnr.
Assault & battery. Robert Gullery £50, Timothy Shaw £5, on condition that Robt. Gullery Junr appear at next court & not to depart without licence.

Page 85
The King vs Robert Gullery
Assault & battery.

The King vs John South
Felony. Saith he is not guilty. Jury; Daniel Williams, Mathew Miller, John A Dugo, Robert Pelenon(?), Andr. Parker, Erwin __, Saml. Lamb, John Reed Junr, James Graham, John Burgess, Rowland Chambers, Patrick Robins came who say that the defendant is guilty. Fined £40 and be whipped with 21 lashes.

The King vs Hugh McCully & al
Felony. Be whipped the first Tuesday of March next, make restitution of the goods, pay the costs & charges of prosecution, stand committed.

Page 86
Benjamin Diever £100, James Dicort £50, on condition that Benj. Diever appear at next Court. Danl Nathery £50, Richd. Prarter £50

James McBride £25, Alexr. McBride £12, on condition that James McBride appear at next court to prosecute his __ on a certain bill of indenture & not depart without license.

Patrick Robinson £10, Martha Hannah £10, on condition that they appear at the next court to give evidence & not depart Court without license.

The King vs John Singleton & William McDowell
Deceit.

Page 87 April Term 1764
The following were sworn on the grand inquest; Tobias Hendericks, foreman, Samuel Cunningham, Allen Leeper, William Patton, James Love, Samuel Brison, George Woods, Thomas John, Richard Nickelson, John Nailor, William Wood, John Gregg, Richard Rankin.

Page 88
The King vs John Hamilton & Alice Hogan
Commitment for felony brought from July Term 1763. Defendants plead not guilty. Jury; John Sina (?). Robert Campbell, Abraham Stanford, Robert

McIlinney, Petter Smith, Andrew Galbreath, John Hardy, John Hamilton, Samuel Fisher, William Rodman, Archibald Miller, & James Kennedy do say that the defendant is guilty, it is considered he make restitution of the goods stolen or the value thereof to the owners & make fine to the governour of the value of the goods stolen & receive on his bare back at the common whipping post in Carlisle between the hours of 9 & 11 oclock on the 20th day of April instant 21 lashes well laid on, stand committed till fine & fees be paid.

Page 89
Upon the application of John Montgomery. Ordered that Margaret Craig servant of the said John Montgomery do serve the said John Montgomery and his assigns the full term of six months over and above the time specified in her indenture for run away time charges & expenses.

Upon application of inhabitants of Allen and Middleton townships in the County of Cumberland, it is ordered that Jonathan Holmes, Robert Patterson, William Abernethy, Thomas Rankin, Walter Gregory and Joseph Gaily or any four of them to view the road laid by a former order of this Court, leading from the town of Carlisle to the line of York County in the nearest direction to Dill's Gap, whether the same can or may be laid out in a different manner what the same is now laid out by virtue of the same order for the benefit of the inhabitants, and make report of their proceedings to the next Court.

Page 90- blank

Page 91
At Carlisle, 22 April 1760, before William Smith, Esq., and his associates. [There is no record of any Grand Jury being summoned to this Court.]

The King vs George Anssell(?)
Felony. Defendant pleads not guilty. Jury; John Kincaid, George Saunderson, John Hastings, James Stuart, John Read, Junr, Saml. Thompson, Thomas Hotmer (?), William White, James Starkpole, William Furguson, Patrick Robinson and John Kennaday say he is guilty. 5 Shillings Maryland Curry the goods and chattes of Michael __ & not guilty as to the __. Ordered 20 stripes on his bare back & make restitution to Michael D__ in the sum of 5 shillings the like money to the Governor, pay the cost of prosecution 2 pounds, 12 shillings & stand committed till fine and fees are paid.

The King vs Robt. Gullery Senr.
Assault & battery. Defendant is not willing to contend with our Sovereign Lord the King submits himself to the Court. Fined 5 shillings, pay the cost of prosecution & stand committed till fine and fees be paid.

Page 92
The King vs Robt. Gullery, Senr
Assault. Defendant not being willing to contend with our Sovereign Lord the King submits himself to the Court. It is considered by the Court that the Defendant make fine to the King of 3 pounds & cost of prosecution, stand committed till fine and fees be paid.

Page 93
Upon application of James Dunning. It is ordered that Mary Martin servant to the said James Dunning do serve the said James Dunning and his assigns the full term of six months over and above the time specified in her indenture, for run away time charges & expenses lost.

Page 94- blank

Page 95
At Carlisle, 22 July, before Francis West and his associates. The sheriff Ezekiel Smith returned the following list of grand jurors; John Agnu, Timothy Shaw, Peter Title, William Davenport, Thomas Calhoun, George Sruart, Thomas Holt, James Smith, Thomas Anderson, John Wood, James Barclay, John McCartney, Joseph Smith, William Line, Robert Armstrong. Ordered that James Carouthers and David Wilson Esq., be fined 30 shillings each for their non appearance.

Page 96
The King vs William Drillison(?)
Assault & battery. Alexander Brown £40, on consideration that said Alexander Brown & Leonard appear at next session and give evidence. The defendant not willing to contend with the King protesting his innocence submits to said Court, prays to be admitted to a small fine. The Court do order that he pay a fine of six pence to his Honor the Governor, likewise the cost of prosecution and stand committed til find and fees are paid.

The King vs William Patterson
Assault & battery. William Patterson £50, Francis McNichols £25, on condition that William Patterson appear at next Court & not depart the Court without licence. January 1761 the Defendant not willing to contend with out Sovereign Lord the King protests his innocence, submits to the Court and prays to be admitted to a small fine. The Court do order he pay a fine of 5 shillings to the Governor, likewise the cost of prosecution, stand committed till fine and fees are paid.

Page 97
The King vs Smith & Nugent
Felony. Curtis Smith one of the defendants being arraigned pleads not guilty. Jury; John Hart, William Mall(?), James Starkpole, John Lusk, Wm. Querry, William Carthers, Saml. Thompson, John Pollack, John James, James Elder,

Abraham Holmes & James Montgomery do say that Curtis Smith is guilty.
Thomas Nugent the other of the defendant being arraigned pleads not guilty
and George Ross __. Jury; John Hart, William Wallis, James Starkpole, John
Lusk, William Jerry, William Cruthers, Saml. Thompson, John Pollock, John
James, James Weir, Abraham Holmes & James Montgomery being sworn do
say that Thomas Nugent is guilty. Ordered by the Court that Curtis Smith and
Thomas Nugent restore the goods stolen to the right owner, or shall pay the
value of said goods, the costs of prosecution & other disbursements.

The King vs Smith & Nugent
Felony. Curtis Smith being arraigned pleads not guilty. Jury; William Wallis,
James Starkpole, John Lusk, William Quarry, William Carruthers, Samuel
Thompson, John Polls, John James, James Elder, Abraham Holmes & James
Montgomery do say that Curtis Smith is guilty of the felony. Thomas Nuggent
the other of the defendants being arraigned pleads not guilty. Geo. Ross __ __.
Jury; John Kerr, William Wallis, James Starkpole, John Lusk, Wm. Quarry,
William Caruthers, Samuel Thompson, John Pollock, John James. James Elder,
Abraham Holmes, & James Montgomery do say that Thomas Nuggent is guilty.
It is ordered by the Court that they the said Curtis Smith and Thomas Nuggent
restore the goods so stolen to the right owner or pay the value thereof said
goods as also the cost of prosecution.

Page 98
The King vs Curtis Smith & Thomas Nugent
Curtis Smith pleads not guilty. Jury; William Wallis, James Starkpole, John
Lusk, William Quarry, William Carruthers, Samuel Thompson, John Polls,
John James, James Elder, Abraham Holmes & James Montgomery say that
Curtis Smith is guilty. Thomas Nugent the other of the defendants being
arraigns pleads not guilty and George Ross __. [same jury as above] that
Thomas Nugent is guilty. It is ordered by the Court that they the said Curtis
Smith and Thomas Nugent return the goods stolen to the right owners or pay
the value of the said goods as also the cost of prosecution and other
disbursements, likewise the __ and Prosecutor had and __ shall forfeit and pay
the value of the good __ to the Governor & shall be committed to the __ and
shall be publickly whipped at the publick whipping post this evening between
the hours of 5 and 7 of the clock with 15 lashes on their bare back, the 31 day
of July at the same place and on the 2nd day of August aforesaid.

Page 99
The King vs Eliz Dougherty
Felony. That the Sheriff of Cumberland County bring in the body in the space
of one __ __ be fined in the sum of 50 pounds showed cause within the time.

Page 100- blank

Page 101
At Carlisle, 31 October 1760. The sheriff Ezekiel Smith returned following grand jurors; John Sample, John McClure, David Bee, Matthew Holmes, Joseph Smith, William Wallace, George Hoake, George Stuart, James Armstrong, William Ross, William Grayhame, John Bigham, William Patterson, Samuel Culbertson, Thomas Blair.

Page 102
Ordered by the Court that Constable of Hamilton Township Robert Kerr, Constable of Lurgan Township, Middleboro Township, Westbrough township, Allen Township be fined __ shillings lawful money of Pennsylvania for his non appearance. The Court do order that the above order be reviewed.

Upon application of Mr. John Mather on behalf of Mr. William McClay praying that he may be admitted to Attorney of this Court and having taken the Oath provided by Act of Assembly in such case & admitted accordingly.

The King vs Eliz. Jack
Felony. Defendant being arraigned pleads not guilty. Jury; William Reynolds, James Dunlap, William Piper, Saml. Marlyn, James Read, William Davenport, John Degg, Robert Patterson, John Quin, James Reynolds, William Boyles, & John Robinson, say that Elizabeth Jack the defendant is not guilty.

Alexander Brown for David Brown & Leonard __, conditioned that said David Brown & appear to give evidence at the next Court.
James Hunter £20, conditioned that he appear to give evidence before the next Court of General Quarter Sessions.
Clement Horall   £20, conditioned that appear to give evidence before the next Court of General Quarter Sessions.
Andrew Drew £20, John Steel £20
Andrew Drew & John Steel for Mary Gibson £20, conditioned that said Drew, Steel and Gibson be and appear to give evidence before the next Court.

Page 103
The King vs Bridget Debourne (?)
Felony. Jury; Jonathan Glarsley(?), Daniel Williams, Samuel Anderson, James Mathius, David Scott, Robert Owen, William Ridle, John Elder, David Couther (?), William Cunningham, John Lusk, James Wilson do say that the defendant is guilty. Ordered that she return the goods if not already returned to the owners and pay fine of [nothing written in] to the Governor, costs of prosecution and shall be publickly whipped at the publick whipping post with 10 lashes on her bare back between the hours of 8 and 10 and stand committed until fine and fees are paid.

The King vs John Burns
Felony. Jury; William Reynolds, James Dunlap, William Piper, Samuel Martyn, James Read, William Davenport, John Gregg, Robert Patterson, John Erwin, James Reynolds, William Boytas (?) and John Robinson do say that John Burns is guilty and therefore the Court do order that the said John Burns restore the goods so stolen to the owner or pay the value of said goods and also the cost of the prosecution, likewise shall pay the value of said goods to the Governor and tomorrow to wit the 25th day of Oct shall be publickly whipped at the publick whipping post with 15 lashes on his bare back at 10 oclock in the forenoon and stand committed until fine and fees are paid.

Page 104 October 1760
The King vs William Patterson
Assault & battery. William Paterson £40, Andrew Greer £40, conditioned that said Patterson appear at the next Court and not depart the Court without licence. Jan 1761 Defendant not willing to contest with the King protests his innocence submits to the Court and prays to be admitted to a small fine. The Court order that the defendant pay fine of 5 shillings to the Governor likewise pay costs of prosecution and stand committed until fine and fees are paid.

The King vs Samuel Thompon
For keeping publick house with licence. Defendant being solemnly called appeared not. Process award January 1761. Defendant submits to the Court.

Page 105
The King vs John Gray
For keeping publick house without licence. Defendant being arraigned pleads guilty. The Court order and that he pay a fine of 5 pounds to the King, the costs of prosecution and stand committed until the fine and fees are paid.

The King vs Robert Guthery
Assault and battery.

Page 106
The King vs Dennis Dougherty
For keeping a tavern without licence. Defendant being solemnly called appeared not. Janry 1761 the defendant submits to the Court.

The King vs William White
For keeping a publick house without licence. Defendant being solemnly called appeared not.

Page 107
The King vs Ralph Whitsides
For keeping a Publick House with licence. Defendant being solemnly called appeared not. Janry 1761 the defendant pleads non cul (?)

The King vs Peter Title
For keeping a publick house without licence. Defendant being solemnly called appeared not. Peter Title £20, John McCartney £20, conditioned that said Peter Title appear at the next Court and not to depart the Court without licence.

Page 108 October 1760
Curtis Smith and Thomas Nugent now in prison at Carlisle, being indicted for three several indictments in July Sessions 1760, in all of which said indictments they the said Thomas Nugent and Curtis Smith were found guilty, and remanded back to prison until the fines and fees were paid the amount of the said fines and fees being 50 pounds and 4 shillings, besides the cost of the prosecutors and the said Thomas Nugent and Curtis Smith having not the wherewith to satisfy the, therefore the said Curtis Smith and Thomas Nugent by Ezekiel Smith Esq., high sheriff of said Court, prays the Court that the said Curtis Smith and Thomas Nugent may be sold out of the said prison in service to satisfy the fees and fines aforesaid. The Court do order that the Curtis Smith for 5 years and the said Thomas Nugent for 7 years be sold by Ezekiel Smith, sheriff as aforesaid, and that the money arising from, be disposed of in manner following: that first of all the legal fees be paid and next the cost of the several prosecutors and that the remainder if any, be remitted to the Governor.

Page 109- blank

Page 110
At Carlisle, 20 January 1761, before John McKnight Esq., and his associates. The sheriff Ezekeil Smith returned the following grand jury; John Davis, John Holmes, Andrew Holmes, Joseph Boyd, Andrew Miller, Ralph Whitsides, John McClure, Stephen Duncan, Samuel Colter, William Armstrong, Christopher Brandon, Hugh Hunter, Charles Patterson, Robert Walker, James Weakley, Peter Tittle.

Page 111 January 1761
Upon the petition of sundry of the inhabitants of Earl township, setting forth that a bridle road leading from the town of Carlisle in Letort spring to foot of sidling hill by Larrabys Gap, so as to intersect said provincial road leading to Pittsburgh and praying the court to appoint proper persons to view the same and if they see cause to lay out a road from Carlisle aforesaid. Ordered that John Houston, James Dickey, John McDowell, Joseph Smith, Francis Patterson, Henry Anderson and any four of them view the premises as aforesaid and if they think convenient lay out the same and make report to said court whether the same be of public or private use.

Upon application of Thomas Donnellan it is ordered by the Court that Bridget Eagan servant to the said Thomas Donnellan do serve the said Thomas Donnellan or his assigns the full term of 9 months over and above the time specified in her indenture for ran away time charges lost by the said Thomas for and on account of said Bridget and by reason of her deserting his service.

Upon application of Francis West, Esq prior to an order of Court appointing Alexander Anderson, Junr., William Waddel, James Henderson. George Sanderson, William Davidson and William Fleming for making a road from the Town of Carlisle to Upper Gap in the North Mountain and by the return of William Fleming, William Davidson, George Saunderson, and Alexander Anderson having __ said road the Court do hereby order that the said road shall be laid out as aforesaid.

Page 112 January 1761
The King vs James Dunkin, Thomas Dunkin and Wm Bennett
Felony. April 1761. Jury; Ezekiel Dunning, Saml. Derry (?), James Young, John Brady, Robert Newel, John Shelby, Allen Naper, John Greg, Wm. Patton, Walter Denny, Saml. Lindsay and William Aberthany do say that the defendants are guilty, that William Bennett is not guilty therefore the Court do order that the said James Duncan and Thomas Duncan make restitution to the party for the goods stolen and the value thereof which is 4 pounds 10 shillings to the Governor, to stand committed till fine and fees are paid and on the 24th day of May next to be carried to the publick whipping post and then to receive 10 lashes and their bare backs well laid on, and that William Bennett be discharged and paying his fees.

The King vs Henry Duncan
Felony. Defendant pleads guilty. Adjudged the goods be delivered to owner, that the Defendant do pay a fine of 3 pounds current money to the Governor and that he pay the cost of prosecution and be publickly whipped at the publick whipping post with 5 lashes upon his bare back on tomorrow morning between 8 and 10 of the clock, stand committed until fine and fees are paid.

Page 113 January 1761
The King vs James Dunkin, Thos. Dunkin and Wm. Bennett
Felony. Thomas Dunkin £50, James Dunkin £50, James Wakely £50, William Bennet £100, Andrew Farril £100. April 1761. Jury; Ezekiel Dunning, Sam. Derry, James Young, John Brady, Robt Newill, John Shelby, Allen Naper, John Gregg, William Patton, Walter Denny, Saml. Lindsey and William Abethernathy do say that the defendants are guilty and that the said James Duncan and Thomas Duncan make restitution to the party for the goods so stolen and the value thereof which is 13 pounds to the Governor and to stand committed til fine and fees are paid and on the 24th day of May next to be carried to the publick whipping post and there to receive 10 lashes on their bare backs well laid on and that William Bennett be discharged paying his fees.

The King vs Dudley Dougherty
Felony.

Page 114
The King vs David Scott, Andrew Miller, Patrick Miller, Ezekiel Smith, Thos. Jefferies, Moses Jefferies
Riot. April 1761. Defendant being charged and being unwillingly to contend with the King protests their innocence, prays that they may be remitted to a small fine, the Court do order that the defendants David Scott pay a fine of 2 shillings and sixpence and James Duncan pay a fine of 2 shillings and sixpence. Thomas Duncan pay a fine of 2 shillings and sixpence, James Stackpole pay a fine of 1 shilling and sixpence, Robert Gutherty Senr pay a fine of 2 shillings and sixpence, Robert Guthery Junr pay a fine of 2 shillings and six pence and Margaret Stackpole pay a fine of 1 shilling and sixpence to his honor the Governor and stand committed until fine and fees are paid.

The King vs William Huskell
Assault and battery. April 1761, defendant being unwilling to contend with the King protests his innocence, prays to be admitted to a small fine. Court order that he pay a fine of 5 shillings to his honor the Governor together with the cost of the prosecutor and prosecution and to stand committed til fine and fees are paid.

Page 115
The King vs Isaac Brubaker, Margt. Hegar (?)
Felony.

The King vs Rose Young
Felony. Michl. Carney, James Warden and Thomas Nugent, being witness on
__ part the King, confined in said prison of the County are ordered by the Court to be brought by said Sheriff in Court to give testimony.

Page 116 January 1761
The King vs James Warden
Assault and battery. Jury say he is guilty, fined 10 shillings, cost of the prosecution.

The King vs James Warden
Assault and battery. Defendant pleads not guilty and a jury said he is guilty, fined 10 shillings and cost of prosecution.

Page 117
The King vs James Warden
Assault and battery. Defendant being arraigned pleads not guilty and by jury say he is guilty fined 10 shillings and cost of prosecution.

The King vs Rose Young
Felony.

Page 118
The King vs Alexr. McB__ (?)
Felony.

The King vs Oliver Culberson
Assault and battery.

Page 119
The King vs Thomas Woods
Felony. Defendant pleads not guilty. Jury; Ezekiel Dunning, Saml. Derry, James Young, John Brady, Robt. Newell, John Shelby, Allen Nasper (?), John __, William Patton, Walter Denny, Saml. Laird and William Aberthny say that the defendant is not guilty, the Court do order the defendant be discharged and paying his fees.

The King vs Conrad Myer (?)
Felony. Defendant pleads not guilty. Jury; Jonathan Stersley (?), Daniel William, Robt. Irwin, John Lusk, David __, James Wilson, James __, John Edler, Samuel Anderson, William Cunningham, David __, William Riddle, do say that the defendant is guilty and it is ordered and by the Court that the defendant restore the goods so stolen or the value therefore to the owner and the value thereof to the Governor and to be publickly whipped at the public whipping post between the hours of 8 and 10 oclock in the forenoon on Saturday next with 10 lashes on the bare back and stand committed until fine and fees are paid.

Page 120 January 1761
The King vs Saml. White, John Beaty
Assault and battery.

The King vs Patrick Miller
Assault and battery.

Page 121
The King vs James Pollock
Tippling house without licence.

The King vs Stephen Jordan
Trespass.

Page 122
The King vs Thomas Kinnsliss (?)
Riot.

The King vs Andrew Blackhart, Jacob Haman
Trespass.

Page 123

At Carlisle, 21 April 1761 before John Armstrong and his assistant justices. The sheriff, Ezekiel Smith, returned the following as grand inquest; James Guthry, John Trindle Junr, William Brown, Richard Parker, Moses __, Daniel Duncan, John Crunkeleton, Robert Wilson, Walter David, Richard Rankin, James Jack, Alexander Scraggs, John Thompson, William Dunbar, James Sharron, John Elliot, John Smiley, Alexander Sanderson, Alexander Robinson, Rowland Chambers, John Vaughan, James Long, Saml. Martin, George Armstrong, Robert McClure, John Patton, __ Johnson, and John Brown.

The King vs Thomas McLoughlin
Defendant ordered to be__ by the Court on his own recognizance, on condition of his entering into his Majestys service and paying his fees.

Page 124   April Term 1761

Sundry of the inhabitants of Peters township preferred their petition, setting forth that they have no prospect of a standing market for the product of their country only at Baltimore in Maryland, and having no road leading from this township to the said town and flour being one principle commodity said township produceth and having as mills in said township namely, John McDowell's and William Smith's that does not accommodate said inhabitants. Said inhabitants pray the Court that they would appoint men to view and lay out said road from each of said mills to meet at or near the house of William Maxwell and from thence the highest and best way toward the said town and with it intercept the temporary line on the line of York county.

The Court do order that Henry Daulin, James Jack, John Allison, Joseph Bradner, John McCleland Jr., and William Holliday or any four of them do view and lay out the above road and make report thereof to the next Court. By the Court, Herman Aldricks

Quarter Session Docket 2 1761-1765

Page 1

At Carlisle, 31 July 1761, before John Armstrong and his associates for appointment of township officers,

Antrim Township; John Erwin, Constable

Guilford Township; James Jack, constable, John Farming, John McCartney, overseers of poor; John Jack, Frederick Crafts, supervisor of roads; Thomas Binea, Thomas Baird appraisers and viewers of fences.

Hamilton Township; John Campbell, constable; Thomas Barnitz, John Burns over-seers of the poor; James Eaton, Samuel Moorehead supervisors of roads; John Craig, James Guthery, appraisers &viewers of fences.

Lurgan Township; William Linn, constable; John Cummins, John Weir supervisors of roads; Abram Weir, Archibald Mahon, appraisers and viewers of fences.

Peter Township; John Daugherty Constable; John Holiday, Thomas Orbison overseers of poor; John Houston, Robert Elliot, supervisors of roads; John McClellan, John Martin, appraisers and viewers of fences.

Aire Township; William Linn, constable; John Cunningham, James Bellow, overseers of poor; William Wallace, John Elliot, supervisors of roads.

Lack Township; (no officers appointed for this year.)

Tyrone Township; James Scott, constable; Thomas Ross, George Robinson, supervisors of roads.

Page 2 July Sessions 1761

The sheriff returns the following list of grand jurors; John Agnu, William Miller, James McFarland, Joseph Hunter, Abram Holmes, Thomas Holt, James Smith, William Davenport, Robert Semple, William Linn, James Barelay, George Stuart, Richard McCune, William Pipper, Wilson Thomson, John Stell, James Bolt, William McCrosky, Thomas Donnellan, William Wallace, William Patterson, John Tunnel, Roger Walton, John Gemmel.

Page 3

Ordered that the following gentlemen being summoned on the Grant Inquest, having made default be fined for their non-attendance 20 shillings each; James McFarland, Thomas Holt, James Braidy, Richard McClure, William Pipper, William Wallace, William Patterson.

Ordered that fines be levied on the following gentlemen for their non-attendance pursuant to summons at the last April Session; James Guthery, John Trindle, Jr., William Brown, Richard Parker, Moses Stan, John Cruncleston, Robert Wilson, Walter Davis, Alexander Scroggs, John Thompson, William Dunbar, James Shannon, John Elliot, John Smily, Alexander Sanderson, Alexander Robinson, Roland Chambers, James Long, Samuel Martin, Robert

McClure, John Patten, and James Brown, 20 shilling each and Daniel Dumont 10 shilling and Robert Rankin 5 shillings.

Page 4 July Sessions 1761
The King vs Hugh Preston
Felony. Jury; John Keer, Daniel Duncan, James Bell, John McCardy, John Prack, John Chapman, Samuel Montgomery, John Lyttle, John Hunter, John Kenedy, Timothy Sherd (?), and John Hastings do say that the defendant is guilty and it thereupon adjudged by the Court that restitution be made to the party aggrieved, fine to the Governor to the value of the thing stole pay costs, and be publickly whipped on his bare back at the whipping post in Carlisle on the 23 instant between the hours of 12 and 3, stand committed till this judgement be complied with.

The King vs George Ross
Assault & battery. Jury; Robert Erwin, John Chapman, James Bechensidger, Thomas Baird, James Henderson, John Urer, William Ride, Robert Litle, John Paton, Joseph Boyd, John McKemey, James Hunter do say that the defendant is guilty. It is considered by the Court and the defendant is fined 20 shillings and to pay the costs of the prosecution and of the prosecutor, stand committed till the judgement be complied with.

The King vs James Stackpole
Assault & battery. The defendant being charged saith that being unwilling to contend with the King, therefore submits to the Court and prays to be admitted to a small fine. It is considered by the Court and the defendant is fined 2 shillings and six pence and is to stand committed till fine and fees are paid.

Page 5
The King vs Lawrence Goodjohn
Assault and battery. Lawrence Goodjohn £20, John Lytle £10, defendant being charged pleads not guilty.

The King vs Robert Gutherson
Assault & battery. Defendant pleads not guilty. Jury; Robert Erwin, John Chapman, James Beckenridge, Thomas Baird, James Henderson, John Elder, William Ridle, Robert Litle, John Paton, Joseph Boyd, John McKemey, James Hunter who say that the defendant is guilty and fined 10 shillings and to pay the costs of prosecutor, prosecution and stand committed till the fees fulfilled.

The King vs James Stackpole
Assault & battery. And now the defendant being charged saith that being unwilling to contend with the King therefore submits to the Court and prays to be admitted to a moderate fine. The defendant is fined 2 shillings and stand committed till fine and fees are paid.

Page 6 July Sessions 1761
The King vs George Sanderson
Assault & battery. Defendant being pleads guilty, being unwilling to contend with the King, and prays the Court to be admitted to a small fine. Defendant is fined 20 shillings and to stand committed till fine and fees are paid.

The King vs John Crooker
Felony.

The King vs Jacob Card
Felony. Jacob Card £100, George Hoke £50, William Davenport £50, on condition that Jacob Card appear at the next Court. Henry Snively £30, on condition that he and Barbara Snively appear at next Court.

Page 7
The King vs Andrew Irons
Felony. Defendant pleads not guilty. Jury; John Keer, Daniel Duncan, James Belly, John McCurdy, John Poach, John Chapman, Samuel Montgomery, James Starkpole, John Little, John Hunter, Timothy Shard, John Hustinger say that the defendant is guilty. It is adjudged that he make restitution of the things stolen, pay all costs of the prosecutor, make fine to the Governor to the value of the things stolen and be publickly whipped on his bare back with 21 lashes well laid on, on the 26th day of this instant at the publick whipping post in Carlisle.

The King vs Thomas Kemplin
Assault and battery.

The King vs Edward Davies
Felony. Defendant pleads not guilty. Jury; John Kee, Daniel Duncan, __ Bell, John McCurdy, John Procker, John Chapman, Samuel Montgomery, James __, John Little, John Hunter, Timothy Sheid and John Hastings say that the defendant Edward Davies is guilty and to make restitution to the party of the things stolen and make fine to the Governor to the value of the things stole, pay the costs of prosecution, be publickly shipped on the with 21 lashes well laid at the publick whipping post in Carlisle between the hours of 12 and 2 in the afternoon of the __.

Page 8
The King vs James Henderson
Indictment for keeping tavern without licence. Defendant pleads guilty being unwilling to contend with the King, fined 5 pounds according to act of assembly and to stand committed till fine and fees are paid.

James Mitchel Free (?) £100, Andrew Holmes £25, Charles McCormick £25, on condition that James Mitchel Free (?) do well and truly observe the __ of the King, towards all his Majestys subjects especially toward Robert Guttery Jun.

Robert Guttery Jun £100, Robert Guttery Sen. £25, William Wite £25, on condition that Robert Guttery Junr. do well and truly observe the peace of the King toward all his Majestys subjects especially towards James Mitchell.

Page 9
The King vs George Sanderson and Matthew Miller
Indictment for not repairing the highway. Defendant being charged say, that being unwilling to contend with our Sovereign Lord the King, therefore submit to the Court. It is considered by the Court, defendants are fined 6 pence each, and to stand committed till fines and fees are paid.

Ordered that no licences for keeping taverns be filled up to any persons whatsoever not withstanding the recommendation of this Court until such person or persons so applying shall produce to the Protonotry or other person so granting or filling up licences, receipts from the Collector of the Exes.

Page 10
Petition of sundry of the inhabitants of Middleton Township setting forth that a road being from the Town of Carlisle to Craigheads Mills was greatly granted and that the same road be of publick use, was read whereupon it is considered by the Court. And John McKnight, Esq, Robert Robb, Walter __, James Young, John Davies and Joseph Griley or any four of them as appointed to view and if they see cause lay out a road from the Town of Carlisle aforesaid to Craigheads Mills aforesaid and make report of the proceedings to the next Court of and whether the same road if of publick or private use.

Page 11
William Brown vs John Elder

Appeal from the judgement of John Montgomery and William Spear. Judgment of the Court is that the original action was wrong brought therefore they confirm the judgement of the Magistrate and reverse the appeal with costs.

Page 12
At Carlisle, 20 October 1761, before James Galbraith and his associates. The sheriff makes return of the following list of grand jurors; Ezekiel Dunning, Robert Chambers, Richard Parker, James Young, Thomas Duncan, Daniel Duncan, William Parker, Robert Peoples, Andrew McFarland, Samuel Culbertson, Samuel Rippey, Laird Burns, James Smith, John McCartney, James Sharp, Robert Mickey, John Myer Jr., James Chambers, William Thompson, Cleary Campbell, James Culbertson, John Dunning, John Thompson, William Carneyhan.

Page 13 October Sessions 1761
Ordered by the Court that the fines imposed on the following gentlemen at the last July Session of their non attendance in pursuance of summons to serve on the Grand Inquest and who have not now appeared; James Barclay 20 shillings, William __ 20 shillings, William Wallace 20 shillings, William Patterson 20 shillings, for the use of the poor of the respective townships.

Page 14
The King vs James Allison
Assault and battery. Defendant being charged saith that being unwilling to contend with the King, submits to the Court and prays to be admitted to a small fine. It is considered by the Court and the defendant is accordingly fined 40 shillings and to stand committed till fine and fees are paid.

The King vs James Clark
Felony. Andrew Boggs £40, Adam Hoops (?) £40, John Bray £40, Andras Bonjour (?) £40, Thomas Donnallan £40, Patrick Leekin £40, on condition that they personally be and appear at the next Court to give evidence.

Page 15
The King vs Charles Duffy
Felony. Defendant being charged pleads guilty, it is considered by the Court that he make restitution of the goods stolen and fine to the Governor in 6 pounds pay the costs of prosecution and receive on his bare back 15 lashes well laid on at the common whipping post in Carlisle on Friday the 23rd instant between the hours of 10 and 2 of the same day and to stand committed till this judgment complied with.

The King vs James Hammel
Indictment for a Ch__. April Term: the recognizance of James Hammel and Robert Gibson being solemnly called came not, recognizance is forfeited. James Hammel £80, Robert Gibson £40, conditioned that James Hammel be and appear at next quarters session. Oct 1762. James Hammel £80, Robert Gibson £40, on condition that James Hammel be and appear at the next court to answer and not depart without leave and acknowledged in Court. Oct 1761

The King vs Conrad Hoke
Felony.

Page 16
John Titus £40, Peter Titus £20, on condition that the above named John Titus do personally appear at the next Court to answer and not depart.

The King vs William Parker
Fornication.

The King vs Charles McCormick
Assault and battery. Defendant being charged pleads not guilty but being unwilling to contend with our Lord the King retracts his plea and protesting his innocense submits to the Court and prays to a small fine. Fined to the Governor 2 shillings and 6 pence, 5 shillings for being drunk with __ committed to the __ __ till fine and fees are paid.

Page 17 October Sessions 1761
The King vs Charles Boyle
Indictment for keeping tavern without licence. Defendant being charged pleads whereupon it is considered by the Court that he make fine to the Governor the fine being in 5 pounds, pay the costs of this indictment and stand committed till fine and fees are paid.

The King vs William Patterson
Adultery.

Page 18
The King vs Thomas Duncan
Indictment for keeping tavern without license. Defendant pleads guilty, fined 5 pounds, pay all the costs, to stand committed until fine and fees are paid.

Petition of sundry of the inhabitants of Sherman's Valley setting forth that they labor under considerable disadvantage for want of a public road leading from the said valley to the town Carlisle and praying that a road may be viewed and laid out etc. It is considered by the Court and James Galbraith, Thomas Wilson, John McCormick, John Davis, James Young, Alexander Roddy, and George Robinson are appointed to view and if they see cause to lay out a road from the valley aforesaid the nearest and best way to the town of Carlisle aforesaid and make report to the next Court and whether it shall be of public or private use.

Page 19
Petition of sundry of the inhabitants of Sherman Valley, to this Court setting forth that they labored under considerable disadvantage for want of a publick road leading from the said valley to the Town of Carlisle and praying that the road maybe viewed and laid out. Whereupon it is considered by the Court and James Galbreath, Thomas Wilson, John McCormick, John Davies, James Young, Alexander Roddy and George Robinson are appointed to view and if they see cause to lay out a road from the Valley aforesaid the nearest and best way to the Town of Carlisle aforesaid and make report to the next Court and whether the same be of publick or private use.

Petition of inhabitants of Middletown Township setting forth that a road is greatly wanted from Town of Carlisle to the county line between Cumberland and York County leading through Mahaffes Gap and from thence to be continued by the inhabitants of York County into the Baltimore Road.

Whereupon it is considered by the Court and John Byers, Ezekiel Dunning, John Davies, Robert Miller, Robert Robbard, James Young, are appointed to view and if they see cause, to lay out a road the nearest and best way to the Line aforesaid through the Gap aforesaid, who are to make report of their proceedings to the next Court and if the road be for publick or private use.

Page 20-blank

Page 21
At Carlisle, 19 January 1762, before John Armstrong and his associates. The sheriff Ezekiel Smith returns the following panel of grand jurors; Capt. William Armstrong, James Blair, James Allison, Robert Urcy, Matthew Miller, James Matthias, Benjamin Varner, William Miller, John Beerd, William Abernathy, George Armstrong, Archibald Ross, John Craig, John Clarke (excused), William Armstrong, Thomas Holt.

Page 22 January Sessions 1762
Summoned to grand inquest; William Armstrong, foreman; James Blane, James Allison, Robert Urey, Mathew Miller, James Mathews, Benjamin Varnor, John Reed, Archibald Ross, John Gregg, William Abernathy, George Armstrong, William Boyd, John Wilson, Thomas Rankin, William Armstrong, Thomas Holt.

Page 23
The King vs John Noreast
Felony. Defendant pleads not guilty. Jury; William Miller, William Fleming, Andrew Armstrong, David Hog, Jonathan Holmes, Andrew Holmes, Edward Horten, Samuel Perry, John Nailer, John Lusk, John Vanleer, William Ganethers, say that the defendant is guilty, considered by the court that the said John Northeast make restitution of the things stole pay the costs of prosecution, receive on his bare back at the common whipping post in Carlisle between the hours of 10 and 12 on the 22 instant 15 lashes well laid on and stand committed till this judgment is complied with.

The King vs James Stackpole and others
Riot. James Stackpole £50, John Kinkerd £25, James Stakpole for his wife £50, Hugh Walker £50, condition that James Stackpole & others appear at next court.

Transposed from July Session 1761
The King vs Jacob Card
Felony. Jury; William Miller, Wm. Fleming, Andrew Armstrong, William Chesney, David Hog, Andrew Holmes, Ekeread Morten, Samuel Pery, John Nailer, John Ludk, John Vanleer and William Caruthers say that the defendant is guilty and it is considered by the Court that the defendant make restitution of the things stole being 11 pounds, 7 shillings and six pence, make fine to the

Governor to the value of the things stole and receive on his bare back 15 lashes
well laid on at the common whipping post in Carlisle on the 20th day of April
next between the hours of 12 and 4 of the same day pay all the costs of this
prosecution and stand committed until this judgment be complied with.

Page 24 January Sessions 1762
The King vs William Mushett
Indictment tippling house.

The King vs Thomas Fowler
Felony. Jury; William Miller, William Fleming, Andrew Armstrong, William
Chesney, David Hog, Andrew Holmes, Edward Morten, Samuel Perry, John
Nailer, John Lask, John Vanleer, William Garuthers say that the defendant is
guilty and it is considered by the Court that the defendant make restitution of
the goods stole or the value thereof, make fine to the Governor in the value of
the things stole pay the costs of this prosecution and receive on his bare back
21 lashes well laid on at the common whipping post in the town of Carlisle on
the 22 instant January between the hours of 10 and 12 in the forenoon of the
same day, stand committed till this judgment is complied with.

The King vs Davis & Governor
Trespass.

The King vs Benjamin Nugent
Assault.

Page 25
The King vs Robert McCulley
Indictment for keeping tavern.

The King vs Thomas Forsler
Felony. It is considered by the Court that the defendant make restitution of the
goods stolen or the value of the same, make fine to the Governor to the value of
the goods stolen, pay all the costs of prosecution, receive upon his bare back at
the common whipping post in Carlisle on the __ 9th of this instant January 39
lashes well laid on, stand committed until this judgment be complied with.

The King vs Barnabas & William Humhey (?)
Trespass.

Page 26 January Sessions 1762
The King vs John Crawford
Trespass.

Benjamin Nugent £50, William McCoskey £30, on condition that Benjamin

Nugent be and appear at the next Court to answer and not depart.

Charles Magill £50, William McCoskey £30, on condition as above.

John Jack £20, on condition that Ann Thomas personally be at the next Court then and there to give evidence. James Jack £20, on condition that Rebecca Boon be and appear as above.

Page 27
The King vs Timothy Connaway & Matthew Coletrap (?)
Indictment felony. Defendant being arraigned plead not guilty. Jury; William Miller, William Fleming, Andrew Armstrong, Jonathan Holmes, David Hogg, Andrew Holmes, Edward Morten, Samuel & John Nailer, John Lusk, John Vanleer, William Caruthers, say that the defendants are guilty. It is considered by the Court that the defendants make restitution of the goods stole or the value of the same, make fine to the Governor to the value of the things stolen, pay all the costs of prosecution and that Mathew Coletrap (?) receive on his bare back 21 lashes well laid on at the common whipping post in Carlisle on the 22nd instant January between the hours of 10 & 12 of the same day and that Timothy Conaway at the same time and place receive 10 lashes on his bare back well laid on, and that both stand committed until this judgment be complied with.

Upon the petition of sundry of the inhabitants of this township of Carlisle, setting forth that said inhabitants labor under sundry inconveniences by reason of the public streets of the town not being laid out and confirmed as public roads, by reason thereof the repairs of the said streets were neglected by the over-seers of the high-ways of the said township. It is ordered by the Court that William Linn, Robert Miller, Robert Robb, Stephen Duncan, William Miller, John Agnu and Thomas Donnellan are appointed to view and if they see cause to lay out the streets or as many of them as to them seem meet into public roads, and make report of their proceedings thereon to the next Court.

Page 28- blank

Page 29
At a Court of Private Sessions, at Carlisle 25 March 1762 for the appointment of officers, before James Galbraith and his associate justices.
Lurgan Township; Arthur Miller, constable; Samuel Rippey, supervisor of
        roads; Davie Herron, Thomas McCombs, over-seers of the poor;
        Abram Weir, Archibald Mahon, viewers of fences.
Letterkenny Township; William Brackenridge, constable; Samuel Culbertson
        supervisor of roads.
Guilford Township; Thomas Birnley, constable; Thomas Baird supervisor of
        roads; Samuel Thompson, William Brotherton overseers of poor;
        James Lindsay, Joseph Crawford viewers of fences.
Hamilton Township; John Erwin, constable; James Guthery overseer of roads.

Antrim Township; Frederick Foreman, constable; James Potter, Henry Pauling
supervisors of roads; John Moorehead, Thomas Pow overseers of
poor.

Peters Township; William Wilson constable; John Shelby, John McClelland
over-seers of roads; John Holiday, Thomas Orbison overseers of
poor.

Fannet Township; Francis McConnell, constable; John Blair, supervisor of
roads; John Elliot, Robert Baker, overseers of poor; John Weir,
Phillip McGuire, viewers of fences.

Air Township; William Hains, constable; Daniel McConnell, supervisor of road

Tyrone Township; John Morrow, constable.

Lack Township; Ralph Street, constable ; William Anderson, John McKeeken,
supervisors of roads.

Farmanagh Township; John White, constable

Page 30
Constables are appointed at the April Term 1762; James Dickey, Richard
Gilston, Stephen Duncan, Edward Lasey and William Willson.

Page 31
At Carlisle, 20 April 1762, before James Galbraith and his associates. The
sheriff returns the following list of grand jurors; John Davis, William Kunkle,
John Miller, William Piper, John Braidy, Richard Long, Charles Patterson,
Andrew Wilkins, James McCall, William Davenport, James Barlay, John
Lindsay, Cleary Campbell, George Daivson, Ralph Whitsides, James Robb,
William McKinney, John Sterritt, Joseph Gailey, John Mickey, Thomas Gay,
Robert Smith, Daniel Reed, James Lawton.

Page 32 April Sessions 1762
The King vs John Ury and others
Indictment riot. Defendant being charged pleads guilty and submits to the
Court. Considered by the Court that the John Ury make fine to the Governor in
the sum of 7 pounds and that John Woods make fine to the Governor in the
sum of 20 shillings, pay all the costs of the prosecutor and the prosecution,
stand committed until this judgment be complied with and give security for the
good behaviour and appearance.

John Eurey £100. condition that he appear at next Court and in the mean while
be of good behaviour. Robert Ury £50, on the same condition. John Wood £20,
condition that he appear at next Court and in the mean while be of good
behaviour. David Hog £10, on the same condition.

Page 33

The King vs Benjamin Nugent

Indictment assault & battery. Benjamin & Joseph solemnly called came not and therefore the recognizance is forfeited. Joseph McForrin (?) £100, on condition that Benj. Nugent appear & not depart.

Alexr Finney is held in £50, on condition that he and Ann Thomas appear at next Court to give evidence.

John Matchel is held in £50, condition that he appear to give evidence.

Rebecca Boon £50, condition to give evidence

The King vs Benjamin Nugent

Indictment assault & battery. Benj. Nugent £200, Joseph McFernan £100, on condition that Benj. Nugent appear at next Court and not depart. July Sessions. Benjamin & Joseph being solemnly called came not, recognizance is forfeited.

Page 34

The King vs Robert Guttery

Assault & battery. Defendant being charged plead guilty and submits to the Court is accordingly fined 5 shillings pay the cost of the prosecutor and of the prosecution, stand committed till fine and fees be paid.

The King vs Moses Jefferies (?)

Assault & battery. Defendant being charged plead guilty and submits to the Court, is fined 10 shillings and six pence, pay the costs of the prosecutor and prosecution, stand committed till judgment be complied with.

Page 35 April Sessions 1762

The King vs William Ferguson

Indictment fornication. William Ferguson £50, William McCroskey £25, on condition that William Ferguson appear at next Court to answer and not depart. July Term, William Ferguson being solemnly called came not and thereupon this recognizance is forfeited and by order of the Court respited till next court. William Ferguson £50, William McCroskey £25, on condition that Wm Ferguson appear at next Court to answer and not depart.

The King vs Moses Jefferies

Assault & battery.

Page 36

The King vs Charles Boyle

Assault.

The King vs John Urie and others
Riot.

Page 37
The King vs Mathew Carr
Assault & battery. Defendant being charged plead guilty and submits to the Court. It is adjudged that he make fee to the Governor in the sum of 5 pounds, pay the costs of prosecutor and prosecution and stand committed till fine and fees are paid. July 22 1762. Ordered by the Court that Mathew Carr __ James Smith two years & a half in the Station of a __.

The King vs John Kennedy
Indictment for tippling house. Defendant pleads not guilty. Jury; Peter Smith, Jonathan Keasley, Wm. Reaney, Saml. Coulter, John Lush, Willm Calonell, Thos. Jeffries, John McCurdy, Thos. Porter, James Thompson, James Alcorn and Mathew Willson who being duly elected and sworn upon their oaths respectfully do say that the defendant is not guilty.

Page 38 April Sessions 1762
The King vs John Davison
Assault & battery. Defendant being charged pleads guilty and submits to the Court. It is considered and fine in 6 pence, to pay costs of prosecution and stand committed till fines and fees are paid.

The King vs John Walker
Indictment felony. The defendant being called plead not guilty. Defendant retracts his plea and pleads guilty. Considered by the Court that the said John Walker make restitution of the things stole, fine to the Governor in 6 pounds, be whipped on his bare back at the publick whipping post in Carlisle on the 23 instant between the hours of 12 & 3, 21 lashes well laid on & stand committed until fine and fees, costs of the prosecutor and this prosecution be paid.

The King vs James Eckles
Trespass. James Cauthers £100, on condition for his good behaviour and complying with a certain order of Court for his delivery __ of certain children. William Caruthers £50.

Page 39
Came into Court William Wallace and by petition set forth that a certain Eleanor Harrison an indented servant to him the said William had at sundry times absented herself from the service of her said master for the space of 6 days and her said master was put to sundry expense in following and recovering the said servant to his service amounting in the whole to 34 shillings. It is considered by the Court and that the said Eleanor Harrison serve her said master or his assigns for the space of three months over and above the time mentioned in her indenture in order to the satisfaction of her said master.

Petition of sundry of the Inhabitants of the township of Allen to the Court
setting forth that the inhabitants of said township labored under sundry
inconveniences for want of a publick road leading from or beginning near __
__ Mills on Yellow Britches Creek the near and best way to Harris Ferry or
into the County road leading by Tobias Hendricks and praying the Court to
appoint proper persons to view and if they see cause to lay all the same, it is
considered by the Court and Tobias Hendricks, Edward Norton, William
Abernathy, James Konnel, Isaac Hendrick, Thomas Rankin, appointed to view
and if they see cause to lay out a road as aforesaid and make report of their
proceedings to next Court and whether the same be for publick or private use.

Page 40- blank

Page 41
At Carlisle, 20 July 1762. The sheriff returned of the following list of grand
jurors; Thomas Hendricks, foreman, Ezekiel Dunning, John Miller, Robert
Robb, John Agnu, William Line, Thomas Donnellan, James Pipper, John
Braidy, David McGuire, John Van Luire, William Brown, John Pollock,
Abram Wood, William McLaskry, William Denny, Joseph Fleming, James
Pollock, Oliver Culbertson, John Patterson, Joseph Boyd, John Gamble, James
McClintock, Charles Pattison,.

Page 42 July Sessions 1762
The following gentleman were sworn on the grand inquest; Tobias Hendrix,
Ezekiel Dunning, Robert Robb, Joseph Galbreath, Thomas Donnalan, James
Piper, John Bready, David Magani, William Brown, John Pollock, Abrm.
Wood, William Denny, James Fleming, James Gullery, John Pattson

Page 43
The King vs William Waddle
Felony. William Waddle £100, Timothy Shaw £50, on condition that Wm.
Wadle appear at next Court & not depart. Wm Waddle £100, Timothy Shaw
£50, Joseph Griley £50, condition that Wm. Wadle be and appear at next Court
& not depart.

The King vs Samuel Moorhead
Indictment battery. The defendant being charged plead guilty and submits to
the Court. It is adjudged that he make a fine to the Governor in the sum of 10
shillings, the cost of the prosecutor and of this prosecution and stand committed
till fine and fees are paid.

Page 44
The King vs Daniel McGinly
Indictment felony. The defendant being solemnly called came not therefore the
recognizance is forfeited.

Came into Court John Gray and by petition set forth that a certain Sarah Hughes an indented servant to him the said John had at sundry times absconded herself from the service of her said master for the space of 43 days and that her said master was put to sundry expense in following and recovering the said servant to his service amounting in the whole to 5 pounds, __ shilling it is adjudged by the Court that Sarah Hughes serve her said master or his assigns for the space of 14 months over and above the time mentioned in her indenture.

Page 45 July Sessions 1762
Came into Court John M. Nichols who was bound to appear at this session in presence of the Court and no person appearing to P__ after publick proclamation & no prosecutor or any recognizance appearing the said John M. Nichols is discharged from the said recognizance.

Came into Court James Moore, Archibald M. Grew, James Weakly, William Smith and Robert Walked being five of the persons appointed by order of a former Court of to view and if they should see cause to lay out a road from the line of York County which might conveniently coincide with the road leading from Carlisle to York Town and made report that they had met in pursuance of their appointment and had accordingly laid out the same road beginning at the Line of York county where a road laid out by order of Court for York County ends and proceeding __ north 252 perches & north 26 degrees, east 240 perches & North 20 degrees, west 120 perches & north 11 degrees, west 172 perches and north __ degrees , East 140 perches and north 12 degrees, east 223 perches into the aforesaid road. The whole being 3 ½ miles, 27 perches, to be of publick use. It is ordered that the same road as aforesaid described and laid be to all intents and purposes a publick road and high way.

Page 46
The petition of sundry of the inhabitants of Guilford and Hamilton township to this Court set fourth that the inhabitants labor under sundry inconveniences for want of a publick road leading from the mountain above Edward Craffords and __ go from thence with a straight course to Adam Hoops Mill and from thence to fort Lowden and prayed the Court to appoint proper persons to view and if they see cause to lay out the same __ whereupon it is considered by the Court and Thomas Poe, Captain James Potter, Jacob Cook, Fredrick Craft, George Brown, and Peter Schnyder are appointed to view and if they see cause to lay out the road as aforesaid, make report of their proceedings to next court and whether the same be of publick or private use.

Page 47
At a Court, 19 October 1762, grand jury men; James Young, Jonathan Holmes, John McClure, Wm Ferguison, Saml. Lindsay, Peter Smith, John Murdough, John Kennedy, Willm Dunbar, Robert McWheney, Richd Venable, Clarey Campbell, Willm Davenport, James White, Andrew Gregg, Joseph McEdy,

Robert Bevard, Saml Gutter, Willm Wallace, Joseph Smith, William Gettis, John Patterson, George Davis, James Garden.

Ordered by the Court that John Murdough be fined the sum of 10 shillings for refusing to take the oath of jury man as proscribed by law and to stand committed till fine and fees are paid.

John Hastens is fine by this Court in the sum of 20 shillings for breaking the Sabbath Day.

Page 48 October Sessions 1762
The following gentlemen were according sworn on the Grand Inquest; James Young, John McClure, Petter Smith, Willm Dunbar, Robert McWhiney, Richd Venable, Willm Davenport, Andrew Gregg, William Gettis, James Borden, Joseph Smith, Daniel McAllester, Robert Sevard, John Kennedy.

Page 49
The King vs William St__ (?) Alias Small
James McMorris (?) £20, on condition that he appear to give evidence.

John Hurt (?) £20, on condition that he appear to give evidence.

Garret Enoch is held in £20, on condition that he appear to give evidence.

The King vs John Martin
Assault & battery.

Page 50
The King vs William Huston
Trespass.

The King vs William Waddle
Indictment felony.

Page 51
The King vs Mary Wallace
Indictment felony. The defendant pleads guilty as to one quarter of a Cambrick and not guilty as to the rest. Jury; Robert Erwin, Joseph Boyd, Culbert Nicholson, William Riddle, James Al__, John Denny, Archd. Miller, James Long, Henry Creighton, Robt Litle, Thos Porter and Saml Lambsay that the defendant is guilty, that the defendant make restitution of the goods stolen or the value thereof, make fine to the Governor in the sum of 19 shillings pay the costs of prosecution and prosecutors, receive on her bare back at the common whipping post in Carlisle between the hours of 9 and 11 on the third Tuesday of November next 5 lashes well laid on and stand committed till this judgment is complied with.

The King vs Mark Chambers
Indictment felony. Pleads not guilty. Jury; Robert Erwin, Joseph Boyd, Culbert Nicholson, Willm Riddle, James Alcorn, John Denny, Arch. Miller, James Long, Henry Creighton, Robt. Litle, Thos Porter and Saml. Lamb say that the defendant is guilty, the defendant make restitution of the money stolen, make fine to the Governor the sum of the money stolen and receive on his bare back at the common whipping post in Carlisle between the hours of 9 and 11 on the 22 October, 21 lashes well laid on, pay all the costs of prosecution & the costs of the prosecutor and stand committed until this judgment be complied with.

Page 52 October Sessions 1762
The petition of sundry of the inhabitants of Lorgan & Hopewell Township to this Court set fourth that the inhabitants of said township labored under sundry in conveniences for want of a publick road being cut leading from James McAllesters Mill near the old Treading (?) Gap in the North Mountain and from thence with a straight course to the town of Carlisle and prayeth the Court to appoint proper persons to view and if they see cause to lay out the same was read. Whereupon it is considered by the Court and John Maclay, James McCormick, James Laughlin, Willm Laughlin, Allen Leeper and Daniel McAllester or any five of them, are appointed to view and if they see cause to lay out the road as aforesaid and make report of their proceedings to next Court ad whither the same be of publick or private use.

Came into Court the report of George Brown, Thomas Poe, James Potter, John Scnider and Jacob Cook and Frederick Croft being the persons appointed by order of a former Court to General Quarter Sessions of the peace to view and if they should see cause to layout a road leading from the mountain above Edward Craffords and __ from thence with a straight course to Adam Hoops Mill and from thence to Fort Lowden the said report being red and considered by the Court they do now appoint and order John Reynolds Esq, William Br__, George Brown, Thomas Pie, James Potter and Joseph Cook __ and if they think proper to lay out the above road and make report of their proceedings the next Court and whither the same be of publick or private use.

Page 53
Petition of divers of the inhabitants of Carlisle and places adjacent there to the Court setting forth that a road from Carlisle to a Gap called Mahaffy's Gap to the county line to enter the road to be laid out through York County towards Baltimore would greatly shorten the way for the person traveling from Carlisle to Baltimore. Was presented to Court and viewers appointed.

Page 54- blank

Page 55

At Carlisle, 8 January 1763. Grand jurymen; Benjamin Blyth, foreman; Ralph Whiteside, Andrew Holmes, Joseph Boyd, Joseph Rook, Saml. Culbertson, Junr; Charles McGill, William Campbell, John Mitchael, Francis McGuire, Robert Gilbreath, John McKay, Edward Morten, Isaac Hendrix, Samuel And__, Thomas McCormick, Joseph Hon, Robert Reed, Even Griffith, Robert Denny, George Hamilton, Robert Hunter, Joseph Elliot.

Page 56 January Sessions 1763

The following gentlemen appearing sworn on the grand inquest; Ralph Whiteside, foreman; Andrew Homes, Joseph Boyd, Charles McGill, Senr; John Mitcheel, Francis McGuire, Edward Morton, Thomas McCormick, Even Griffith, Robert Denny, John Luckey, Joseph McFerron, Mathew Miller, William Campbell, James Grahames.

Upon the motion of Mr. George Ross to the Court, Mr. Thomas Jennes is admitted as attorney of this Court and is sworn as such.

Page 57

The King vs William Waddle

Indictment felony. Defendant pleads not guilty. Jury; Robert __, Samuel Lamb, James Shanks, Thomas Davis, Samuel Morehead, Daniel Williams, William Riddle, Thomas Chidy, Walter Denney, John Kinherd, James Fleming, John Defrance say that the defendant is guilty. It is considered by the Court that the defendant make restitution of the goods stolen and make fine to the Governor in the sum of 7 pounds and receive on his bare back at the common whipping post in Carlisle between the hours of 10 and 12 on the 20th day of January instant 21 lashes well laid on, pay all the costs of prosecutor and the costs of the prosecution and stand committed until this judgment is complied with.

The King vs Benjamin Rio (?) And William Calewell (?)

Page 58

The King vs William Caldwell

Indictment assault & battery.

The King vs John Patterson

Indictment trespass. The defendant being solemnly called pleads not guilty.

Page 59 January Sessions 1763

The King vs William Woods

Indictment felony. The defendant being charged pleads not guilty. Jury; Robert Erwin, Samuel Lamb, James Shank, Thomas Davie, Saml Moorhead. Judgment for the defendant.

The King vs William Woods
Indictment felony. Defendant being arraigned pleads not guilty. Jury; Robert Erwin, Samuel Lamb, James Shanks, Thomas David, Samuel Moorehead, Daniel Williams, William Riddle, Thomas Christy, Walter Denny, John Kinhead, James Fleming, John Defrance say that the defendant is guilty. It is considered by the Court that he make restitution of the goods stolen or the value thereof to the owner, make fine to the Governor in the sum of six pounds and receive on his bare back at the common whipping post in Carlisle between the hours of 9 and 12 on the 21st day of January instant 21 lashes well laid on and pay the costs of prosecution and the costs of the prosecutors and stand committed until this judgement is complied with.

Page 60
The King vs John Defrance
Indictment tippling house. Defendant plead guilty.

The King vs Agness Leath
Indictment felony.

Page 61
The King vs William Christy & Andrew Serroll
Indictment felony. Andrew Serrol £40, John Chapman £40, on condition that Andrew Serrol appear at next Court and not depart.

Saml Lamb £10, Jams Slackpole £10, Wm Lamb £10, on condition that they be and appear to give evidence.

Willm Christy & Andrew Serol £20 each, Thomas Christy & John Chapman £10 each, on condition that Wm Christy and Andrew Serol be and appear and not depart. James Maxwell £10, that he be and appear to give evidence. Recognizance forfeited as to Serrol. January Sessions 1764. Jury; Walter Denny, Robert __. William Armstrong, Robert Litle, Moses Barrick, William Livingston. Abraham __, [can't read the rest]

The King vs William Christy
Indictment felony. Jury; Walter Denny, Robert Walker, William Armstrong, Robert Little, Moses Barnet, William Levingston, Abraham Sandford, Arthur Forster, James Hunter, James Weakby, Robert Campbell, and Roger Clark say that William Christy is guilty of the felony. It is considered by the court that he make restitution of the goods stolen and make fine to the Governor to the same value and that he receive 5 lashes on the bare back on the 26th day of March next and stand committed until the same be complied with.

Page 62 January Sessions 1763
The King vs William Woods & William Shane
Indictment felony.

The King vs William Woods
Indictment felony. Motion to the Court the said Bill is quashed the defendant upon a __ to a former bill this session of the said felony having had judgment in his favor.

Page 63
Came into Court Thomas Wilson, John Davis, Alexander Roddy, and James Young , four of the persons appointed by an order of a former Court to view and lay out the nearest and best way for a public road from the head of Sherman's Valley to the town of Carlisle make a report and return under their hand that a public road well opened and made through the lands of William Smiley, Francis West, William McClure, James Dick, and John Mitchell's to Alexander Logan's, from thence to the gap in the Tuskarora Mountain leading to Aughwich and Juniata road the nearest and best way from the head of Sherman's Valley to the town of Carlisle and as most convenient for the inhabitants thereabouts which road we return of public use. It is accordingly ordered by the Court that the said road be opened agreeable to the report.

Page 64
Came into Court Rowlin Chambers and by petition to said Court setting forth the great disconveniency and damage done to the petitioner by a road being laid out leading from Ralph Whitesides Mill near Yellow Breeches Creek to Tobias Hendrix which road goes __ best of petitioners land and prayeth the Court to grant him a second __ in order to turn the road from doing him so great damage was __. Whereupon it is considered by the Court and James Hunter, John McCormick, Francis McGuire, Thomas McCormick, George Woods and John Trindle are appointed to view the road as aforesaid and make report of their proceedings to next court.

Page 65
At Carlisle, 25 March 1763, for the appointment of officers before John Byers and his associates. The following officers were appointed.
Lurgan Township; Samuel Breckenridge, constable; Samuel Culberston Sr., Archibald Mahon, supervisor of roads; Thomas Montgomery , Will Linn Jr., over-seers of the poor.
Letterkenny Township; John Mitchell, constable.
Guilford Township; John Hammond, constable; Thomas Baird, James Guthery supervisors of roads; Thomas Baird, Matthew Wilson over-seeker of poor; John Forsyth , James Lindsay, viewers of fences.
Hamilton Township; John Hindran, constable; Thomas Patterson, James Eaton overseers of poor; Samuel Sloan, Joseph Swan, viewers of fences.
Antrim Township; James Lane, constable; George Brown, Henry Pritter, supervisors of roads; George Brown, James McKee, overseers of poor; William Rankin, Samuel Smith, viewers of fences.
Peters Township; William More, constable

Fannet Township; John Elder, constable; Phillip McGuire, David Scott
supervisors of roads; David Campbell, William Wallace, overseers of
poor; John Sanns, Samuel Parker, viewers of fences.
Aire Township; Richard Stephens, constable.
Tyrone Township; John Hamilton, constable; Hugh Kilgore, Joseph Adam
supervisors of roads; Thomas Rose, George Robinson, overseers of
poor.
Tiboyne Township; James Wilson, constable; John Crawford, John Byers,
overseers of poor.
Lack Township; John McClellan, constable; Robert Campbell, Robert Houston
supervisors of roads; William Graham, John Erwin, overseers of
poor.
Farmanach Township; Arthur Moody, constable; John Nicholson, Samuel
Mitchell, supervisors of roads; Andrew Keever, George Hays,
overseers of poor; Alexander Laverty, Samuel Gallacher, viewers of
fences.

Page 66
Upon application of some of the inhabitants of Tyrone Township to this Court
setting forth that the said township is too large, it is adjudged by the said Court
that Alexander Roddy Mill Run be the line and the name of the Upper
Teboyne, Alexander Logans being in Teboyne township.

Ordered by the Court that Hugh Kilgor and James Adams be overseers of the
road in Tyrone township for the ensuing year.

Page 67
At Carlisle, 19 April 1793. List of grand jurymen; Benjamin Glyh (?) Foreman,
James Dunlap, James Randles, John Piper, William Piper, William Randles,
Robert Culberson, James Piper, James Boggs, Cleary Campbell, Samuel
Culberson, Robert Peoples, Johnston Smith, John Blair, Taussey Miller,
Samuel Rippey, John Nailor, James Kibbin, John Jack, Daniel Duncan,
Mathew Willson, Alexander Finney, Isaac Hendrix

Page 68 April Sessions 1763
The following gentlemen were sworn on the inquest; Benjamin Blyth, William
Piper, William McKinney, Clerry Campbell, Robert Peoples, Johnston Smith,
Samuel Rippey, John Nailor, John Jack, Daniel Duncan, Mathew Willson,
Isaac Hendrix.

Upon the application of Mr. James Smith to the Court Nicholas Waln was
admitted an attorney of this Court & was duly qualified according to the Act of
Assembly in that case provided.

A motion of Mr. Smith the person's appointed to view & lay out the road from James McCallisters Mill to near the gap of the North Mountain to Carlisle town, having been disappointed in getting a surveyor, so that they could not report to the Court, are continued & ordered that they view & if they see cause to lay our this road and make report to the next Court.

Page 69
The King vs Laurence Kelly
Laurence Kelly £20, Thomas Donalling £10, on condition that Laurence appear & not depart.

Isaac Hendrix £20, Isaac Baker £20, on condition that he appear the said Isaac Baker at next court to give evidence.

Christian Runnion £20, Isaac Baker £20, on condition that Christian Rummion & others be and appear at next quarter session.

Page 70
The King vs William Dunlap & John Dunlap
The defendant being called upon their recognizance for their good behaviour appeared and are discharged.

The King vs Margaret Dunsmore
The defendant being called upon the recognizance for his good Behaviour.

John Dinsmore £10, on condition that Margaret Dinsmore be of good behaviour & also that she be and appear at next quarter session.

Page 71
Came into Court Tobias Hendrick, Edward Morton, Isaac Hendricks and James McConnell being 4 of the persons appointed by order of a former Court to view and if they should see cause to layout a road from or beginning near Ralph Whitesides Mill on Yellow Britches Creek the nearest and best way to Harris Ferry or into the County road leading by Tobias Hendricks and made report that they had met in pursuance of their appointment and have accordingly laid out the same road beginning at a white oak tree & from thence North 41 degrees west 294 perches from thence north 66 degrees west 100 perches from thence north 31 degrees west 50 perches from thence north 23 degrees west 30 perches from thence north 34 degrees west 90 perches from thence north 62 degrees west 30 perches from thence north 41 degrees west 50 perches from thence north 24 degrees west 65 perches from thence north 12 degrees east 320 perches from thence north 20 degrees east 540 perches to the Carlisle road, and that the same is of publick use. Ordered the road as aforesaid described laid out be to all intents and purposes as a publick road and high way and that the same as such be fourth with opened cleared and repaired.

Page 72
Came into Court John Rannells, George Brown, Joseph Cook and Thomas Poe being four of the persons appointed by order of a former court to view and if they should see cause to lay out a road from or beginning at the Gap of the Mountain above Edward Crawfords to Adam Hoops Mill and from thence to Fort Lowden, and made report that they had met in pursuance of their appointment and have accordingly laid out the same road beginning at the Gap or forks of the road above Edward Crawfords to Adam Hoops Mill following the old road to John Harmonnys north 70 degrees west 8 miles and 60 road and from Adam Hoops Mill to Back Creek at John Glens following the Warm Spring Road west 5 miles and from Back Creek to Lowden Road at William McDonalls north 50 degrees west 3 miles and 280 roads in all 17 miles and 10 hands and that the same is of publick use. Ordered the road described and laid out be to all intents and purposes as a publick road & High way and that the same as such be forth with opened cleared and repaired in pursuance of an act of Assembly of this Province in such case made and provided.

The petition of sundry of the inhabitants of Sherman's Valley of this county, praying the Court to grant them an order for laying out a road in the most convenient manner from the head of the valley aforesaid to the road leading from Crogham's Gap to Alexander Logan's.

It is considered by the Court and that James Blain, Alexander Logan, John Crawford, John Gardner, Francis West and Alexander Roddy or any four of them view and if they see cause lay out said road, make return to next Court.

Page 73
At Carlisle, 19 July 1763. The sheriff returned the following gentlemen to serve the Grand Inquest; Joseph Hunter foreman, John Egnen, John Steel, James Barclay, John Mitchell, Thomas Holt, William Wallace, John Gray, William Donney, John Pollock Carpr, John Holmes, Abraham Holmes, John Pollock, Mallster, William Blaire, Robert Sample, Samuel Tromple, Thomas Patton, William Lyon, Abraham Wood, William Divenpoart, Joseph Jaffries, Robert Campbell Thomson.

Page 74- blank

Page 75   July Sessions 1763

The King vs John Hamilton
Felony.

Baptist Scot £25, on condition that he appear at next Court to give evidence.

Margaret Nilson £25, on condition that she appear at next Court to give evidence.

John Glen £25, on condition that he appear at next Court to give evidence.

John Glen £25, on condition that he appear at next Court to give evidence.

John Buyers £25, on condition that Margaret Nilson appear at January Court to give evidence.

Baptist Scot £25, on condition that he appear at January Court to give evidence.

The King vs Mary Stewart
Recognizance to answer. Defendant being called appeared & no grand jury appearing she is continued on former recognizance till next Court.

Page 76- blank

Page 77
At Carlisle, 18 Oct 1763. The sheriff returned the following list of gentlemen who were summoned to be on the Grand Inquest; John Michell foreman, Robert Gibson, William Gammel, Samuel Leard, Robert McWhinney, Abraham Holmes, James Pollock, John Kerr, Stephen Folk, John Gray, John McCurdy, William Brown, Stephen Duncan, John Pollock, John Van Lear, James Barclay, John Kinkead, James Thomson, Thomas Parks, William Kenney, Jonathan Kearsley, John Ballison, John Hastings, James Magussage

Page 78 October Sessions 1763
The following gentlemen were sworn on the Grand Inquest; John Michell, Robert Gibson, Robert McWhinney, Stephen Folk, John Gray, John McCurdy, Stephen Duncan, John Van Lear, James Barclay, John Kinkend, James Thomson, William Keaney, Jonathan Kearsley, James Magussage.

The King vs Robert Stewart
The Defendant being called upon the recognizance for his good behaviour appeared.

Robert Stewart £20, Thomas Patton £10, for the good behaviour of Robert Stewart. The defendant being solemnly came not therefore the defendant came.

Page 79
The King vs Thomas Gullory
James Gordon £10, James Gullery £10, for appearance during this Session.

The King vs Margaret Dinsmore
Assault & battery.

Page 80
The King vs Samuel Harper

The King vs John Hamilton
Felony. Defendant being called & being arraigned plead not guilty.

Page 81
The King vs Allen Ralston
Assault & battery.

The King vs Petter Goodlink
Trespass.

Page 82 October Sessions 1763
The King vs James Guttery
Assault. The defendant being charged & not being willing to contend with the King submits to the Court & prays to be admitted to a small fine. Whereupon it is considered by the Court that the said James Guttery make fine to the Governor in the sum of 20 shillings & stand committed till fines are paid.

The petition of sundry of the inhabitants of Midelton township to this Court setting fourth that sundry of the inhabitants of said township laboreth under sundry inconveyencies for want of a private road leading from Thomas Johnsons plantation on Conesogavanet and to run from thence and fall into the Great Road leading to Carlisle near Ezekiel Smiths & that it would be of great advantage the inhabitants of the said township which road the petition will maintain at their own expense and prayeth the Court to appoint proper persons to view and if they see cause to lay out the same was read. It is considered by the Court and James Waugh, James Kenney, Andrew Armstrong, George Sanderson, William Fleming and Andrew McBeath or any five of them do view & is they see cause to lay out a road agreeable to the pray of the petition.

Page 83
At Carlisle, 24 January 1764, the Sheriff returns list of gentlemen summoned to serve on the Grand Inquest; Ezekiel Smith foreman, Andrew Holmes, Robert Nemell, William Marshell, George Gillespey, William Moore, George Kinkead, John Orr, John Hastens, James McGussoge, James Crawford, Ralph Whitesides, George Hamilton, John Giles, Edward McMurrey, John Forgey, Richard Parker, William Fleming, Samuel Marten, William Ferguson, John Davison, Robert Lowry, John Andrew, Francis McGuire.

Page 84 January Term 1764
The following gentlemen appearing were sworn on the Grand Inquest; Ezekl Smith foreman, Andrew Holmes, Robert Nevel, William Marshel, George Gillespie, William Moore, George Kinkead, John Orr, John Haslens, James Maussoge, James Crawford, Ralph Whitesides, George Hamilton, John Giles, Edward McMurrey, John Forgey, Richard Parker, William Fleming.

The King vs Ann Means

Felony. Defendant pleads not guilty. Jury; to wit [blank] do say who upon their oath respectively that the defendant is guilty. The Court do adjudge that the she be whipped at the publick whipping post tomorrow between the hours of 10 & 12 o'clock with 5 lashes on her bare back well laid on, make restitution the goods stolen or value thereof, make fine in the like to the Governor, pay the costs of prosecution and stand committed till fines and fees are paid.

Page 85

The King vs James Barkley

The Defendant being unwilling to contend with the King protests his innocence & submits. The Court fines the defendant 2 shillings & six pence & costs of suit & he is committed until fine & fees are paid. James Barkley £40, John Mitchell £20, for the appearance of James Barkley at next Court & good behaviour in the mean time especially to Alexander Bremer.

The King vs Andrew Ferrol

Andrew Ferrol £50, Benjamin Kid £25, on condition that Andrew Ferrol be & appear at next Court & not depart.

Page 86

Came into Court James McColough and by petition to said Court setting forth the great disadvantage & damage done to the petitioner for want of a road to the said petitioners and which Lyes Belmix, John Hansys (?) & Arthur Clark which formerly was a road to said Meacon. Whereupon it is considered & ordered by the Court the road by laid out on the line between Arthur Clark & John _nansy equal on each side of the line and also to continue its former course & that the said petitioner is to cut & keep open said road at his own expense.

The King vs John Donnellan

Assault & battery.

Page 87

At a Private Sessions held at Carlisle, 5 March 1764 for the appointment of officers before John McKnight and his associates.

Lurgan Township; Thomas Grier, constable; John Weir supervisor of roads; Samuel Rippey, John Weir overseers or poor.

Letterkenny Township; Samuel Mitchell, constable ; John Finely Supervisor road

Guilford Township; Henry Thompson, constable; Thomas Baird supervisor of roads; Matthew Wilson, Samuel Thompson overseers of poor; John Forsyth, John Lindsay viewers of fences.

Hamilton township; John Glen, constable: James Guthery, supervisor of roads.

Antrim township; Henry Snively, constable; James Potter, James Cook,
supervisors of roads; George Brown, James McKee, overseers of
poor; William Rankin, William Wallace, viewers of fences.
Peters township; John Erwin, constable; William Campbell, Robert McCay s
upervisors of roads; John Holliday, Thomas Orbison overseers of
poor; William McDowell, James Davis, viewers of fences.
Fannet Township; Phillip McGurie, constable; Alexander Walker, Francis
Elliot overseers of poor; John Blair, Francis McCormick, viewers of
fence.
There were no officers appointed this year for either of the townships of Aire,
Tyrone, Tiboyne, Lack or Farmanagh.

Page 88
At Carlisle, 17 Apr 1764, the sheriff returned the following list of gentleman
who were summoned to serve on the Grand Inquest; Tobias Hendrick foreman,
Samuel Cunningham, Moses Starr, Allen Leeper, William Patton, James Love,
Paul Pierce, Thomas Clark, Thomas McCormick, David Hog, George Woods,
Thomas Holmes, Samuel Brison, Richard Nickleson, David Cruchlow, John
Nailor, Edward Morton, William Woods, George Sanderson, John Gregg,
James Grahams, Richard Rankin, James McConnel, John Finley.

Page 89- blank

Page 90
At Carlisle, 24 July 1764, the Sheriff, Ezekl Dunning, returned the following
list of gentlemen who were summoned to serve on the Grand Inquest; Robert
Robb foreman, William Lion, Abraham Wood, William Denny, John Pollock
Carpr, John Starret, John Agnem, John Pollock Malstr, Stephen Duncan,
William Wallace, John Van Lear, James Parker, William McCroskry, James
Ramsey, John Kerr, John Kinkead, Charles Patterson, John Kennedy, Peter
Smith, John Gamble, John McCurdy, Hugh Wallace, William Devenport,
James Robb.

Page 91 July Sessions 1764
The following were sworn on the Grand Inquest; Robert Robb foreman,
William Lyon, Abraham Wood, William Denny, John Starrel, John Pollock
Malster, Stephen Duncan, William Wallace, William McCroskry, John Kerr,
Charles Pattison, John Kennedy, Peter Smith, John Gamble, John McCurdy.

The King vs Ephraim Blain
Assault & battery.
The Defendant acknowledged his fault & submits himself to the Court. It is
considered by the Court that the said Ephraim Blain make fine to the Governor
the sum of 10 shillings & stand committed till fine are paid.

Page 92
The King vs Thomas Kempleton
Felony. Defendant pleads not guilty. Jury; John Steel, Saml Laird, Thomas
Holt, James Thompson, Joseph Boyd, John Hasten, Robert Guttery, James
McClinlock, James Brandon, Joseph Neeper, William Ramey, Andrew
Kinkead who being duly elected & sworn who their oaths respectively do say
that the defendant is not guilty and is discharged upon his payment of the fees.

The King vs George Jacob Houseman
Assault & battery. Defendant submits under protests of his innocence. It is
considered by the Court that the said George Jacob Houseman make fine to the
Governor of 10 shillings & stand committed until fine & fees are paid.

Page 93
The King vs James Stackpole
Assault & battery. James Stackpole now present in Court being unwilling to
contend with the King & submits to the Court and prays to be admitted to a
small fine, it is considered by the Court & the said he is fined in the sum of 3
pounds to the Governor with costs of prosecution and stand committed till fine
and fees are paid.

The King vs John Beard
Assault& battery.

Page 94
The King vs James Patton
Felony.

The King vs Samuel Holliday
Assault & battery.

Samuel Holliday now present in Court & being unwilling to contend with the
King, protesting his innocence submits to the Court, prays to be admitted to a
small fine and is thereupon considered by the Court & the said Samuel
Holliday is fined to the Governor in the sum of 5 shillings, with costs of
prosecution & stand committed till fine & fees paid.

Page 95
The King vs John Dougherty
Assault & battery.

The King vs Thomas Duncan
Assault & battery.

Page 96 July Sessions 1764
The King vs Hanna Brown
Felony. Defendant pleads not guilty. Jury; Robert Gibson, John Dunning, John Sisna, John Leach, Phillip Miller, Alexr McConnel, Robert Erwin, David McNear, Patrick Robison, Saml Reock, George Woods & John Kinkead say that the defendant is not guilty and is discharged upon her payment of her fees.

The King vs William Proctor
Tippling house.

Page 97
The King vs Jeremiah Reese
Trespass. Defendant being arraigned plead not guilty & George Ross who prosecutes for our Sovereign Lord the King in like manner [blank]

The King vs Sarah Reynolds
Assault & battery.

Page 98
The King vs Thomas Beard & James Gullery
For not clearing the highway. Defendant Thomas Beard being arraigned pleads not guilty. Retracts his plea & on motion the In__ is quashed by the Court.

Thomas Beard £20, James Gullery £20, Benjamin Chambers£20, on condition that Thos Beard & James Gullery be & appear at Next Court & not depart.

The King vs John Glen
Assault & battery. John Glen £20, Joseph McFarren £20, on condition that John Glen be & appear at next court & not depart without leave.

Defendant pleads not guilty. Jury; William Wallace, John Mitchell, William Stewart, Jacob Houseman, Thomas Paton, John Wallace, Barnabas Hughs, John McCay, Samuel Skinner, William Rodman, Joseph Connally & Samuel Coulter who say that the defendant is not guilty.

Page 99 July Sessions 1764
The King vs Thomas Patten
Tippling house.

The King vs Nathan Andrews
Tippling house.

Page 100- blank

Page 101
At Carlisle, 23 Oct 1764, sheriff returned the following list to serve on the Grand Inquest; John Miller foreman, David Magan, Robert McDowel, William Stewart, Thomas Guy, William Laughlin, Andrew Wilkey, James Carmaghan, Daniel Duncan, James McCall, John Montgomery, James Dunlap, William Reynolds, Samuel Montgomery, Arthur Parks, Cleary Campbell, Charles McCormick, Charles McGill, James Henderson, George McCamey, William Brotherton, Robert Peoples, Samuel Rippey, George Taylor.

Ordered by the Court that Willm Stewart, Thomas Guy, Willm Laughlin, James Carmahan, James McCall, John Montgomery, Arthur Parks, Charles McCormick, James Henderson, Willm Brotherton, Robert Peoples, Saml. Rippey, George Taylor be find 20 shillings each for non attendance agreeable to summon on the Grand Jury.

Page 102 October Sessions 1764
The following appearing were sworn on the Grand Inquest; John Miller foreman, David Magam, Robert McDowel, Andrew Eilkey, Daniel Duncan, William Reynolds, Cleary Campbell, Charles McCall, George McCamey.

The King vs Thomas Morehead
Thos. Morehead £20, Saml. Sloan £10, on condition that Thos. Morehead be & appear at next Court & not depart.

Page 103
The King vs James McCurdey
James McCurdey £20, Thomas Patton £10, on condition that Saml McCurdey be & appear at next Court & not depart.

Page 104- blank

Page 105
At Carlisle, 22 January 1765, the sheriff returned the following list summoned to serve on the Grand Inquest; Andrew Holmes foreman, Robert Peoples, James McCall, Arthur Parks, Charles Kimmins, Benjamin Blyth, William Brown, John Gray, John Procter, Samuel Weer, Robert McComes, William Clark, John Vanlear, John McClure, Joseph Boyd, Thomas Guy, William Ferguson, Samuel Willson.

Page 106 January Sessions 1765
The following appearing were sworn on the Grand Inquest; Andrew Holmes foreman, Robert Peoples, James McCall, Arthur Parks, Charles Kimmins, Benjamin Blyth, William Brown, John Gray, John Kimmins, John Vanlear, John McClure, Joseph Boyd, Thomas Guy.

Page 107
The King vs Phillip Connelly
Assault & battery. Defendant pleads guilty, submits to the Court, fined 10 shillings, pay the cost of the prosecution and stand committed till fine and fees be complied with.

The King vs John Murphy
Felony. Defendant pleads guilty, submits to the Court, fined 50 shillings, receive on his bare back at the common whipping post in Carlisle between the hours of 10 & 11 oclock on 25 January, 21 lashes well laid on and pay all costs of prosecution & prosecutors, stand committed until find and fees be complied with.

Page 108
The King vs Phillip Connelly
Assault & battery. Defendant pleads guilty, submits to the Court, fined 10 shillings, pay the costs of the prosecution and stand committed till fine and fees be complied with.

The King vs Thomas Morehead
Assault & battery. Defendant pleads not guilty. Thomas Morehead being unwilling to contend with out Lord the King & pretesting his innocence retracts his plea & submits to the Court & prays to be admitted to a small fine and it is fined one shilling by the Court & to stand committed till fine & fee are paid.

Page 109
The King vs James McCurdy
James McCurdy came into Court in proper person in pursuance of his recognizance and by James Smith his attorney prayed to be discharged from his recognizance, no person appearing to prosecute he is thereupon discharged from his recognizance.

The King vs John Robinson
John Robinson £40, Stephen Duncan £30, on condition that John Robinson appear next session to answer & not depart the Court without license.

Page 110 January Sessions 1765
The King vs James Gullery
Tippling house. Jury; Abraham Woods, Daniel Laurance, William Waugh, Thomas Beard, Thomas Davis, William Denny, Petter Smith, Robert Guttery, John Hastin, John Pollack, John McCallester & John Kinhead say that the defendant is not guilty.

The King vs Hugh McDonnald
Tippling house.

Page 111
The King vs Thomas Perkins
Assault.

The King vs Thomas Williamson
Tippling house.

Page 112
The King vs John Wilcocks, William Morrow, James McMahan
Riot.

The King vs John Nicholson
Assault & battery.

Page 113
The King vs Samuel Finley
Assault.

Came into Court William Laughlin, Daniel McCallester, James Laughlin, Allen
Leeper, John McClear being 5 of the persons appointed by order of a former
Court to view and if they should see cause to lay out a road from James
McCallesters Mills to Carlisle & made report that they had met in pursuance of
their appointment & had accordingly laid out the same road beginning in the
great road leading from Carlisle to Shippensburg to a marked hickory & thence
north 84 degrees 30 minutes west 75 persons to Sam Henrys & thence North 85
degrees 40 minutes west 80 perches thence north 40 degrees west 230 perches
thence north 66 degrees west 410 perches thence south 88 degrees west 130
perches thence 56 degrees west 400 perches thence south 75 30 minutes west
292 perches thence south 54 degrees 45 minutes west 348 perches thence south
81 degrees west 242 perches thence north 42 degrees west 18 perches thence
south 61 degrees 30 minutes west 69 perches thence north 60 degrees west 80
perches thence south 51 degrees 30 minutes west 60 perches thence south 72
degrees west 92 perches thence south 60 degrees west 46 perches thence south
82 degrees 30 minutes west 155 perches thence north to Connogquinn Creek
79 degrees 30 minutes west 249 perches thence north 60 degrees 30 minutes
west 54 perches thence south 80 degrees west 70 perches thence south 55
degrees 30 minutest west 174 perches thence south 73 degrees west 72 perches
thence south 84 degrees 30 minutes west 126 perches thence south 63 degrees
30 minutes west 298 perches thence south 71 degrees west 46 perches thence
south 28 degrees west 210 perches thence south 58 degrees 30 minutes west 58
perches thence south 81 degrees 30 minutes west 220 perches thence south 50
degrees west 198 perches thence south 84 degrees 30 minutes west 94 perches
thence north 29 degrees west 59 perches thence south 79 degrees west 123
perches thence south 62 degrees 30 minutes west 150 perches thence south 80
degrees 30 minutes west 24 perches thence north 78 degrees west 34 perches
thence south 54 degrees west 80 perches thence south 74 degrees west 74

perches thence south 82 degrees west 134 perches thence south 85 degrees west 44 perches thence south 50 degrees west 30 perches thence south to James McCallesters Mill 80 degrees west 204 perches & that the same is of public use whereupon it is ordered by the Court that the same road as aforesaid described & laid out be to all intents and purposes as a publick road.

Page 114
The Petition of Sundry of the inhabitants of the Township of Carlisle, Middeton and West Pennsborough praying the Court to appoint men to view and if they see cause to lay out the same was read whereupon it is considered by the Court that John Davis, James Gordon, Robert Little, Robert McClu__, William Logan & William Gettys or any four of them are appointed to view and if they see cause to lay out the road as aforesaid and make report of their proceeding to the next Court.

Page 115
At Carlisle, 25 March 1765, for the appointment of officers and before John McKnight and his associates.
Lurgan Township; James Stuart, constable.
Letterkenny Township; William Breckenridge, constable.
Guilford township; Anthony Snyder, constable; John Erwin, John Lindsay supervisors of the roads; William Gass, William Brotherton overseers of poor; Hugh Thompson, George Smith viewers of fences.
Hamilton township; Thomas Paterson, constable.
Antrim township; John Moorehead, constable; John McBath, James Roddy viewers of fences.
Peters township; James Rankin, constable.
Fannet township; John Elliot, constable.
Aire township; Malcum McFall, constable.
Tyrone township; Thomas Ross, constable.

Page 116
Upon application made to this Court that a constable is wanted at Bedford. The Court appointed Samuel Drennen to serve as constable in Bedford and the parts adjoining the said town for the ensuing year.

Page 117
At Carlisle, 23 April 1765, before James Galbraith and his associates. The sheriff Ezekiel Dunning returns the following list of grand jurors: John Mitchell, Thomas Burney, Ralph Whitsides, James Gregiry, William Morrison, William Marshall, Carns Sterett, William Hudson, John Clark, John Daugherty, Samuel Davis, John Naylor, Nathaniel Wilson, William Ore, John Flannigan, Robert Crawford, William Pipper, Richard Long, John Pipper, Joseph Hudson, James Pipper, David Davis, Richard Carson, William Bennet.

Page 118 April Sessions 1765
The following were sworn on the Grand Inquest; Thomas Burney foreman,
Ralph Whitesides, James Gregory, William Morrison, William Marshell, Crons
Starret, William Hudson, John Clark, Samuel Davis, John Nailor, Nathaniel
Nilson, William Orr, John Flenigan, Robert Crawford, Joseph Hudson, Richard
Carson, William Bennet.

Page 119
The King vs William Porter & others
Riot.

The King vs George McGonagle
George McGonagle £40, Daniel Lawrance £10, Abraham Wood £10, James
McLee £10, John Bain £10, condition that George McGonagle appear at next
Court.

Page 120 April Sessions 1765
The King vs William Campbell
Assault. Defendant pleads guilty, submits to the Court, fined 2 shillings, six
pence to the Governor, pay the costs of prosecution and stand committed till
fine and fees be complied with.

The King vs Michael Cotterel
Felony. Defendant pleads guilty, submits to the Court, fined 40 shillings to the
Governor, make restitution of the goods stolen, receive on his bare back at the
common whipping post in Carlisle between the hours of 10 & 12 oclock on the
25th day of April instant 20 lashes well laid on and stand committed till fine &
fees & the cost of prosecution be paid.

Page 121
The King vs Barnabas Hughs
Assault & battery. Barnabas Hughs £20, James Reed £10, conditioned that
Barnabas Hughs appear at next Court of July 1765. Defendant retracts his plea,
submits to the Court, fined 5 shillings to the Governor, pay the costs of
prosecution & stand committed till fine and fees are paid.

The King vs James Foley
Assault & battery.

Page 122
The King vs John Dunning
Assault & battery. James Foley £10, on condition he appear at the next Court to
give evidence in behalf of the King. John Dunning £20, John Steel £10, on
condition that John Dunning appear at the next Court & not depart without
leave. July 1765 Defendant submits to the Court with protestation of his
innocence, fined 2 shillings and 6 pence to the Governor, pay the costs of

prosecution & stand committed till fine and fees be complied with.

Page 123
Petition of sundry of the inhabitants of the Township of Hopewell & Lurgan to the Court setting forth that sundry of the inhabitants of said townships labor under sundry inconveniences for the want of a publick road from McCallestors Mills to Shippensburg & from thence across the South Mountain to York County line which would be of great advantage to the inhabitants of said townships & prayeth the Court to appoint proper persons to view and if they see cause to lay out the same was read. Whereupon it is considered by the Court & James McGillester, John McClay Junr, James McCall, William Piper, James Dunlap and William Reynolds were appointed to view the road as aforesaid & make report of their proceedings to the next court.

Petition of sundry of the inhabitants of the township of Guilford, Hamilton & Petters for this Court setting forth that sundry of the inhabitants of said townships laboreth under sundry inconveniences for want of a publick road from the fork of the road above Edward Crafords the nighest and best way to Fort Loudon which wold be of great advantage to the inhabitants of said townships & prayeth the Court to appoint proper persons to view and if they see cause to lay out the same was read. Whereupon it is considered by the Court & William Holland, Nathan McDomatt, Samuel Sloan, Captain James Potter, Samuel Lindsay & Thomas Beard or any four of them are appointed to view and if they see cause to lay our the road as aforesaid and make report of their proceedings to the next court.

Page 124
Came into Court Jonathan Holmes, Andrew Holmes, Joseph Hunter, James Crocket, Robert Robb being five of the persons appointed by order of a former Court of General Quarter Sessions of the peace to view and if they should see cause to lay out a road from Carlisle to the York County Line near Dills Gap Beginning at the Great Road leading to Herrises ferry near Carlisle & extending & thence south 55 degrees east 243 perches thence north 88 degrees east 53 perches thence north 7_ degrees east 67 perches thence south 66 degrees east __ by 6 perches thence south 31 degrees east 56 perches thence south 49 degrees east 160 perches thence south 21 degrees & ½ degree east 240 perches thence south 56 degrees east 164 perches thence south 40 degrees east 64 perches thence south to Bank (?) Spring 21 degrees east 54 perches thence South 87 degrees east 366 perches thence south 37 degrees east 160 perches thence south to Yellow Breeches Creek 4 degrees east 42 perches thence south 67 degrees east 96 perches thence south to the county line 57 degrees east 344 perches being in all 8 1/4 miles & 77 perches & that the same is of publick use. Whereupon it is ordered by the Court that the same road as aforesaid described & laid out be to all intents & purposes as a publick road & high way & that the same as such be forthwith opened cleared & repaired in pursuance of an Act of Assembly of this province in such case made & provided.

Page 125

Account of roads confirmed commencing July Sessions 1762.

1. Beginning at the line of York county to coincide with the road leading to Yorktown.

Tyrone divided, the name of the upper Tiboyne. January Sessions 1763

2. Beginning at Ralph Whitsides' Mill to Harris Ferry, April 1763

3. Beginning at the Gap of the mountain near Edward Crawford's (say Roxbury)

4. Beginning at McAllaster's to Shippensburg, January 1765

5. Beginning at Carlisle to York County line near Dill's Gap, April 1765

6. Beginning at Mr. Rock and the McAllaster's Gap, January 1765.

Quarter Session Docket 3 1765-1768

Page 1
At Carlisle, 23 July 1765 before John Armstrong Esq and his associates. The Sheriff returns the following jury men; Robert Kobb, foreman, Samuel Leard, James Ransey, James Pollock, Stephen Duncan, Thomas Donnallan, John VanLear, Robert Gamble, Joseph Hunter, James Gibson, Jacob Honeyman, Samuel Gamble, James Barcley, John Pollock (Malster), William Denney, Jonathan Kesley, Stephen Folk (?), Ephraim Blain, John McCurdey, Abraham Wood, Charles Patterson, John Carr, Jacob Cart, Robert McWhiney

Page 2 July Session 1765
The following were recorded on the Grand Inquest; Robert Kobb, Foreman; Samuel Leard, James Ransey, Stephen Duncan, Thomas Donnallan, Jacob Honeyman, Samuel Gamble, John Pollack, (Malster), William Denny, Jonathan Kearnly(?), Ephraim Blain, John McCurdey, Charles Patterson, John Carr, Robert McWhiney.

Page 3
The King vs John Smith
Felony. Defendant pleads guilty, fined 12 pounds, receive on his bare back at the common whipping post in Carlisle between the hours of 9 & 11 o'clock on the 25 July, 21 lashes well laid on, to make restitution to the owner of the value of the goods stolen, pay all costs of prosecution and the costs of the prosecution and stand committed until fine and fees be complied with.

The King vs John Smith
Felony. Defendant pleads guilty, submits to the Court, fined 7 pounds to the Governor and received on his bare back at the common whipping post in Carlisle between the hours of 9 and 11 o'clock on 25 July, 20 lashes well laid on, make restitution to the owner of the value of the goods stolen and pay all costs of prosecution, stand committed until fine and fees be complied with.

Page 4
The King vs Elizabeth Brooks
Defendant pleads guilty, goods stolen, to receive on her bare back at the common whipping post in Carlisle between the hours of 9 and 11 o'clock on the 26 July, 21 lashes well laid on, pay all costs of prosecution, until fine and fees be complied with.

The King vs William Cochran
Barnard Dougherty paid £20 on condition that he appear at the next court to give evidence on behalf of the King. Came into Court William Cochran and no person appearing to prosecute he is discharged by proclamation of his bail.

Page 5
The King vs George Jacob Housean
Defendant pleads guilty, fined six pence.

The King vs Elizabeth Morrison
Elizabeth Morrison paid £40, Hugh Morrison paid £30 for the appearance of Elizabeth Morrison next session.

Page 6 July Session 1765
The King vs William Harris and others
Mary Bryan £10, Mary Cummins £10, on condition that they appear at next court to give evidence on behalf of the King.

The King vs Patrick McCardel
Issued recognizances Patrick McCardel £40, Dennis Dougherty £30, on condition __.

Page 7
At Carlisle, 5 August 1765, before John B.(?) Knight, Robert Miller and John Holmes Eight justices of said Court. Came into Court James Moore and made complaint that a certain Ann Connely in indented servant to him the said James had at sundry times absconded herself from the service of her said master for the space of 45 days ad that her said master was put to sundry expense in following and recovering the said servant to his service amounting in the whole to 14 pounds, 7 shillings and 3 pence. It is considered by the Court that the said Ann Connily __ and master on his assigns for the space of 3 years over and above the time mentioned in her indenture in order to the satisfaction of her said master in pursuance of the laws of this providence made and provided.

At the Court of Private Sessions, at Carlisle, 10 October 1765 before Andrew Colhoun, Robert Miller and Am. Alrich. Came into Court John Duffey and made complaint that a certain Dinnis Conner an indented servant to him the said John had absconded himself from his service of said master for the space of 1 year, 7 months, 19 days and that his said master was put to sundry expenses in following and recovering the said servant to his service amounting in the whole to 7 pounds, 17 shillings and 6 pence. It is thereupon considered by the Court that the said Dinnis Conner serve the said master or his assigns for the space of 2 years __ months [cont on page 8]

Page 8
and 12 days over and above the time yet remaining and of the said indenture as a satisfaction to his master for his expenses and loss of time aforesaid.

The petition of sundry of the inhabitants of Lowther Street in the Town of Carlisle and other in the County adjoining said town to the Court humbly requesting that there may be a road from the eastern of the aforesaid street and to be joined into the Great Road leading to John French's and that the same be for publick use. The Court order the road be to all intent and purposes a publick road and high way and that the same as such be forth with opened cleared and repaired..

The petition of John Cox Jr and of sundry inhabitants of the lower parts of Cumberland County and parts adjacent setting forth that whereas a new town has been lately e__ on the east side of the River Susquehanna by the said John Cox Jr. where Stores are now existing and where it is expected then will be a market for all kinds of County produce and that the inhabitants of the said lower part of the said County have long labored more especially more to the northward of the Conedogainet (?) Creek under many inconvenience for want of a road and ferry the nearest and best way toward the upper parts of Paxton and Hannover toward and into the Reading Road and praying the Court to appoint men to view and if they should see cause to lay out a road the nearest and best way from the [cont on page 9]

Page 9
Town of Carlisle to the aforesaid town of Susquahanna received to accommodate in the best manner as well the inhabitants of the Old Valley as those of Sheamans and other places over the mountain __ it is considered by the Court and Thomas Wellson , Andrew Armstrong, Francis Silver, John Orr, John Dickey, and James Hardy or any four of them to view and if they see cause lay out a road agreeable to the prayer of the petitioner and make report of their proceedings to the next Court and whether it is for publick or private use.

Came into Court James McCall, James Dunlap, William Reynolds, William Piper 4 of the persons appointed by an order of last sessions to view and if they should see cause to lay out a road the nearest and best way from McCallesters Mill to Shippensburgh and from thence to the York County line and did report to the Court that in pursuance of the said order they had survey and according to their __ laid out the said road in the most advantageous manner and the nearest way from McCallesters Mill to Shippensburg and from thence to the York County line as follows. To the South Mountain beginning from the south east end of Queen Street south 60 degrees east 880 perches to Blyths __ Mill from thence south 60 degrees east 320 perches to the Mountain Run thence south 10 degrees east eighty 88 perches to a spanish oak thence south 40 degrees east 42 perches to a pine thence south 50 degrees east 40 perches to a post __ thence south 30 degrees east 66 perches to a __ [cont p.10]

Page 10
south 55 degrees east 25 perches to another stake thence north 88 degrees east 120 perches to __ dead pine thence south 55 degrees east 468 six perches to the County line in all 6 ½ miles to the North Mountain Gap. Beginning from the west end of King street and north 67 degrees west 1326 perches to John Weirs Forge from thence south 70 degrees west to a white oak sapling by Weirs old road 168 perches from thence north 85 degrees west 136 perches to the near end of Turners field thence north 52 degrees west 72 perches to the far corner of said field thence north 30 __ west 140 perches to James H. Callaster Mill in all 8 1/4 miles and 2 perches and that the same is of publick use where upon it is ordered by the Court that the same road as aforesaid described and laid out be to all intent and purposes as a publick road and high way and that the same as such be forth with opened cleared and repaired in pursuance of an Act of Assembly of this province in such case made and provided.

Page 11
At Carlisle, 22 October 1765, before John Armstrong Esq and his associate justices. Grand jury men; William Miller, Foreman, John Agnen, Joseph Hordson (?), John Miller, John Dunning, William Henvard, Francis Silver. Robert McWhiney, Ralph Nailor, John Pollock, Malster, John Pollock, Carpenter, John Criegh. Ephraim Blain, John Glen, Samuel Kyle, John Kennedy, John Henry, Samuel Skinner, James McCallester, Patrick McCardell, Ellias Davis, Charles McCormick, Thomas Holmes, Robert Robb.

Page 12 October Session 1765
The following gentlemen were on the Grand Inquest; William Miller, John Agnen, Robert McWhinney, John Criegh, John Glen, Samuel Kyle, John Kennedy, John Kenner, Samuel Skinner, James McCallester, Patrick McCardle, Ellias Davis, Thomas Holmes, Robert Robb.

Upon the application of Mr. James Sayre to this Court to be admitted an attorney and having taken the oath prescribed by the Act of Assembly in such case and upon consideration be and admitted an attorney of the Court of Common Pleas and General Quarter Sessions for the County aforesaid.

Upon the application of Mr. William Sweeny and of Mr. Robert Galbreath to this Court to be admitted attorneys and having taken the oath prescribed by Act of Assembly in such __ upon consideration they and each of them are admitted attorneys of the Court.

Page 13
Upon application made to the Court by General of the inhabitants of Lurgan and Hopewell townships that a constable is wanted at Shippensburg the Court therefore order that a constable be appointed to serve from Shippensburg and the places adjacent for this present years and __ Francis Campbell and Samuel Perry Esq to choose said Constable and qualify him.

The King vs Thomas Czar
Felony. Pleaded guilty, fined 14 pound, 10 shillings and receive 21 lashes on
his bare back at the common whipping post in Carlisle between the hours of 9
and 12 o'clock on the 25 October. To make restitution to the owner of the value
of goods stolen and pay all costs of prosecution.

Page 14 October Session 1765
The King vs James Johnston and Dinnis Argan
Felony. Defendant pleads not guilty. Jurors; Abraham Woods, Daniel
Lawrence, Wm. Waugh, Thomas Beard, Thomas Davis, William Denny, Petter
Smith, Robert Gillery, John Haskins, John Gray, John McCallester, and John
Kinkead say that the Defendant is guilty. It is considered by the Court that they
restore the goods stolen or the value thereof to the owners __ fine to the
Governor of the value of the goods stolen and receive on the bare back at the
common whipping post at Carlisle between the hours of 3 and 5 o'clock in the
afternoon on 25 October, 21 lashes.

The King vs James Gibson
Tippling house.

Page 15 & 16 blank

Page 17
At Carlisle, 26 January 1766, before John Armstrong and his associate justices.

Page 18 January Sessions 1766
The King vs William Anthony
Sur recognizance, Robert Morgan £40.

The King vs Jacob Hernuck (?)
Sur recognizance.

Page 19
The King vs John Hasting
Sur recognizance.

The King vs James Ferguson
Sur recognizance. James Ferguson £40, Robert Robb £20, on condition __
acknowledge in Court. Came into Court James Ferguson no cause appearing to
the Court why he should __ to his recognizance he is discharged from his said
recognizance.

Page 20- blank

Page 21

At Carlisle, 22 October 1765, before John Armstrong and his associate justices. Upon application made to this Court by several of the inhabitants of Lurgan and Hopewell townships that a constable is wanted at Shippensburg Court therefore orders that a constable be appointed and serve in Shippensburg and the places adjacent for the present year and allow Francis Campbell and Samuel Perry Esqs., to choose said constable and qualify him.

At a Court of Private Sessions held at Carlisle, 25 March 1766, for the appointment of officer etc., in the said county before James Galbraith Esq., and his associate justices in the said county.

Lurgan township; James Stuart, constable; John Brechinridge, road supervisor
Letterkenny township; Josiah Ramadge, constable
Guilford township; David Hoskins, constable; Thomas Baird, Samuel
        Thompson over-seers of the poor; Henry Thompson, George Smith,
        Paul Barnet over-seers of the poor; Thomas Knox, Isaac Patterson,
        viewers of fences.
Antrim township; Andrew Miller, constable; Robert McCrea, Joseph Cook,
        supervisors of roads; William Rankin, Adam Robinson viewers of
        fences.
Peters township; John Shelby, constable; William McDowell, Robert Elliot,
        William Shannon, John Clelan Jr., overseer of the poor.
Fannet township; Philip McGuire, constable; Thomas Blair, Francis Elliot
        supervisors of roads; James Walker, Robert Elder, overseer of poor;
        Randel Alexander, Samuel Mair, viewers of fences.
Air township; William Evans, constable
Tyrone township; Hugh Alexander, constable; Hugh Gilgore, John Hamilton
        supervisors of roads; George Robinson, Thomas Ross overseers of
        the poor.
Tiboyne township; Robert Miller, constable; Alexander Morrow, James Bole,
        supervisors of roads; Joseph Neefer ,Thomas Adam overseer of poor.
Rye township; Samuel Baskins, constable; Frederick Watts, William Poor,
        supervisors of roads.
Lack township; George McConnel, constable; Hugh Quigley , John Armstrong,
        supervisors of roads.
Farminaw township — (no appointments made)

Petition of several of the inhabitants of Tyrone township to this Court, setting forth that said township is too large. Is adjudged and ordered by the said Court that from the North Mountain to the Tuskarora mountain by Mr. West's and from that to Darlington's and the strip to Tuskarora about William Noble's be the line and the name of the lower to be called Rye Township. Considered and decided by the Court that Joseph Chaneywooth to serve as constable in Bedford and parts adjoining to said town for their ensuring year.

Page 22
At Carlisle, 9 September 1766, before John Byers, Robert Miller and Andrew Calhoun Esq., justices of said Court.

Upon the information of Mr. Joseph West setting forth that the township of Rye was destitute of supervisors, the Court order that Frederick Watts and William Poor be supervisors of high-ways in the said township for the current year.

Page 23
At Carlisle, 22 April 1766, before John Armstrong and his associate justices. The Sheriff, John Holmes return list of grand jury men; Robert Thornburg, foreman; Ezek. Dunning, Ezek. Smith, Tobias Hendrick, John Miller, John Davis, Jonathan Holmes, Andrew Holmes, William Carithers, Daniel McClaster. James Parker, Robert Urey, William Fleming, Walter Denney, John McClure, James Erwin, James Love, James McGalluck, Henry Cevin, Ralph Hariet (?), Andrew Armstrong, Richard Lasher (?), Andrew Miller, Samuel Williamson.

Page 24 April Session 1766
The following appearing were accordingly sworn the Grand Inquest; Robert Thornburg, Foreman; Ezekial Dunning, Ezekiel Smith, Tobias Hendricks, John Davis, Jonathan Holmes, Andrew Holmes, Daniel McClester, Robert Uray, William Fleming, Walter Denney, John McClure, James Love, James McGalluck, Andrew Armstrong.

On motion of Mr. Smith on behalf of Thomas Creaghead and James Kenny overseers of the poor for Middletown Township praying an appeal from an order of John McKnight, Robert Miller and Andw. Calhoon __ for the maintenance of a Negro man named Jack may be entered __ April 1766 agreeable to the act of Assembly on such case made and provided the Court thereupon will take time to advise.

James Bell £20, Thomas Bell Senr. £10, on condition that James Bell __ maintain and teach David Colhoun __ apprentice to said James Bell according to the tenor of his __.

Page 25
The King vs Phillip Connally
Felony. Defendant being arraigned pleads not guilty. Robert Hagan prosecutor, jury; John Nickels, John Davis, John Patton, John Colhoun, Hance Morrison, Richd. Carson, Robert Campbell, Patrick Hartford, Willm Gray, Wm. Gray, John __, Sr, Thomas Armstrong. Defendant is guilty of felony. He is return the stolen goods, or the value of, and to receive __ lashes on his back at the common whipping post at Carlisle between the hours of 10 and 1.

The King vs Henry Praller
The defendant pleads guilty and is fined 2 shillings and sixpence to the Governor and pay the cost of prosecution and stand committed til fine and fees are completed with. Henry Praller £20, Robert McCreve £10, on condition that Henry Praller be of good behavior toward John Horn until next Court.

Page 26
The King vs Thomas Davis
Felony.

The Kings vs Abraham James
Trespass.

Page 27 April Sessions 1766
The King vs James McAdams
Felony.

The King vs Patrick McMullen
William Bennett £20, for the appearance of Thomas Cuthbert next session to give evidence.

Page 28
At a Court of Private sessions held in Carlisle, 26 May 1766, before Andrew Calhoun, John McKnight and Robert Miller Esqs., justices of the said court.

Upon petition of John Holmes Esq high sheriff of the county aforesaid, to the Court setting forth in a petition before four of the magistrates of the said county, his Honor, the Governor, hath remitted the fines due him from John Smith, Elizabeth Brooks and Thomas Erzar, prisoners in the jail of this county, severally convicted of grand larceny, that the said prisoners now remain in jail for their fees, witness expenses and restitution money, that they are chargeable to said county, and prayeth the Court to adjudge each of the said prisoners to serve a certain term of years to satisfy the fees and restitution money aforesaid that he may have order to sell them out of the same agreeable to the said adjudication. The Court therefore adjudge that the said Elizabeth Brooks do serve for a term of 4 years, that the said John Smith do serve for a term of 4 years, and the said Thomas Erzer for a term of 4 years, and that the said sheriff sell them respectively out of jail for the respective terms aforesaid to satisfy their fees, restitution money and witness expenses aforesaid, for the highest bid he can get for them.

Page 29
At a Court of Private Session held at Carlisle, 28 May 1766, before Andrew Calhoun, Robert Miller, William Lyons Esq, justices of said court.

Whereas Abel Gibbon the above assigned before us three of his Majesty's Justices of the Peace for the said County. James indented servant absconded himself from said master for the term of one years and eleven months and also that he said Abel Gibbon has been at 10 pounds expenses in finding the obtaining the said servant. Wherefore we do judge that there be added to the term or fine mentioned in the writing indenture 4 years given under our hand the day and year above said. The within indenture expires the 4 July 1766.

Page 30
Court of Private Session held at Carlisle 14 June 1766, before Andrew Colhoun and Robert Miller Esq., justices of same Court.

Came into Court Abraham Holmes and set forth that a certain Charles McCormick an indented servant to him the said Abraham hath at sundry times absconded himself from the service of his said master for the space of fifteen days and that his said master was put __ sundry expenses in following and recovering the said servant to his service amounting in the whole to four pounds ad it is thereupon considered by the Court and __ judged by the Court that the said Charles McCromick serve his said master of his assigns for the space of one year over and above the time mentioned in the indenture in order to the satisfaction of his said master in pursuance of the same of this province and such case made and provided.

At a Court of Private Session, held at Carlisle, 14 Jul 1766, before Andrew Colhoun, Robert Miller and William Lyons, Esq., Justices of said Court.

Came into Court Thomas Donnallan and set forth that a certain Derby Collins an indentured servant to him the said Thomas hath at sundry times absconded himself from the service of his said master for the space of 5 days and that his said master was put to sundry expenses in __ and recovering the__ amounting to the whole to 2 pounds 17 shillings and 6 pence it is thereupon considered by the Court and adjudged by the Court that the said Derbey Collins to __ his said master or his heirs or assigns for the space [to be cont.]

Page 31
of 5 months over and above the time mentioned in his indenture in order to the satisfaction of his said master in pursuance of the laws of this Province in such case made and provided.

Page 32- blank page

Page 33
At Carlisle, 22 July 1766, before John Armstrong Esq., and his justices. The Sheriff, John Holmes, returns the following grand jury men; William Denny, foreman, Robert Robb, Charles Pallison, Robert Gilson, William Miller, Abraham Wood, Abraham Holmes, John Pollock, Malster, William McCrosky,

Ephraim Blain, John Gray, James Pollock, John Gamble, James Thompson, Robert Robb, Samuel Coulter, John Fulton, William Gray, Daniel Laurence, John Agnen, Robert McCully, George Hamilton, James McClintock, John Kennedy.

Page 34 July Sessions 1766
The following gentlemen appearing were sworn on the grand jury; William Denny, foreman, Robert Robb, Charles Pallison, Robert Gibson, Abraham Holmes, John Pollick, Malster, William McGrosky, Ephraim Blain, John Gray, James Pollock, James Thompson, James Robb, James Coulter, William Gray, Daniel Laurence, Robert McCully, James McClintock.

Page 35
The King vs Sarah Danvill (?)
Felony.

The King vs Patrick McMullan
Felony, true bill, defendant pleads not guilty. Jury; Stephen Duncan, Samuel Leard, John Kinhead, John Steel, John McKee, Ralph Nailor, John Hastings, John Hays, John Holmes, Mattew Sailor, William Ervin, say defendant is guilty of felony as he stands charged and the judgement is considered by the Court.

Page 36
The King vs John Silver and William Nugent
Defendants plead not guilty. Jury; Stephen Duncan, Samuel Laird, John Kinkead, John Steel, Peter Smith, John McKee, Ralph Nailor, Willm Erwin, John Hastings, Math__ Sailor, John Hays, John Holmes, say defendants are guilty. It is considered by the Court that John Lefavour (?) Make restitutions of the goods stolen of the value thereof __, make fine in the sum of __ pounds and receive on his bare back at the common whipping post on the 25th day of July between the hours of 10 and 12 o'clock, 21 lashes well laid on.

The King vs John Woods
Assault and battery, true bill, defendant pleads not guilty.

The King vs John Lefavort and William Nugent
Felony.

Page 37
The King vs John Kinner
Assault and battery. Defendant fined 5 pounds to the Governor with costs of prosecution.

The King vs Richard Stewart
Assault and battery.

Page 38 July Sessions 1766
The King vs James Forsyth
Felony, defendants pleads not guilty.

The King vs Richard Parker
__ Ignoramites (?)

Page 39
The King vs Elizabeth Smith
Felony. Defendant pleads guilty, submits to the Court, fined 9 pounds and 10 shillings to the Governor for the support of the Government. Makes restitution of the goods stolen and to receive on her bare back at the common whipping post in Carlisle between the hours of 10 and 11 o'clock on the 25th day of the instant, 21 lashes.

The King vs John Dunbar
Defendant pleads not guilty and Benjamin Che_ prosecutes. Jury; Daniel Duncan, John Brandy, William Piper, Wm. Rospotos (?), John Cunningham, Jonathan Call, Joseph Culbertson, __ Culbertson, James Colhoun, Joseph Park, Joshua Hannark (?) And Robert Culbertson who say he is not guilty.

Page 40
The King vs William Harris
Riot.

The King vs Mary Buchanan
Assault and battery.

Page 41
Upon motion of James Smith, attorney, that an attachment be made of contempt issue against William Hunton, constable of Shippensburg for presuming under color of execution of Justice Perry to take and sell a horse of property of Thomas Duncan when in fact and in truth he held no such execution or any order for doing so, it is considered by the Court and ordered that an order to show cause why an attachment should not issue for the contempt aforesaid, be issued, and so forth. And now on motion and the Court being informed that the said William Hutton is about to remove out of the jurisdiction of this Court, further orders the party to show cause and attachment issue.

The King vs John Dougherty and William Dougherty

Page 42
At a Court of Private Sessions, at Carlisle, 1766, before Jonathan Hoge, Robert Miller and Wm. Snyder.

Came into Court Robert Hannan in behalf of John McCool and set forth that a certain William Hannah an indented servant to the said John McCool hath absconded himself from the service of his said master for the space of 9 months and that his said master was put to sundry expenses in following and recovering the said servant to his service, amounting to the whole to the sum of 4 pounds, 4 shillings and 4 pence, it is ordered by the Court that the said William Hannah serve his said master or his assigns for the space of 4 years over and above the time mentioned on his indenture in order to the satisfaction of his said master.

At a private Session, at Carlisle, 23 August 1766, before John Byvis, Robert Miller and Andrew Colhoun.

Came into Court William Miller and set forth that Rasmond Cassidy an indented Servant woman to him and by her own confession saith that she the said servant woman was delivered of two __ born children at one birth in the time of her servitude, the Court having considered the matter, has adjudged that she the said servant __ her said master or his assigns one year over and above her former time, mentioned in her indenture.

Page 43
At a Court of Private Sessions, at Carlisle, 9 September 1766, before John Byoud, Robert Miller and Andrew Colhoun.

Came into Court John Homes Esq., in behalf of Doctor William Plunkett and set forth that a certain Peter Willson an indented servant to the said William Plunkett hath absconded himself from his said master for the space of 4 days and that his said master was put to sundry expenses in following and recovering the said servant to the service amounting in the whole to the sum of 4 pounds, 10 shillings. Its considered by the Court that the said Peter Willson serve his said master or assigns, the space of 6 months over and above the time mentioned in his indenture in order to the satisfaction of said master.

Page 44-46 blank

Page 47
At Carlisle, 1 October 1766, before John Armstrong. The sheriff, John Holmes, returned the following jurymen; James Dunlap, foremen, Daniel Duncan, James McCall, Samuel Culbertson, Senr, Samuel Culbertson, Junr, Oliver Culbertson, Samuel Montgomery, William Ripply, Andrew Boyd, Joseph Park, Joseph Mitchell, John Johnston, David Johnston, Archibald Machan, James Caldwell, James Brackinridge, John Brackinridge, John Brackinridge, William McKnett, William Piper, William Erwin, John McKnett, James Randles, David Timrill (?), John Finley.

Ordered by the Court that James McCall, Sam Culbertson Senr, Sam
Culbertson Junr, Sam Montgomery, Joseph Park, Joseph Mitchel, John
Johnson, Arch Macan, James Calwell, James Brackinridge, John Breckinridge,
William Piper, William Erwin, John McKnight, James Ranchles, David Timill
and John Finley be fined 20 shillings each for non attendance.

Page 48 October Session 1766
The following gentlemen appearing were according sworn to the grand inquest.
[note: no one listed]

The King vs James Bigger

Page 49
The King vs Samuel McCune

The King vs Charles McCormick

Page 50
The King vs William Gammond

The King vs William Dennet

Page 51
The King vs George McGonnigal

The King vs John Bird

Page 52
The King vs Samuel Harper

The King vs Robert Guy

The King vs William Thompson

Page 53
The King vs James Forsyth
Felony. Pleads not guilty. Jury; Benjamin Blyth, James Torrance, Peter Dickey,
Thomas McCombs, Charles Cummins, John Cummins, Andrew Wilkey, John
Given, James Arthur, Thomas Fleming, John Bird, James Knox, say defendant
is guilty of the felony. January Sessions, 1767, jury; Daniel Duncan, John
Bready, William Piper, William Ray__, John Cunningham, James McCall,
Joseph Culbertson, Sam Culbertson, James Colhoun, Joseph Park, Joshua
Hannah, Robert Culbertson say defendant not guilty in the felony and larceny.

The King vs James Forsyth

Page 54 October Sessions 1766
Ordered William Randles, James Finley, James Sille, Adam Torrence, Thomas Greer, Francis Campbell Taylor, John Cunningham, James Calhoun, Samuel Culbertson, Robert Culbertson shoemaker, Joseph Culbertson, Atrch Machon Junr, Jeremiah Gohvin, John McClay, Samuel Culbertson, wagoner fined 20 shillings each for non attendance.

Page 55
Before John Armstrong and his associate justices, 21 October 1766..
Upon the petition of the inhabitants of Guilford, Hamilton and Peters township to the Court, setting forth that the petitioners hath long and doth still report under many difficulties for want of a road leading from the forks about Edward Crawford's to Fort Loudon as many of us petitioners are deeply sensible that the road being laid out betwixt the above mentioned places, the straightest and best course must directly lead by John Jack's Merchant Mill which will be a means of making said road much more beneficial for both public and private interests, prays that your Honor would be pleased to grant an order for viewing and laying the same. The Court appoints Edward Crawford, George Brown, Joseph Cook, James Arthur, Samuel Holiday and James McDowell or any 4 of them and make report to the next Court of their proceedings.

Page 56- blank

Page 57
At Carlisle, 20 January 1767, before John Armstrong. The Sheriff, John Holmes, summoned the following gentleman to serve on the Grand Inquest; Robert McCrea, foreman, Samuel Lindsey, Patrick Jack, Mathew Wilson, James Chambers, James Parker, Paul Pierce, Richard Parker, Richard Carson, John Calhoun blacksmith, Robert Cannor, Anorem Miller, John Glen, Charles McGill, Senr., Sam Culbertson wagonmaster, John Breakinridge, John Patton, Samuel Gibson, David Herron, Thomas Creigherd, John Culbertson, Robert Culbertson, William Patten, William Bennel.

Page 58 January Sessions 1767
Following sworn on the Grand Inquest; Robert McGrea foreman, Patrick Jack, Mathew Wilson, Paul Pierce, Richard Parker, John Colhoun blacksmith, Charles McGill, Senr, Samuel Culbertson, John Breakinridge, John Patton, Samuel Gibson, David Herron, John Culbertson, Robert Culbertson, William Patton.

Page 59
The King vs Robert Guy

The King vs Samuel Harper
Assault and battery. Defendant fined 2 shillings, 6 pence to the governor for the support of Government, stand committed until fine and fees be complied with.

Page 60

The King vs James Bigger

Felony. Defendant pleads guilty, fined in the sum of 10 pounds to the Governor for the support of Government, make restitution of the goods stolen if not already restored, receive on his bare back at the common whipping post between the hours of 10 and 11 oclock in the forenoon on Friday the 23 of this instant, 21 lashes well laid on his bare back, stand committed until fees paid.

The King vs James Bigger

Felony. Defendant pleads guilty, fined in the sum of 10 pounds to the Governor for the support of Government, make restitution of the goods stolen if not already restored and receive on his bare back at the common whipping post between the hours of 10 and 11 oclock in the forenoon on Friday the 23rd day of this instant twenty one lashes well laid on his bare back and stand committed until fine and fees are complied with.

Page 61 January Session 1767

The King vs James Moore

Felony. Defendant pleads not guilty

The King vs James Bigger

Felony. Fined 27 pounds to the Governor for the support of the Government for the support of Government, make restitution of the goods stolen if not already restored and receive on his bare back at the common whipping post between the hours of 10 oclock in the forenoon on __ day, 21 lashes well laid on and stand committed til fine and fees be complied with costs of prosecution.

Page 62

The King vs John Burd

Riot and assault.

The King vs John Graham and others.

Felony. Defendant pleads guilty and is accordingly fined in the sum 8 pounds to the Governor for the support of Government and make restitution of the goods stolen if not already restored and receive on his bare back at the common whipping post on Friday, 23 January, 21 lashes well laid on and stand committed until prosecution be complied with.

Page 63

The King vs John Graham and others

Felony. Defendant pleads guilty, fined 5 pounds to the Governor for the support of Government, make restitution of the goods stolen if not already restored, receive on his bare back at the common whipping post on Saturday the 24th day of this instant January, 21 lashes well laid on Saturday at 10 oclock in the forenoon, stand committed until fine and fees with the costs of the prosecution and prosecutors be complied with.

The King vs William Thompson
Assault and battery.

Page 64 January Sessions 1767
The King vs William Dennel
Felony. The defendants pleads guilty, fined in the sum of 10 pounds to the Governor for the support of Government, make restitution of the goods stolen if not already restored, receive on his bare back at the common whipping post at the hour of 10 and 11 oclock in the forenoon, 21 lashes well laid on and stand committed until fine and fees with costs of the prosecution and prosecutors be complied with.

Page 65
The King vs Saml Dinsmore
Assault and battery.

The King vs Willm. Thompson
Assault and battery. Defendant pleads not guilty. Jury; John Mitchell, James Kenny, Willm Davison, Samuel Williamson, John Gragg, James Young, Richard Rankin, Allen Neiper, Thomas Guy, James Clark, Anoene McBar, William Smith say that the defendant is not guilty, discharged paying his fees.

Page 66
The King vs James White

The King vs Christopher Quigly

Page 67
The King vs Alexander Work, William Work, John Work and James Dunning

The King vs Saml McCune

Page 68
The King vs George McGonigal
Fornication. Defendant pleads guilty, fined 10 pounds to give County for the maintenance of the bastard child and stand committed till fine and fees be complied with.

The King vs Rose Cassidy
Fornication.

Page 69 January Sessions 1767
The King vs John Burd
Tippling house. Pleads guilty to submit to the Court, fined 5 pounds to the Governor for the support of Government, stand committed until fine and fees be complied with.

The King vs James Moore
Felony. Defendant pleads not guilty. Jury; John Mitchell, James Kenny, William Davison, Saml Williams, John Gregg, James Young, Richard Rankin, Allen Neiper, Thomas Guy, James Clark, Andrew McBay, and William Smith who say that the defendant is not guilty of the felony as he stands charged in the indictment.

Page 70
Petition of sundry of the inhabitants of Rye township to this Court, setting forth to the worshipful Courts the prayer of the said petitioners to have a road put between James Baskin's Ferry on the Susquehanna in Rye township to Andrew Stephen's Ferry on the Juniata, beginning at said Baskin's thence the most straightest and convenient way to Frederick Watt's plantation, and from thence straight to the Narrows at Juniata and from thence straight from Stephen's Ferry in the township aforesaid. The Court do consider and appoint Duncan McCoon, Thomas Dugen, John Mitchell, Francis Ellis, John Anderson, and Thomas Larimer or any of them are appointed to view and if they see cause to lay out the road as aforesaid, and make report of their proceedings to the next Court.

Page 71-72 blank

Page 73
At a Court of Private Session held at Carlisle, 25 March 1767, for the appointment of officers, before John Byers Esq., and his associates.
Lurgan township; Thomas Pomeroy, constable; Thomas McCombs, Abraham Weire, supervisors of roads.
Letterkenny township; John Boyd, constable; John Findey, Joseph Culbertson supervisors of roads; John Baird, Richard Hananle, overseers of poor; Samuel Robinson, Alexander McComb, viewers of fences.
Guilford township; William Brotherton, constable; Thomas Baird, Samuel Lindsay, supervisors of road; John Andrew, Patrick Manne, overseers of poor; Henry Thompson, George Smith, viewers of fences.
Hamilton township; William McBrier, constable; Joseph Swain, Thomas Freeman, overseers of poor.
Antrim township; Thomas Long, constable; Elias Davison, David Stoner, superintendent of road; Joshua Harris, John Lovell, viewers of fences.
Peters township; Thomas Orbison, constable; Samuel Andrews, William Waddle, supervisors of roads; William Halloday, David Brown, overseers of poor; William Dunwoody, Samuel Davis, viewers of fences.
Fannet township; Samuel Montgomery, constable; John Elliot, John Hallowday, supervisors of roads; Randel Alexander, Francis Elliot overseers of poor; Felix Doyle, John Clark, viewers of fences.
Air township; Thomas John, constable; Evan Shelby, James Liddel, overseers of poor; Benjamin Dunn, Daniel McOgnele viewers of fences.

Tyrone township; Edward Elliot, constable; Alexander Roddy, Daniel William
    Jr., supervisors of roads; Thomas Ross, George Robinson, overseers
    of poor; William McClure, Robert Robinson, viewers of fences.
Tiboyne township; James Bolex, constable; James Williamson, Robert Pollock
    supervisors of roads; James Blain, Alexander Morrow, overseers of
    poor; John Morrow, James Adams, viewers of fences.
Rye township; Thomas Barnet, constable; Andrew Stephens, William Smilie,
    supervisors of roads; Duncan McCenue, Samuel Galbraith, overseers
    of poor; James Watts, Cornelius Wilson, viewers of fences.
Lack township; Samuel Chrisly, constable.
Farmanagh township; James Purdy, constable.

Page 74
Considered and appointed by the Court that John Cochran do serve as
constable in Bedford and the parts adjoining for the ensuing year.

July 22, 1767— appointed by the Court that Charles McCull Jr., to serve as
constable to the 25 March next in Derry township, and that Michael Rager do
serve as constable in Penns township to 25 of March next and that John
Balingham do serve as constable in Greenwood township to the 25 March next.

Page 75
At Carlisle, 21 April 1767, before John Armstrong. The Sheriff, John Holmes,
following gentlemen were duly summoned to serve on the Grand Inquest;
Robert Thornburg, foreman, Ezekiel Dunning, Jonathan Holmes, Andrew
Holmes, Ezekiel Smith, John Davis, Robert Ury, Walter Denny, Daniel
McCallester, Andrew McCallester, John McClure, William Flemming, Andrew
McFarling, Thomas Butler, Richard Carson, Mathew Miller, John Miller,
James Parker, James Love, John Morrow, James Morrow, James Freeman,
James Smith, George Woods.

Page 76 April Sessions 1767
The following appearing were according sworn, Grand Inquest; Robt.
Thornburg, foreman, Ezekiel Dunning, Jonathan Holmes, Andrew Holmes,
John Davis, Robert Ury, Walter Denny, Daniel McCallester, John McClure,
William Fleming, Andrew McFarling, Mathew Miller, John Miller, James
Parker.

Page 77
The King vs Alexander Work and others.
Defendants is discharged upon paying the fee.

The King vs Joseph Shansswolf.
Misdemeanor.

Page 78

The King vs John Burd

Assault and battery. Defendant pleads not guilty. Jury; John Mitchell, James Kenny, William Davison, Saml Williamson, John Gregg, James Young. Richard Rankin, Allen Neiper, Thomas Guy, Saml Clark, Andrew McBay and William Smith say that the defendant is guilty. It is considered that the defendant make fine to the Governor in the sum of 2 shillings and six pence and that his adjudged to pay the fine with the costs of prosecution and stand committed until fine and fees are paid.

The King vs Robert McKinney

Assault and battery. Defendant pleads not guilty. Jury; John Mitchell, James Kenny, William Davison, Samuel Williamson, John Gregg, James Young, Richard Rankin, Allen Neiper, Thomas Guy, Saml Clark, Andrew McBay, and William Smith say that the defendant is not guilty.

Page 79

The King vs Saml McCune

The King vs John Gorman and Giles Bowenalia.
Burglary.

Page 80

The King vs Christopher Quigly

Page 81

At a Court of Private Sessions held at Carlisle, 25 March last Rye township made their complaint before the Court with respect __ between it and Tyrone township. Your worship was pleased to appoint us to attend this court in order to have justice done us; therefore, we hope the Court will be please to appoint some men that may impartially consider the same and if a division must take place to have the line fun so as justice be done to each township both with respect to road and inhabitants. Signed by order of Rye township. Frederick Watts, Robert Erwin. The Court order that Robert Erwin, David English, Thomas Ross, John Hamilton and John Lewis do determine the line between Rye and Tyrone townships and make report to the next court.

Petition of some of the inhabitants of Peters and Antrim townships to the Court most humbly showeth that some years ago same petitioners were favored with an order of the court for viewing and laying out a road between Smith's Mill and John McDowell's mill to meet at or near William Maxwell's and from thence the nearest and best way to Baltimore Town in Maryland; but as some of the men that were appointed to lay out the said road have since died and others left the parts, praying the Court to appoint other men in their places to view and lay out the same and to extend the aforesaid branches as far as the bounding of Peters township to accommodate Air and Fannet townships.

It is ordered by the Court that James Jack, John Allison, George Brown, John McClellan, James Dickey and Robert Smith are appointed or any four of them to view the road aforesaid make report of their proceedings to the next court.

Page 82- blank

Page 83
At a Court of Private Sessions held at Carlisle, 6 May 1767, before John McKnight, Andrew Calhoun and Robert Miler Esq., justices. John Homes, Esq, high sheriff, came into Court setting forth that the Governor admitted the fines due him from Elizabeth Smith, John Grahames, James Bigger and William Dennet, prisoners in the jail of the county and asked the court to judge each said prisoners to serve a term of years to satisfy the fees and restitution money and the have an order to sell them out of jail, whereupon the Court orders them to serve for a term of 4 years and that the sheriff sell them respectively out of the jail of the respective terms.

Page 84-86 blank

Page 87
At Private Session, held at Carlisle, 20 June 1767, before Andrew Calhoun, Robert Miller and William Lyon.

Came into Court Stephen Fordan and set forth that a certain John O'Donnall indented servant to him the said Stephen saith at sundry times absconded himself from his said master and his said master was put sundry expenses in following and recovering the said servant to his service and the Court do consider and adjudge that the said John O'Donnall do serve his said master of his heirs of assigns for the space of three months over and above the time specified in his indenture in order to the satisfaction of his said master is pursuance of the laws of this Province in that case made and provided.

At Private Sessions, held at Carlisle, 27 June, 1767, before Robert Miller, William Lyon and Andrew Calhoun, justices of the said Court. Came into Court Samuel Rodgers and set forth that a certain John McLougall an indentured servant to him the said Samuel Rodgers hath absconded himself from his said master for the space of 2 months and that his said master was put to sundry expenses in following and recovering said servant to his service amounting to the whole of 8 pounds 16 shillings and __ pence __ considered by the Court that the said John McLougall serve his said master or his assigns for the space of 2 years over and above the time mentioned in his indenture in order to the satisfaction of his said master in pursuance of the Laws of this Providence in such case made and provided.

Page 88
Court of Private Session, held in Carlisle, twenty first day of July, 1767, before
[note: the rest of the page is blank]

Page 89- blank

Page 90
At Carlisle, 21 July 1767 before John Armstrong. The Sheriff, John Holmes,
summons the following gentlemen to serve on the Grand Inquest; William
Miller, foreman, Richard Tea, John Agnen, Ephraim Blain, Samuel Laird,
Charles Patterson, John Pollack Carpenter, William Denny, Stephen Folk,
Ralph Nailor, Joseph Hunter, William Erwin, James Pollock, William
McCroskey, William Wallace, James Ramsey, James Thompson, John Creigh,
John Glen, John Fulton, Stephen Duncan. Christopher Vanlear, Samuel
Coulter, Thomas Donnellan.

Page 91 July Sessions 1767
The following persons were sworn on the Grand Inquest; William Miller,
foreman, Richard Tea, John Agnen, Ephraim Blain, Samuel Laird, Charles
Patterson, John Pollock Carpenter, William Denny, Stephen Folk, James
Pollock, William Wallace, James Ransey, James Thompson, John Glen,
Stephen Duncan.

Page 92
George Roseberry being held over under recognizance to this Court on
suspicion of a burglary committed in the Province of Maryland is discharged
from his recognizance on the __.

Page 93
The King vs Thomas Robinson
Felony. Defendant pleads not guilty. Jury; William Brown, Joanthan Kearsley,
Peter Smith, John __, Robert McWhiney, John Kinkeard, __ Robert, William
Corran, John Hasting, William Reney, Arch Miller and Andrew Gilbreath say
that the defendant is guilty. It is considered by the Court that the defendant
make fine of the Governor of the sum of 4 pounds for the support of
government, restore and receive on his bare back at the common whipping
between the hours of 10 and 4 oclock 25 lashes well laid on the 24th.

The King vs Thomas Plunket, Margaret Plunket and Jossee Harris
Felony. Defendants plead not guilty. Jury; William Brown, Jonathan Kearsley,
Peter Smith, John Hay, Robert McWhiney, John __ James Robert, William
Corran, John Hasting, William Reney, Arch Miller and Andrew Galbreath do
say that the Thomas Plunket is not guilty of the felony whereof he stands
indicted, Margaret Plunket is not guilty of the felony whereof she stands
indicted, and Jesse Harris is not guilty of the felony whereof he stands indicted.

Page 94
The King vs Samuel Miller
Assault and battery.

The King vs Samuel Miller
Assault and battery.

Page 95
The King vs Thomas Plunket, Margaret Plunker, and Jesse Harris
Felony. Defendants plead not guilty. Jury; Willm Brown, Peter Smith, John __,
Robt McWhiney, John Kinkerd, James Robb, William Reney, Archd Miller,
Jonathan Kearsley, Andrew Galbreath say that Thomas Plunket is not guilty of
the felony whereof he stands indicted. Margaret Plunket is not guilty and Jesse
Harris is not guilty of the felony whereof he stands indicted.

The King vs John Marsdel
Assault and battery.

Page 96 July Sessions 1767
The King vs William Bennett
Assault and battery.

The King vs Andrew Armstrong, William Armstrong, James Armstrong, John
Cook, Margaret Armstrong, Ann Armstrong, Agnes Erwin and Eliz Sharron.

Page 97
The King vs Willm Harris and William Cook, Samuel Simpson, Rebecca
Simpson and Jane Simpson.
Defendants plead not guilty. Judgement that William Harris pay a fine of 20
shillings to his Honor the Governor, William Cook to pay a fine of 20
schillings to his Honor the Governor, Samuel Simpson pay a fine of 20 shilling
to his Honor the Governor, Rebecca Simpson pay a fine of 1 shilling to his
Honor the Governor and Jane Simpson a fine of 5 shillings to the Governor.

The King vs Paul Pierce
Assault and battery. Defendant to pay a fine of two shillings and six pence to
his Honor the Governor.

Page 98
The King vs Paul Pierce
Assault and battery. Judgement that he pay a fine of 2 shillings and six pence
to his Honor the Governor.

The King vs Edwd Marshel
Assault and battery. Judgement that he pay a fine of two shillings and six pence
to his Honor the Governor.

Page 99

The King vs Jane Fisher

Fornication. The defendant to pay to the Governor 10 pounds and the costs of prosecution and stand committed be complied with.

The King vs Hugh Sharron

Fornication. Jury; Hugh Laird, Alexander Work, John Willson, William Meteer, Thomas Donalson, William Hodson, William Abernathy, Samuel Cunningham, Henry Quigly, Christopher Quigley, George Armstrong and John Nailor say that the defendant is not guilty, judgment that the defendant be discharged upon his paying the costs.

Page 100 July Sessions 1767

The King vs Stephen Jordon

Felony.

The King vs Christopher Quigley

Misdemeanor.

Page 101

Upon the application of Henry Cunningham to the Honorable court, setting forth that a certain Charles Feeley and William Riley, run-away servant, is cumbersome to the jail and notwithstanding their master hath been notified long ago of their being in jail, he hath neither come or sent for them; it is therefore ordered by the Court that the said Henry Cunningham sell them respectively for their prisoners fees and expenses.

Page 102

Court of Private Sessions, held at Carlisle, 7 August 1767, before Andrew Colhoun, Robert Hillery, William Lyons, Esqs., Justices of the same Court.

Whereas Thomas Plunket and Margaret his wife __ for __ in general __ sessions last __ for the same by their county and the fees of there ever indictments and the costs of prosecuting __ in the whole to 19 pounds, 4 shilling and 4 pence, it is there upon considered and ordered by the Court that the said Thomas Plunket and Margaret be sold out by the sheriff for the term of 3 years and order for the __ of the __ and the prosecution.

Whereas Jesse Harris __ tried for grand larceny at July Sessions last and was acquitted for the same by is County and the __ of the several indictment and he costs of prosecution and __ in the whole to the sum of 10 pounds, 8 shillings and 2 pence. It is there upon considered and ordered by the Court that the said Jesse Harris be sold out by the sherif for the term of 3 years in order for the satisfaction of his fees and the prosecution for the above sum.

Page 103

The petition of sundry of the inhabitants of West Pennsborough township to this Court setting forth that a road leading from James Smith Mill in said township to the Walnut Bottom Plantation would be of great use to several of the inhabitants of said township and prayeth the Court to appoint proper persons to view and if they see cause to lay out the same __. Where upon it is considered by the Court and John Miller, James Weakley, William Woods, Andrew __, William Querary and David McCuroy or any four of them are appointed to view and if they see cause to lay out a road the nearest and best way to the plantation aforesaid and make report of their proceedings to the next court.

The petition of sundry of the inhabitants of Kishacoquillis Jack Creek Lost Creek Juniata Tuscarora __ to this Court setting forth that the inhabitants laborer under many inconveniences for want of a road leaving this the settlement in such __ as might best __ inhabitants there fore your petitioners humbly pray the Court would take the same into consideration and appoint men to view and to lay out a road leading from the road already laid out in Sherman's valley the best nearest and most convenient way up Juanita into Kisharquellis Valley whereupon it is considered by the Court and Thomas __, William Brown, William Bell, William Paterson, Thomas Ross, and John Black or any four of the said appointed to new and if they see cause to lay out a road to the nearest and best way to the __ aforesaid and make report of their proceedings to next court.

Page 104

At a Court of Private Sessions held at Carlisle, 4 September 1767 before Robert Miller, William Lyons and Andrew Colhoun.

Came into Court John Anderson and set forth that a certain John McFall an indented servant to him the said John Anderson hath absconded himself from the service of his said master for the space of 10 days and that his said master was put to sundry expenses in following and recovering the said servant to his service amounting in the whole to 3 pounds, 8 shillings, 6 pence, it is there upon considered by the Court and adjudged by the Court that the said John McFall serve his said master or his assigns for the spare of 6 months over and above the time mentioned in his indenture in order to the satisfaction of his said master.

Page 105-108 blank

Page 109

At Carlisle, 20 October 1767 before John Armstrong. The Sheriff, John Holmes, summoned the following gentlemen to serve the Grand Inquest; Ezekial Dunning, foreman, William Carrithers, Ralph Starrel, Charles McGill, Ellias Davis, Richd McClure, Robert Gullery Senr, James Knox, James

McCamish, Michael Bargle, Charles McCormick, John Abernathy, John Scott, John Davison, Arch Miller, John Cessney, Thomas Poe, John Hindman, George Smith, James McCall, David Sample, Adam Hays, Andrew Meas, John Kennedy.

Page 110 October Sessions 1767
The following persons appearing were accordingly sworn on the Grand Inquest: Ezekl Dunning, foreman, William Caulters, Charles McGill, Senr, Richard McClure, Robert Gullery Senr, James Knox, James McCamish, Michael Bargle, Charles McCormick, John Scott, Archibald Miller, David Sample, Adam Hays, Andrew Meas, John Kennedy

The King vs John Robinson and Wm Dillon
Felony. Defendant pleads guilty. Fined 10 pounds to the governor for the support of government and make restitution of the goods stolen if not already restore, receive on his bare back at the common whipping post between the hours of 10 and 12 oclock in forenoon on Friday the 23rd day of this instant .21 lashes well laid on and stand committed until fees and cost of prosecution be complied with.

The King vs Charles Smith
Felony. Defendant pleads guilty. Fined in the sum of 3 pounds, 10 shillings to the Governor for the support of government and make restitution of the goods stolen if not already restored and to stand one hour in the pillory between the hours of __ after receive on his bare back 30 lashes well laid on Friday the 23 day of this instant, be imprisoned for the space of two months and stand committed until fines and the costs of prosecution be complied with.

The King vs William Ramsey

Page 111 October Sessions 1767
The King vs George Woods
Assault and battery. Defendant fined in the sum of 2 shillings and six pence to the governor for the support of Government and stand committed until fine and fees be complied with.

The King vs Michael Gungle

Page 112
The King vs Mary Foley
Assault and battery. Defendant pleads guilty.

The King vs James Starkpole

Page 113
Dublin township bounded by Air and Fannet townships on the one side, and Colraine and Barre townships on the top of Sidling Hill on the other side. John Ramsey, constable.

Colraine township bounded by Dublin township as above, the provincial line and the top of Dunnings Mountain so as to join Cumberland and Bedford townships to the gap of Morrison's Cove, then to the mouth of Yellow Creek joining Baie township to strike Sidling Hill. William Parker, constable.

Cumberland township bounded by Colraine township as above, the provincial line to the Allegheny mountain and along the Allegheny Mountain to the top of the ridge that divides the waters of the Willis Creek thence to Juniata to strike Dummungs Mountain and Thomas Sim's gap. Thomas Colter, constable.

Bedford township bounded by the above mentioned east line and Dummings Mountain to the Gap of Morrison's Cove and form thence to the top of Tessess mountain joining Barre township so as to include Morrison's Cove and from end of Morrison's Cove cross by Franktown to the Allegheny. John Cochran, constable.

Barre township bounded by Dublin, Colraine and Bedford townships as already mentioned along the Allegheny until a line struck from thence to Jack's mountain so as to include the water of the Little Juniata and Shavers and Standing Stone Creek. John Foresee, constable.

Page 114
The petition of sundry inhabitants of Middleton township to this Court setting forth that the petitioners labor under many in__ for want of a road from Chambers Mill to Robert Uries and the settlement there abouts wherefore your petitioners prays your Worships to appoint proper persons to view and lay out a road as foresaid was __ where upon it is considered by the Court and Thomas Willson, Jonathan Holmes, William Heming, William Davison, Hugh McCormick, and Andrew Holmes or any four of them are appointed to view and if they see cause to lay out a road the nearest and best way to the place aforesaid and make report to the next Court.

Came into Court William Querey, James Weakley, Andrew Johnston, and John Miller four of the persons appointed by an order of last session to view and if they should see cause to lay out a road from James Smiths Mill in West Pennsborough township to the Walnut Bottom and did return to the Court that in pursuance of the said order they finding the road in the said order mentioned exceedingly necessary did lay out the same in manner following, that the said road lead from said Mill to a certain surveyed line between James Smith and John Lusk or as Nigh as the Commo__ of said road will allow as by our master and Blazes Mill appear being nigh a westerly course through a certain

Alexander __ Field and between two rows of apple trees and to pass the south
end of said Arwins House and between two __ trees at the head of a spring
belonging to the Walnut Bottom. Whereupon it is ordered by the Court that the
same road as aforesaid described and laid out be to all intents and purposes as a
publick road and high way and that the same as such be forth with opened
cleared and repaired in pursuance of an act of assembly of this providence.

Page 115
At a Court of Private Session, held at Carlisle, 7 December 1767, before John
Armstrong.

Came into Court Francis Campbell and set forth that a certain Thomas McCue
an indented servant to him the said Francis Campbell hath absconded a
considerable time from the service of his said master and that his said master
was put to sundry expenses in following and recovering the said servant to his
service amounting in the whole to two pounds 6 shillings, 6 pence, it is
thereupon considered by the Court and adjudged that the said Thomas McCue
serve his said master or his assigns for the space of 2 years from this date in
order to the satisfaction of his said master in pursuance of the laws of this
providence in such case made and provided.

Page 116 &117 blank

Page 118
At Carlisle, 19 January 1768 before John Armstrong. The Sheriff, John Holms,
summoned the following gentlemen to serve on the Grand Inquest; Tobias
Hendricks, foreman, Robert Callender, John Sample, David Hoge, George
Woods, Isaac Hendricks, David Bell, John Tindle, John Quigley, Francis
Silvers, Joseph Sample, William Marshall, John Orr, Jeremiah Rees, James
McConnel, Samuel Adams, Abraham Adams, Francis McCuire, Thomas
McCormick, Thomas Calbert, John Carrithers, James McCormick, Andrew
Erwin, John McCormick.

Page 119 January Sessions 1768
Of whom the following appearing were accordingly sworn on the Grand
Inquest; Tobias Hendricks, foreman, John Sample, David Hoge, George
Woods, David Bell, John Trindle, John Quigley, Francis Silvers, Joseph
Sample, John Orr, Jeremiah Rees, James McConnel, Samuel Adams, Thomas
McCormick, Thomas Calbert, John Carithers, James McCormick, Andrew
Erwin, John McCormick

The King vs William Bennet
The defendant submits to the Court protesting his innocence, judgment that he
pay fine to Governor of the Town of 10 shillings, with the costs of prosecution
and stand committed until fine and fees be complied with.

Page 120
The King vs James Norton
Assault and battery.

The King vs Richard Smith
Felony. The defendant pleads guilty judgement that the defendant receive on
his bare back at the common whipping post in Carlisle on Friday the 22nd day
of this instant 21 lashes, between the hours of 10 and 11 oclock in the
forenoon, make fine to the Governor of the sum of 45 shillings for the support
of the Government, stand committed until the costs of the prosecution be
complied with.

Page 121   January Term 1768
The King vs Andrew Armstrong, William Armstrong, Saml Armstrong, John
Cook, Margaret Armstrong, Anne Armstrong, Agnes Erwin and Eliza Thomas.
Riot. Defendants submit to the Court protesting their innocence judgement that
they pay a fine to the Governor the sum of three pence each with the costs of
prosecution and stand committed until fine and fees by be complied with.

The King vs Joseph Sheneyvol
Misdemeanor. Now the defendant being charged submits to the Court
protesting his innocence judgement and that he pay a fine to the Governor in
the sum of six pence with the costs of prosecution and stand committed until
fine and fees be paid.

Page 122
The King vs John Dunning
Assault and battery.

The King vs John Anderson
Misdemeanor. Jury; Hugh Laird, Alexander Work, John Wilson, William
Metser, Thomas Donnelson, William Hodson, William Abernathy, Samuel
Cunningham, Henry Quigley, Christopher Quigly, George Armstrong, and
John Nailor say that the defendant is guilty of the misdemeanor, indicted
judgement that John Anderson be whipped at the publick whipping post 21
lashes on the 22nd instant on his bare back and on the 29th instant to again
whipped with 21 lashes at the public whipping post between the hours of 12
and 2 in the afternoon of the same day, stand in the pillory for the space of two
hours, the same time to pay the costs of prosecution, give security for himself
in 200 pounds and two good sureties in 100 pounds each for his good behavior
for one year, stand committed till this judgement be complied with.

Page 123
The King vs John Dunning, John Davis, James McIvinee, Ezekiel Dunning and
William Carithers Junr.

The King vs Nathaniel Wallace
Assault and battery.

Page 124 January Sessions 1768
The King vs Robert Allison
Felony.

Page 125
The petition of sundry of the inhabitants of the County of Cumberland residing
between Carlisle from Works and Croughans Gap in the North Mountains and
in Shermans Valley humbly __ that there is great need for a road leading out of
the road that comes from Croughans Gap to Carlisle at Chamber's Mill on the
Mouth of Letorts Spring and from thence the nearest and best way to
Carlisle from Works and prayeth the Court to Grant the above road and to
appoint proper persons to view the ground and lay it out the Court do consider
the same and appoint John Mitchell, James Young, Walter Denny, William
Moor, James Erwin, and John Pollock or any four of them to view and if they
see cause to lay out a road the nearest and best way to the place aforesaid and
make report to the next Court.

The petition of the inhabitants of the township of Lack and parts adjacent most
humbly __ that your petitioners have great need of a bridle road from said
township to cross the Tuscarora Mountain at the run Gap and from thence to
Carlisle your Petitioners therefor doth most humbly pray that your Worship
would appoint men to view and if they see cause to lay out a road from the
mouth of the Long Narrows to the Run Gap in the said Township from thence
the nearest and best way to McAlrichs Plantation in Shearmans valey. The
Court do consider the same and appoint Clement Horrell, Robert Huston, John
McClennand, John Hamilton, William McClure and David McClure or any
four of them are appointed to view and if they see cause to lay out a bridle road
to the places aforesaid and make report to the next Court.

Page 126
The petition of the inhabitants of Peters, Hamilton and Guilford townships to
the Court, setting forth that the petitioners labor under many difficulties for
want of a road leading from James Campbell's near Loudon through
Chambersburg to the county line in Black's Gap, praying the Court to appoint
proper men to view and lay out a road as aforesaid; whereupon, it is considered
by the Court and Edward Crawford, Joseph Cook, George Brown, William
McBrier, William Halloday, Nathan McDowell or any 4 of them are appointed
to view and if they see cause to lay a road as aforesaid and make report to the
next Court.

Page 127- blank

Page 128 & 129

At a Court of private Sessions held at Carlisle, 25 March 1768 for the appointment of officers, before James Galbraith Esq., and his associate justices.

Lurgan township; Thomas Pumery, constable; Robert Peoples, James McKibbens, superintendent of road; John Baird, Samuel Culbertson, overseers of poor.

Gilford township; Moses Lamb, constable; Edward Cook, Matthew Wilson, supervisors of roads; Patrick Vance, John Miller, overseers of poor; Samuel Thompson, Peter Schnyder, viewers of fences.

Hamilton township; Thomas Aspy, constable; James McFarland, Thomas Barnet supervisors of roads; Isaac Patterson, James Eaton, overseers of poor; Johnson Elliot, William McCord, viewers of fences.

Antrim township; Samuel McCrea, constable; Abram Smith, John Wallace, supervisors of roads.

Peters township; James McDowell, John Andrem, constable; William Waddle, William Duffield, superintendent of road; Harry Anderson, William Halliday overseer of poor; Samuel Davis, William Dunwoody, viewers of fences.

Fannet township; Randel Alexander, constable; John Elliot, John Hallowday, supervisors of roads; Robert Anderson, John Clark, overseers of poor; Phillip McGurie, James Ardy, viewers of fences.

Air township; Moses Wilson, constable

Tyrone township; Daniel Williams, constable; George Robinson Cooper, Henry Gass, supervisors of roads; William McClure, Thomas Ross, overseers of poor; Samuel Fisher, John Scott, viewers of fences.

Tiboyne township; John Rhea, constable; John Gardner, Anthony Morrison, supervisors of roads; John Irwin, Archibald Ross, overseers of poor; William Townsley, James Morrison, viewers of fences.

Rie township; Thomas Walker, constable; William Richardson, Finley McCoune, supervisors of roads; Neal McCoy, David English, overseers of poor; Robert Jones, Joseph Marshall, viewers of fences.

Lack township; Jacob Pyate, constable; William Kirk, Robert Little, supervisors of roads; William Bell, James Stoner, overseers of poor; James Gray , William Stewart, viewers of fences.

Framanagh township; Samuel Mitchell, constable; James Purdy, John William, superintendents of roads.

Bedford township; John Height, constable; Thomas Hinto, Robert Adams, supervisors of roads; John Frazer, John Miller, overseers of poor; Phillip Baltimore, James McAsham, viewers of fences.

Derry township; Samuel Sander, constable; George Bell, Thomas Holt, supervisors of roads.

Penn township; Casper Reed, constable.

Greenwood township; Stophel Monce, constable; Nathaniel Barber, overseer of road.

Dublin township; Charles Bole, constable; Watson supervisors of roads.

Colraine township; Christian Miller, constable; Oliver Miller, Joseph Morrison, supervisors of roads; William Parker, Hugh Ferguson, overseers of poor; Thomas Wire, Thomas Croile, viewers of fences.

Cumberland township; Edward Anderson, constable; Thomas Jones, John Birris, supervisors of roads; Samuel Barret, Thomas Davis, overseers of poor; Charles Cissna, Matthew Kerr, viewers of fences.

Barre township; Samuel Anderson, constable; John Braidy, Jacob Hair, supervisors of roads; George Jackson, Zebulin Moore, overseers of poor.

Page 130
At Carlisle, 9 April 1768, before John Armstrong Esq., and his associate justices, the sheriff, with John Homes returns the following gentlemen are duly summoned to serve on the grand jury; Robert Thornburg, foreman, John Miller, James Erwin, Samuel Williamson, Ezekiel Dunning, Walter Denny, Robert Fry, Richard Parker, John Clark, James Parker, John Davison, John Holmes, William Carouthers, John McClure, George Davison, Matthew Miller, Patrick McFarland, John Davis, James Young, Hugh Cook, William Fleming, James Love, Paul Pierce, William Davison.

Page 131 April sessions 1768
The following were sworn on the Grant Inquest; Robert Thornburgh, foreman; James Erwin, Ezekiel Dunning, Walter Denny, Robert Ury, Richard Parker, Jonathan Holmes, John Clark, Patrick McFarlan, James Young, James Love.

The King vs David Bard
Assault & battery.

Page 132
The King vs Robert Allison
Felony. Mr. Magan his attorney retracts his plea & submits to the Court and is fined 20 shillings to the Governor and make restitution of the goods stolen or the value thereof if not already restored & stand committed until fine and fees by complied with.

The King vs James Forsyth
Felony. Defendant pleads not guilty. Jury; Richard Rankin, James Kenny, George Kindead, James Clark, William Smith, Robert Walker Junr, Robert McLovel, Thomas Holmes, Thomas Craighead, Andrew McBath, John Bennet & Patrick Jack who say the defendant is guilty of the felony & larceny in __ the watch laid in this indictment, fined 9 pounds to the Governor, make restitution of the watch stolen or the value thereof to the owner if not already done, receive on his bare back at the common whipping post in Carlisle between the hours of 9 & 11 oclock in the forenoon 15 lashes on Saturday the 23rd, stand committed until the above judgment complied with, the costs of prosecution.

Page 133 April Sessions 1768
The King vs James Forsyth
Felony for stealing a watch the property of James Temple (?). Defendant being arraigned pleads not guilty. Jury; Richard Rankin, James Keny, George Kinkead, James Clark, William Smith, Robert Walker Junr, Robert McDowel, Thomas Holmes, Thomas Craighead, Andrew McBath, John Bonnet, & Patrick Jack say that the defendant is guilty, 9 pounds to the Governor, make restitution of the watch stolen or the value thereof to the owner thereof if not already done, receive on his bare back at the common whipping post in Carlisle between the hours of 9 & 11 oclock in the forenoon with 15 lashes & stand committed until the above judgment be complied with & the costs of prosecution & prosecutors.

The King vs Jonathan Ross
Assault & battery.

Joseph Carrel £ 100, on condition that Joseph Carrel appear at next court & not depart without leave.

Page 134
The King vs John Coner
Felony. Defendant pleads guilty, submits to the court, fined in the sum of 45 shillings, that he restore the goods stolen or the value thereof to the owner & receive on the 22 day of this instant April being Friday between the hours of 6 & 10 Oclock, 21 lashes well laid at the common whipping post at Carlisle and stand committed until fine and fees be complied with and the costs of the prosecutor & prosecutors.

The King vs Benjamin Jolly
Misdemeanor. Defendant being charged submits to the Court, ordered that he pay a fine of 5 pounds to the Governor & stand committed until fine & fees be complied with.

Page 135 April Sessions 1768
The King vs John Dunning, Ezek Dunning, James McIver, John Vavis, Willm. Carrithers Junr.
Forcible entry & detainer. Jury; Richard Rankin, James Kenny, George Kinkead, James Clark, William Smith, Robert Walker Junr, Robert McDowel, Thomas Holmes, Thomas Creighead, Andrew McBrith, John Bonnet & Patrick Jack say that John Dunning is not guilty of the forceable entry & detainor, that Ezekiel Dunnng is not guilty of the forcible entry & detainor, that James McIlver is not guilty of the forcible entry & detainor, that John Davis is not guilty of the forcible entry & detainor & that William Carrithors Junr is not guilty of the forcible entry & detainor said in the indictment.

Timothy Tate being three times solemnly called appear not but makes default recognizance forfeited.

John Stewart being three times solemnly called to bring forth the body of Timothy Tate __forth the same body. Recognizance forfeited.

Page 136
The petition of sundry of the inhabitants of Gilford and Hamilton townships to the Court, setting forth that several of the petitioners hath formerly petitioned your worship to appoint fit persons to view and lay our a road beginning at the forks of the road above Edward Crawford's proceeding from thence the nearest way to John McDowell's, there notwithstanding it is notoriously known to many, the same will be of practical advantage and utility to many of the inhabitants of the townships, through it passes, yet the same hitherto miscarried from all manner of people adjoining and application, therefore prays your worship once more to appoint suitable and fit men to view and lay out the same road. It is considered by the Court and George Brown, George Calvin, David Stephenson, William Bannels, William Hallowday and John McCoy or any four of them are appointed to view and if they see cause to lay out the aforesaid road and make report of their proceedings to the next Court.

Petition of sundry of the inhabitants of Middleton, Hopewell and West Pennsborough townships, and others, humbly showeth that the road from the town of Carlisle leading from thence the nighest and best way to Walnut Bottom so as to come into the old road leading from thence to Shippensburg which old road is to be cleared, straightened to be of greater benefit to the inhabitants of said townships, the subscribers beg your worshipful justices of the bench to appoint proper persons to view, lay out a road aforesaid to the same. Whereupon it is considered and ordered by the Court that James Piper, James Dunlap, Thomas Wilson, John Erving, David McCendy and William Rennells or any four of them are appointed to view and if they see cause to lay out the road aforesaid and make report to the next Court.

Page 137
At a private sessions held at Carlisle, 13 July 1768 before Andrew Colhoun, Robert Miller, William Lyon.

Came into Court Samuel Wilson, set forth that a certain Patrick Glinnenan indented servant to him the said Samuel Willson, hath absconded himself from his said master for the space of 14 days, that the said master was put to sundry expenses in following & recovering the said servant to his service amounting to the whole to 3 pounds, 12 shillings, it is thereupon considered by the Court that the said Patrick Glinnen serve his said master or his assigns for the space of 6 months over and above the term mentioned in his said indenture in order to the satisfaction of his said master in pursuance of the laws of this province for such cases made & provided by.

Page 138
Came into Court John McClellan, John Allison, George Brown and James Dickey being four of the persons appointed and ordered of the former Court of general quarter sessions of the Peace and make report to the Court as follows: We the subscribers by order of the Court to view or lay out a road beginning at William Smith's and John McDowell's mill and to meet at or near William Maxwell's and from thence the nearest and best way to Baltimore Town in Maryland. We therefore agreeable to the said order have viewed from the aforesaid mills and do give it as our opinion that the appoint of contact of these branches ought to be at or near James Erwin's in Peters township, from thence crossing Conococheague Creek at the mouth of Muddy Run and proceeding through Antrim township to the gap commonly called Nicholson's in the South Mountain, we imagine the most direct course to the town of Baltimore and that the same will admit of a good road, be of public advantage and utility to the greatest parts of the upper end of the county. Courses and distances which is all affixes or annexed underneath, also we find that it will admit of a bridle road from the 2 miles aforesaid to boundaries of Peters township for the accommodation of Air and Hamilton townships. Courses and distances of the branch beginning at John McDowell's mill is south 34 degrees east 5 miles and 117 perches to James Erwin's, then south 61 degrees east 260 perches, thence south 92 degrees east 692 perches to the fording at the north of Muddy Run: the other branch beginning at M. Smith's mill thence south 66 degrees east 438 perches to Dongall Campbell's, thence south 77 degrees east 309 perches, then north 84 ½ degrees, east 693 perches to the point of contact with other branch near James Erwin's, thence from the fording at Muddy Run extending through Antrim township north 78 degrees east 138 perches, then south 74 ½ degrees east 7 1/4 miles to Samuel McCrea's, then south 64 ½ degrees east 5 miles and 256 perches to the cove of the mountain called Nicholson.

Page 139
Ordered that the road, aforesaid described and laid out be for all intents and purposes a public road and highway, that the same as such be forth with opened, cleared and repaired in pursuance of an act of the assembly of the province in such cases made and provided.

Page 140- 141 blank

Page 142
At a Court of Private Sessions held the 6 May 1768, before John Byers, Andrew Calhoun and Hiram Aldricks Esq, justices of the said Court.

Whereas John Commer was tired for criminal larceny at April Sessions last and he pleaded guilty and appearing to the Court that the fines and fees against the said John Commer amount to the sum of 10 lbs, 7 shillings and 2 pence, it is therefore considered by the Court that the said John Commer be sold out by the sheriff for the term of 3 years in order for the satisfaction of his fees and fines.

Page 143

William Brown, Thomas Holt, Thomas Ross, William Patterson, John Black, 5 of the men appointed by an order of the said Court made July Sessions then last past to view & if they saw cause to lay out a road leading from the road already laid out in Shearmans valley the best & most convenient way up Juniata into Kishecochquillis Valley came into Court and made report that the subscribers having met in pursuance of their appointment aforesaid & carefully viewed the places mentioned in said appointment find that a carriage road leading between said places is much wanted & will be of general utility & have accordingly proceeded & laid out the said road from the road already laid out in Shearmans valley Beginning at a marked white oak in said road about 2 miles & 3/4 from Croghans Gap & from thence through Rye township & across Juniata at the North of Lugan Run into Fermanagh Township & thence thro the same & Derry Township up the north side of Juniata into Kiskacoquillis Valley the courses & distances of which are hereunto annexed and are of opinion that the said road so laid and marked is the nearest and best publick road that the nature of the County will admit of and likewise most convenient for the inhabitants in general the courses & distances of the above mentioned road beginning at marked white oak in the old road 860 perches from Croghans Gap leading thro Rye Township north 18 degrees west 64 perches to a white oak north 55 degrees west 64 perches to a white oak north 55 degrees west 64 perches to a hickory north 18 degrees west 132 perches to a post north 22 degrees east 140 perches to a pine north 60 perches to a pine north 42 degrees west 92 perches to a post north 12 degrees west 44 perches to a pine north 65 degrees west 20 perches to a black oak north 19 degrees east 92 perches to a pine north 45 degrees east 78 perches to a black oak north 13 degrees west 42 perches to a black north 32 degrees.

Page 144

East 50 perches to a pine north 64 perches to a black oak north 21 degrees west 172 perches to a spanish oak north 25 degrees east 112 perches to a pine north 35 degrees east 112 perches to a pine north 35 degrees east 38 perches to a pine north 25 degrees east 20 perches to a black oak north 8 degrees west 94 perches to a chestnut north 64 degrees west 34 perches to a black oak north 35 degrees west 128 perches to a chestnut north 25 degrees west 28 perches to a pine north 41 degrees __ 34 perches to a pine north 25 degrees east 80 perches to a white oak north 43 degrees east 34 perches to a __ north 25 degrees east 28 perches to a white oak north 20 degrees west 32 perches to a white oak north 8 degrees east 80 perches to a white oak north 30 degrees east 70 perches to a white oak north 10 degrees west 62 perches to a pine north 32 degrees west 80 perches to a white oak north 15 degrees west 26 perches to a white oak north 15 degrees west 26 perches to a white oak north 63 degrees west __ perches to a white oak north 58 degrees west 20 perches to a white oak north 87 degrees west 28 perches to a white oak north 29 degrees west 62 perches to a white oak north 2 degrees west 46 perches to a white oak north 20 degrees east 64 perches to a white oak north 55 degrees east 210 perches to a white oak north 74 degrees east 80 perches to a white oak north 7 degrees east 64 perches to a black oak north 21 degrees west 16 perches to a white oak north 20 degrees east 60 perches to a post north 20 degrees west 130 perches to a pine north 5 degrees west 26 perches to a pine north 36 degrees west 20 perches to a spanish oak north 20 degrees west 34 perches to a maple north 10 degrees east 32 perches to a white oak north 25 degrees west 46 perches to a white oak north 20 degrees east 50 perches to a pine north 45 degrees west 22 perches to a post north 10 degrees east 32 perches to a hickory north

Page 145
30 degrees west 42 perches to a white oak north 7 degrees west 60 perches to a pine north 21 degrees east 52 perches to a black oak north 20 degrees west 34 perches to a chestnut north 3 degrees west 38 perches to a white oak north 43 degrees west 26 perches to a hickory north 8 degrees west 32 perches to a white oak north 42 degrees west 18 perches to a white oak north 8 degrees west 26 perches to a white oak north 22 degrees east 24 perches to a white oak north 40 degrees east 44 perches to a white oak north 10 degrees east 26 perches to a post north 5 degrees west 56 perches to a post north 20 degrees east 38 perches to a dogwood north 13 degrees west 46 perches to a hickory north 48 degrees west 40 perches to a white oak north 7 degrees west 60 perches to a maple north 31 degrees west 48 perches to a white oak north 128 perches to a pine north 13 degrees east 122 perches to a black oak north 44 degrees east 108 perches to a white oak north 20 degrees east 172 perches to a post north 25 degrees east 162 perches to a pine north 55 degrees east 162 perches to a pine north 55 degrees west 44 perches to a white oak north 16 degrees west 20 perches to a white oak north 38 degrees west 44 perches to a gum north 53 degrees east 26 perches to a white oak north 63 degrees east 56 perches to a post north 73 degrees east 232 perches to a locust north 35 degrees east 24 perches to an elm north 30 degrees west 8 perches to a locust and crossing Juniata north 41 degrees east 40 perches to a black oak north 30 degrees west 38 perches to a black oak north 5 degrees east 22 perches to a black oak north 15 degrees west 92 perches to a black oak north 15 degrees west 92 perches to a black oak and north 30 degrees west 92 perches to a black oak north 48 degrees west 30 perches to a white oak north 36 degrees west 43 perches to a gum north 45 degrees west 38 perches to a hickory north 38 degrees west 28 perches to a chestnut north 30 degrees __

Page 146
perches to a hickory north 46 degrees west 36 perches to a black oak north 66 degrees west 64 perches to a __ south 85 degrees west 226 perches to a white oak north 65 degrees west 64 perches to a black oak north 52 degrees west perches to a white oak north 44 degrees west 28 perches to a white oak north 31 degrees west 74 perches to a black oak north 89 degrees west 48 perches to a black oak north 78 degrees west 84 perches to a black oak south 65 degrees west 94 perches to a black oak south 75 degrees west 318 perches to a black oak south 87 degrees west 284 perches to a locust south 70 degrees west 1276

perches to a white oak south 82 degrees west 141 perches to a white oak south 75 degrees west 140 perches to a black oak west 160 perches to a post north 41 degrees and a half west 1026 perches to a post north 3 degrees east 66 perches to a post north 19 degrees east 32 perches to a white oak north 8 degrees west 18 perches to a locust north 1 degree east 32 perches to a spanish oak north 13 degrees west 116 perches to a mulberry north 8 degrees west 46 perches to a spanish oak north 35 degrees west 48 perches to a stump north 8 degrees west 48 perches to a chestnut oak north 5 degrees east 24 perches to a chestnut oak north 37 degrees west 14 perches to __ north 78 degrees west 42 perches to a black oak north 52 degrees west 122 perches to a white oak north 15 degrees wet 52 perches to a post north 67 degrees west 52 perches to a post north 67 degrees west 34 perches to a __ north 48 degrees west 54 perches to an elm north 69 degrees wet 56 perches to a white oak south 70 degrees west 26 perches to a black oak north 56 degrees

Page 147

west 54 perches to a black oak north 44 degrees west 80 perches to an elm north 49 degrees west 40 perches to a white oak north 48 degrees west 86 perches to Odgens north 65 degrees west 32 perches to an ironwood north __ 6 degrees west 26 perches to a spanish oak at the foot of long narrows north 57 degrees west 130 perches south 84 degrees west 120 perches south 75 degrees west 365 perches south 70 degrees west 336 perches to a black oak 62 degrees west 102 perches south 65 degrees west 288 perches south 48 degrees 96 perches south 69 degrees west 120 perches south 76 degrees west 68 perches south 57 degrees west 36 perches to an elm south 48 west 42 perches south 65 degrees west 66 perches to a white oak south 82 degrees west 52 perches to a locust south 70 degrees west 22 perches to a white oak south 80 degrees west 65 perches to a white oak north 58 degrees west 72 perches to a white oak north 28 degrees west 122 perches to a hickory on Jacks Creek north 55 degrees west 54 perches to McMeens north 52 degrees west 174 perches to a black oak north 4 degrees west 130 perches to a white oak north 17 degrees east 134 perches to a white oak north 20 degrees east 282 perches to a white oak north 27 degrees wet 230 perches to a white oak north 47 degrees west 88 perches to a spanish oak north 35 degrees west 100 perches to a white oak north 4 degrees west 82 perches to a maple north 23 degrees east 50 perches to a dogwood north 4 degrees west 40 perches to a white oak north 29 degrees west 100 perches to a maple north 63 degrees west 24 perches to a Kisagulllis (?) Crossed south 84 degrees west 58 perches.

Page 148

to a white oak north 65 degrees west 24 perches to a white oak north 49 degrees west 30 perches to a pine north 35 degrees west 42 perches to a pine north 22 degrees west 30 perches to a white oak north 5 degrees west 42 perches to a maple north 10 degrees west 34 perches to a walnut east branch crossed north 12 degrees west 50 perches to a pine and James Reeds north 64 degrees west 26 perches to a hickory north 37 degrees west 10 perches to a white oak crossing the middle or north branch north 67 degrees west 34 perches to a white oak at William Browns. The Court having taken the above report into consideration do thereupon order the same road as aforesaid described and laid out be to all intents and purposes a publick road and highway and that the same as such be forthwith opened cleared and repaired in pursuance of the Acts of General Assembly of this Province in such case made and provided of which the Supervisors of the roads in the respective townships through which same passes are to take notice.

Page 149
Acct of roads confirmed commencing July Sessions 1765
1. Beginning at McCallisters Mill to Shippensburg   July Sessions 1765
   Tyrons divided the Lower called Rye   Jany 1766
   Fermanagh Penns, Greenwood & Derry townships boundaries July 1767
2. Beginning at Smiths Mill to Walnut Bottom   October 1767
3. Beginning at McDowells Mill to Neepolsons Gap   apt. 1768
4. Beginning at a road laid out in Sherman Valley up Juniata to Kickacog (?)
   Apt 1768

Page 150- blank

Page 151
At a court of Private sessions for appointing officers, held at Carlisle, 25 __ 1753, before Samuel Smith and his associates.
Antrim Township; Constable- John Scott; Supervisors of highways- John
          Mitchel, John Homer; Appraisers- Henry Palin, Abr. Miller
Gilford Township; Constable- Patrick Jack; Overseers of Poor- John Reynolds,
          William Smith; Appraisers- John Forsyth, Thos Urie
Hamilton Township; Constable- Joseph Barnet; Overseers of Poor- Willm
          McCamish, James Hamilton; Supervisors of highways- William
          Rankin, Thomas Barrel; Appraisers- Andrew Bratton
Lurgon Township; Constable- Alex. Culbertson; Overseers of Poor- David
          Harrin (?), Joseph Stephenson; Supervisors of highways- John Finly
          Elder, William Karr; Appraisers- Francis Harrin
Middleton Township; Constable- John Creighead; Overseers of Poor- Willm.
          Parkison, Willm Grimes; Supervisors of highways- Robt. Campbell,
          Willm. Armstrong

Page 152
Peters Township; Constable- John Beard; Overseers of Poor- Willm. Lowry,
          Mashac Jamas; Supervisors of highways- Mathw. Patter, John Patten;
          Appraisers- Willm. Sample, John Beard
East Pensbro Township; Constable- John Waugh; Overseers of Poor- Joseph
          Green, Saml. Fisher; Supervisors of highways- Nathl. Nellson, Sam.
          Martin; Appraisers- Harvey Quigley, Andw. Miller

West Pensbro Township; Constable- Thos. Parker; Overseers of Poor- John McClure, John Logan; Supervisors of highways- Robt. Walker, Robt. McQuesp_; Appraisers- Willm. Patten, Robt. Breverd
Carlisle Township; Constable- Robt. McHenny

Quarter Session Docket 4 1768-1772

Page 1
At Carlisle, 9 July 1768, before John Armstrong and his associate justices.
Sheriff John Holmes returns the following grand jurors; William Miller,
foreman, Robert Sample, Samuel Laird, Robert Gibson, John McKee, James
Mays, James Pollock, William Denny, Ralph Naylor, William Wallace, John
Pollock, Charles Patteron, James Ramsey, John Agnem, Thomas Donnellan,
William Erwin, Paul Pierce, Abrah Woods, Jonathan Kershley, Stephen Folk,
John Pollock Carpenter, Joseph Hunter, John Fulton, John Kinkead.

Page 2 July Sessions 1768
The following were sworn on the Grand Inquest; William Miller foreman,
Samuel Laird, Robert Gibson, John McKee, James Mays, James Pollock,
William Denny, Ralph Nailor, William Wallace, John Pollock, Charles
Patterson, James Ransey, Thomas Donnallan, William Ervin, John Fulton, John
Kinkead.

The King vs William Chambers
Tippling house. David Sample £40, conditioned for the appearance of Wm.
Chambers at next court

Page 3
Richd Kirkpatrick Senr, Richd Kirkpatrick, Junr, James Lee
Tent. in £50 each on condition that the said Richd Kirkpatrick Senr and Richd
Kirkpatrick Junr, Joseph Kirkpatrick and Moses Kirkpatrick do severally keep
the peace and be of good behaviour to all his Majestys loyal subjects for the
space of one year.

Samuel Fisher Sen. £50 each on condition that Samuel Fisher Junr and Fisher
Senr do keep the peace and be of good behaviour to all his Majesties subjects
for the space of one year.

The King vs Jesse Harris
Felony.

Abiah Rees £15, on condition that Jessie Harris do keep the peace and be of
good behaviour to all his Majesties Siege subjects for the space of two years
next ensuing.

Page 4
The King vs William Irwin
Assault & battery.

The King vs Ameas Willson
Felony. Defendant pleads not guilty. Jury; Stephen Duncan,, William Brown, James McClinlok, William Corren, Samuel Coulter, John Holmes Cooper, Peter Smith, John McCurdey, William Reaney, Thomas Holmes, Mathias Sailor, James Lee say that the defendant is guilty , fined 3 pounds 16 shillings to the Governor, make restitution of the value thereof to the owner if not already done, receive on his bare back at the common whipping post in Carlisle between the hours of 9 & 11 oclock in the forenoon 21 lashes well laid on, on Thursday the 21st and stand committed until the above judgement be complied with and the costs of the prosecution & prosecutors.

Page 5 July Sessions 1768
The King vs Robert Kerr
Felony. Robert Kerr £100, George Kerr £50, on condition that Robert Kerr appear at next Court & not depart the court without leave.
John Willy, Hugh Willy, Robert McNight, in £30 each on the condition for the several appearance at next court to give evidence.

The King vs Catherine May Alias Eatton & James Eatton
Pleads not guilty. Jury; Stephen Duncan, William Brown, James McClintock, William Corren, Samuel Coutler, John Holmes Cooper, Peter Smith, William Keaney, Thomas Holmes, John McCurdy, Mathias Sailor & James Lee say the defendant Catherine May is guilty, fined in the sum of 7 pounds for the support of Government & restore the good stolen or the value thereof to the owner if not already restored & receive on her bare back at the common whipping post on Friday the 22nd day of this instant between the hours of 9 & 11 oclock in the forenoon 10 lashes well laid on.

Page 6
The King vs Robert Taggert
Tippling house. Defendant retracts his plea and submits to the Court protesting his innocence & is accordingly fined in the sum of 5 pounds to the Governor & stand committed until fine & fees be complied with.

The King vs John Clark
Forcable entry & detainor. John Clark £200, John Agnew £100, on condition that John Clark appear at next Court & not depart without leave.

David Reed £50, on condition for his own __ testify at the next Court.

Page 7
The King vs John Glen
Assault & battery.

The King vs Lewis Still

Felony.

Page 8 July Sessions 1768
The King vs Andrew Holmes
Misdemeanor. James Holmes £50 conditioned for the appearance of Andrew
Holmes at next Court.

The King vs Andrew Boyd, James Davis & Christopher Vanlear
Rescue. John Holmes £20, James David £50, Christopher Vanlear £50, on
condition for the appearance of James Davis, Christopher Vanlear at next Court
& not depart without leave.

Page 9
At Carlisle, before Jonathan __, Andrew Colhoun, Robert Miller & William
Lyon.

It is ordered that Giles Boners allies Giles Lowel & Catherine May (?) __ in the
_ of said County are each adjudged to serve 4 years and that the sheriff shall
them forthwith for what he can get.

Page 10
Came into Court Thomas Wilson, James Piper, David McCurdy & John Ering
being four of the person appointed by order of a former Court of General
Quarter Sessions of the peace to view and if they saw cause to lay out a road
from Carlisle the nearest & best way to the walnut bottom as to fall in the old
road leading to Shippensburgh & repair & straighten the said old road & made
report as that they had viewed & laid out a road as follows to wit. Beginning at
Carlisle thence S 60 degrees west 40 perches thence south 52 degrees 410
perches thence south 51 degrees west 310 perches to David McCords thence
south 40 degrees west 510 perches thence south 53 degrees west 573 perches to
the Walnut Bottom road thence south 72 degrees west 600 perches to Thomas
Wilson thence 65 ½ degrees west 192 perches thence south 71 degrees west 74
perches thence south 77 degrees west 162 perches thence south 63 degrees wet
65 perches thence south 55 degrees west 154 perches thence south 68 degrees
west 54 perches thence south 78 degrees west 460 perches to James Ewing
thence south 62 degrees west 1510 perches thence south 68 degrees west 500
perches to the Town of Shippensburg. Whereupon it is ordered by the Court
that the same road as aforesaid described & laid out be to all intents & purposes
a publick road and highway & that the same as such be forthwith opened
cleared & repaired in pursuance of an act of Assembly of this Province in such
case made & provided by.

Page 11
The petition of several of the inhabitants of Gilford and Hamilton townships to
the Court, setting forth that the petitioners understand a late application has
been made to have a road reviewed and laid out from the gap at Edward

Crawford's the nearest and best way to Fort Loudon and whereas we are informed the same has been lately surveyed and laid out in such a manner as will be __ tious to a great majority of the inhabitants of the different townships through which same passes and being laid out to answer a private interest and not to be an advantage of the whole, besides it will not be practicable to make and keep the same in repair without laying an intolerable burden on the people. We therefore pray your worship not to accept returns respective to same at present but to order a review that the same may be disposed to the common advantage and utility of most people.

James McKee, Joseph Cook, George Crawford, William McBrice, Thomas Aspey and Robert Sloan or any four of them are appointed to review and see cause to lay out the same road as and make report of their proceedings.

Page 12
Petition of several of the inhabitants of Guilford & Hamilton township to the Court setting forth that your petitioners understand a late application hath been made to have a road reviewed & laid out from the Gap at Edward Crawfords the nearest & best way to Fort Loudon & whereas we are informed the same has been lately survey and laid out in such a manner as will be __ to __ majority of the inhabitants of the different townships through which the same passes it being laid out to answer a private interest & not the good advantage of the whole __ it will not be practicable to make & keep the same in repair without laying an intolerable burden on the people we therefore pray your Worships not to Accept of any return respecting the same at present but to order a review that the same may be disposed & calculated to answer the common advantage and utility of the whole. Whereupon it is considered by the Court and James McKee, Joseph Cook, George Crawford, William McBryan, Thomas Askey and Robert Sloan or any four of them are appointed to review and if they cause to lay out the same road as aforesaid & make report.

Page 13- blank

Page 14
On 18 October 1768, before John Armstrong and his associate justices, the sheriff, Daniel Hogg, returns these jurors; Samuel Sloan, foreman, James Paper, William Rennels, John Guthery, Thomas Knox, John Miller, Samuel Rippey, William Reppey, James Calhoun, James Clark, William McCune, James Finley, James Chambers, Samuel Culbertson, William Lindsay, Samuel Moorehead, George Crawford, William Breckinridge, Thomas Poor, Robert Jack, Robert Calowell, Stephen Calowell, William Mitchell, Isaac Martin.

Ordered that Samuel Sloan, James Piper, William Rennells, James Guthery, William Rippey, James Calhoun, James Finley, James Clark, James Chambers, Samuel Culbertson, William Lindsay, Samuel Moorehead, George Crawford, William Breckinridge, Thomas Poor, Robert Jack, Robert Calowel, Stephen

Calowell, William Mitchell and Isaac Martin, fined 40 shillings each for non appearance.

Page 15 October Sessions 1768
1. Thomas Knox, 2. Samuel Rippey, 3. William McCune
Ordered by the Court that Daniel Duncan, John Campbell, Samuel Thomson, James Young, John Burns, Samuel Culbert, Richard Benson, James Kelly, John Hineman, Samuel Ligget, William Rippy, Thos. McCaine, Paul Barnet, William Beard, James McCaine, John Y. Thorn, Patrick Vance, John Noble, & Willm. McCamish be fined 40 shillings each for non attendance agreeable to a summons on the Traverse Jury & agreeable to an act of Assembly.

The King vs Samuel White
Joseph Jacobs __, for his appearance at next Court to testify.
Samuel White £50, William Wallace £25, on condition that Sam White appear at next Court & not depart without leave.

Page 16
The King vs John White
Recognizance John White upon proclamation upon paying costs.

The King vs John Clark
Forceable entry & detainor. John Clark £200, John Holmes £100, on condition that John Clark appear at next Court & not depart without leave.

David Reed £50, on condition & for his own appearance & Joseph Reads appearance for testified at the next Court of General Quarter Sessions.

Page 17
The King vs Robert Campbell
Robert Campbell £50, Alex Brown £25, on condition that Robt. Campbell, Saml. Camble, & __ Campbell be & appear at next Court & not depart without leave.
Thoms. Wilson £20, on condition for his appearance at next Court.

The King vs Andrew Holmes
Andrew Holmes £50, John Holmes £25, on condition that Andrew Holmes do appear at next Court to answer.

Page 18 October Sessions 1768
The King vs Robert Kerr
Hugh Willy £30, Robert McKnight £30, on condition that they appear at next Court of General Quarter Session to give evidence.

Robert Kerr £100, George Kerr £50, on condition that Robert Kerr appear at next Court & not depart without licence.

The King vs James Davis & Christopher Vanlear
James Davis £50, Christopher Vanlear £50, John Holmes £25, on condition for the appearance of James Davis & Christopher Vanlear at next Court & not depart without leave.

Page 19
The King vs Alexr. Brown
Alexander Brown £50, Robert Campbell £25, on condition that Alextr. Brown do keep the peace & be of good behaviour to all his Majesties Seige subjects & especially to William Hood for the space of three months. January Sessions 1769 Wm. Hood being called three times & no person appearing against Alexr. Brown he is thereupon discharged from his recognizance.

The King vs James Mitchel
James Mitchel £200, Henry Cunningham £100, on condition that James Mitchel be & appear at next Court & not depart the same without licence.

Robert Sample £50, on condition that Mary Steel appear at next Court to give evidence.

Page 20
The King vs Danmark
Charles Patterson £20, on condition that he appear at next Court to give evidence. James Pollock £20, on condition that he appear at next Court to give evidence.

James Duncan £50, Hugh Killgore £25, conditioned for the appear of James Duncan at next Court & not depart without license.

The King vs John Bird
John Bird £30, Rowland Harris £15, on condition that John Bird appear at next Court & not depart the same without license.

Joseph Glenn £20, on condition that he appear at next Court to give evidence.

Page 21
The petition of John Sutton of Hamilton township this county, setting forth that the said petitioners under great difficulties for want of a road from where the petitioners now lives through the lands of Jane McKinney and others to a great road leading to Carlisle, to mill and meeting and refused the same. Your petitioners therefore prays your worship to grant liberty for the same. It is considered by the Court and Matthew Wilson, William Bretherton, Thomas Baird, Patrick Vance, William Gass and John Vance, or any four of them are appointed to view and if they see cause to lay out the same as aforesaid and make report of their proceedings to next court.

The petition of several of the inhabitants of Middleton Township to the Court setting forth that whereas there was an order of Court obtained for laying out a road from Carlisle town to Creigheads Mill was wanted and of the same would be of publick use, was read. Whereupon it is considered by the Court and Robert Robb, Walter Denny, James Young, John Davies, Mathew Miller & Robert Urie or any four of them are appointed to view and if they see cause to lay out a road from the Town of Carlisle aforesaid to Creigheads Mill aforesaid & make report of their proceedings at the next Court of General Quarter Sessions & whether the same road be or publick or private use.

The petition of sundry inhabitants of Westpennsborough Township setting forth that there is a very great necessity for a road leading from James Smiths Mill in said township to fall into the Walnut Bottom road near where the men laid out road from Carlisle & the old Walnut Bottom road meet that such a road would be very advantageous & serviceable to the inhabitants of said township & others coming to said Mill from Carlisle & other places, therefore your petitioners prays your Worship to appoint proper men to view and if the see cause to lay out a road as aforesaid. Whereupon the __ [page torn]

Page 22
any four of them are appointed to view and if they see cause to lay out as aforesaid & make report of their proceedings to the next Court.

Came into court John Mitchel, James Young, James Irvin, & John Pollick being four of the persons appointed by Order of a former court of General Quarter Sessions of the peace to view and if they should see cause to lay out a road the nighest & best way from Chambers Mill in Middletown Township to Carlisle Ironworks and made report that they had met in pursuance of their appointment & had accordingly laid out the same road beginning at Chambers Mill aforesaid thence south 27 degrees east 80 perches thence south 36 degrees east 72 perches thence 65 degrees east 1605 perches thence south 7 degrees 260 perches to Carlisle Ironworks aforesaid & that the same is of publick use. October Sessions, 1768. The Court having taken the report into consideration do thereupon order that the same orad as aforesaid described & laid out be to all intents and purposes a publick road and highway and that the same as such be forthwith opened cleared and repaired in pursuance of the acts of General Assembly of this province in such case made and provided of which the supervisors of the roads in the respective townships through which the same passes and to take notice.

Page 22 [note, there are two page 22's]
At a Court of Private Sessions held at Carlisle, 4 November 1768, before Robert Miller, Andrew Calhoun, & John Holmes.

Came into Court Abraham Holmes & set forth that a Charles McCormick an indented servant to him the said Abraham Holmes hath absconded himself from his said master for the space of 20 days & that the said master was put to sundry expenses in following & recovering the said servant to his service amounting in the whole to 5 pounds, 17 shillings & three pence it is thereupon considered by the Court that the said Charles McCormick serve his said master or his assigns for the space of one year & three months above the time mentioned said indenture in order to the satisfaction of his said master in pursuance of the laws of this province in such case made & provided.

And also came into Court Abraham Holmes and set forth that a certain John Carpenter an indented servant of him the said Abraham Holmes hath absconded himself from his said master for the space of 23 days & that the said master was put to sundry expenses in following & recovering his said servant to his service amounting in the whole to 5 pounds, 17 shillings and 3 pence it is thereupon considered by the Court that the said John Carpenter serve his said master or his assigns for the space of one year & three months over & above the time mentioned in his said indenture ___ order to the satisfaction of his said master in pursuance of the Laws of this province in such case made & provided.

Page 24
At a Court of Private Sessions, held at Carlisle, 7 November 1768 before Robert Miller, Andrew Calhoun & John Holmes.

Came into Court William Nunan & set forth that a certain Thomas Tolbot an indented servant to him the said William Nunan hath absconded himself from his said master for the space of one year & a half and the said master was put to sundry expenses in following and recovering the said servant to his service amounting in the whole to 7 pounds, 10 shillings it is thereupon considered by the Court that the said Thomas Tabot serve his said master or his assigns for the space of 4 years over and above the time mentioned in his said indenture in order to the satisfaction of his said master in pursuance of the Laws of this province in such case made & provided.

Came into Court William Neenan & set forth that a certain Elenor Clement an indented servant to him the said William Nunan hath absconded herself from his said master for the space of one & a half years that the said master wads put to sundry expenses in following & recovering the said servant to his service amounting in the whole to 7 pounds, 10 shillings it is thereupon considered by the Court that the said Elenor Clement serve her said master or his assigns for the space of four years over & above the time mentioned in her said indenture in order to the satisfaction of her said master.

Page 24 [there are two page 24's]
Millford Township. Bound by Lack township & to run across the Valley by James Grays & William Scots throwing these two inhabitants into lack or the uper part of the Valley, the lower part hereafter to be known by the name of Millford Township.

Upon the petition of the inhabitants of East pennsburgh Township to the Court setting forth that they labor great inconvenience for want of a road being laid out and opened from Captian Robert Callenders Mill the nighest & best way into the Baltimore great road to terminate at Dogwood run or the County line would be of publick benefit to the inhabitants and praying the Court to order men to view and lay out the same agreeable to the above prayer. The Court do order and appoint James Galbreath Esquire, Edward Morton, John Nailer, David Wilson, Andrew Miller, & Thomas McCormick or any four of them to view the above mentioned premises and if they see necessary lay out the same by courses & distances the most useful for the Publick and least injurious to private property and make report to next Court.

Page 25
Court, 24 January 1769, before John Armstrong and his associate justices, the sheriff David Hogg returns the following panel of grand jurors; Tobias Hendricks, Francis Silver, Edward Morton, George Woods, Abram Adam, John Naylor, Sam Adam, Hugh White, John Quigley, John Galbraith, Joseph Judson, Isaac Hendricks, John K. Carouthers, Samuel Gates, Robert Gilfillin, John Abernathy, William Mateer, John Douglas, Jeremiah Reese, Joseph McClure, Joseph Simple, Thomas Martin, William Holmes, David Harkness.

Page 26 January Session 1769
The following appearing were sworn on the Grand Inquest, to wit. Francis Silver, John Nailor, Samuel Adams, Hugh White, John Galbraith, Joseph Hudson, Isaac Hendricks, John Carrithers, Samuel Galles, John Duglass, Jeremiah Kregs, Joseph McClure, Joseph Sample, William Holmes.

Page 27
The King vs David English
Recognizance of Wm. Patterson. On motion the Court asks that the recognizance taken in the pro__tion by Mr. Stephen Patterson for a felony supposed to be __ by the defendant in the __ the goods and chattels of Philip __ be discharged.

The King vs William Chambers
Tippling house. Defendant retracts his plea & submits to the Court protesting his innocence the Court fines him 5 pounds to the Governor for the support of Governor & costs of prosecution & __ his fees.

Page 28
The King vs Andrew Boyd, James Davis & Christopher Vanlear
Rescue. Pleads not guilty. Jury; Alexr. Work, Thomas McCormic, John
Trindle, Jams. Gregory, Thoms. Martin, Alexr. Trindle, John Caruthers Junr,
Rowland McDonn__, George Hudson, William Marshall, James Maten &
William Maleer say that Andrew Boyd is not guilty of the rescue assault &
battery. James Davis is not guilty of the rescue assault & battery & Christopher
Vanlear is not guilty of the rescue assault & battery whereof he stands indicted,
discharged paying a cost.

The King vs Andrew Holmes
Misdemeanor. Defendant pleads not guilty. Jury; Alexr. Work, Thomas
McCormick, John Trindle, James Gregory, Thomas Martin, Alexr. Trindle,
John Carithers Junr, Rowland McDonneld, George Hudson, William Marshell,
James Statter, & William Maleer say that Andrew Holmes is not guilty.

Page 29
The King vs James Moore alis Bigger & John Denmark
Felony. Defendant pleads not guilty. Jury; Alexander Work, Thomas
McCormick, John Trindle, James Gregory, Thomas Martin, Alexander Trindle,
James Canthers Junr, __ Donnald, George Hudson, William Marshell, __
Maleer, William Maleer, say that John Danmark is not guilty.

The King vs James Tenel (?) & Thomas Run
Felony.

Page 30
The King vs George Moore alis Bigger & John Danmark
Felony. John Danmark pleads not guilty. Jury; Alexander Work, Thomas
McCormick, John Trindle, James Gregory, Thomas Martin, Alexander Trindle,
John Carithers Junr, Rowland McDonnald, George Hudson, William Markshel,
James Mateer, & William Mateer say that John Danmark is not guilty.

The King vs Robert Carr
Felony. Defendant pleads not guilty. Jury; Alexander Work, Thomas
McCormick, John Trindle, James Gregory, Thomas Martin, Alexander Trindle,
John Carithers Junr, Rowland McDonnald, George Hudson, William Marshell,
James Mateer & William Mateer say that Robert Carr is guilty. Judgment that
Robert Carr be whipped at the publick whipping post in Carlisle on 25 March,
with 39 lashes and stand in the pillory one hour of the same between hours of
10 and 12 hours of the said 25 March, make fine to the Governor for the
support of government of the sum of 14 pounds, 10 shillings, make restitution
for the like sum of 14 pounds, 10 shillings if not already, to stand committed
with and pay the costs of the prosecution and the prosecutor.

Page 31 January Sessions 1769
The King vs Andrew Galbraith
Assault & battery. Andrew Galbraith £50, James Thompson £25, on condition
that Andrew Galbreath appear at the next Court, at Carlisle and in the mean
while to keep the peace and be of good behaviour to all his Majesties subjects.

The King vs John Clark
Forceable entry & detainor. Defendant pleads not guilty. Jury; Alexr Work,
Thoms. McCormick, John Trindle, James Gregory, Thomas Martin, Alexander
Trindle, John Carithers Junr, Rowland McDonnald, George Hudson, William
Marshell, James Mateer, & William Mateer say that the defendant John Clark
is guilty, judgment that the defendant pay 10 shillings & the costs of
prosecution & stand committed until fine & fees be complied with.

Page 32
The King vs John Overend
Felony.

The King vs James Mitchell
Fornication with Mary Steel.

The King vs Mary Steel
Fornication with James Mitchell.

The King vs James Little
Fornication with Mary Lather.

The King vs Mary Lather
Fornication with James Little.

James Andrew £50, condition of Mary Lather appear at next Court to testify

James Little £100, Robert Little £50, on condition that James Little appear at
next Court.

Page 33
John Homes bound in £50, for the appearance of Mary Steel at the Quarter
Sessions & give evidence

James Mitchel £100, Henry Prather £50, on condition that James Mitchel
appear at next Court & not depart without leave.

Henry Cunningham bound in £10, for the appearance of John Glen at next
Court.

Phillip Miller bound £20, for the appearance of himself & wife Elenor at next Court to testify.

Joseph Jacobs £20, on condition for the appearance of said Jacobs at the next Court to testify.

Page 34
The King vs Robert Campbell, James Campbell & Lincoln Campbell
Defendants discharged paying costs.

The King vs James Duncan
Defendant discharged paying costs.

Page 35
John Bird being three times solemnly called, appears not, makes default, recognizance forfeited.

Rowland Harris being three times solemnly called to being forth the body of John Bird brings not forth the body of the __ John bur makes default. Recognizance forfeited.

Joseph Green Junr being three times solemnly called appears not but makes default. Recognizance forfeited.

Samuel Hunter being 3 times solemnly called on his several recognizances to bring forth the body of Charles __ & Robert Armstrong brings not forth the bodies of the same Charles & Robert, but makes default. Recognizance forfeited.

Samuel Hunter being three times solemnly called on his several recognizances, appear not but makes default. Recognizance forfeited.

Robert Callender being three times solemnly called on his several recognizances to bring for the body of Samuel Hunter, brings not forth the body of same Samuel, but makes default. Recognizance forfeited.

John Defew Senr. Being three times solemnly called, appearth not, but makes default. Recognizance forfeited.

Robert Mateer (?) Being three times solemnly called to bring forth the body of John Defew Senr brings not forth the body of the said John, but makes default. Recognizance forfeited.

Page 36
At a court of Private sessions, held at Carlisle, 31 January 1769 before Andrew Colhoun, Robert Miller & John Holmes.

Quarter Session Docket 4 1768-1772 121

Whereas James Forsyth was tried for grand larceny at April Session last & was found guilty for the same & an application to the Governor his fines are omitted & the fees of his several indictments & the cots of prosecution & a amounting in the whole to 28 pounds, 10 shillings it is thereupon considered & ordered by the Court that the said James Forsyth be sold by the Sheriff for the term of 4 years for the satisfaction of his fee & the prosecution.

Whereas Enos Wilson was tried for Grand Larceny at July Sessions last & was found guilty for the same & on application to the Governor his fine was omitted & the fees of his indictment & the costs of prosecution & a amounting in the whole to 5 pounds, 18 shillings & six pence it is thereupon considered & ordered by the Court that the said Enos Wilson be sold and by the Sheriff for the term of two years in order for the satisfaction of is fees & the prosecution.

Page 37
Upon reading the petition of sundry inhabitants of Middleton township and others in said County setting forth that a __lling Mill, grist and merchant Mill have been lately built under the Mouth of Letort spring to the benefit of the petitioners & others in the adjacent parts that the petitioners and __ the Court would be of opinion that rendering publick road to places of this nature as near & easy as possible must be of great advantage to the neighbourhood. That a road or any from the publick road which comes from Croghan Gap to strike off a few perches from where the same crosses Canedoguinet Creek & from thence to the said mill across Letrot Spring near the mouth over which the owner of said Mill purposes building a bridge would be much more convenient & near that now made use of for the inhabitants of Shearmans Valley & those of said township living on the North side of said creek that the said road will run but a few perches and the petitioners apprehend can be injurious to none and prayeth the Court to appoint proper persons to view and lay out a road as aforesaid. Whereupon the Court do consider and order that James Irvine, Andrew McBath, Alexander Brown, Robert Sanderson, William Smith & James Armstrong or any four of them view and if they see cause lay out a road agreeable to the prayer of said Petition and make report of their proceedings to the next Court.

Page 38
At a Court of Private Sessions, 31 January 1769 before Andrew Calhoun, Robert Miller and John Holmes, justice. Upon a petition of a number of the inhabitants of the western side of the township of Peters, setting forth that whereas said petitioners labor under a great many disadvantages for the want of a wagon road leading from the mill of Robert Fleming, crossing west of the south east path to strike a road leading to Georgetown in Maryland or as near the house of Allen Killough and to extend near westardly from said mill on a former road as far as the house of William Marshall thence along a bridle road to the little Cove Mountain. The whole extent of this road according to the best computation will not exceed 9 miles and will be a very easy cut. It will be of

practical benefit to your petitioners as at Georgetown is deemed the most continuous best place for your petitioners to carry their salable commodities besides that it will be of great profit to the owner of said mill and also be commodious to a number of your petitioners in regard to their attendance on sermon at the meeting house formerly known by the name of Mr. Campbell's. We recommend it to your worships consideration, praying yo if it is consistent with your more superior judgement to grant an order for path, appointing men to view and lay out the same. Whereupon the Court do consider and order that William Patten, John Shelby, Dongall Campbell, David Davis, John Miller and Patrick Maxwell or any four of them view and if they see cause lay out the road aforesaid, agreeable to the places of the petition and make report of their proceedings to the next court.

Page 39 & 40 - blank

Page 41- 42
At a Court of Private Sessions, 25 March 1769 for the appointment of officers, before Andrew Callhoun Esq. and his associate justices.
Lurgan township; Hugh Willy, Jr, constable; James McAllaster, James
        Rennels, supervisors of roads; Charles Maclear, James McKee
        overseers of poor; William Young, William Erwin, viewers of fences.
Letterkenny township; James Kelly, constable; Joseph Culbertson, Albert
        Torrence, supervisors of roads; John Baird, Samuel Culbertson.
        overseers of poor.
Gilford township; Andrew Frees, Peter Gooshead, constable; Frederick Graft,
        Thomas Binney, supervisors of roads; John Andrew. John Miller,
        overseers of poor; Peter Snyder, Thomas Thompson, viewers of
        fences.
Hamilton township; Forgus Moorehead, constable.
Antrim township; William Cross, constable; James Roddy Sr, Frederick
        Foreman, supervisors of roads; John Moorehead, John Rule,
        overseers of poor; John Wallace, Roger Hart, viewers of fences.
Peters township; Josiah McKenney, constable.
Fannet township; David Elder, constable; Allen Brown, Felix Doyle,
        supervisors of roads; James Howe, Archibald Elliot, overseers of
        poor; William Moore, Patrick McGuire, viewers of fences.
Air township; Lewis Davis, constable; David Scott, James Liddle,
        superintendent of road; Evan Shelby, James Liddel, overseers of
        poor.
Tyrone township; Hugh Kilgore, constable; Samuel Fisher, Robert Wilson,
        supervisors of roads; John Sharpe, William Raugh, overseers of poor;
        Jonathan Ross, David McClure, viewers of fences.
Tiboyne township; Thomas Clark, constable; James Morrison, William
        Anderson, supervisors of roads; Alexander Rodger, Robert Nelson,
        overseers of poor; John Wilson, William Hunter, viewers of fences.

Rie township; Robert Hearse, constable; John Marshal, Benjamin Abraham, supervisors of roads; James Watt, William Parkinson, overseers of poor; John English, Samuel Godney, viewers of fences.

Lack township; John Collins, constable; William Kirk, William Bruce, supervisors of roads; James Stoner, William Wallace, overseers of poor; James Gray, William Pyate, viewers of fences.

Milford township; James Scott, constable; John Erwin, John Hamilton, supervisors of roads; Clement Horrel, Alexander Robinson over seers of poor; Robert Campbell, Thomas Benger, viewers of fences.

Farmanagh township; James Mitcheltree, constable; James Gibson, Hugh McCormick, over seers of poor; Hugh McAllister, Samuel Patterson viewers of fence.

Bedford township; (no officers appointed)

Derry township; Daniel Jones, constable; William Brown and Samuel Sander, superintendent of road; John Carmichael, George Bell, overseers of poor; James Lime, James Ross, viewers of fences.

Penns township; (no officers appointed for this year)

Greenwood township; William McLeavy, constable.

Dublin township; Robert Ramsey, constable; James Elliot, Charles Boles, over seers of poor.

Colraine township; (no officers appointed for this year)

Cumberland township; (no officers appointed for his year)

Bane township; Samuel Anderson, constable; Zebulon Moore, Robert Calewell, overseers of poor; Samuel Little, Charles Calewell, viewers of fences.

Page 43
At Carlisle, 18 April 1769, the sheriff David Hogg returned the following panel of grand jurors; Robert Thornburgh, foreman — Ezekile Dunning, Jonathan Holmes, William Clark, William Moore, Paul Pierce, Andrew Homes, William Chambers, Robert Galbraith, John Calhoun (Lisburn), John Moore (fuller), James Parker, Robert Rob, Andrew Miller, James Smith, John Clark, John Gragg, Jarret Erwin, William Carouthers, George Sanderson, Sr., John McClure, Robert Wire, Robert Walker.

Page 44 April Sessions 1769
The following were sworn on the Grand Inquest; Robert Thornburgh foreman, Ezekiel Dunning, Jonathan Holmes, William Clark, Andrew Holmes, William Chambers, Robert Galbreath, John Calhoun of Lisburn, James Parker, Andrew Miller, John Clark, William Carrithers, John McClure, Robert Urie, Robert Walker Junr.

Page 45
The King vs John Overend
Felony. Jury; John Steward, Richd. Rankin, William Waddle, Richd. Gillson (?), James Crocket, Alexr. McBride, Robert Armstrong, John Dickey, Andrew Johnston, David Lusk, Samuel Hogg, David Elliot say that the defendant is

guilty & is fined 15 shillings for the support of Government & return the goods stolen or the value thereof to the owner if not already restored & receive on his bare back at the common whipping post in Carlisle on Thursday the 20th day of this instant, between the hours of 9 & 4 oclock of the same day 21 lashes well laid on & stand committed until fine & fees be complied with.

On motion of Mr. Johnston Hugh McCormick is discharged from his recognizance.

Ann Gorman is discharged from her recognizance paying fee.

William McConnel £50 for the appearance of Mary McCommel at next Court, to testify against Wm. Bealy Junr.

William Bealy £100 for the appearance of William Bealy Junr at next Court.

Robert Allison £100, John Montgomery £50, on condition for the John Allison at next Court.

Page 46
The King vs Andrew Galbreath
Assault & battery. Defendant retracts his plea and submits to the Court protesting his innocence. Judgment that he pay a fine 10 shillings & the costs of prosecution & stand committed until fine & fees be complied with.

The King vs Samuel White
Felony. Defendant pleads not guilty. Jury; John Stewart, Richard Rankin, John Waddle, Richard Gillson, James Crocket, Alexander McBride, Robert Armstrong, John Dickey, Andrew Johnston, David Lusk, Samuel Hogg & David Elliot say that the defendant is not guilty, discharged paying costs.

Page 47 April Sessions 1769
The King vs James Little
Fornication & basterdy. Jury; John Stewart, Richard Rankin, John Waddle, Richard Gillory, James Crocket, Alexander McBride, Robert Armstrong, John Dickey, Andrew Johnston, David Lusk, Samuel Hogg & David Elliot say that James Little is guilty, judgment that he pay 10 pounds to the Governor with the costs of prosecution & stand committed until fine be complied with.

The King vs Mary Lather
Fornication. Defendant pleads guilty. Judgment that she pay a fine to the Governor of 10 pounds & stand committed until the fees be paid.

Page 48
The King vs Elinor McSwine (?)
Assault & battery.

The King vs Mathias Taylor & Elizabeth Taylor
Assault & battery. Submits to the Court protesting their innocence judgment that they pay fine of the sum of six pence each with the costs of prosecution & stand committed until fines & fees be complied with.

Page 49
The King vs John Quigley
Assault & battery. Defendant submits to the Court protesting his innocence, judgment that he pay a fine of 10 shillings to the Governor with the costs of prosecution & stand committed until fine & fees be complied with

The King vs James Mitchel
Fornication & bastery. Jury; John Stewart, Richard Rankin, John Waddle, Richard Gillson, James Crocket, Alexr. McBride, Robert Armstrong, John Dickey, Andrew Johnston, David Lusk, Samuel Godd & David Elliott say that James Mitchel is guilty, pay 10 pounds to the Governor with the costs of prosecution & stand committed until fine & fees be complied with and the court order that the above said James Mitchel defendant in the above action pay or cause to be paid into the hands of Mary Steel the Mother of the said bastard child under whose care the said child is hereby ordered at the rate of 13 pounds & __ monthly until the said child is 2 years old & that a property __ part thereof now become due be forth with paid & when the said child is arrived at the age of 2 full years that the said children and her so keep as not to become chargeable to the township as in the mean time give security to the Court for the due performance of this order.

Page 50 April Sessions 1769
The King vs John Quigley

The King vs Mary Steel
Fornication & bastardy. Defendant pleads guilty, fined 10 pounds to the Governor with the costs of prosecution & stand committed until fine be complied with.

The King vs William Holmes
Tippling house.

Page 51
The King vs John McMahon
Felony.

The King vs John Glen
Assault & battery. Defendant submits to the Court protesting his innocence judgment that he pay a fine of the sum of six pence with the cots of prosecution & stand committed until fine & fees are complied with.

Page 52

The King vs John Pollock, Andrew Murphy, William Murphy
Larceny. John Pollock pleads guilty. Andrew Murphy & William Murphy
being severally arraigned plead not guilty. Jury; John Stewart, Richd Rankin,
John Waddle, Richard Guillory, James Crocket, Alexander McBride, Robert
Armstrong, John Dickey, Andrew Johnston, David Lust, Samuel Hogg, David
Elliott say that Andrew Murphy is guilty & that Wm Murphy of the
misdemeanor whereof the stands indicted. Judgment that John Pollock be fined
4 pounds 10 shillings to the Governor for the support of Government & restore
to the owner thereof if not restored & receive on his bare back 21 lashes well
laid on at the whipping post at Carlisle between the hours of 10 & 4 oclock of
said 22nd instant & that Andrew Murphy is fined 4 pounds to the Governor for
the support of Government & restore to the owner thereof if not restored &
receive on his bar back 21 lashes well laid on at the whipping post in Carlisle
between the hours of 10 & 4 oclock of 22 day of said day & that Wm. Murphy
is fined in the sum of 4 pounds to the Governor for the support of Government
& restore to the owner thereof if not restored & receive on his bare back 21
lashes well laid on the 22nd day of the instant at the common whipping post in
Carlisle & stand committed until fine and fees be complied with.

The King vs Bartholomew David, & Ann his wife, Jane Drennan & James
Tweed (?)

Page 53

Came into Court David Scott and prayeth the Court to appoint a fit person to
make a division line between the townships of Peters and the township of Air.
The Court do consider the same and appoint Elias Davison, James Johnson, of
Antrim township and Allen Brown and William Elliot of Fannet township to
make a division between the two townships aforesaid, and make report of their
proceeding to the next Court.

Came into Court Thomas Craignhead & set forth that a certain John Green
indented servant to him the said Thomas Craighead hath absconded himself
from his said master for the space of 4 days & that the said master was put to
sundry expenses in following & recovering his said servant to his service
accounting in the whole to 3 pounds, 2 shillings & 4 pence it thereupon on
considered by the Court that the said John Green do serve his said master or his
assigns for the space of 5 months over & above the time mentioned in his said
indenture in order to the satisfaction of his said master in pursuance of the laws
of the Province in such case made & provided.

At a Court of private sessions held at Carlisle, 2 July 1769 before John
Armstrong, Robert Miller, William Lyon.
At a private Court of Quarter sessions held the 12 day of July 1769 by us the
subscribers three of his Majesties Justices of the peace for the mid County;
Benjamin Blyth brought before us into Court his servant man in the within

indenture bound and made appear before us that the said servant named William George absconded himself from his service the space of 17 days & that he the said Benjamin Blyth has expended in finding and getting into his custody the said servant the sum of 8 pounds, 12 shillings and 3 pence in consideration of [cont]

Page 54
which time & the above damage sustained by the said Benjamin Blyth we do adjudge that the said servant William George shall serve the further term or time of 12 months, over the term in the within indenture is expired given under our hands and seals the day and year above written.

Page 55, 56, 57- blank

Page 58
At Carlisle, 18 July 1769, the sheriff of the county David Hogg returns the following list of grand jurors; Richard Tea, William Miller, James Pollock, William Thompson, John Wilkins, Charles Pettison, Thomas Donnelan, John Prentice, William McGlosky, John McCurdy, John Glen, Samuel Laird, John Grier, Stephen Duncan, Stewart Rowan, John McKee, John Gray, Robert Calhoun, Matthew Sellers, Christopher Van Lear, Ralph Naylor, James Sheron, Joseph Speer, John Fulton.

Page 59 July Sessions 1769
The following appearing were sworn on the Grand Inquest; Richard Tea-foreman, William Miller, James Pollock, William Thompson, Charles Pattison, John Prentice, William McCroskey, John McCurdy, John Glen, Samuel Laird, John Jreir, Stewart Rowan, John McKee, Ralph Nailer, James Sharon

Samuel Hastins, John Hastins Junr & John McIntire being severally bound over by recognizance to appear at this sessions are discharged on motion paying costs.

John Wilkins, Thomas Donnellon & Stephen Duncan being respectively summoned as Grand Jury men to appear at this sessions and being present in Court and offering sufficient excuses for not serving, the Court dispenses with their attendance.

Henry Boil £50, James Thomas £50, conditioned that Henry Boils keep the peace and be of good behaviour to all his Majesties subjects and particularly to John Wilkey for 3 months and that be shall appear at the next Court.

George Hopaher (?) Is discharged paying fees.

Page 60
The King vs Robert Gutherie Junr
Assault & battery.

The King vs John Hastings
Assault & battery. Defendant pleads guilty, judgment that he pay a fine to support the Government of six pence and the costs of prosecution and stand committed until fine & costs be complied with.

Henry Thompson being 3 times solemnly called appears not and forfeits his recognizance.

James McCall on motion is discharged from his recognizance to give evidence on behalf of our Lord the King.

John McClann being 3 times solemnly called appears not or brings forth the body of Daniel McClark therefore recognizance forfeited.

William People being 3 times solemnly called to bring forth the body of John Amberson appears not nor brings forth the body of the same John therefore recognizance forfeited.

William Piper £50, conditioned for the appearances of David Lewiston at the next Court to answer to such matters and things as may be subject against him in this Majesties behalf.

On motion of Mr. Ross James McAffee is discharged from his recognizance paying costs.

Page 61
The King vs Laughlin Lee (?)
Felony in steeling the goods of John Kersley (?). Prisoner being pleads guilty. Judgment that the prisoner pay a fine of 5 pounds, 18 shillings to his Honor the Governour and the costs of prosecution and further be whipped at the publick whipping post on the morrow being the 20th instant between the hours of 10 & 12 in the forenoon of the same day, with 21 lashes on his bare back well laid on and stand committed till judgment be complied with.

The King vs James Elliot
Assault & battery on Mary Martin. John Martin indorsed prosecutor and now the defendant by Mr. McGaw pleads not guilty.

The King vs James Elliot and Barbara Elliot
Forcible entry. Defendants by Mr. Magaw pleads not guilty. James Elliot £50, conditioned for the appearance of the said James Elliot and Barbara Elliot at the next Court to answer and not depart without licence.

October Sessions 1769 and now James Elliott being 3 times solemnly called appearth not and therefor the recognizance of the said James Elliott is forfeited.

Page 62 July Session 1769
Came into Court James Johnson, Elias Davison, William Elliot and Allen Brown the persons appointed by order of the former Court to make division between the townships of Peters and Air, and make report that in pursuance of which order, we have viewed and fixed the top of the dividing ridge from the waters of Conococheague and Licking creek running through and townships of Air, the line beginning at the provincial line and continuing as far as said township are connected. The Court having taken the report into consideration do thereupon order the same division as above described and laid out be to all intents and purposes the dividing line between the townships of Peters and Air.

The Petition of sundry of the inhabitants of Middleton and West pennsbrough townships and parts adjacent to this Court setting forth that a road leading from Carlisle to the Mills of the Revd. William Thompson is much wanted and would be of great use to the Publick and in particular the inhabitants of the said townships to carry the produce of their plantations to market our Petitioners therefore humbly pray your Worship to take the premises under consideration and appoint proper persons to view the ground and if they see cause lay out a road the nearest and best way the ground will admit of as aforesaid. Whereupon it is considered by the Court that John Davis, Captain William Thompson, John McClure, Richard Parker, John Dunber and Alexander Parker or any 4 of them be appointed to view and if they see cause to lay out the same road as aforesaid and make report of their proceedings to the next Court.

Petition of several of the inhabitants of Shermans Valley & others setting forth that a road is much wanted from the __ parts of said Valley to and from Carlisle and also in going to and from Moores Mills to begin at Thomas Clarks thence to John Neepers thence to Moores Mills and thence the nighest and best road to Carlisle wherefore your petitioners pray your worship to appoint proper persons to view and lay out a road as aforesaid. Whereupon it is considered by the Court that John Byers, James _iffon, John Neiper, John Sharp, Hugh Alexander and Alexander Roddy or any four of them be appointed to view the said road and make report to the next Court.

Page 63- blank

Page 64
At a private sessions held at Carlisle, 4 Aug 1769 before John Armstrong, Robert Miller, William Lyon. Whereas Laughlin McFee was tried for grand larceny at July Sessions last and was found guilty of the same and on application for his discharge. It is ordered and considered by the Court that the said Laughlin McFee be sold out by the Sheriff for the term of 4 years.

Page 65- blank

Page 66
24 October 1769, the sheriff returns the following list of grand jurors; Samuel Lindsay, Samuel Sloan, Samuel Culbertson, John Sutton, Benjamin Chambers, William Baird, Edward Crawford, Roland Hanes, Robert Patterson, Robert English, John Rule, William Thompson, Albert Thompson, Thomas Baird, John Comboni, Thomas Daugherty, Patrick McLane, Albert Culbertson, William McCune, Thomas McKeen, Thomas Pooe, James McKee, William Swan, James Breckenridge.

Page 67   October Sessions 1769
An application of Mr. Johnston to the Court James Biddle, Edward Biddle, Daniel Levan and Thomas Hartley having taken the oaths prescribed by act of assembly are admitted attorneys of this Court.

Peter Roweleater £50 on condition that he appear at the next Court to testify.

James Lee £50, on condition that Mary Lee the wife of the said James Lee shall appear at the next Court testify on behalf of our Sovereign Lord the King.

James Elliott and Barbara Elliott being three times solemnly called appear not therefore the recognizance of the said James Elliott is forfeited.

On Motion of Mr. Smith Jacob Grove is discharged from his recognizance paying costs.

William Derrough (?) £50, William Patrick £50, conditioned for their several appearances at the next Court and to give evidence for the King and not depart.

William Patrick applying to the Court setting forth that he had become bound for the appearance of James Hugh at this sessions to testify and that the said James is now sick ad unable to travel the Court respites the recognizance of the said James & Patrick at the next Sessions.

Page 68
William Wilson £50, John Willson £50, conditioned that William Wilson shall appear at the next Court & give evidence and not depart the Court.

George McGonagle £50, James Thomas £50, conditioned for the appearance of George McGonagle at the next Court to answer and not depart the Court.

Robert Smith £100, Robert Robb £100. Conditioned for the appearance of Robert Smith at the next Court to testify and not depart the Court.

George Beard £40, John Robb£20, conditioned for the appearance of George Beard at the next Court not depart the Court.

Philip Tabor £200, John Wilson £100, conditioned for the appearance of Philip Tabor at the next Court to answer and not depart the Court.

Robert Guthry £40, John Guthry £20, conditioned for the appearance of Robert Guthry at the next Court to answer and not depart the Court.

Page 69
James Patton £50, Joseph Greenwood £50, conditioned for the appearance of James Patton at the next Court to answer and not depart the Court.

George Girty £50, James Dolton £50, conditioned for the appearance of George Girty at the next Court to answer and not depart the Court.

John Rhoades being three times solemnly called appears not therefore his recognizance forfeited.

Frederick Dhyam being three times solemnly called to bring forth the body of John Thoades, brings not forth his body therefore his recognizance forfeited.

John McClelland being three times solemnly called appears not but makes default therefore recognizance forfeited.

Charles Camelon being three times solemnly called appears not but makes default Therefore his recognizance forfeited.

James Hunter being three times solemnly called to bring forth the body of Charles Camelon brings not forth his body therefore his recognizance forfeited.

The several recognizance of George Truck, John Roades, James Hughes, George Wolf, Miahcel Wallock, George Twegar, Leonard Twegar, Samuel Blair and Patrick Hartford are respited until the next session.

Page 70 October Sessions 1769
On Motion Francis Owen is discharged from his recognizance paying costs.

On Motion William Gardner Junr and William Gardner Senr are discharged from their recognizance paying costs.

On Motion of Wm. Wilson and argument John Wilson is discharged from his recognizance paying costs.

On Motion of Wm. Wilson, it is ordered that David Walker of Milford Township, show cause at next January Court, why an order not be made upon him to maintain his wife.

Petition of sundry of the inhabitants of the townships of Derry and Barre setting forth that the petitioners labor under great difficulty for the want of a bridle road from the mouth of Aughwich Creek to the mouth of Keshecokoles Creek and into the road laid out part Mr. McClays the petitioners humbly praying the Court would grant an order for said road and appoint men to view and lay it out the nearest and best way. It is thereupon considered by the Court that Joseph Howard, John Brown, Samuel Holiday, Thomas Holt, James Lyon and Andrew Bratton or any four of them be appointed to view and if they see cause to lay out the same roads as aforesaid and make report of their proceedings to the next Court.

Came into Court Alexander Roddy, John Sharp, James Wilson, John Neeper and Hugh Alexander being five of the persons appointed b order of a former Court of General Quarter Sessions of the Peace to view and if they should see cause to lay out a road from the western parts of Shermans Valley to and from Carlisle and in going to and from Moores Mills to begin at Thomas Clarks thence to John Neaper thence to Moores Mills and thence the nighest and best way to Carlisle and make report that they had met in pursuance of their appointment and adjudged it necessary to begin at said Clarks [cont]

Page 71 October Sessions 1769
Clarks and end at the great Road leading from Mr. Francis Wests (?) to John Fargus's near the place called Red Rock, as appears by the trees marked on the different Courses. The Court having taken the report into consideration do thereupon order that the same road as before described and laid out be to all intents and purposes a publick roads and high way and the same as such be forthwith opened and cleared and repaired, and the supervisors of the roads in the respective townships through which the said passes are to take notice.

Upon reading the petition of several of the inhabitants of Antrim, Gilford townships, setting forth that said petitioners labor under great difficulties for want of a road leading from the mouth of Adam Cook's lane to the Dutch Meeting House as your petitioners has opened two or three roads to said Meeting House already and they are constantly stopped, so we have no road at present without going a great way round, your petitioners humbly beg your worship will take the matter into serious consideration and grant us a road. The Court appoint John Harmony, Peter Snyder, Anthony Snyder, Robert Baird, Joseph Rower and Daniel Royer or any four of them to view and if they see cause to lay out a road as aforesaid and make return to next Court.

Upon reading the petition of a number of the inhabitants of Shermans Valley setting forth that a road is much wanted from the western parts of said valley in going to and from Carlisle your petitioners therefore pray your Worship to appoint proper persons to view and lay out a road as aforesaid to begin at Widow Dame's thence past Robert Millers Field and then into the road already laid out to Thomas Clarks. The Court do thereupon consider and appoint Thomas Ross, Obediah Garwood, John Scott, Robert Pohe, Robert Adams and John Watt or any four of them to view and if they see cause lay out a road as aforesaid and make report of their proceedings to next Court.

Page 72
At a private sessions, held at Carlisle, 1 December 1769, before John Reynolds, Andrew _oth__, and Bernard Dougherty. Came into court John Fulton and set forth that a certain John Kind an indented servant to him the said John Fulton hath absconded himself from his said master for the space of 14 days and that the said master was put to sundry expenses in following and recovering the said servant to his service amounting in the whole to 7 pounds and 10 shillings. It is considered by the Court that the said John Kind serve his said master or his assigns a 14 months and an half exclusive of the time mentioned in his indenture aforesaid to the satisfaction of his said master in pursuance of the Laws of this Province in such case made and provided.

Page 73- blank

Page 74
At Carlisle, 23 January 1770 before John Rennell, Jonathan Hope, Andrew Calhoun Esq. the sheriff David Hogg returns the following juryman; George Brown, James Irvin (Conococheague), William Davison, James Campbell, Archibald Irving, James Piper, Johnson Elliot, James Waugh, James Parker (Yellow breeches), Richard Parker, John Baird, William Little, Adam Hays, John McClure, Alexander Officer, William Campbell, John Moorehead, Samuel Hanne, James McDowell, John Dunbar, Samuel Culbertson Jr., William Sharpe.

Page 75 January Sessions 1770
Upon reading the petition of several of the inhabitants of Kishohoguillis Great Valley saying they labor under the burthen of being in one township with Derry and as Jacks Mountain lies between the Great Valley and the rest of the township which cuts away all communication only at the Narrows. The petitioners therefore humbly prayed that the Court would take them under due consideration and strike the great valley off into a township by itself saying Jack Mountain to be the division line. The Court order that Jacks Mountain be the division line between the Township of Derry and the part struck off from said township which is called by the name of Armagh township, allowing the township of Armagh to include Kishochaquillis Narrows to where the road now crosses Kishochaquillis Creek.

Petition of the inhabitants of the West side of Peters township, saying they labor under some inconvenience for want of a bridle-path leading from Dunn gap to the Rev. John King's meeting-house, the petitioners pray the Court to appoint men to view and lay out the same and make return to the next Court.

The Court order that James Campbell, Robert McFarland, Richard Brownston, James Rankin and Patrick Campbell or any four of them are appointed to view and if they see cause to lay out the road and make report to the next Court.

Page 76 January Sessions 1770
The King vs Henry Davis
Felony. Defendant pleads guilty. Ordered that the said Henry Davis restore that goods so stolen to the right owner or shall pay the value of said goods, costs of prosecution and other disbursements in apprehending and prosecuting him, also pay the like value of the goods stolen to the Governor and shall be committed to the common goal until he makes satisfaction as aforesaid and shall be publickly whipped at the publick whipping post to morrow between the hours of 10 and 4 with 21 lashes on his bare back well laid.

The King vs Francis Lassly (?)
Felony. Jury; Joseph McKinney, Samuel McCune, William Evan, Robert Culbertson, George Sanderson Junr, Benjamin Allsworth, Thomas McClelland, James Barnes, John Brackenridge, William Linn, Peter Dick and Samuel Mitchell say that the defendant Francis Lassly is guilty. It is ordered that the said Francis Lassly restore the goods so stolen to the right owner or pay the value of the said goods as also the costs of prosecution and other disbursements in apprehending and prosecuting him and likewise the cost of time the owner and prosecutor had and moreover shall forfeit and pay the value of the goods so stolen to the Governor and shall be committed to the common goal there to remain till he makes satisfaction for all the sums adjudged and shall be publicked whipped at the publick whipping post between the hours of 10 and three to morrow with 5 lashes on his bare back.

Page 77
The King vs Moses Skinner
Felony.

The King vs Samuel Paxton, James Smith, William Thompson, Thomas Paxton
Rescue. Defendants are discharged by the Court on payment of fees.

The King vs John Peery, William Neely, James Neely, Alexander Dunlap, John Dunlap, James Erwin, John Willson, John Newell, William Newell, Robert Newell, James Peery, Samuel McFanan
Rescue. Defendants are discharged by the Court on payment of fees.

Page 78

Motion of William Johnson, Andrew Ross was admitted and sworn as an attorney of court.

Upon reading the petition of the inhabitants of Lurgan, Letterkenny, Gilford and Antrim townships, setting forth that whereas there is a necessity for a road to be laid out from Shippensburg by John Pennells Mill to John Andrew's mill from thence the nearest and best way to the road leading to Fredericktown in Maryland which would be of the petitioners, and also it would save much trouble and charges by having a nearer road to Carlisle to go to Court and other business, the petitioners request the Court that they would take their grievances into consideration and make an order to lay out the straightest and best course that the nature of the country of the country will admit of. The Court order that James Rennells, John Vance, Anthony Snyder, James M. McClear, James Johnson, Joseph Cook to view and if they see cause to lay out the same.

Upon reading the petition of the inhabitants of Tuskorora Valley praying the Worshipful Court to appoint six men to view and lay out a road beginning at or near John Fergues in Shermans Valley round Tuskorora Mountain and by _ailis's (?) Mills thence to cross Juniata below William Pattersons and to intersect a road lately made up the east side of Juniata. The Court do thereupon consider and appoint Thomas Wilson, Clement Horrel, Hugh Quigley, William Bell, Robert Morrow and Alexander Morrow to view and if they or any four of them see cause to lay out the same road agreeable to the prayer of the petitioners and make report of their proceedings to next Court.

Page 79

At a Court of Private Sessions of the Peace, at Carlisle, before John Armstrong, Robert Miller, and William Lyon.

Whereas Henry Davis was tried for grand larceny at January Sessions last and he pleading guilty and it appearing to the Court that the fine and fees against the said Henry Davis amounted to the sum of 19 pounds, 9 shillings and six pence. It is thereupon considered and ordered by the Court that the said Henry Davis be sold out by the Sheriff for the term of 5 years in order for the satisfaction of his fine and fees of prosecution.

Page 80

At a Court of private sessions held at Carlisle, 26th day of March 1770.

Page 81- 82

At a Court of Private Sessions held at Carlisle the 20 March 1770 before Jonathan Hoge, Esq.

Lurgan township; Hugh White, constable; Thomas Grier, Peter Dickey supervisors of roads; Chas. McClay, Jas. McKeehan overseers of poor; Wm. Krimmer Jr., John McKnight, viewers of fences.

Letterkenny township; Robt. Petterson, constable; Wm. Shapr, Saml.
    Culberston, supervisors of roads; John Ferguson, Wm. Mitchell,
    overseers of poor; Alexander McConnell, Jas. Robinson, viewers of
    fences.
Gilford township; Saml. Thompson, constable; Geo. Smith and Geo. Crawford
    superintendent of roads; John Andrews, John Miller, overseers of
    poor; Peter Fry, Wm. V. Lear, viewers of fences.
Hamilton township; Fergus Moorehead, constable.
Antrim township; Thos. Pough, constable; Frederick Foreman, Robert
    Crunkleton, supt.roads.
Peters township; Jas. McDowell, constable; Jas. Rankin, Wm. Hallowday
    overseers of poor.
Fannet township; Jas. Moore, constable; Allen Brown, Saml. Gamble,
    superintendent of roads; Robt. Little, Archibald Elliot over seers of
    poor; Phillip McGuire and Nathaniel Paul, viewers of fences.
Tyrone township; Jas. Roddy, constable; Alexander Sanderson, Jonathan Ross,
    superintendent of roads; Wm. Waugh, Jas. Sharpe, overseer poor;
    Ths. Elliot, Obadiah Carwoos viewers of fences.
Tyboyne township; Jos. McClintock, constable; Alexander Murry, Jas. Wilson,
    overseers of poor; Jos. McClintock, Robt. Hunter, viewers of fences.
Rye township; Jas. Carson, constable; Jas. Watts, David Miller, superintendent
    of roads; Robert Taylor, Robert Larmon, overseers of poor; John
    Ramsey, Robert Watso, viewers of fences.

Page 83- blank

Page 84
At Carlisle, 20 April 1770, before John Armstrong Esq. and his associates the
sheriff David Hoge returns following panel of grand juror; Robert Callender,
Jonathan Holmes, Wm. Clark, John McClure, Andrew Holmes, Wm. Moore,
Wm. Fleming, Andrew McFarland, Robert Wire, Jas. Parker, Walter Paul
Pierce, Robt. Walker, Jr., John Mitchell, John Holmes, Jr. John Davis, Jr., Jas.
Weakley, Jr., John Stewart, Saml. Williamson.

Page 85 April Sessions 1770
The King v Moses Skinner
Felony. Jury; Richard Rankin, William Smith, Thomas Craighead, James
Gordon (?), William Clark, John Gregg, John Bowman, Samuel Harper,
Thomas Wilson, John Dunbar, John Kendey (?), and George Kinkead say that
the defendant Moses Skinner is guilty. It is ordered that the said Moses
Skinner restore the goods so stolen to the right owner or the value thereof as
also the costs of prosecution and other disbursements in prosecuting him and
shall also pay the Governor the like value of the goods so stolen and shall be
committed to the common goal till he makes satisfaction as aforesaid and shall
be whipped at the publick whipping post to morrow morning between the hours
of 9 and 4 with ten lashes on his bare back well laid on.

The King vs Hannah Irwin
Fornication., October Session 1770, defendant pleads guilty. Judgment is that the defendant Hannah Irwin pay 10 pounds to the Governor and costs of prosecution and stand committed until the whole be complied with.

Page 86 April Sessions 1770
The King vs George Smilie
Fornication and bastardy. Jury; Richard Rankin, William Smith, Thomas Craighhead, James Gordon, William Clark, John Clark, John Bowman, Thomas Wilson, John Dunbar, John Henderson, George Kenkead and John Ewing did not agree on their verdict during the sessions. Now October Sessions 1770, Jury; Joseph McHenry, William Duncan, Joseph Brady, Samuel Stewart, William Montgomary, John Moorhead, John Mahan, Thomas Pomroy, William Mitche, Stephan Coldwel, James Kelly and William Cunningham say that the defendant George Smilies is guilty. The judgement, defendant pay 10 pounds to the Governor also that the pay Hannah Irwin for her dyeing (?) In 2 pounds and 4 shillings and __ for the maintenance of the child for one year if it shall __ __ the township pay the costs of prosecution and stand committed until the whole be complied with.

The King vs John Houser & Elizabeth his wife
Felony. Jury; Richard Rankin, William Smith, Thomas Craighead, James Gordon, William Clark, John Cregg, John Bowman, Thomas Wilson, John Dunbar, John Henderson, George Kinkead and John Ewing say that the defendants John Houser and Elizabeth his wife are not guilty, it is ordered by the Court that the said John Houser and Elizabeth his wife be discharged on payment of costs of prosecution.

Page 87
The King vs Elisha Pittman
Misdemeanor. Defendant pleads non cul.

Henry Gass £50, John Gass £50, Elisah Pitman £50, conditioned for the appearance of Elisha Pitman at the next Court.

Robert Ewin £40, conditioned for the appearance of Hannah Erwin and Jane __ at the next General Court.

Page 88
Upon reading the petition of sundry of the inhabitants of Westpennsburgh, Hopewell, and Newtown townships, setting forth that a very advantageous trade in wheat and flower have been for some time past carried on by your petitioners and other farmers in said county to the Baltimore market and the trace of proper encouraged must conduce to raise the value of lands and promote industry in the inhabitants of said county. And that a continuance and increase said trade the particular object of publick attention ought to be __ to

render the roads to said marked as near and easy as possible. That a good wagon road can be made at a small expense from James Smiths Merchant Mill near the Walnut Bottom through the South Mountain to the York County Line and that your petitioners have reason to believe the inhabitants of York county will concur in their good intentions and lay out and open a road from where this petitioned for __ the nearest and best way thro York County toward Baltimore. Ordered that Allan Leeper, William Quiery, Alex McBride, Robert Walker, John Ewing, John Scooler, are appointed to view and if they or any our of them see proper to lay out the same agreeable to the prayer of the petition they make report of their proceedings to next Court.

Upon reading of the petition of sundry of the inhabitants of Fermanagh township, setting forth that your petitioners labor under great hardships for want of a bridle road leading from the upper parts of Loss Creek to the Meeting house in said township and Capt. James Pattersons Mill and the landing for Water Carriage and if your Worships in your wisdom see proper appoint 6 men to view and lay out the same on or near the old path and __. Ordered that William Maclay, James Purdy, Hugh McCallister, Samuel Mitchel, William Hinder (?), and John McCartney are appointed to view and if they or any 4 of them see proper to lay out the road agreeable to the prayer of the petition they make report of their proceedings to next court.

Page 89

Upon reading the petition of sundry of Inhabitants of Sheamans Valley setting forth a road is much wanted from the western part of said Valley in going to and from Carlisle your petitioners pray your Worships to appoint proper persons to view and layout the same as aforesaid to being at Widow Adams thence past Robert Millers field and then into the road already laid out to Thomas Clarkes and your Petitioner. Ordered that Thomas Ross, Obadiah Garwood, John Scot, Robert Pook (?), Robert Adams, John Watt are appointed as above said to go upon the premises and measure the nighest of two roads that the inhabitants contend for if they or any four of them agree they make report of their proceedings to next Court.

Upon reading the petition of sundry of the inhabitants of Fannet twp., setting forth that the inhabitants and all other persons who have occasion to travel therein, labor under many difficulties for reason of there not being a wagon road laid out and cleared through the same, your petitioners pray your worship would issue an order that a wagon road may be laid out and cleared the nearest and best way from Colter's saw-mill to Elliot's grist mill and from thence to McDowell's grist mill in Peter's twp. By inhabitants of the respective twps., through it passes. Ordered that David Elder, Thos. Blair, Robt. Hardy, Jno. Clark, Allen Brown, Saml. Walker are appointed to view and lay out the same.

Page 90 April Sessions 1770
At a court of Private Sessions, at Carlisle, 28 May 1770, before Jonathan Hoge, Robert Miller, and William Lyon. Came into Court Thomas Willson and set forth that a certain Agnus Cogley indented servant to him the said Thomas Willson did within the term specified in her indenture bear a bastard child. We therefore adjudge that she the said Agnus Cogley shall serve her said Master Thomas Willson or his assigns the further term or time of one year over and above the time specified in her said indenture.

Upon reading the report of Wm. Paten, John Miller, John Shelby, and Douglas Campbell being majority of six men appointed by the Court of Private Session held at Carlisle the 31 February 1769 to view and make report in regard to a public road petitioned for my the inhabitants of the west side of the twp. of Peters extending near the westerly from the mill of Robt. Fleming to the house of Wm. Marshall and from the said mill near south east strike the Maryland line at or near Allen Keelough's to answer in particular the valuable end of going to market at Georgetown in Maryland etc., we present to your worshipful court a draft of the said road which in our judgement appears very necessary and well calculated to answer the valuable and represented by the petitioners and therefore desire the same may be inserted in our report according to the above plan and the necessary orders forth with given the same may be opened according to law, submitting ourselves to your worshipful court, your subscribers etc. Ordered that the road as above laid out be confirmed and that it be opened by the next Court to be held in July.

Page 91
At a Court of private sessions, at Carlisle, 22 June 1770 before Robert Miller, Andrew Colhoone, William Lyon. Came into Court James Elliot and set forth that a certain Patrick Glennan an indented servant to him the said James Elliot did abscond himself from his said master the space of one month and that the said master was put to sundry expenses in following and recovering the said servant to his service amounting in the whole to 3 pounds. 17 shillings. It is considered that the said Patrick Glennan serve his said master or his assigns for the space of 12 months over and above the time mentioned in his said indenture in order to the satisfaction of the said master.

Page 92- 93 blank

Page 94
At Carlisle, 24 July 1770, before John Armstrong Esq, and his associate justices. the sheriff David Hoge returned the following panel of grand jurors; Wm. Thompson, Jas. Pollock, John Pallock. Jos. Spear, John Welkins, Stephen Duncan, Ralph Mayer, John McAndy. Chas. Patterson, Stewart Robinson, Christopher Vanlear, John Glena, John Kinkead, John Grier, Jas. Ramsey. Wm. Thomas, John Pollock (carpenter), Jas. David, Thos. Moore. Michael Finley, Robt. Calhoun, Jos. Dobson, James Sharon. John Prentic.

Page 95 July Sessions 1770
The following constables have been called appeared not, the Court fines each of the said delinquents, orders that the same be levied of them unless they show sufficient cause by the next Court why they made default. Lurgan, Hugh Wiley; Gilford. Saml. Thompson ; Hamilton, Fergus Moorhead; Antrim, Thos. Pough; Peters. Jas. McDowell; Fannet, Jas. Moore

List of townships and constables; Hopewell- Samuel Montgomery; Newburn- John McCune; Lurgan- Hugh Wiley; Guilford- Samuel Thompson; Hamilton- Fergus Moorhead; Antrim- Thomas Pough; Peters- James McDowell; Fannet- James Moore; Air- George Bush; Tyrone- James Roddy; Bedford- [none listed]; Derry- Robert Chambers; Teboyne- Joseph McClinbet(?); Lack- James Glenn; Milford- Clemen Horrel; Fermanagh- Hugh McCallister; Penns [none listed]; Dublin- James Watson; Colerain- John Cresna; Cumberland- [none listed]; Barree- John Wilson, Armagh- William Brown.

Page 96
His Honor. 14 July 1770, to Jas. Hamiton Jr., Jas. Turner, Wm. Logan, Richard Peters, Linford Lardner, Benj. Chew, Thomas Cladwalder, Richard Penn and Jas. Tilgnan, members of proprietary and governors council and to John Armstrong, Jas. Galbraith, John Byers, Jas. Carouthers, Hermanis Aldricks, John Rennels, Jonathan Hoge, Robt. Miller, Wm. Line, Robt. Collender, Andrew Calhoun, Jas. Maxwell, Saml. Perry, John Holmes, John Allison, Christopher Simms, Benj. Daugherty, George Robinson, Wm. Patterson, Turbett Frances, Wm. McClay, Arthur St. Clair, Henry Prather, Wm. Crawford, Jas. Milligan. Thos. Gist, Dorsey Petcost and John Agnu, assigns them justices of the peace and assigns all or any three of them justices as well the peace in the said county to keep as also divers felonies and other misdeeds within the same county perpetrated to hear and to determine.

His honor, the governor's commissions bearing date 1 May 1770 to Col. Torbott Frances Esq. commissioning and appointing him the said Torbott Frances clerk of the peace of the Court.

Dom. Rex vs Henry Keer
Felony in stealing the goods of William Smith. Defendant being arraigned pleads guilty. Judgment that the said Henry Kerr be taken tomorrow between the hours of 10 in the forenoon and 4 of the clock in the afternoon to the publick whipping post and there receive 21 lashes on his bare back well laid on that the pay a fine to the Governor of 40 shillings, that the make restitution of the goods stolen to the owner, and that the pay the costs of prosecution and stand committed until his judgement be complied with.

Page 97

Dom Rex vs William Baker and Hugh Teaft(?)

Forcible entry and detainer. April 1771, jury; Samuel Culbertson wagoner, Samuel Culbertson Junior, John Brackenridge, Robert Patterson, Samuel McCormick, David Bowen, Robert Stockton, John Kunble, Samuel McIlhaney, William Smith, William Sanderson, Robert Culbertson say that the defendant William Baker is not guilty.

Dom Rex vs Daniel McCoy

Assault & battery. October sessions 1770 the defendant retracts his plea and submits to the Court and protesting his innocence, judgment that the defendant Daniel McCoy be fined two shillings, sixpence, pay the costs of prosecution, stand committed until the whole be complied with.

Dom Rex vs Alexander Armstrong

Forceible entry.

Page 98

The King vs Elisha Bateman

Misdemeanor. Jury; William Irwin, William McCreshey, James Wilson, John Hamilton, John Kerr, Andrew Boyd, John McKee, James Gregg, John Jordon, Peter Smith, Jacob Taylor, & John Holmes say that Elisah Bateman is [blank].

William Baker £100, William Middle £50, conditioned for the appearance of the said William Baker at the next Court then and there to answer to a certain bill of indictment found against him and not depart the Court without license.

Alexander Armstrong £40, John Gulliford, conditioned for the appearance of the said Alexander Armstrong at the next Court then and there to testify in his Majesties Behalf and not depart the Court without licence.

John Guildord £40, Alexander Armstrong £40, conditioned for the appearance of the said John Gulliford at the next Court there to testify in his Majesties behalf and depart the Court without licence.

Daniel McCoy £50, Samuel Campbell £25, conditioned for the appearance of the said Daniel McCoy at the next Court then and there to answer to a certain bill of indictment found against him and not depart the Court with licence.

The King vs George Smylie

Page 99 July Sessions 1770

Alice Adams £25, conditioned for her appearance at the next Court then and there to testify in his Majesties behalf & not depart the Court without licence.

Hannah Irwin £25, William Sanderson £25, Andrew Irwin £25, conditioned for the appearance of Hannah Irwin, William Sanderson & Andrew Irwin at the next Court then and there to testify in his Majesties behalf and depart the Court without license.

Elisha Bateman- being 3 times solemnly called appeared not recognizance forfeited.

Henry Gass and John Gass being 3 times solemnly called to forth the body of Elisha Bateman bring not forth the body of the same Elisha. Recognizance forfeited.

The Court appointed Ezekiel Heckman constable of the township of Red Stone Creek for the present year.

John Pollock, Jas. Pollock, Thos. Donnelan, Wm. Ervin, Christopher Van Lear, Ephraim Blain, John Gray, Ralph Naylor, Jas. Ramsey, Peter Pence, John McAudy, Jas. Greenwood, John Miller, Henry Cunningham, Robt. Hendricks, Geo. Sharp. Jas. Davis, Jas. Gallocher, Jas. Bell, Thos. Miller, Robt. Jack, Jas. McCall, Geo. Mineur, Wm. McKune, having petitioned the Court to recommend to the governor, for his license to keep public houses of entertainment and the Court taking the same under consideration the above parties were accordingly recommended and allowed.

Page 100
Upon the application of Jasper Yeates Esquire to the Court Praying that John Hubley be admitted an attorney of this Court and having taken the oaths prescribed by Act of Assembly he is admitted an Attorney of the Court.

Upon the petition of the inhabitants of Carlisle and Middelton townships to the Court setting forth that they labor under great inconvenience for a road to begin at the north end of Hanover street to the corner of James Pollock & James Stackpoles lots from thence the same road that is laid out in the plan of the lots which goes to the outside of them from thence proceeding the nearest and best way over the Forty Shillings Gap, from thence the most convenient way until it fall in with the great road that goes through Shermans valley, there bring no tollerable way of passing and repassing to Shermans valley without going to Croghans Gap which is very impracticable as well for the inhabitants of Shermans valley as for your petitioners. And praying the Court that a road might be allowed beginning at the North end of Hanover Street to the Corner of James Pollocks lots and James Stackpoles lots from thence as aforesaid the same road that is laid out in the plan of the out lots which goes to the outside of them and from thence proceeding the nearest and best way to and over the Forty Shilling Gapp until it fall in with the great road through Shermans valley, and that men be appointed to view and lay out the same as aforesaid. The Court do appoint Thomas Wilson, William Fleming, John Stuart, John Mitchel, John

Titus and Henry Gass who are to view the premises above mentioned and that they or any four of them, if they see cause lay out the same by courses and distances and make report to the next court.

Upon petition of the inhabitants of Letterkenny twp. to the Court setting forth that they labor under great inconveniences for a road beginning at Jas. Fulton's to Rocky Spring Meeting House and praying the Court to appoint men to view and lay out the same road from Jas. Fulton's to the Rocky Spring Meeting House the nearest and best way.

The Court do appoint John Bevins, Saml. Thompson, Jos. Swan, Wm. Lindsey Sr., Jos. Laton and John Finley to view the premises above mentioned and that they or any four of them if they see necessary lay out the same by courses and distances most useful to the public and least injurious to private property and make report of their proceeding to next Court.

Page 101 [skipped in filming]

Page 102 July Sessions 1770
Upon the petition of the inhabitants of Greenwood township to the Court setting forth they labor under great inconvenience for a road or cartway to begin the lower end of Baskens Island situate in the mouth of Juniata, to intersect the road already laid out between Croghans Gap and William Brown or James Reeds in Kesacocquellas Valley, also at James Galloghers. Appointed; Leonard Foutz, Graft Goz (?), John Bringham, William McAleavey, William English and John Sturgeon to view the premises above mentioned and that they or any four of them if they see cause lay out a road by courses and distances the most useful for the publick good in general and least injurious to private property and make report thereof to the next Court.

Upon the petition of the inhabitants of Allen Township to the Court setting forth they labor under great inconveniences for want of a road from Hugh Lairds Mill to intersect the great Road leading from Susquehannah to Carlisle at or near Samuel Williamsons. Praying the Court to appoint men to view and lay out a road from Lairds Mill to Intersect the great road at Samuel Williamsons as above. Appointed Christopher Quigley, Samuel Lamb, Samuel Williamson, Robert Galbraith, William McTeer, and Anthony McKew to view the premises and if they or any four of them see cause, lay out the above road by courses and distances the least injurious to private property and for the best utility of the publick and make report to next Court.

Petition of the inhabitants of Sheermans valley setting forth that they labor under great inconvenience for want of a road for carrying out their produce and praying the Court to appoint men to view and lay out a road beginning at Croghans Gap the best and nearest to Obadiah Garwoods Mill or to Thomas Ross Fording and from thence upward the nearest and best way to the great road leading upwards. Appointed James Blaine, Hugh Alexander. Thomas Ross, Daniel Williams Sen., Daniel Evans and John Byers or any four of them if they see necessary to lay out the same by courses and distances the least injurious to private property and for the best utility of the publick and make report there of to the next Court.

Page 103 July Sessions 1770
Upon petition of the inhabitants of Guilford twp. to the Court, setting for that they labor under great inconvenience for the want of a great road leading from Jas. Campbell's to the York Co. Line and from thence to Blacks Gap and prays the Court to appoint men to view and lay out a road beginning at Jas.Campbells near Loudon through Chambersburg to the York line and thence to John Miller's at Black's Gap.

The Court appeared Saml. Lindsay, Edw. Crawford, Matthew Wilson, Wm. Gass, Jas. Campbell being four of the men appointed by an order of last Jan. Session to view and if they should see cause to lay out a road leading from Dunn's Gap to the Rev. Mr. John King's Meeting House and make report that they had met in pursuance of their appointment and adjudge it necessary to begin at Wm. Houston's house and by courses and distances as by the marked trees appear to the Rev. Mr. King's Meeting House and do return the same for public use. The Court having taken the report into consideration do thereupon order that the same road as before described and laid out be to all intents and purposes a public road and highway and the same as such be forth with opened 20 feet wide and cleared and repaired in pursuance to the act of assembly.

Came into Court Allan Leeper, John Erwin, William Querey, and Alexander McBride being four of the men appointed by order of the Court of General Quarter Sessions of the Peace held at Carlisle in April last and did set forth that in pursuance of said rule or order they did meet and report that they viewed the premises in said order mentioned agreeable to the Prayer of the Petition that is to say beginning at James Smiths Merchant Mill on Yellow Britches Creek and from thence though the South Mountain to the York County line will be of great advantage to the inhabitants of Westpennsbro township and the publick and do return the same for publick use. Ordered and that the same road as before described and laid out be to all intents and purposes a publick road and high way, and the same as such be forth with opened 30 feet wide and cleared and repaired in pursuance of the Acts of General Assembly of this Province in such case made and provided, of which the supervisors of the roads in the respective townships through which the same passes are to take notice.

Came into Court James Camble, Robert Fleming, James Renken, Patrick Campbell being four of the men appointed by an order of last January Sessions to view and if they should see cause to lay out a road leading from Dunns Gap to the Rev. Mr. John Kings Meeting house and made report that they had met in pursuance of their appointment and adjudged it necessary to begin at

William Hustons house and by courses and distances as by the marked trees may appear to the Revd. Mr. Kings Meetinghouse and do return the same for publick use. Ordered that the same road as before described and laid out be to all intents and purposes a publick road and highway and the same as such be forthwith opened 20 feet wide and cleared and repaired in pursuance of the Acts of Assembly of this Province in such case made and provided of which the supervisors of the roads in the respective township through which the same passes are to take notice.

Page 104 July Sessions 1770
On Motion in behalf of Gawin Haffey (?). It is ruled that the overseers of the Poor of the Township of Middleton to show cause at the next Sessions hy they have not paid the sum of 3 pounds, 2 shillings and six pence the remainder of his account allowed by the Court for the maintenance of a certain negroe man named Jack under an order of three Justices bearing date the 31 January 1765. October Sessions 1770, on motion of Mr. Willson the Court order that the above be argued next January Sessions.

At a Court of Private Sessions held at Carlisle, 13 July 1770, before Andrew Colhoone, William Lyon and John Agnew. Came into Court John Kerr and set forth that a certain Morgan McIntosh and indented servant to him the said John, did run away and carry with him sundry goods belonging to his said master and having been absent from his said master s service in the space of one day, his said master was put to sundry expenses to the amount of 4 pounds and 10 pence in following and taking up said servant. Prays the Court that the said Morgan McIntosh may be adjudged to serve such longer time as shall be thought sufficient to satisfy the above sum. Ordered that the said Morgan McIntosh do serve the said John Kerr, his master, or his assigns the further term of time of 12 months over and above the time specified in his indenture in order to make satisfaction for the above sum expended as aforesaid.

Page 105- blank

Page 106
At Carlisle, 23 October 1770, before John Armstrong Esq. and his associates. The sheriff David Hoge made return of this panel of grand jurors; Thos. Butler, David Duncan, Geo. Davison, Jas. Smith, John Young, Jas. Rennells, Robt. Anderson, Jas. Carothers, Adam Leiper, Hugh Kilgore, Peter Kickey, Saml. McClure, Jas. McKee, Jas. Breckenridge, Jos. Graham, Saml. Lindsay, Matthew Wilson, David Hopkins, Alexander Stewart, Thos. Rose, Thos. Bard, John Shelby, Patrick Maxwell, John Barr.

Page 107   October Sessions 1770
The King vs James Stackpole
Assault and battery, on the body of Andrew Murphy. January Sessions 1771
the defendant retracts his plea and submits to the Court and protesting his
innocense. Judgment that James Stackpole be fined sixpence and pay the costs
of prosecution and stand committed until the whole be complied with.

The King vs William Bond
Felony in stealing 1 sheep the property of William Carrothers. Defendant being
pleads not guilty. Jury; Joseph McKinny, William Duncan, Joseph Brady,
Samuel Stuart, William Montgomery, John Moorhead, John Mahan, Thomas
Pomeroy, William Mitchel, Stephan Caldwell, James Kelly and William
Cunningham say that the defendant William Bond is guilty. Judgment that the
said William Bond restore the goods stolen to the owner or the value thereof if
not already restored and the value of the goods so stolen to the Governor for
support of Government and that he be taken to the common whipping post
tomorrow the 26th instant and receive 15 lashes on his bare back well laid on,
between the hours of 10 and 4 in the afternoon, stand committed until costs of
prosecution and Governors fine be paid. On motion of the Attorney General the
Court awards habeas corpus to bring up Wm. Bond a prisoner under execution
in the jail of this county to give evidence on the part of the Commonwealth.

Page 108
The King vs Richard Thompson
Felony in stealing 1 hat (?) the property of Jonathan Kearsley. Judgment of the
Court is that the defendant Richard Thompson return the goods stolen to the
owner or the value thereof if not already restored, that he pay an equal value as
a fine to the Governor that the be taken to the common whipping post between
the hours of 10 and 4 of the clock on Thursday the 25th day of this instant and
there receive 15 lashes on his bare back well laid on, that he pay the costs of
prosecution and stand committed until the sentence is fully complied with.

The King vs Daniel McCoy
Assault and battery.

The King vs James Stackpole
Assault and battery upon James McEvoy. January Term 1771, jury; Hugh
Laird, James Oliver, James McCormick, Thomas Donaldson, William
Abernathy, Richard Beard, Thomas Stuart, Thomas Ranken, William Starret,
William McTeer, Mathew Kenny and John Trimble say that the defendant
James Stackpole is guilty. Judgment the said James Stackpole is fined 2
shillings and six pence, pay the costs of prosecution, stand committed until the
whole be complied with.

The same vs the same

Assault and battery upon Ann McEvoy. January Term 1771, jury; Hugh Laird, James Oliver, James McCormick, Thomas Donaldson, William Abernathy, Richard Beard, Thomas Stuart, Thomas Ranken, William Starret. William McTeer, Mathew Kenny and John Trimble, say that the defendant James Stackpole is not guilty.

Page 109 October Sessions 1770
The King vs Samuel Quin
Felony in stealing 1 roan mare the property of James McCammon.

Richard Stewart being three times solemnly called to bring forth the body of Js. Stewart brings not forth his body. Recognizance forfeited.

James Stewart being three times solemnly called appears not, recog. forfeited.

Joseph Armstrong is discharged from his recognizance, paying costs.

The King vs John Smith
Felony. The defendant is discharged by proclamation paying costs.

The King vs James McEvoy
Assault & battery. The defendants is discharged by proclamation paying costs.

The King vs James Patterson, William Henderson, and Thos. McFadden
Forcible entry and Detainer, defendants are discharged paying costs.

David English is discharged by proclamation no person appearing against him.

William Beard is discharged from his recognizance paying fees.

Page 110
William Baker £100, William Riddle £50, conditioned for the appearance of the said Wm. Baker at the next Court then and there to answer all certain bills of indictment and not to depart the Court without license.

James Stackpole £50, Felix Doyle £25, conditioned for the appearance of said James Stackpole at the next Court then and there to answer to certain bills of indictment found against him and not depart the Court without licence.

Andrew Murphy £20, James £10, conditioned for the appearance of the said Andrew Murphy at the next Court then and there to testify in his Majesties behalf and not depart the Court without licence.

Jane Butlar £10, conditioned for her appearance at the next Court then and there to testify in his Majesties behalf and not depart the Court without licence.
Page 111

Upon the petition of the inhabitants of East Pennsborrough township to the Court setting forth that they labor under great inconvenience for want of a road being opened from John Beard Senr of John Carrothers in the aforesaid township or from any part in that settlement as may be thought most convenient for use to Edward Wards Mills. Praying the Court to order men to view and lay out the same from the most convenient part in that settlement to said Edward Wards Mills. The Court do appoint Thomas McCormick, Edward Morton, George Wood, James McCormick, John Nailer, and Casper Weaver to view the premises above mentioned and that they or any four of them if they see necessary layout the same by courses and distances the most useful for the public and least injurious to private property and make report to next Court.

Upon the petition of the inhabitants of Allan township setting forth to the Court that a road being laid out and cleared Begging at Crochans Gap on this side the North Mountain from thence to run the straightest and best course to John Clark's Mill, and from thence the nighest and best course to the great road leading from Carlisle to Baltimore past Mr. Sills Tavern would be of publick benefit to the inhabitants. Praying the Court to order and appoint men to view and lay out the same agreeable to the above prayer. Appointed Robert Urie, James Irwin, Andrew Armstrong, James Gregory, John Trindle, and Andrew McBeath to view the premises above mentioned and that they or any four of them if they see necessary lay out the same by distances the most useful for the public, least injurious to private property and make report to next Court.

Upon the petition of the inhabitants of Hopewell twp. to the Court, setting forth that they labor under great inconvenience for the want of a great road or the old road opened from Three Square Hollow at the foot of the North Mountain to the old forgeage at Conodoquinet Creek at Cats Cabins from thence to the old road or the nighest and best way to the Middle Spring Meeting House, from thence to Mr. Robt. Camber's bill. Appointed Robt. Culbertson, Saml. McKune, David Sterrit, John Moorehead, Saml. Montogmery and Saml. Gibb to view and lay out the same and make report to the next Court.

Page 112

Came into Court Jos. Easton, Jos. Swan, Wm. Lindsay and Saml. Thompson being 4 of the men appointed by an order of the July Sessions to view and if they see cause to lay out a road leading from Jos. Fulton's to Rocky Spring Meeting House, make report that they had met in pursuance to their appointment, adjudge it necessary having carefully examined the ground to begin as follows, that a straight course from a hickory grub nigh the end of said Fulton's land north 172 degrees, east 255 perches to the Meeting House will best answer the public goo and as little injury to private property as any other way that will admit of a good road. Ordered allow that the same road as before described and laid be to all intents and purposes a public road and highway and the same as such be forthwith opened 20 feet wide, cleared and repaired.

At a Court of Private Sessions held at Carlisle, 24 November 1770 before John
Homes, Saml. Perry and John Agnu, justices. Whereas Wm. Bond was tried for
grand larceny at October Sessions last and was found guilty of the same and on
application for his discharge, it is ordered by the Court that the said Wm. Bond
be sold out by the sheriff for the term of two years in order for the satisfaction
of fines, fees and cost of prosecution amounting to 8 lbs.

Page 113
At a Court of Private Sessions, 4 December 1770, before Robert Miller,
William Lyon and John Agnew. Came into court Robert Gillispie and set forth
that a certain John Butler an Indented servant to him the said Robert did run
away from his said master and did absent himself the space of 2 months and 15
days from his said masters service and that he his said master was put to sundry
expenses to the amount of 5 pounds, 13 shillings in following advertising and
taking up said servant and praying the Court that the said John Butler be
adjudged to serve such longer time as should be through sufficient to satisfy the
above sum. Ordered that John Butler do serve the said Robert Gillispie his said
master or his assigns the further term or time of one year over and above the
time specified in his indenture.

At a Court of Private sessions held at Carlisle the 29th [blank]

Page 114- blank

Page 115
At Carlisle, 23 January 1771, before John Armstrong and his associate justices.
The sheriff David Hoge returned the following list of grand jurors; Jas.
Hendricks, Robt. Galbraith, Ephraim Blain, Frances Silver, Geo. Woods, Edw.
Morton, John Carouthers, Isaac Hendricks, David Bell, Jas. Gregory, Jno.
Trindle, Wm. White, Robt. McClure, Adam Adams, Willis Pettis, Saml. Lamb,
Jas. Hudson, John Quigley, Frances McGuire (excused), John Carothers,
Alexander Trindle, David Harkness, Jas. McClure, Saml. Culbertson.

Page 116 January Sessions 1771
The King vs John Cogden als Cougley
Felony. Jury; Hugh Laird, James Oliver, James McCormick, Thomas
Donaldson, William Abernathy, Richard Beard, Thomas (?) Stuart, Thomas
Kinden, William Starret, William McTerr, Mathew Kenny and John Trinble
say that the defendant John Cogden alias Cougley is not guilty.

The King vs Martin McDonald
Felony in stealing one black mare the goods of John Lambert. Jury; Hugh
Laird, James Oliver, James McCormick, Thomas Donaldson, William
Abernathy, Richard Beard, Thomas Stuart, Thomas Renken, William Starret,
William McTeer, Mathew Kenny, and John Trimble say that the defendant
Martin McDonald is not guilty.

Page 117

King vs Wm. Quirk

Indictment, felony for stealing one black horse saddle and bridle the goods of Chas. Stuart. Judgement the prisoner Wm. Quirk restore the horse as stolen to the owner if not already done or may the full value thereof and also pay the cost of prosecution with all such sums of money as will be allowed by the Court to the owner for his trouble and expense in the prosecution and also pay the value of the horse so stolen to the governor and shall stand in the pillory tomorrow being the 25 instant, during the space of one hour, be publicly whipped at the common whipping post upon his bare back with 39 lashes well laid on, between the hours of 10 and 4 o'clock, be committed to the jail for the said county for the space of one month until the whole be compiled with.

The King vs David Semple

Assault & battery on the body of Ralph Nailer. Defendant by Mr. James Smith submits himself to the Court protesting his innocence. Judgment is that the defendant David Semple is fined 2 shillings and six pence.

Page 118 January Sessions 1771

Hugh Swan £200, James Patterson £100, John Mitchel £100, conditioned for the appearance of the said Hugh Swan at the next Court then and there to answer to such things as shall be objected against him on his Majesties behalf and not depart the Court without licence.

Thomas McCamish £100, William Thompson £50, conditioned for the appearance of Thomas McComish at the next Court then and there to answer such things as shall be objected to him on his Majesties behalf and not depart the Court without Licence.

Andrew Mann £60, conditioned for the appearance of John Houser and Elizabeth his wife and Edward Combs at the court then and there to answer such things as shall be objected to him on his Majesties behalf, shall not depart the Court without Licence, in the mean time to keep the peace, be of good behaviour to all his Majesties subjects, in particular to Edward Smithson then the same to be void otherwise to be and remain in full force and virtue.

William Stewart being three times solemnly called appeareth not forfeits his recognizance.

James Davis being three times solemnly called to bring on the body of William Stewart appearyh not forfeits his recognizance.

Page 119

Edward Armstrong being three times solemnly called appeareth not forfeit his recognizance.

William Irwin being three times solemnly called to bring in the body of
Edward Armstrong appeareth not forfeits his recognizance.

John Houser, Elizabeth Houser and Edward Combs not appearing agreeable to
their recognizance. The Court respite their recognizance until next Sessions.

An argument as well on behalf of the overseers of the poor of Middleton
township as of Gawin Mahafy. Ordered that the rule made at last July Sessions
absolute and further directs that the present overseers of the poor for the said
township do forthwith pay and satisfy to the said Gawin Mahaffy the sum of 3
pounds, 2 shillings and 6 pence the amount of his account allowed by the Court
for the maintenance of a certain Negro man named Jack under an order of 3
Justices bearing date 31 January 1765.

Petition of the inhabitants of Air township living along the water of Conolowais
setting forth that they labor under great inconvenience for want of a wagon road
laid out to the best advantage of the whole settlement leading to meetings, mills
and markets beginning at Mr. Samuel Truaxe's along by Mr. Thomas Reynolds
and along by Mr. Francis Bushe's and Mr. Joseph Warfords, thence straight to
the Provincial line leading toward the Warm Springs, praying the Court to
order men to view and lay out the same. Court appoint William McConnell,
Evan Shelby, Edward Combs, James Graham, William Hart and John Reynolds
to view the premises above mentions and that they of any four of them if they
see necessary lay out the same by courses and distances the most useful for the
publick and lest injurious to private property and make report to next Court.

Page 120 January Sessions 1771
Upon the petition of sundry Inhabitants of the Township of West Pennsburgh
to the Court setting forth that they labor great inconvenience for want of a road
leading from James Smiths Mill in the said Township to __ into the Walnut
Bottom road near the place where the new laid out road from Carlisle and the
old Walnut Bottom Road meet and that such road would be very useful to the
inhabitants of the said Township and others coming to the said Mill and other
places. Praying the Court to appoint men to view and lay out the same from
James Smith's aforesaid. Appointed John Davison, Thomas Wilson, George
Davidson, Thomas Greer, John Ewing, and David McCurdy to view the
premises and if they or any four of them see necessary lay out the same by
courses and distances the nighest and best road the least injurious to private
property and for the best utility of the publick and make report to next Court.

Petition of sundry inhabitants of Carlisle and Middleton Township to the Court
setting forth that they labor under great inconvenience for want of a publick
road leading from the north end of Bedford Street in Carlisle, running between
the lot of John Wilkins and Wm Lyons Esquires, then thence through the North
west Corner of Thomas Wilsons Lane thence though the south east corner of
Hugh McCormicks land by Robert Robbs house and across the creek at said

Rob Boarding thence nearly between the lands of Wm __ing and Mathew Brown and through part of said Browns land to the plantation of John Stewart the Elder thence through the said plantation the nearest and best way to Richard Cranes Gap in the Mountain that such a road will be of great __ to the inhabitants of Carlisle and Middleton Township as there is already a good bridle road from said gap into the valley and the gap found to be easy and good. Praying the Court to appoint men to view and if they see cause lay out a road the nearest and best way agreeable to the above __. Appointed John Davis, Wm. Davison, James Clark, William __ing, __ John Stewart to view the premises and if they or any four of them see necessary __ the same __ courses and distances the nearest and best way the least injurious to private property and In the best utility for the publick and make report the next Court.

Page 121 January Term 1771
Upon the petition of sundry of the Inhabitants of Carlisle and Middleton Townships setting forth to the Court that they labor under many inconveniences for want of a publick road beginning on Carlisle Common near where the road from York and Trindles Road meet and from thence across Letart Spring thro Pompel Street and from the west end of said street to fall into the great road leading to Shippensburgh as at present each end of said Street is able to be stopped up and the communication between the same and the West Road cut off. Praying the Court to appoint proper persons to view and lay our a road as aforesaid. Appointed Stephan Duncan, James Pollock, Tavern keeper, Samuel Coulder, Jonathan Holmes, John Davis and John Mitchel to view the premises and if they or any four of them see necessary to lay out the same by courses and distances the nearest and best way the least injurious to private property and for the utility of the publick and make report to next Court.

Upon the petition of sundry inhabitants of Middleton and Allen Townships in Cumberland County to the Court Setting forth that they labor under great disadvantage for want of a road from Capt. Robert Callenders and Chamber's Mills at the Mouth of Letort Spring to fall into the Baltimore Road at the most convenient place between Carlisle and James Dills. That such road would not only be of great use to the petitioners and other inhabitants of said townships who have no direct roads from said Mills to the Baltimore Market but also very serviceable to the inhabitants of Shermans valley passing at Croghans Gap and going from thence to York and Baltimore. Praying the Court to appoint proper men to view and lay out the same as aforesaid. Appointed Thomas Wilson, Mathew Muir, Robert Robbs, Samuel Hay, William Miller and William Blair to view the premises and if they or any four of them see necessary to lay out the same by courses and distances the nearest and best way, the least injurious to private property and for the utility of the publick, make report to next Court.

Page 122

Upon the petition of John Byers and Robert Robinson in behalf of sundry inhabitants of Toboyne and Tyrone Townships to the Court setting forth that they labor under great Inconvenience for want of a Road from Croghan Gap by the back of Peter Titus's and from thence the nighest and best way to intersect the road already laid out in said Valley and praying the Court to appoint proper men to view and lay out the same as aforesaid.

The Court do appoint Henry Cunningham, Henry Gap, Hugh Alexander, Thomas Ross, John Black, and William McClure to view the premises and if they or any 4 of them see necessary lay out the same by distances the nighest and best way the least injurious to private property, of the best utility for the publick, make report to next Court.

Petition of sundry of the inhabitants of Rye and Greenwood Townships to the Court setting forth that being conscious of the many reviews of roads already made to pass through said township a communication of which would be of publick utility praying the Court to appoint men to view and lay out a publick road to commence at James Gallohers on Juniata River, from thence to William Patterson's Esquires and from thence to James Bashens's Ferry on Juniata River which will be for the benefit of the publick utility and intercourse of both Townships. Appoint William Richardson, Frederick Wall, James Watt, David English, James Carson and Joseph Martin to view the premises and if they or any four of them see necessary lay out the same by distances the nighest and best way the least injurious to private property , best utility for the publick and make report to next Court.

Upon the petition of sundry inhabitants of Cumberland County to the Court setting forth that a great road is much wanted from near McClures Gap in the North Mountain the nearest and best way to Morris Mill on Yellow Britches Creek in order for the better carrying their produce to Baltimore and praying the Court to appoint men to view the premises and lay out a public road as aforesaid. Appoint William Clark, James Brown, William Carrothers, Senr., Adams Hays, John Miller and Paul Pierce to view the Premises and if they or any four of them see necessary lay out the said by courses and distances the nighest and best way the least injurious to private property and for the best utility of the publick and make report to next Court.

Page 123 January Sessions 1771

Upon the petition of sundry inhabitants of Cumberland County to the Court setting forth that they labor under many difficulties for want of a publick road from Carlisle to Craigheads Mill and from thence through the Forge Gap to the county line and leading by Mr. Stevensons plantation formerly known by Keytons Tavern as the said road will be __ of __ on around of passing and recrossing to the different mills and praying the Court to appoint men to view the premises and lay out a road the nighest and best way as aforesaid.

Appointed Samuel Laird, Samuel Kay, Robert Urie, Jonathan Holmes, John Glenn and John Kinhead to view the premises, if they or any 4 of them see necessary lay out the same by distance the nighest and best way the least injurious to private property, for the utility of the publick, make report to next Court.

Upon petition of sundry of the inhabitants of Lurgan and Letterkenny twps. and others of the co. of Cumberland setting forth that the want of a public road from the west end of the town of Shippensburg to Cisna's Gap and from thence across the mountain to intersect the great road leading to Fort Pitt near the Burnt Cabins or Littletonis of great inconvenience to the petitioners and the public in general who have occasion to travel to the extensive new country to the west and that they conceive such a road will be the nearest and best way of any now in use of that can be made to that part of the country and praying the Court to appoint proper persons to view and lay out a road from the west end of Shippensburg aforesaid to Herron's Ford where the road now crosses Herron's Branch and from thence the nighest and best way to Cisna's Gap by Andrew Naylor's old place now the property of John Cisna and from thence to lay out a bridle road leading from Fort Pitt. Appointed John Johnson, Saml. Culbertson, Wm. Young, Jas. Moore, Alexander McConnell, Jas. McCammon to view and lay out the same.

Page 124
Came in to Court Robt. Culbertson, Saml. McCune, Saml. Montgomery, Saml. Gibbs, and John Moorehead, 5 of the men appointed by an order of the last Oct. Sessions to view and lay out a road from the Three Square Hollow at the foot of the North Mountain to the old gorging place on Conodoguinet at Catts Cabin, from thence to Middle Spring Meeting House and from thence to Robt. Chamber's Mills and report to the Court that they had met and viewed the same and return the same for public use by distances as follows: beginning at a place known by the name of Three Square Hollow, thence through vacant land and land of John Kanagh south 50 degrees, east 113 perches, south 90 degrees, west 160 perches and south 40 degrees, west 73 perches, thence by vacant land and land of Saml. Mitchell south 50 degrees west 208 perches, south 75 degrees east 160 perches to land of Jas. Dysert, thence through the same and last mentioned course 32 perches thence south 2 degrees west 117 perches to a line between said Dysert's and said John Moorehead's, thence through vacant lands the same course 24 perches, thence south 27 degrees, east 220 perches, thence partly by fences and partly on land between Wm. Trimble and Sam. Hanna south 20 degrees east 226 perches, thence though lands of John Trimel and land of the heirs of Neil Wain crossing Cocodoguinet creek near Catts Cabbins south 40 degrees, east 354 perches, thence through the land of Saml. Gibbs south 120 perches to land of Wm. Duncan, thence through the same south 66 degrees, west 60 perches and north 6 degrees, east 60 perches to a line of land between said Duncan and Adam Cunningham thence on or near said line south 36 degrees, east 38 perches to land of Geo. Cunningham, thence

through said land south 13 degrees, east 84 perches, south 5 degrees, east 136 perches to or near Saml. McCune's line, thence through said McCune's land 20 degrees west, south 120 perches, south 14 degrees, west 92 perches thence through the same and land of the late Saml. Rippey south 5 degrees, east 120 perches, south 15 degrees, west 74 perches to the said Chambers mill door.

Page 125
The Court having taken the report into consideration do hereupon order and allow that the said road before described and laid out be of all intents and purposes a public road and highway and the same as such be opened forth with 30 feet wide and cleared and repaired according to an act of assembly.

At a Court of Private Sessions, at Carlisle, 28 March 1771 before Robert Miller, Andrew Colhoone and William Lyon

Came into Court William Thomas and set forth that a certain Thomas Oneal an indented servant to him the said William did absent himself from his said master's service a considerable time and that he had some expense gaining him again to his said service. The Court adjudges that the said Thomas Oneal serve his said Master William Thomas his heirs or assigns the term of three months over and above the Time mentioned in his Indenture also over and above the time adjudged by a former Court at Lancaster in full satisfaction for the __ of time and expenses aforesaid.

Page 126
At a Court of Private Sessions, at Carlisle, 25 March 1771, for the appointment of officers etc. before John Byers Esq. and his associate justices.
Lurgan Twp: John Maclay, constable; Adam Turner, Wm. Rippey, supervisors of roads; Jas. McKibben, Alexander Stewart, overseers of poor.
Letterkenny twp: John Immel, constable; Saml. Culbertson (fourth), Wm. Sharp, superintendent of roads; John Wade, Saml. Cumbertson (Irish), over seer poor.
Guilford Twp; Jacob Flack, constable; Wm. Gass, Peter Snyder, superintendent of roads; Wm. MacBrier, Richard Binson, overseers of poor.
Antrim Twp; Henry Gordon, constable; Wm. Rankin, John Price, superintendent of roads; Jas. Coil. Wm. Hannah, over seers of poor.
Peters Twp; Jos. Dunlap, constable; Jas. Stuart, David Hareston, supervisors of roads; Jonathan Smith, Nathan McDowell, overseers of poor.
Fannet Twp; Noah Abraham, constable; David Elder, Robt. Harvey, supervisors of roads; Robt. Little, Archibald Elliot, overseers of poor.

page 127
Tyrone- constable Owen McCabe; supervisors of roads Edward Elliott, William Sanderson; Over seers of poor Hugh Kilgore, Wm. McClure.
Teboyne- constable John Erwin; Supervisors of roads- Robert Adams Jr, Robert Pollock; over seers of poor John Nesbit, John Garner.

Rye- constable Will Robinson; supervisors of roads- Michael Marshal, James
        Baskins; over seers of poor John McCoy, Duncan McKowen.
Lack- constable David Wallace; supervisors of roads- William Arbuckle,
        Jacob Royal; over seers of poor James Gray, William Kirk.
Millford- constable, Hugh Quigley; Supervisors of roads- Thomas Hardy,
        William __ son; over seers of poor Robert Hoge, John Wilson
Fermauagh- constable James Gibson; supervisors of roads- William Sharron,
        John McKeever: over seers of poor William Redmon, Jonathan
        Parshghell
Derry- constable Jonas Balm; supervisors of roads- Edward Johnson, Henry
        Dreymond; over seers of poor George Moway, Duncan McDonald
Armagh- constable James Alexander Junior; supervisors of roads- James
        Alexander Jr; over seers of poor Robt. Brotherton, Willm Brown
Greenwood- constable Craft Coast; supervisors of roads- Marcus Huslins,
        Charles Burgher: over seers of poor John Brougham, Wm
        McIllenney
Barree- constable William Shirley; supervisors of roads- Saml. Thompson,
        Daniel Lego; over seers of poor Zebulon Moor, Robt Caldwell
Bedford- constable Michael Feather
Dublin- constable James Toaley; over seers of poor Charles Boyle, Benj. Elliot

Page 128 April Session 1771
At Carlisle, 23 April 1771, before John Armstrong, Esq., and his associates.
The sheriff David Hoge made the following return of grand jurors; Wm.
Duffield, Wm. Clark, Thos. Orbison, Matthew Miller, Jas. McAllister, Wm.
Hallowday, Richard Nicholson, David Davis, Wm. Davison, Jas. Finley, Jas.
Parker, Nathan McDowell, Robt. Smith, John McClure, Richard Parker,
Andrew Holmes, Jas. McCall, Andrew Boyd, Wm. Gray, Alexander Roddy,
Thos. Elliot, Charles Pollick, Obadiah Garwood.

Page 129
His honor, the Governor's commission's hearing date the 6 April to Jas.
Turner, Jas. Hamilton, Jos. Tilgham, Wm. Logan, Richard Peters, Linwood
Lardner, Benj. Chew, Thos. Caldwalder, Richard Penn, Andrew Allen and
Edw. Shiffen Esq., members of the proprietary and Governors Council and to
John Armstrong, John Byers, John Rennels, Jonathan Hoge, Robert Miller,
Wm. Line, Andrew Calhoun, Jas. Maxwell, John Holmes, John Allison,
George Robson, Wm. Petterson, Turbutt Frances, Henry Prather, John Agnu,
Wm. Thompson, Jas. Oliver, Matthew Henderson, John McClay Jr., Wm.
Elliot, Wm. Brown, Saml. Lyon, and Jas. Dunlap Esq., assigns them jointly and
severally justices of the peace & also assigns them or any three of them justices
as well of the peace in the said county to keep as also divers felonies and other
misdeeds within the same county aforesaid to hear and determine.

The King vs John Thomas

Felony, stealing a great __ the property of Thos Wilson. Jury; Samuel Culbertson Junior, Samuel Culbertson Wagr, John Brackenridge, Robert Patterson, Samuel McCormick, David Bowen, Robert Stockton, John Kimble, Samuel McIlheaney, William Smith, __ Sanderson and Robert Culbertson say the defendant John Thomas is guilty. Judgement that John Thomas restore the goods so stolen to the owner if not already done or the full value thereof also pay the full value thereof to the Governor for the support of Government Likewise pay the costs of prosecution with all such sums of Money as shall be allowed by the Court to the owner for his trouble and expense in the prosecution and also shall be taken to the common whipping post tomorrow the 26th instant, receive 15 lashes upon his bare back well laid on between the hours of 10 and 4 of the clock in the afternoon, committed to the common goal until the whole be complied with.

Page 130 April Sessions 1771

The King vs George Jeffries

Felony in stealing 15 yds of Linnen cloth. Jury; Samuel Culbertson Junior, Samuel Culbertson Wagoner, John Brackenridge, Robert Patterson, Samuel McCormick, David _owen, Robert Stockton, John Kimble, Samuel McIlheany, William Smith, William Sanderson, and Robert Culbertson who being duly impaneled chosen and sworn upon their respective do say that the defendant George Jeffries is guilty. Judgement, George Jeffries restore the goods so stolen to the owner if not already done for the full value thereof the like value thereof to the Governor for support of Government also pay the cost of prosecution with all such sums of money as shall be allowed to the owner for his trouble and expense in the prosecution and also shall be taken to the common whipping post tomorrow the 26th instant, receive 15 lashes upon his bare back well laid on between the hours of 10 and 4 of the clock in the afternoon, stand committed until the whole be complied with.

The King vs David English

Assault and battery. Defendant pleads his innocence. Judgement is that David English pay a fine of 10 shillings to the Governor for the support of Government also pay the costs of prosecution and stand committed in the custody of the Sheriff until the whole be complied with.

Page 131

The King vs David Hannah

Assault and battery. Jury; Samuel Coulter, William McCune, John Holmes, John Hastings, James McAfee, Peter Smith, Robert Coulhoun, Alexr Peoples, Jonathan Kearsley, Duncan McDonald, John Norris and George Hamilton say that the David Hannah is guilty. Judgement that David Hannah is fined 20 shillings, pay the costs of prosecution, stand committed until the whole be complied with.

The King vs William Kelso
Indictment for keeping a tippling house.

Page 132 April Sessions 1771
The King vs Hugh Swan
Perjury. April 1772 Jury; Robert Urie, Andrew McBeath, William Carrithers, Walter Denny, William Clark, James McCullough, Thomas Craighead, Robert Denny, James Kinney, George Sanderson and James Elliot say that Hugh Swan is not guilty.

The same vs the same
Perjury. April 1772 Jury; Robert Urie, Andrew McBeath, William Carrothers, Walter Denny, William Clark, James McCullough, Thomas Craighead, Robert Sanderson and James Elliot say that Hugh Swan is not guilty.

Page 133
The King vs David Stowall
Indicted for not repairing the highways.

The King vs James Irwins
Assault and battery. Jury; Samuel Coulter, Wm McCune, John Bay, John Hastings, Thomas McAfee, Peter Smith, Robert Calhoun, Alexander Peoples, Jonathan __ly, Duncan McDonald, John Norris and George Hamilton who say that the defendant James Irwin is guilty. Judgement that the defendant James Irwin is fined in the sum of 2 shillings and six pence, pay the costs of prosecution, stand committed until the whole be complied with.

Page 134
The King vs James Watt and David Miller
Indicted for not repairing the highroads.

The King vs Thomas Miller
Assault and battery upon Robert Lard.

The same vs the same
Assault and battery on David Christy.

The King vs Thomas Moor
Assault and battery on James Irwin.

The same vs the same
Assault and battery on Edwd. Armstrong.

Page 135 April Sessions 1771
The King vs James Graham
Assault and battery on David Hannah.

The King vs Andrew Gibson
Assault and battery on James Graham.

The King vs Edward Armstrong
Assault and battery on Thomas Moor.

The King vs David Hannah
Assault and battery upon John Patton.

The King vs the same
Assault and battery upon Robert Patton.

Thomas McCormick £100, Ephraim Blaine £50, conditioned for the appearance of Thomas McCormick at the next Court then and there to answer such things as shall be objected to him on his Majesties behalf and not depart the Court without license.

Robert Brackenridge £40, David Hoge £20, conditioned for the appearance of the said Robert Brackenridge at the next Court then and there to answer such things as shall be objected him on his Majesties behalf and not depart the Court with license.

Page 136
David Sterrat £40, Alexander McKeeghan £20, conditioned for the appearance of David Sterrat at the next Court then and there to answer to a certain bill of Indictment found against him and not depart the Court without license.

David Hannah £40, Charles Largu£20, conditioned for the appearance of the David Hannah at the next Court then and there to answer to a certain bill of Indictment found against him and not depart the Court without license.

James Erwin £40, Andrew Armstrong £20, conditioned for the appearance of the said James Erwin at the next Court then and there to answer to a certain bill of indictment found against him and not depart the Court without license.

John Guilliford £50, Alexander Armstrong £30, conditioned for the appearance of John Guilliford at the next Court then and there to answer to such things as shall be objected to him on his Majesties behalf and depart the Court without license.

William Henderson £25, David Evans £25, conditioned for their several appearance at the next Court then and there to testify in his Majesties behalf and not depart the Court without license.

Page 137 April Sessions 1771
Robert Elder £50, James Pollock £50, Robert Whenie £50, conditioned for their several appearance at the next Court then and there to testify in his Majesties behalf and not depart the Court without license.

David Wills £20, conditioned for his appearance at the next Court then and there to testify in his Majesties behalf and not depart the Court without license.

James Graham £20, Moses Donald £20, Charles Luper £20, conditioned for their several appearance at the next Court then and there to testify in his Majesties behalf and not depart the Court without license.

Samuel Wharton £20, conditioned for his appearance at the next Court then and there to testify in his Majesties behalf and not depart the Court without license.

Thomas Moor £40, Ephraim Blaine £20, conditioned for the appearance of the said Thomas Moor at the next Court then and there to testify in his Majesties behalf and not depart the Court without license.

Page 138
Daniel Smithson £60, conditioned for his appearance and Sarah his wife at the next Court then and there to answer such things as shall be objected to them on his Majesties behalf and not depart the Court without license and in the mean time to keep the peace and be of good behaviour to all his Majesties subjects and in particular to John Houzer and Elizabeth his Wife then the same to be void otherwise to be and remain in full force and virtue

John Houzer £40, Andrew Mann £20, Edward Combs £29, conditioned on the appearance of the said John Houser and Elizabeth his wife at the next Court then and there to answer such things as shall be objected to them on his Majesties behalf and not depart the Court without license and in the mean time keep the peace and be of good behaviour to all his Majesties subjects and in particular to Daniel Smithson and Sarah his wife then the same to be void, otherwise to be ad remain in full force and virtue.

Page 139
Upon application of George Ross Esq. To the Court praying that Jas. Lucamb admitted an attorney of this court and having taken the oath prescribed by an act of assembly, he is admitted as an attorney of the Court of Common Pleas and General Sessions of said county.

Upon application of Jas. Smith Esq. praying that David Grier be admitted and upon taking oath, he was likewise admitted.

Upon application of Gasper Yeates Esq. praying that David Aspie be admitted and upon taking oath, he was likewise admitted.

Upon petition of sundry of the inhabitants of Antrim twp. to the Court setting forth that they have been at a considerable expense in building a house of worship in conjunction with their neighbors and also been at the trouble of laying out and cutting roads thereto which afterwards have been stopped and turned such being made by owners of different plantations. Have now been at the trouble of laying our a road beginning at Wm. Rankin's and running thence south 63 degrees, west 160 perches, to a hickory, thence south 57 degrees, west 220 perches to the great road at Robt. McCrea's filed and as the same doth no interfere with any improvements and the distance so small pray the Court do appoint men to view and lay out the same which shall be kept in order at the expense of the petitioners and not at the expense of the township that free and open intercourse and access may be had to said place of worship. Appointed John Kennedy, Andrew Robison, Wm. Croil Jr., Henry Paulining, Andrew Miller and Jas. Mitchell to view and lay out the same.

Page 140 April Sessions 1771
Upon the petition of sundry inhabitants of Middleton, Allen and Carlisle Townships to the Court setting forth that the road heretofore used from Carlisle to James Dills Gap and there falling into the road leading to York has not ben laid out by __ order of Court and by reason of the inhabitants adjacent extending their fields across the same at will the distance is not only un__ much greater but the passage difficult and troublesome. This inconvenience is likely to increase as some of said inhabitants intend shortly to extend their improvements and consequently throw the Road still further out of the direct course. That altho some years ago a road was petitioned for laid out and confirmed by Order of Court from Carlisle to said Dills Gap yet the same was laid out contrary to the prayer of the petitioners and contrary to the useful purpose they intended. Praying the Court to appoint proper men to view and if they see cause lay out a road the nearest and best way from Carlisle to Dills Gap. The Court do appoint Robert Miler, Esqr, William Lyon Esqr, Robert Magraw Esqr, Samuel Hay, Hugh Gibson, and Joseph Hudson to view the premises and if they or any four of them see necessary to lay out the same by courses and distances the nighest and best way the least injurious to private property and for the best utility of the publick.

Upon the petition of sundry inhabitants of Newton, and West Pennborrough Townships to the Court setting forth that they labor many inconveniences and difficulties for want of a public road leading from McCastions Gap in the North Mountain to the Town of Carlisle Crossing Canedoquenet Creek at or nigh a place called the broad Foard and praying the Court to appoint proper men to view and if they see cause lay out a road the nighest and best way from McCastions Gap to Carlisle. Appointed James Brown, William Clark, James Kilgore, George Brown, John Aspie, and Andrew McFarland to view the premises and if they or any four of them see necessary lay out the same distances the nighest and best way the least injurious to private property and for the best utility of the publick and make report to next court.

Page 141 April Sessions 1771
Upon the petition of sundry of the inhabitants of Lurgan and Letterkenny twps. to the Court setting forth that they being members of the Presbyterian Church at Middle Spring hath no way to pass and repass and that their roads are so much stopped and turned that they are likely to be deprived of any convenient way to their house of worship praying the Court to appoint men to view and lay out a road from said Middle Springs House Meeting along the old course to Herron's Ford into the road from Shippensburg to Cessna's Gap the nighest and best way. Appointed Wm. Power, David Miller, Robt. Lowmore, Wm. English, Wm. McKerbry, and Jas. Ervine to review the premises etc.

Upon the petition of Andrew McBeath of Middleton Township in the County of Cumberland to the Court Setting forth that he labors under many inconveniences for want of a great road from his dwelling house to the dwelling house of William Henderson as nigh as possible to an old __ented road and from thence to follow the course of the said old road until it falls into the Great Road leading from Croghans Gap to Carlisle which Road he is willing to clear and Maintain at his own proper cost and Charges. Praying the Court to appoint proper men to view and lay out the same as aforesaid. Appointed Andrew Armstrong, James Irwin, William Chambers, Thomas Armstrong, James Bell, and Robert Sanderson and if they or any four of them see necessary lay out the same by courses and distances the nighest and best way the least injurious to private property and for the best utility and make report to next Court.

Page 142
Upon the petition of Samuel Coulter of the Town of Carlisle setting forth to the Court that he purchased of James How in the Path Valley a plantation and the improvements thereon since which the inhabitants of that place obtained an order from the Court for a road through said Valley the viewers and layers out of which has thought proper to take said road through the improved part of said plantation and has thereby rendered his orchard and meadow useless when at the same time it might be taken thro's other parts of said premises nigher straighter and on better ground not twenty rods from where it is now marked and would not be of any prejudice to te Inhabitants nor the petitioners. None of the inhabitants having any of their improvements any way infringed on __ the Petitioners. Praying the Court to grant them a viewer of the said and appoint men to view and lay out the same the nighest and best way. Appointed Robert Anderson, James Montgomery, James Moor, William Campble, James Ardrey and Randle Alexander to review the premises and if they or any four of them see necessary lay out the same by courses and distances the nighest and best way the least injurious to said plantation and for the best utility of the publick and make report to the next Court.

Upon the petition of sundry Inhabitants of Rye Township to the Court setting forth that six men were appointed by an order of this Court to view and lay out a road to Lead from James Gallohers to James Baskins's and having met agreeable to said order four of them did agree to carry the said road from said Gallohers to Andrew Stephens and from thence to James Baksins which they look upon as a great grievance as it would be a great expense to open and maintain a road on such ground and praying the Court to grant a review of the said road and appoint proper men to review the premises and lay out the same the nighest and best way. Appointed William Power, David Miller, Robert Lawrence, William English, William McIllevey and James Irwin to review the premises and if they or any four of them see necessary to lay out the same by courses and distance the least injurious to private property and of the best utility of the publick and make report to next Court.

Page 143 April Sessions 1771
Upon the petition of sundry inhabitants of Westpennsburgh Township to the Court Setting forth that they labor under great Inconvenience for want of publick roads to the place of market, and praying the Court to appoint proper men to view and lay out a road from the late dwelling house of John McClure near McClures gap the nearest and best way to James Smiths gap and to fall into the road already made near said Smiths Mill good roads being of great utility to the publick. Appointed James Brown, George Brown, William Gaddis, Richard Parker, James Carrothers junr and John Young to view the premises and if they or any four of them se necessary lay out the same by distances the nighest and best way the least injurious to private property and for the best utility of the publick and make report to next court.

Upon the petition of sundry inhabitants of Westpennsburgh Township setting forth to the Court that a road is much wanting from Paul Rerces down the several courses along the Creek to John Dunbars from that the nighest and best way to John McClures along the road leading to Carlisle which road will answer for Mill Meeting and market for a number of the inhabitants about the Creek in said Township. Praying the Court to appoint proper men to view and lay out a road the nearest and best way aforesaid. Appointed John McClure, Richard Parker, John Dunbar, John Forbes, James Love, Paul Pierce to view the premises and if they or any four of them see necessary lay out the same by courses and distances the nighest and best way the least injurious to private property and for the best utility of the publick and make return to next Court.

Petition of __ inhabitants Pennsborough Township and parts adjacent to the Court setting forth that upon the petition of __ inhabitants of Pennsborough Township and parts adjacent many years since for a road from a ferry on Susquehanna called commonly by the name of Taafs (?) Ferry to Carlisle such a road was laid out and confirmed but that such confirmation cannot now be found. That the said road has been used constantly and been of real service to the people passing and repassing between the said Ferry called Taaffs Ferry and

Carlisle that such road is necessary and of great utility to the inhabitants there abouts as well as Travelers and that it is likely that the said road will now be __ there being no record of its confirmation

Page 144
Praying the Court to appoint proper persons to view and lay out the said road from Yellow Britches Creek if they find the same necessary and of publick utility. Appointed Edward Morton, George Woods, John Galbreath, John Orr, John Orr Junior, William Gaddis and if they or any four of them sees necessary lay out the same by courses and distances the least injurious to private property and for the best utility of the publick, make report to next Court.

Upon the report of John Johnson, Jas. McKammond, Wm. Young, Saml. Culbertson and Alexander McConnel to the Court setting forth that by order of last Jan. Sessions they were appointed to view and if they should see cause lay road by courses and distances from the west end of the town of Shippensburg by Herron's Ford to Cessna's Gap and having met and viewed the premises are of the opinion that there is necessity of a road there and have laid out the same by courses and distances as follows: Beginning at the west end of the town of Shippensburg by Herron's Ford to Cessna's Gap and having met and viewed the premises are of the opinion that there is necessity for a road there and have laid out the same by courses and distances as follows. Beginning at the west end of Shippensburg west 76 perches, north 74 degrees, west 835 perches, north 40 degrees, west 150 perches, south 75 degrees, west 310 perches, south 54 degrees, west 280 perches, south 70 degrees, west 186 perches, to Andrew Neil's old place, north 70 degrees, west 186 perches, south 86 degrees, west 263 perches, north 68 degrees, west 165 perches, 644 perches, south 60 degrees, west 9 perches to Cessna's Gap. Ordered the road laid out be to all intent and purposes a public road and highway and the same as such be opened forth with 20 feet wide, cleared and repaired.

At Court of Private Sessions held at Carlisle, 6 June 1771 before John Rannels, Andrew Colhoone, John Allison and James Dunlap. Adjudged that Cornelius Larry Indented servant to John Beard do__ his said master John Neard the space or term of one year over and above the time specified in his indenture in compensation for run away time and expenses amounting to 2 pounds 10 shillings.

Page 145
At a Court of Private Sessions held at Carlisle, 10 June 1771 before John Armstrong, Robert Miller, John Agnew. Adjudged by the Court that Henry Stewart indented servant to William Steel do serve his said master William or his assigns the further time of one year and three months over and above the time specified in his indenture in compensation for run away time and expenses amounting to 7 pounds, 19 shillings and 4 pence.

At a Court of Private Sessions held at Carlisle 25 June 1771 before Robert Miller, William Thompson and John Agnew. Adjudged by the Court that Francis Leslie indented servant to Christopher Vanlear do serve his said master Christopher Vanlear or his assigns the further time of six months over and above the time specified in his indenture, compensation for run away time and expenses amounting to 3 pounds, 19 shillings and 6 pence.

At a Court of Private Sessions held at Carlisle 9 July 1771 before Robert Miller, William Thompson and John Agrew. Whereas David Hannah was indicted last April sessions and found guilty of an assault and battery on the body of James Graham and on application for his discharge, ordered that the said David Hannah be sold out by the Sheriff of the said County for the term of 19 months in order for the satisfaction of his fine fees and costs of prosecution, amounting in the whole to 13 pounds, 18 shillings, 8 pence.

Page 146 October Sessions 1771
The King vs William McKee

The King vs Samuel Quin

The King vs Barth David

The King vs Hugh Taaft

Page 147
At Carlisle, 23 July 1771. Sheriff David Hoge returns the following panel of grand jurors; Wm. Denny, Jas. Pollock, John Pollock (tavern keeper), Robt. McKnight, John Wilkins, Jos. Sample, Jas. Sample, Jas. Hendricks, Joseph Spear, Stephen Dunca, Edw. Ward, Wm. McCosky, Michael Findley, Christopher Van Lier, Jas. Ramsey, Joseph Pollock (carpenter), John Grier, Anthony Harwick, Wm. Thomas, John McCurdy, Jas. Davis, John Glen, Jacob Sailor, Thos. Moore.

Page 148 July Sessions 1771
The King vs William Morrow
Felony in stealing sundry goods the property of Cornelius Athison. Judgement that the prisoner Wm Morow restore the goods so stolen to the owner if not already done or the value thereof the like value thereof to the Governor for support of Government also pay costs of prosecution, be taken to the common whipping post tomorrow the 26th instant, receive 15 lashes on his bare back well laid on between the hours of 10 and 4 of the clock in the afternoon, stand committed in the custody of the Sheriff until the whole be complied with.

The same vs the same
Felony in stealing sundry goods the property of Benjamin Walker. Judgement that the prisoner Wm Morow restore the goods so stolen to the owner if not already or the value thereof the like value thereof to the Governor for support of government also pay costs of prosecution and also be taken to the common whipping post tomorrow the 26th instant, receive 15 lashes on his bare back well laid in between the hours of 10 and 4 of the oclock in the afternoon. stand committed in the custody of the Sheriff until this whole be complied with.

The same us the same
Felony in stealing one ax the property of [left blank]. Judgement that the prisoner Wm Morrow restore the goods so stolen to the owner if not already done and value thereof the like value thereof to Governor for the support of government also pay costs of prosecution and also be taken to the common whipping post tomorrow the twenty sixth instant, receive 15 lashes on his bare back well laid on between the hours of 10 and 4 of the clock in the afternoon, stand committed in the Sheriffs custody until the whole be complied with.

Page 149
The King vs Sarah McCorth
Assault and battery on the body of Samuel McCall. Judgement that the defendant Sarah McCorth be fined one shilling, pay the costs of prosecution, stand committed until the whole be complied with.

The King vs Wm McKee
Bastardy.

The same vs Gussill Smith
Bastardy.

Page 150 July Sessions 1771
The King vs Patrick McGrew
Felony. Defendant is discharged by proclamation and paying costs.

The same vs Mary Brien
Felony. Defendant is discharged by proclamation and paying costs.

The Same vs John Guilliford
Forcible Entry. Defendant is discharged by proclamation and paying costs no one appearing against discharge.

The King vs James Watt and David Miller
James Watt £40, David Miller £40, Michael Marshell £20, Frederick Watt £20, conditioned for the of the said James Watt and David Miller at the next Court then and there to answer such things as shall be objected on her Majesties behalf and not depart the Court without license.

Page 151

The King vs John Miller, Chris Walker, Saml Irwin
John Miller £20, Samuel Irwin £20, Chris Walker £20, John Boyd £10,
conditioned for the of the said John Miller and Samuel Irwin and Christian
Walker at the next Court then and there to answer such things as shall be
objected on her Majesties behalf and not depart the Court without license.

Matthew Scott, John Pollock, John Gray, Tobias Hendricks, John Miller, David
Gallagher, Christopher Van Lear, Tarens Davis, Ralph Naylor, Robt. Jack,
Wm. Peoples, Wm. Rippey, Robt. Galbraith, Wm. Smith, John McCurdy,
Ephriam Blain, Geo. Minson, Peter Pence, Jas. Bell, Duncan McDowell, Wm.
Kelso, Geo. Sharpe, Jas. Pollock, Wm. McCune, Jacob Wise, Nicholas Young,
having petitioned the Court to be recommended to his Honor the Governor, for
his license to keep public houses of entertainment and the Court taking such
petitions under consideration, the said Matthew Scott, John Pollock, John Gray,
Tobias Hendricks, John Miller, Jas. Galbraith, Christopher Van Lier, Jas.
Davis, Ralph Naylor, Robt. Jack, Wm. Peoples, Wm. Rippey, Robt. Galbraith,
Wm. Smith, John McCurdy, Ephriam Black, Peter Pence, Geo. Minser, Jas.
Bell, Duncan McDonald, Wm. Kelson, Geo. Sharpe, Jas. Pollock, Wm.
McArve, Jacob Wise, Nicholas Young are recommended and licensed.
Also petitioners for beer licenses Anthony Maule, Conrad Bainer, at Oct. Term,
— John Preentice, Henry Gordon, Robt. Fammel, Jas. McAllaster, — at Jan.
Term Wm. Morrow, and Wm. Finney.

Page 152 July Sessions 1771

Whereas upon the petition of divers of the inhabitants of Eastpennsborough
Township and the Parts adjacent to the last sessions persons were appointed by
the Court to view and lay out a road leading from John Harris's Ferry to
Carlisle in Case they conceived the same road necessary and of publick utility
and whereas the persons so appointed have viewed the same road and made a
report to this Court which said report so made this Court hath ruled to be
informed and insufficient on motion in behalf of the petitions for the said road
the Court here appoint Andrew Armstrong, Wm Abernathy, John Carruthers,
Andrew Miller, John Sample, and James Gregory to view the said Road and if
they or any four of them do see cause to lay out the same as a publick road that
they lay out the same by courses and distances In a manner the least injurious
to private property and most conducive to the publick good and that they make
report of this proceedings to the next sessions.

Upon the petition of sundry of the inhabitants of East Pennsbro Township
setting forth to the Court that they labor under great inconvenience for a road
from the Blue Mountain Foot past John Bards Senr or any other way that may
thought most convenient for the Lower End of said township to go to Major
Edward Wards Mills. Praying the Court to appoint proper men to view and lay
out a public road as aforesaid. Appointed Thomas Mornick, John Semple, John
Nailor, Isaac Hendricks, William McLeer and Rowland Chambers to view the

premises ad if they or any four of them do see cause to lay out the same as a publick road that they lay out the same by courses and distances in manner the least injurious to private property and most conducive to the publick good and that they make report of their proceedings to next sessions.

Page 153
Petition of sundry of the inhabitants of West Pennsboro Township setting forth to the Court that they labor under many inconveniences for want of a publick road, for the benefit of the inhabitants to begin at Charles Kilgores or James Carrothers Junior and from thence to John Moors Mill. Praying the Court to appoint men to view the premises and lay out a publick road as aforesaid. Appointed Ezekiel Dunning, James Carrothers Junior, George Davison, John McClure, Shoemaker, Andrew Miller and Charles Kilgore to view and if they or any four of them do see cause to lay out the same as a publick road that they lay out the same distances in a manner the least injurious to private property and most conducive to the publick good, that they make report to next sessions.

Came into Court David Herron, Thos. Montgomery, Jas. McKee, and Saml. Montgomery, four of the persons appointed by an order of the last April session to view and lay out a public road from the Middle Spring House to Herron's fording place into the road from Shippensburg to Cessna's Gap by courses and distances the nearest and best way and report to the Court that they had met and viewed the premises and that such road is very necessary for public utility and return the same for public use by courses and distances as follows: Beginning at the Meeting House south 48 degrees, west 170 perches to Conrad Fishburn's land, south 39 degrees, west 89 perches, to John Cummins, south 95 degrees, west 208 degrees to Wm. Cox's south 70 degrees, west 124 perches to Arthur Clark's, south 46 degrees, west 125 perches to Alexander Sterritts north 48 degrees, west 27 perches south 70 ½ degrees, west 42 perches, south 64 degrees, west 53 perches to John Herron's ford. The Court having taken the report into consideration do thereupon order and allow that the same road as before described and laid out be to all intents and purposes a public road and highway and the same be forthwith opened 20 feet wide and cleared and repaired in pursuance of an act of assembly etc.

Page 154 July Sessions 1771
Came into Court John Forbes, Richard Parker, Paul Pierce, James Love and John Dunbar five of the men appointed by an order of Last April Sessions to view and if they should necessary to lay out a publick road from Paul Pierces the nighest and best way to John McClures along the road leading to Carlisle by courses and distances. And reported to the Court that they had viewed the premises and do find that such road is very necessary for the utility of the publick and do return the same as such. Beginning at Paul Pierces thence Down the several courses of the Creek to John Dunbar's thence along a partition fence and by marked trees to a line of John McClures and William Carrothers cross the Savany into the old road leading from McDunnings to

John McClures and from thence to Carlisle. Court order the same road as above described and laid out be to all intents and purposes a publick road and highway and the same as such be forthwith opened 20 feet wide and cleared and repaired in pursuance of the Acts of Assembly of this Province in such case made and provided of which the supervisors of the roads in the different townships through which the same passes are to take notice.

Came into Court Andrew Armstrong, James Irwin, William Chambers, Thomas Armstrong, Robert Sanderson and James Bell the men appointed by an order of Last April Sessions to view and if they should see necessary to lay out a private road from Andrew McBeaths House to the dwelling of William Henderson as nigh as possible to an old frequented road and from thence to follow the coarse of said road until it falls into the roads Leading from Groghans Gap to Carlisle by courses and distances the nighest and best way which road the said McBeath engaged to __ and maintain at his own proper costs and charges.

And reported to the Court that they had viewed the premises and laid out the same by courses and distances little injurious to private property as possible viz beginning at the Dwelling house of Andrew McBeath south 5 degrees west 78 perches south 40 west 20 perches south 69 west 37 perches north 55 degrees west 10 perches William Hendersons house south _3 degrees west 92 perches south 65 degrees west 12 perches south 5 degrees west 21 perches south 64 west 9 perches north 84 west 30 perches south 57 west 20 perches south 35 degrees west 69 perches road from Grogans Gap to Carlisle. The Court having taken the said report into consideration , 30 feet wide, clearing and maintaining at his own proper cost and charges as aforesaid of which all persons concerned are to take notice.

Page 155 July Sessions 1771
Petition of divers of the inhabitants of Shermans Valley to July Sessions 1770, persons appointed; Daniel Evans and John Byers to view and lay out a road beginning at Groghans Gap the best and nearest way to Hadiah Garwoods Mill or to Thomas Rofes Fording, from thence upwards the nearest and best way to the great road leading upwards in case they conceived the same road necessary and of public utility and have reported to this Court to wit July Sessions 1771 that they viewed the premises as aforesaid, find the road to be necessary and of public utility, have laid out the same, beginning at a chestnut post South 86 degrees west 140 perches Benjamin Brooks, North 76 W. 130 perches to a chestnut oak south __ W 332 perches White oak south __W 230 Black Oak North _2 W 60 gum James Sharons north 25 W 142 white oak south 76 W 44 white oak west 164 perches to a hickory north 20 W 60 Black oak, west 440 perches hickory North 85 west 126 black oak Josiah Classon north 75 W 203 white oak north 53 W 100 black oak and Hance Ferguson north `0 W 35 to a white oak N 44 perches white oak north 7 east 46 white oak north 7 west 106 white oak John Johnston north 15 W 220 white oak Daniel Evans north 45 west 505 perches to the great road leading up the valley.

The Court having taken the said report into consideration, order and allow that the same road as above described and laid out be to all intents ad purposes a public road and high way and the same as such be forthwith opened twenty feet wide and cleared and repaired in pursuance of the acts of Assembly of this Province in such case made and provided of which the supervisors of the road in the several townships through which the same passes are to take notice.

Page 156 July Sessions 1771
Whereas the petitions of divers of the inhabitants of Fannet Twp, to April Session 1770, the following persons David Elder, Thos. Blair, Robt. Hardy, John Clark, Allen Brown and Saml. Walker were appointed by the Court to view and lay out the road from Colter's saw-mill to Elliot's grist mill and from thence the provincial road near Allen Brown's in case they conceive the same road necessary and of public utility and make report to the Court agreeable thereto at July Sessions 1770, they report to the Court that they had met and viewed the premises and find the same road to be necessary and of public utility and laid out by the same courses and distances and whereas upon the petition of Saml. Colter to the Court praying a review of the above road setting forth that so far as the same went through his plantation it would be distressing and injurious to the same.

The Court ordered at last April other men to wit — Robt. Anderson, Jas. Montgomery, Jas. Moore, Wm. Chapbell, Jas. Ardray and Randall Alexander to review the same road as runs through the improvements of the said Saml. Colter and report to the next Court. Having reported to this Court that they had viewed and laid out the same the least injurious said plantations and best for the utility of public. Ordered and allowed the same to be laid out as described.

Page 157
In a Court of Private Sessions held at Carlisle, 31 Aug 1771 before Robert Miller, William Lyon, John Agnew.

Whereas James Morrow was indicted at last July Sessions and found guilty of felony on three several indictments. And on application of his discharge the Court upon considering the same do order that the said James Morrow be sold out by the Sheriff of the said County for the term of time of four years to commence from the date of said sale in order for the satisfaction of his fines fees and costs of prosecution the amounting in the whole to 16 pounds, 3 shillings and 8 pence.

At a Court of Private Sessions held at Carlisle, 23 September 1771 before Robert Miller, William Lyon and John Agnew. Adjudged that Joan Bryan indented servant to Alexander Irwin do serve the said Alexander Irwin her said master or his assigns the further time of 2 years over and above the time specified in said indenture in compensation for run away time and expenses amounting to 8 pounds, 11 shillings and 8 pence.

Page 158 October Session 1771

22 October 1771, before John Armstrong and his associates. The sheriff Ephriam Blain returns the following list of grand jurors; John Miller, Jas. Smith, Edw. Ward, Ths. Alexander, John Glen, John Rowe, Chas. McClure, John Boyd, Jas. Elliot, __ Davis, John Pollock, Robt. Erwin, Ralph Sterrit, Matthew Miller, John Naylor, Jas. Carothers, John Shelby, Jas. Campbell, Jas. Patten, Wm. Patten, Richard Gibson, Wm. Houston, Richard Stell.

Page 159

The King vs Daniel Farrinsworth

Felony in stealing sundry goods the property of Thomas Alexander. Judgment that the prisoner Daniel Farrinsworth restore the goods so stolen to the owner if not already done or the value thereof the like value thereof to the Governor for support of Government pay cost of prosecution, also be taken to the common whipping post this afternoon between the hours of two and six of the clock and there receive 21 lashes on his bare back well laid on and stand committed in the custody of the Sheriff until the whole be complied with.

The King vs Joseph Hutcheson

Felony in stealing sundry goods the property of Peter Bonebright. Jury; John Miller, Wm. Thompson, Thomas Knox, Charles McPennet, William Corren, Wm. McCune, Thomas McKean, John Read, John Disert, John Moor, Thomas Moor, Wm. Carruthers say that the defendant Joseph Hutcheson is guilty. Judgment is that the Joseph Hutcheson restore the goods so stolen to the owner if not already done or the value thereof the like value thereof to the Governor for support to Government pay costs of prosecution and also be taken to the common whipping post tomorrow between the hours of 10 and 4 in the afternoon, there receive 21 lashes on his bare back well laid on, stand committed in the custody of the Sheriff until the whole be complied with.

Page 160

The King vs Michl Brandon

Fornication and bastardy. Judgement Michael Brandon is fined 10 pounds to the governor for support of Government pay 20 shillings to Elizabeth Parkison for her _ing expense and two shilling __ from the time of the birth of the child until it arrives at the age of seven years that he __ the township where the child was born, pay the costs of prosecution, stand committed till the whole be complied with.

The King vs Elizabeth Parkison

Fornication and bastardy. The defendant being charged pleads guilty, judgment of the Court is that the defendant Elisabeth Parkison pay a fine of 10 pounds to the Governor for support of the Government also pay costs of prosecution.

The King vs Patrick W. Shawn
Felony in stealing goods the property of Thomas Murray. Judgment that the
Prisoner Patrick W. Shawn restore the goods so stolen to owner if not already
done or the value thereof the like value to the Governor for support of
Government and pay costs of prosecution, be taken tomorrow the 25th instant
to common whipping post between the hours of 10 and 4 in the afternoon,
receive 21 lashes on the bare back well laid on and stand committed in the
custody of the sheriff until the whole be complied with.

Page 161 October Sessions 1771
The King vs John Campbell
Felony in stealing and __ gold the value of three pounds the property of
Thomas Ross. Jury; John Miller, William Thompson, Thomas Knox, Charles
W. Jennet, Wm Donan, Willm McCune, Thos McHains, John Read, John __,
John Moor, Thomas Moor, William Carruthers say that the prisoner John
Campbell is guilty. Judgment that he return the money stolen to the owner if
not already done or the value thereof the like value to the Governor for the
support of Government, be taken tomorrow the 25th instant between the hours
of ten and four in the afternoon and their receive 21 lashes well laid on his bare
back and stand committed in the custody of the Sheriff until the whole be
complied with.

The King vs John Crane
Felony in stealing goods the property of Jr. Johnston. Judgment that the
prisoner John Crane return the goods so stolen to the owner if not already done
or the value thereof the like value to the Governor for support of Government,
be taken this afternoon to the common whipping between the hours of 2 and 6,
receive 15 lashes on his bare back well laid on, stand committed in the custody
of the Sheriff until the whole be complied with.

The King vs John Hannah
Indictment assault on John Djert. Judgment that the defendant John Hannah
pay a fine of 5 shillings to the Governor for support of Government fine two
sureties in 100 pound each for his good behaviour toward John Dyert and pay
the costs of prosecution.

Page 162
The King vs John McAlister
Fornication and bastardy. Defendants pleads not guilty.

The King vs Charles McCormick
Keeping a tippling house. Fined 5 pounds for the support of Government and
costs of prosecution, stand committed until the whole be complied with.

The King vs Sarah Cather.
Felony in stealing goods the property of Samuel Kearsly

The King vs the same
Felony in stealing goods the property of Robt W. Kinzie.

Page 163 October Sessions 1771
The King vs the same
Fornication and bastardy.

The King vs William Hunter and Thos Miller
Assault and battery. January 1773 the Defendant William Hunter submits to the
Court protesting his innocence. Judgment that he is fined 2 shillings and six
pence and pay costs of prosecution.

The King vs Joseph Hutchison
Felony.

The King vs William McKean
Assault and battery.

The King vs Sarah Burk
Felony. Defendant by proclamation is discharged on paying costs no one
appearing against her.

Page 164
The King vs John Kenedy
Assault and battery.

The same vs the same
Assault and battery.

The same vs William Hunter
Assault and battery.

The same vs Patrick McShawn
Felony.

John Miller, Christian Walker, Samuel Irwin being three times solemnly called
appeared not forfeit their recognizance.

John Boyd being three time solemnly called to Bring forth the Bodies of John
Miller, Christian Walke, and Saml Irwin appeared not forfeits his recognizance.

On motion of the prosecutor for the Crown that a certain John Lawrence was
Bound over by John Reynolds Esquire to appear at this Court to answer such
matters and things as might be said against him by George Livingston
concerning the Highway Robbery committed by the same John on the same
George and the said John Lawrence now appearing in Court it is ordered by the

Court that he be committed to the custody of the Sheriff for the robbery aforesaid until he be __ discharged from thence by course of law.

Page 165
Upon application of George Ross, Esq. to the Court praying that Geo. North be admitted an attorney of this Court, after having the oath he was duly admitted.

Upon application of Saml. Johnson Esq. To the Court praying the Court Andrew Scott be admitted as an attorney upon taking oath he was admitted.

Page 166 January Sessions 1772
The King vs Bartholomu Davis

The King vs Hugh Swan

The King vs Saml Quin

The King vs Wm Hunter and Thomas Miller

The King vs Willm McKee

The King vs Hugh Toaf

The King vs Chas McCormick

Page 167 April Sessions 1772
The King vs Barthw David et al

The same vs Hugh Swan

The same vs Samuel Quin

The same vs William Hunter and Thomas Miller

The same vs William McKee

The same vs Hugh Toaf

The same vs Charles McCormick

The same vs Isaac Winn

The same vs James Moore

Page 168 October Term 1771
The person appointed by last Court to view and lay out a road leading from Yellow Breeches Creek into the road leading from John Harris Ferry to Carlisle returned to the Court the said road as viewed and laid out by them. According to the following courses and distances. Beginning at Yellow Breeches Creek at a main road Leading from a ferry Commonly Called Teafs Ferry and running along the old road north 30 degrees west 48 perches thence north 58 degrees west 180 perches thence north 78 degrees west 144 perches thence north 60 degrees west 60 perches thence north 65 degrees west 98 perches thence north 23 degrees west 43 perches thence north 80 degrees west 220 perches thence north 50 degrees west 111 perches into the road leading from Harris Ferry to Carlisle and which road viewed and laid out as aforesaid the said Persons viz Andrew Armstrong, Wm Abernathy, John Carrithers, Andrew Miller, John Sample and James Gregory now returns to the Court as a publick road highly necessary and of publick utility and is laid out in a manner the least injurious to private property and most cond__ to the publick interest which said return being now taken into Consideration is accordingly approved of and confirmed by the Court __ further ordered that the said road laid out aforesaid be cut cleared and bridged of necessary by the several supervisors of the respective townships through which the said Road runs forthwith of the breath of 33 feet.

Came into Court John Davis and set forth in the Court that pursuance of an appointment of the Court directed to him to view and judge of a Boundary line to be made between the townships of Tyrone and Rye in the County of Cumberland County and make report of the same and having viewed the Premises is of opinion that a just and equitable Boundary ought to begin at the Tuscarora Mountains at William Nobles Dwelling __ extend by John Darlingtons, Elizabeth Smiley (Widow) and thence the same course to the North Mountain __ of the Plans above mentioning to Include in Rye township The Court upon considering the same do allow and approve of the Boundary as above described.

Page 169 October Session 1771
Upon the Petition of Westpennsborough Township setting forth to the Court that a publick Road leading from McClures Pass in the North Mountain Running from thence the nearest and best way to James Smiths Mill on Yellow Britches Creek and from thence to the York county line at Smiths Pass on the South Mountain will be of public Utility and advantage and praying the court to appoint proper men to view and lay out a publick road as aforesaid, the Court do appoint William Clark, William Carruthers, George Davison, Robt McFarland, John McClure, Creek and Robt McClure to view the premises and if they or any four of them do see cause to lay out the same as publick road that they lay out the same by courses and distances in a manner the least injurious to private property and most conducive to the publick good and that they make report of their proceedings to next session.

Adjudged that bail Blackwell indented servant to James Findley do serve the said James Findlay his said master or his assigns the further time of one year over and above the time specified in said indenture in compensation for runaway time and expenses __ amounting to 8 pounds, 5 shillings.

Adjudged that Thomas Quin indented servant to John Findlay do serve the said John Findley his said master or his assigns the further time of 7 months over and above the time specified in said indenture in compensation for run away time and expenses amounting to 4 pounds, 12 shillings.

Page 170
Adjudged that Patrick Mooney indented servant to John Kinhead do serve the said John Kindead his said master or his assigns the further time of one year and 5 months over and above the time specified in said indenture in compensation of run away time and expense, amounting to 8 pounds, 2 shillings.

Adjudged by the Court that Peter Moor indented servant to James Wilson do serve the said James Wilson said master or his assigns the further time of nine months over and above the time specified in said indenture in compensation of run away time and expenses, amounting to 1 pound, 16 shillings.

Whereas upon the petition of several of the inhabitants of Middletown Township to Last January Sessions Persons were appointed by the Court to view and lay out a road leading from the north end of the Bedford Street in Carlisle thro' the East Corner of Hugh McCormicks land By Robert Robs house and across the Creek at said Robbs Fording thence nearly Between the lands of William Fleming and Mathew Brown, thence the nearest and best way to Richard Evans Gap in the Mountain in case they conceived the same road necessary and of publick utility. Whereas the persons so appointed have viewed the same road and made a report to this Court which said report so made this Court hath ruled in formal and insufficient on motion in behalf of the petitioners for the said road the Court here appoint Thomas Wilson, William Irwin, James Sharron, James Irwin, Andrew Armstrong and Richard Kean to view the said road and if they or any four of them do see cause to lay out the same as a publick road that they lay out the same by courses and distances in a manner the least Injurious to private property and most conducive to the publick good and that they make report of their proceedings to next Court.

Page 171   October Sessions 1771
The persons appointed at last January Court to view and lay out a road leading from the Town of Carlisle past or to Craigheads Mill and from thence through the Forge Gap of the South mountain to York County Line returned to the Court the said road as viewed and laid out by them according to the following courses and distances. Beginning at Craigheads Mill south 63 degrees past 14 perches south 38 degrees East 72 perches south 17 degrees east 39 perches

south 24 degrees east 68 perches South 51 degrees east ff perches South 25 degrees East 8 perches South 14 degrees East 72 perches South 26 degrees east 298 perches south 17 ½ degrees east 292 perches south 9 degrees west 50 perches south 50 degrees west 57 perches south 22 degrees west 40 perches south 4 degrees west 25 perches south 38 degrees west 36 perches South 54 degrees west 42 perches south ten degrees east 243 perches south 18 degrees east 250 perches south 15 degrees east 46 perches south 3 degrees west 74 perches south 26 degrees east 69 perches south 55 degrees east 16 perches to York County Line which road viewed and laid out as aforesaid the said persons viz Jonathan Holmes, Robert Urie, John Kinkead, Samuel Laird, Samuel Hay and John Glenn now return to this Court as a Publick Road highly necessary and of publick utility and is laid out in a manner the least injurious to private property and most conducive to the publick interest which said return being now taken into consideration is accordingly approved of and Bon__ by the Court and it is further ordered that the said road laid out as aforesaid be cut cleared and bridged if necessary by the several supervisors of the respective townships through which the said road runs forthwith of the breadth of 33 feet.

Page 172
Petition of sundry of the inhabitants of Eastpennsborough Township setting forth to the court that they labor under many inconveniences for want of a road for the benefit of the inhabitants to begin at Robert Callenders mill in said township, from thence the nearest and best way to the mouth of Dogwood Run to fall into the great road leading to Baltimore Town. Praying the court to appoint men to view the premises and lay out a publick Road as aforesaid. Appointed Joseph Hudson, David Bell, James Gregory, James McCormick, Francis Silver and Joseph McClure to view the premises and if they or any four of them do see cause to lay out the __ a publick road that they lay out the same by courses and distances in a manner the least injurious to private property and most conducive the publick good and make report to next session.

Upon the petition of sundry of the inhabitants of Armagh Township to the Court setting forth that they __ road already laid out through the narrows into said Township. Praying the court to great them a wagon road the nearest and best way from the road already laid out above the __ eastward to a place called Gap leading to Penns Creek Valley and from the said road above the narrows and then to lead westward through the said township of Wm Millers. Court upon considering the same do appoint James Alexander, James Reed, Wm Dickson, Henry Taylor, William McNulty, Joseph McCibbin to view the premises and if they or any four of them do see necessary to lay out the same as a publick road __ they lay out the same by courses and distances the least injurious to private property and most conducive to the publick good and make report of there proceedings to next sessions.

Page 173 October Sessions 1771
Upon the petition of the inhabitants of Peters Township and parts adjacent, setting forth to the Court that they labor under many inconveniences for want of a road leading through James Campbell's through Chambersburg to the York County line in the gap of the mountain formerly Lindsay of Black's Gap, and praying the Court to appoint proper persons to view the premises and lay out a public road as aforesaid. The Court appointed William Gass, Matthew Wilson, Samuel Lindsay, James Campbell, Thomas Baird, and Patrick Jack to view and lay out the road, etc.

The Persons appointed by last January Court to view and lay out a road leading from Carlisle Commons near where the road from York and Trindles Road __ across Letart Spring through Pom__ street and from the west end of said street to fall into the great Road leading to Shippensburgh by John Millers returned to the court the said road as viewed and laid out by them according to the following courses and distances. North 28 degrees and one half degrees east 90 perches thence south 81 degrees and one half degrees east 94 perches to Letart Spring thence from the west end of said street north 81 ½ degrees, west 36 perches north 26 degrees west 26 perches thence north 63 degrees west 12 perches thence north 52 degrees west 54 perches to the road leading to John Millers which said road

Page 174
viewed and laid out as aforesaid the said persons viz, Steven Duncan, James Pollock, Jonathan Homes and Samuel Coulter now returned to this Court as a publick Road highly necessary and of publick utility and is laid out in a manner the least injurious to private property and most conducive to the publick good, which said return being now taken into consideration is accordingly approved of and confirmed by the Court and it is further ordered that the said road laid out as aforesaid be cut cleared and bridged if necessary by the several supervisors of the respective townships through which the said road runs forth with of the breadth of thirty three feet.

Upon the petition of sundry of the inhabitants of Rye and Greenwood Townships to the Court setting forth that they labor under many inconveniences for want of a bridle road leading from James Gallaghers house to the Ferry Place at the mouth of Juniata River. And praying the Court to appoint six men of Feamanagh and Millford Townships to Review the Premises and lay out a road as aforesaid. The Court do appoint James Grevidy, Robert Neilson, Samuel Mitchell, Robert Taylor, William Bell, Robert Campbell to review the premises and if they or any four of them agree and do see cause to lay out the same that they lay out the same by courses and distances he least injurious to private property and most conclusive to the publick good and make report to next session.

Page 175 October Sessions 1771
Petition of sundry of the inhabitants of Carlisle and Middletown Townships to the Court setting forth that they labor under many inconveniences for want of a publick road leading from Carlisle through McHaffies Gap the South Mountain to York County __ there to Inter__ with a road already laid out confirmed and opened from said line to McCallisters Town and Con__ that the distance between said Town will be 7 miles nearer and praying the Court to appoint men to appoint men to view the premises and lay out a publick road as aforesaid the Court do appoint William Miller, __ Duncan , Christopher Vanlear, James C__ James Kay, John Dickey to view the premises and if they or any four of them do se necessary to lay out the same that they lay out the same courses and distances the least injurious to private property and most conducive to the publick good and make report to next Court.

Page 176
The Persons appointed at last April Court to view and lay out a road from the Town of Carlisle leading toward James Dills Tavern in York County as far as the county line the nearest and best road and the least injurious to private property returned to the Court the said road as viewed and laid out by them according to the following courses and distances, beginning at Letort Spring at the __ing opposite the east end of high street thence south 81 degrees east 60 perches south 55 and ½ degrees east 1123 perches south 55 degrees east 933 perches south 34 ½ degrees east 53 perches south 68 and ½ degrees east 30 perches south 55 ½ east 176 perches south 43 degrees east 38 perches south 2 degrees east 10 perches south 67 and ½ degrees east 321 perches to where the old Road crosses the line between Cumberland and York County the whole length of which from Letort Spring to the County line is 2741 perches being 8 ½ miles and 21 perches. Which road viewed and laid out as aforesaid the said persons viz. William Lyon, Robert Miller, Samuel Hay, Robert Mcgaw and Hugh Gibson now returned to the Court as a publick road highly necessary and of publick utility and is laid out in a manner the least injurious to private property and most conducive to the publick interest which said return being now taken into consideration is accordingly approved of and confirmed by the Court and it is further ordered that the said road laid out as aforesaid be cut cleared and bridged if necessary by the several supervisors of the respective townships through which the said road runs forth with of the breadth of forty feet.

Page 177 October Sessions 1771
Petition of sundry of the inhabitants of __ township and parts adjacent setting forth to the Court that they labor under many inconveniences for want of a Publick road leding from William Pattersons Mill on Cocoham__ Creek to Tobias Bicks Plantation on Middlecreek and praying the Court to appoint six men to view and lay out the same as a publick road aforesaid the Court do appoint John Rickenbough Junr, Henry Moser, William Nees, Frederick Albright, John Rickenbough Senr and Adam __ to view the premises and if

they or any four of them do see necessary to lay out the same that they lay out the same by courses and distances the least injurious to private property and most conducive to the public good and make report to next sessions.

Petition of sundry of the inhabitants of Westpennsborough Township to the last sessions persons were appointed by the Court to view and lay out a road leading from Charles Kilgons or James Carrither Junior and from thence to John Moors Mill in Case they conceived the same road necessary and of publick utility and whereas so appointed viewed the same road and made a report to this Court which said road the Court do appoint William Clark, William Carrithers, George Davison, Robert McFarland, John McClure __ and Robert McClure to view the same road and if they or any four of them do see cause to lay out the same as publick road that they lay out the same by courses and distances in a manner the least injurious to private property and most conducive to the publick road, make report of their proceedings to next Court.

Page 178
Petition of sundry of the inhabitants of Carlisle and Middleton Township setting forth to the Court that an __ was granted and men appointed at last July Sessions 1770 to review a lay out a road from the north end of Hannover __ in the Town of Carlisle nearest and best way to the forty shilling gap from thence the most convenient way to fall in with the great road that __ through the __ Valley but the said persons never met thereon and praying the Court that the same men may be continued or others appointed to review the said road. The Court do appoint Thomas Wilson, William Fleming, John Stewart, John Mitchell, John Titus and Henry Gass to view the premises and if they or any four of them do see necessary to lay out the same that they lay out the same in a manner the least injurious to private property and most conducive to the publick good and make report to next Court.

Page 179   January Sessions 1772
At Carlisle, 21 January 1772. The Sheriff, Ephraim Blain returns the following grand jurors; Edward Morton, Robert Gilfilin, John Quigley, George Woods, John Galbraith, Samuel Gaddver, Stewart Rowen, Robert Whitehill, Thomas Armstrong, John Kimbel, David Bell, James McCormick, Isaac Hendricks, John Bobbs, Joseph McClure, John Ore, Jr., John Sample, William Kelso, Alexander McDaniel, Andrew Erwin, Samuel Adams, Francis Silver, John Ore, Sr., John McCormick, Sr.

Page 180
Thomas Mirion was indicted for felony for stealing one bay horse the property of James Guthrie, and also for stealing one bay horse, the property of Martin Binder, in each of which cases he was convicted to stand in the pillory for the space of one hour and to be whipped at the common whipping post upon his bare back with 39 lashes, well laid on.

Page 181

The King vs John Eagen

Felony in stealing one half of linnen the property of Peter Shoemaker. Jury; Andrew Armstrong, John Trindle, John Dicky, John Baird and James Maugh, John Clark, James McCurdy, Richard Gilstone Senr, John __, John Carruthers, Richard Gilston Junr and Samuel Fisher say the prisoner John Eagen is guilty. Judgment that the prisoner return the goods so stolen to the owner if not already done or pay the value thereof and also pay the costs of prosecution with all such sums of money __ be allowed by the court to the owner for his trouble. Expenses in the prosecution and also pay the like value of the goods so stolen to his honor the Governor for support of Government and be taken tomorrow the 24th instant between the hours of 10 and 4 in the afternoon to the common whipping post and there receive 21 lashes well laid on his bare back and stand committed in the custody of the Sheriff until the whole be complied with.

Page 182 January Sessions 1772

The King vs Thos Burney

Assault and battery on Thomas Baird. Defendant submits to the Court protesting his innocence. Judgment that the defendant Thomas Burney pay a fine of 19 shillings and six pence to his Honor he Governor for support of Government also pay costs of prosecution stand committed until the whole be complied with.

The same vs Thos Burney the younger

Assault and battery on Thos Baird. April 1772 Defendant retracts his pleas and submits to the Court protesting his Innocence. The Judgment the defendant Thomas Burney Junior pay a fine of six pence and pay costs of prosecution and stand committed until the whole be complied with.

The same vs Rebecca Wallace.

Assault and battery on John Hawey. July Sessions 1772 the defendant retracts her plea and submits to the Court protesting her innocence. Therefore the Court fines her in the sum of six pence and that pay costs of prosecution.

Page 183

The King vs Hugh McCurdy

Assault and battery on John Potts. April Term 1772 Jury; Robert Urie, Andrew Mc Beath, William Carrothers, Walter Denny, William Clark, James McCullough, Thomas Craighead, Robert Denny, James Kenny, Matthew Kenny, George Sanderson and James Elliot say that the defendant Hugh McCurdy is guilty. Judgment that he pay a fine of six pence pay costs of prosecution stand committed until the whole be complied.

The same vs the same
April 1772 jury; Robert Urie, Andrew McBeath, William Carrothers, Walter Denny, William Clark, James McCullough, Thomas Craighead, Robert Denny, James Kenny, Mathew Kenny, George Sanderson and James Elliott say that the Defendant Hugh McCurdy is not guilty.

The same vs James Moor
Assault and battery on Anthony Harwick. Defendant January 1773 submits to the Court protesting his innocence. Judgment that the defendant James Moor is fined in the sum of six pence pay costs of prosecution.

Page 184
The King vs Isaac Minor
Assault and battery on John Dunning. April term 1772, defendant submits to the protesting his innocense. Judgment that the defendant Isaac Minor pay a fine of six pence to the Governor for support of Government pay the costs of prosecution, stand committed in the custody of the Sheriff until the fine and costs are paid.

The same vs Thos. Davis
Assault and battery on Wm Carharat. Jury; Robert Urie, Andrew McBeath, William Carrothers, Walter Denny, William Clark, James McCullough, Thomas Craighead, Robert Denny, James Kenny, Mathew Kenny, George Sanderson and James Elliot say that the defendant Thomas Davis is not guilty.

Page 185
The King vs Isabella Carruthers
Indictment felony.

The King vs Sm Bridges and Thos Reynolds
Indictment felony.

The King vs Thos Baird
Assault and battery.

The King vs Joseph Carrol
Thos Duncan of Hopewell £50, conditioned for the appearance of Tom Welsh at the next General Court then and there to testify on his majesties behalf and not depart the court without license.

The King vs Hugh McCurdy
Elizabeth Potts £40, James Elder £20, conditioned for the appearance of Elizabeth Potts at the next Court then and there to testify on his majesties behalf and not depart the court without license.

Page 186 January Sessions 1772
The King vs the same
James Elders £40, conditioned for the appearance of John Potts at the next Court then and there to testify on his majesties behalf and not depart the court without license.

The same vs the same
Hugh McCurdy £50, James McCurdy £25, conditioned for the appearance of Hugh McCurdy at the next Court then and there to answer such things as shall be objected against him on his majesties behalf.

The same vs the same
Hugh McCurdy £50, James McCurdy £25, conditioned for the appearance of Hugh McCurdy at the next Court then and there to answer such things as shall be objected against him on his majesties behalf, not depart the court without license.

Page 187 January Sessions 1772
The King vs Rebecca Wallace
Rebecca Wallace £50, David Wallace £25, conditioned for the appearance of Rebecca Wallace at the next Court then and there to answer such things as shall be objected against her on his majesties behalf, not depart the court without license.

The same vs the same
John Harvey £30, Hugh McCurdy £15, conditioned for the appearance of John Harvey at the next Court then and there to answer such things as shall be objected against him on his majesties behalf, not depart the court without license.

The King vs Thos Burney
Thos Baird £10, Willm Chambers £10, James Galocher £10, John Burns £10 Wm Duffields £10, conditioned for their respective appearance at the next Court then and there to testify on his majesties behalf, not depart the court without license.

Page 188
The King vs Thomas Burney the Younger
Thos Bairds £10, Wm Chambers £10, James Golohers £10, John Burns £10, conditioned for their respective appearance at the next Court then and there to testify on his majesties behalf and not depart the court without license.

The same vs Thos Burney
Thos Burney £50, Wm McCune £25, conditioned for appearance of Thomas Burney at the next Court ,there to answer such things as shall be objected against him on his majesties behalf, not depart the court without license.

The same vs Thomas Burney the Younger
Thos Burney £50, Wm McCune £25, conditioned for the appearance of
Thomas Burney the Younger at the next Court then and there to answer such
things as shall be objected against him on his majesties behalf and not depart
the court without license.

Page 189
The King vs Isaac Winn
John Dunning £20, John Kinkead £10, Thos Burney £50, Wm McCune £25,
conditioned for the appearance of John Dunning at the next Court then and
there to answer such things as shall be objected against him on his majesties
behalf and not depart the court without license.

The King vs Thos Davis
Assault and battery. Thos Davis £40, John Kinkead £20, Thos Burney £50
Wm McCune £25, conditioned for the appearance of Thomas Davis at the next
Court then and there to answer such things as shall be objected against him on
his majesties behalf and not depart the court without license.

The King vs Thos Davis
Conditioned for the appearance of Wm Carhart at the next Court then and there
to testify on his majesties behalf and not depart the court without license.

Page 190   January Sessions 1772
Persons appointed at last October Sessions by the court to review and lay out a
road from Charles Kilgores or James Carruthers Juriors and from thence to
John Moors Mills to wit Wm Clark, Wm Carruthers, George Davidson, Robert
McFarlane, John McClune, Robert McClure have set forth to the court that they
had reviewed the same and are of opinion that no __ is necessary but that the
road laid out by the viewers appointed at last July Sessions to wit E_hiel
Dunning, James Carruthers, Andrew Miller, John McClure, Charles Kilgore
and George Davidson be of publick use and as little injurious to private
property as any that can be laid out. According to the following courses and
distances, beginning at a marked white oak in the line of Charles Kilgores land
thence such 6 degrees and 30 minutes east 1585 perches to a marked white oak
south 12 degrees East 509 perches and south 60 degrees west 40 on perches to
John Moors Mill being 6 ½ miles and 55 perches, which said __ being now
taken into consideration is accordingly approved of and confirmed by the court,
ordered that the said road laid out as aforesaid be to all intents and purposes a
publick road and highway and the same as such be forthwith opened, 30 feet,
cleared and bridged if necessary and the supervisors of the respective
townships are to take notice.

Page 191

The persons appointed by the Court last October sessions to view and lay out a road leading from the Middle Spring Meeting House to Herron Ford, into the road laid out from Shippensburg to Cisna's Gap return to the Court that the said road was viewed and laid out by them according to the following courses and distances, beginning at Middle Spring Meeting House south, 48 degrees west, 25 perches to Conrad Fishburn's; thence south, 50 degrees west, 77 perches to William Coxe's; thence south 51 degrees west, 234 perches to John Cummin to a hickory, thence south, 70 degrees west, 117 perches to Arthur Clark's to a walnut, and thence south, 46 degrees west, 125 perches to John Herron's, north 84 degrees west, 22 perches; thence north 68 degrees west, 64 perches, south 42 degrees, west 27 perches, thence south 64 degrees west 53 perches, to Herron Ford's, which said road, viewed and laid out as aforesaid, the said persons now return as a public road highly necessary and of public utility. Ordered that the said road laid out as aforesaid be to all intents and purposes a public road that the same be opened the width of 30 feet, etc.

Page 192   January Sessions 1772

The Persons appointed by last October Court to view and lay out a road leading from McClures Gap to the road leading past James Smiths Mills to Smiths Gap and near to smith Mills returned to the Court the said road laid out by them according to the following courses and distances, beginning near James Smiths Mills thence north 5 degrees west 40 perches north 5 degrees west 44 perches 35 perches up the said road north 41 degrees west 54 perches north 22 degrees west 54 perches north 8 degrees east 612 perches north 7 degrees west 80 perches north 28 degrees west 38 perches north 33 degrees and half west 87 perches north 54 degrees and an half west 57 perches north 9 degrees east 26 perches north 27 degrees an half east 112 perches north 52 degrees west 26 perches north 8 degrees east 32 perches north 19 degrees and an half east 32 perches and an half north 34 degrees and an half east 64 perches north 10 degrees 66 perches north 49 degrees west 78 perches north 17 degrees west 106 perches north 7 degrees west 550 perches north 11 degrees west 124 perches north __ degree west 40 perches north 30 degrees west 271 north 38 degrees west 14 perches north 1 degrees and an half west 76 perches north 21 degrees west 78 perches north 6 degrees and an half west 20 perches north 8 degrees east 38 perches north two degrees west 21 perches north 14 degrees and an half east fifty perches north 1 degree an half east 94 perches north 70 perches north 21 degrees and half west 164 perches north 7 degrees and an half east 42 perches north 14 degrees and an half west one

Page 193 & 194

44 perches to the deer lick near McClures Gap being 11 miles an 49 ½ perches which said road viewed and laid out as aforesaid the said persons. Viz, Robert McClure, John McClure, Wm Clark. Wm Carothers and George Davison now returned to this Court as a publick road highly necessary and of publick utility and is laid out in a manner the least injurious to private property and most

conducive to the publick good which said return being now taken into consideration is accordingly approved of and confirmed by the Court and it is further ordered that the same road laid out as aforesaid be to all intents and purposes a publick road and highway and the same as such be forthwith opened of the breadth of thirty feet and cut cleared and bridged if necessary and the supervisors of the respective townships through which the said road runs are to take notice.

Persons appointed by last October Court to view and lay out a road leading from the York county line to Black's Gap and passing through Chambersburg to James Campbell's Peters Township, return to the Court that the said road was viewed and laid out by them according to the following courses and distances, namely, north 62 ½ degrees, west 152 perches to the Conococheague creek, thence south 81 degrees, west 28 perches, south 83 degrees, west 63 perches, north 83 degrees, west 184 perches, to the forks of the road, thence north 82 ½ degrees, west 176 perches, north 70 1/4 degrees, west 1323 perches to John Miller's north 85 ½ degrees, west 8 perches, north 32 3/4 degrees, west 84 perches, north 78 1/4 degrees, west 64 perches, and thence by various courses and distances to James Campbell's in Peters township, being in all 18 miles and 17 perches, which road as aforesaid the said viewers have returned as a public road necessary for public utility. Ordered that the said road be laid out as aforesaid as a public road to be laid out as aforesaid as a public road to the breadth of thirty feet.

Page 195 January Sessions 1772
Petition of Sundry of the inhabitants of Allan and Middleton Townships setting forth they labor under many inconveniences for want of a publick road leading from Capt. Robt Callinders Mills on the mouth of Letarts Spring past Carlisle Iron Works and from thence to the said Iron works Gap alias Mahaffies Gap in the south Mountain and through said Gap to the County line there to interfere with a road already laid out and confirmed by York Court and praying the court to appoint proper men to view the premises and lay out a publick road as aforesaid the court do appoint Wm Miller, John Pollock, (Malster), Wm Irwin, Jonathan Holmes, Samuel Hay and William Lamb to view the premises and if they or any four of them do see necessary lay out the same by courses and distances the least injurious to private property and make report of their proceedings to next Sessions.

Petition of sundry of the inhabitants of Westpennsborough Township setting forth to the Court that they labor under many inconveniences for want of a publick road leading from W. Thompsons Mills through a lane between Captain William Thompson, John McClure, and Alexander Parker, the road that ran there formerly has been ___ for some time past and praying the court to appoint proper men to view the premises and lay out a publick road as aforesaid the court do appoint Wm Thompson, John McClure, John Davis (senior), William Coughran, Wm Clark, and John Forbes to view the premises

and if they or any 4 of them do see cause to lay out the same as a publick road
that they lay out the same by courses and distances in a manner the least
injurious to private property and __ conducive to the publick good and make
report of their proceedings to next Court.

Page 196
Petition of sundry of the inhabitants of Newton and Westpennsborough
Townships setting forth to the court that they labor under many inconveniences
for want of a publick raod the nearest and best way from Hugh Torances to
John __ Mills and from thence to John Dennies __ upon Conodogwainet creek
and from thence to Carlisle and praying the Court to appoint proper men to
view and lay out a publick road as aforesaid the court do appoint Erekiel
Dunning, Andrew McFarlane, John Bowman, James Laughlin, Allen Leeper
and Thomas Guy to view the premises and if they or any 4 of them do see cause
to lay out the same as a publick road that they lay out the same distances in a
manner the least injurious to private property and most conducive to the
publick good, make report of their proceedings to next Court.

Upon the petition of the inhabitants of Guilford, Hamilton, and Letterkenny
townships, setting forth that they labor under inconvenience for want of a road,
the nighest and best way between the Falling Spring Meeting House and the
Rocky Spring Meeting House and praying the Court to appoint men to view
and lay out a public road as aforesaid. The Court appoints Samuel Lindsay,
John Alexander, James Finley, William Bear (Rocky Spring), William Lindsay,
Simon and John Neilson to view and lay out the same, etc.

Page 197
Upon the petition of the inhabitants of Peters, Hamilton, and Antrim townships,
setting forth that they labor under great inconvenience for want of a road
beginning at John McDowell's mill, from thence the nighest and best course to
the great road leading from Carlisle to Watkins Ferry on Potomac river at
Charles McCormick's and praying the Court to appoint viewers. The Court
appoints William Hallowday, George Brown, William Bryans, James
Campbell, Jacob Cook, and Poe to view and lay out the road as aforesaid.

Petition of sundry of the inhabitants of Westpennsbough township setting forth
that they labor under many inconveniences for want of a publick road from the
interior parts of said townships leading toward Baltimore, praying the Court to
appoint men to view and lay out a road from the late dwelling house of John
McClure near McClures Gap the nearest and best way to James Weakleys
Merchant Mill and from thence to Trents Gap. Appoint William Clark, William
Carrothers, Robert Walker, Junior, James Byers, John McClure yellow
Britches, and John McClure to view the premises and if they or any 4 of them
do see cause to lay out the same as a publick road that they lay it out by courses
in a manner the least injurious to private property and most conducive to the
publick good and make report of their proceedings to next Court.

Page 198

Court of Private Sessions, at Carlisle on 25 March 1772 before Jonathan Hoge.
Allen Township; Constable; John Nailer; Supr. of Roads- Moses Starr, Jas
Gregory; Overseers of Poor- Rowland Chambers, Wm Abernathy
Antrim Township; Constable- Geo Minser; Supr. of Roads- Wm Benkin,
Gasper Hallan; Overseers of Poor- Wm Hannah, Jas Coyle; Viewers
of Fences- John Wallace, Roger Start
Carlisle Township; Constable- Jonath. Kearsley; Supr. of Roads- Jacob Taylor,
Anthony Harwick; Overseers of Poor- James Pollock, Chris Vanlear
Amagh Township; Constable- Wm Dixon; Sup.of Roads- Henry Taylor, Jas
Reed; Overseers of Poor- John Fleming, J. McKibbens
Derry Township; Constable- Ken Diermond; Supr. of Roads- John Carnshalk,
Daniel Jones; Overseers of Poor- Jas Huston, Thos Howard; Viewers
of Fences- J. Carnshalk, Thos Martin
East Penns Township; Constable- James Waugh; Supr. of Roads- Thos
McCormick, Isaac Hendericks
Fermanagh Township; Constable- David Wright; Supr. of Roads- Jas Purdee,
Fred Swagarthy; Overseers of Poor- John Reed, Robt Aiken; Viewers
of Fences- Hugh McCormick, John Bonir
Guilford Township; Constable- Mathew Wilson; Supr. of Roads- John Keer,
James Bannicks; Overseers of Poor- John Andrews, John Harmony;
Viewers of Fences- Wm Long, Gil Crawford
Fannet Township; Constable- Allan Brown; Supr. of Roads- James Elliot, Ja.
Andrie; Overseers of Poor- Alex McCormick, Alex McConnel;
Viewers of Fences- Robt Lawther, Noah Abraham
Hamilton Township; Constable- Isaac Patterson; Supr. of Roads- Thos Knox,
Thos Freeman; Overseers of Poor- Wm McBrien, Rich Benson
Hopewell Township; Constable- Jas Burns; Supr. of Roads- Andrew Boyd,
David Mills; Overseers of Poor- Wm Duncan, Jos Brady; Viewers of
Fences- Wm Trimble, Jas Caldwell

Page 199

Letterkenny Township; Constable- Wm Baird; Supr. of Roads- John Stevenson,
Wm Smith; Overseers of Poor- John Mahan, Alex McConnel;
Viewers of Fences- Jas Kelly, John Nelson
Lurgan Township; Constable- Robt Peoples; Supr. of Roads- Arthr Clarke,
Abram Wier; Overseers of Poor- Alex Starrel, Adam Turner; Viewers
of Fences- John McKongle, William Turner
Lack Township; Constable- Fran Innis; Supr. of Roads- Wm Arbuckle, Jacob
Pyat; Overseers of Poor- Jas Gray, Jas Stone; Viewers of Fences-
Thos Keer, John McInt_
Middleton Township; Constable- David Drennan; Supr. of Roads- Robt
Sanderson, Thos Mahaffy; Overseers of Poor- Mathw Wilson,
Mathew Kenny
Newtown Township; Constable- Daniel McDonald; Supr. of Roads- John
McCintoch; Overseers of Poor- John Carnahan, John Bowman

Peters Township: Constable- David Brown; Supr. of Roads- Wm Kuston, Rowland Harris; Overseers of Poor- Robt Fleming, Wm McDowel; Viewers of Fences- John Welsh, Robt Scots

Rye Township; Constable- Andw Irwin; Supr. of Roads- John Giles, John McDoy; John McDoy- John Mitchel, Robt Nicholson; Viewers of Fences- Saml Galbraith, Wm Parkenson

Penns Township; Constable- Boston Cashiller; Supr. of Roads- John Ploutz, Michl Weaver

Toboyne Township; Constable- Saml Brown; Supr. of Roads- John Clark, Jas Adams; Overseers of Poor- John McNair, Anthw Morrison; Viewers of Fences- Robt Hunter, Wm Gardner

Tyrone Township; Constable- John Black; Supr. of Roads- Alex Reddy, Henry Cunningham; Viewers of Fences- Dav McClure, Andrew Samson

West Penn Township; Constable- Saml Brice; Supr. of Roads- Geo Brown, Andw Miller; Overseers of Poor- Wm Clarke, Geo Davison; Viewers of Fences- Andrw McFarland, John Forbes

Millford Township; Constable- William Erwin; Supr. of Roads- William Bell, Alex Robinson; Overseers of Poor- Chas Pollock, Robt Taylor; Viewers of Fences- Davd McNeir, Jas Armstrong

Greenwood Township; Constable- Philip Donnelly; Supr. of Roads- Wm English, Joseph Martin; Overseers of Poor- John Kipner, Mathias Gray

Page 200- blank

Page 201

1. Beginning at Carlisle, at the Walnut Bottom to Shippensburg, July '76.
2. Beginning at the western part of Shermans Valley to Moore's Mill October 1769.
3. Beginning at Chambers Mill to Carlisle Iron Works, October 1768.
4. Beginning at Robert Hemmings Mill, to Allen Killough's April, 1770.
5. Beginning at James Smith's mill, to the York county line, July 1, '76.
6. Beginning at William Houston's to Rev. William King's Meeting House July 1770.
7. Beginning at Joseph Fulton's to Rocky Spring Meeting House, Oct. 1770.
8. Beginning at Three Square Hollow to Robert Chambers Mill, Jan. 1771.
9. Beginning at Shippensburg to Cessna's Gap, April 1771.
10.Beginning at Middle Spring Meeting House to Cessna's Gap, July 1771.
11.Beginning at Paul Pierce's to John McClure's July 1771.
12.Beginning at Andrew Macbeth's to William Henderson's, July 1771.
13.Beginning at Crogham's Gap to Obadiah Garwood's Mill, July 1771.
14.Beginning at Colter's saw mill to the provincial line, near Allen Brown's, July 1771.
15.Beginning at Yellow Breeches to the road leading from Harris' Ferry to Carlisle, Oct. 1771.
   Bounding of Tyrone township, by John Davis, Oct. 1771.

16.Beginning at Carlisle by Graighead's Mill to Ford's Gap in the South Mountain, 1771.

17.Beginning at Carlisle Commons across Latort Spring through Pomfret street, Oct.1771.

18.Beginning at Letort spring to the York County line by Dill's tavern, October 1771.

19.Beginning at Charles Kilgore's by James Carothers, to Moores Mill, January 1772.

20.Beginning at Middle Spring Meeting House by Herron Ford to Shippensburg, January 1772.

21.Beginning at the road near McClure's Gap and Smith's Mill to Smith's Gap, April 1772.

22.Beginning at the York County line in Black's Gap by way of Chambersburg to James Campbell. October 1772.

Quarter Session Docket 5 1772-1776

Page 1

At Carlisle, 21 April 1772, before John Armstrong and his associates.

The Sheriff, Ephraim Blain, returns the following panel of grand jurors: John McClure, Robert Robb, Richard Parker, Ezekiel Dunning, George Brown, William Flemming, William Moore, William Gap, William Watson, Thomas McCormick, William Abernathy, Andrew Holmes, Samuel Williamson, William Smith, John Young, James Irwin, Matthew Miller, Edward Weakly, John Moore, Andrew Miller, William Davison, James Parker.

Page 2 April Sessions 1772
The King vs Hugh McCurdy

Assault and battery on John Potts the younger. January 1773 defendant retracts his plea and submits to the Court protesting his Innocence. Judgment that the defendant Hugh McCurdy is fined 2 shillings and six pence and pay costs of prosecution.

The same vs the same

Assault and battery on Elizabeth Potts. January 1773 defendant retracts his plea and submits to the Court protesting his innocence. Judgment defendant Hugh McCurdy is fined 2 shillings and six pence and pay costs of prosecution.

The same vs the same

Assault and battery on Alexander Potts. anuary 1773 defendant retracts his plea and submits to the Court protesting his innocence. The Judgment of the Court is that the defendant Hugh McCurdy is fined two shillings and six pence and pay costs of prosecution.

Page 3
The King vs Philip Hutchinson

Assault and battery on Jane Johnston. October 1772 on Motion of Wm Nelson defendant retracts his pleas submitting to the Court but protesting his innocence. Ordered defendant Philip Hutchinson be fined[blank] pay the costs of prosecution stand committed until the whole be complied with.

The King vs Moses Kirkpatrick

Assault and Battery on William Armstrong. January Term 1773 Jury; David Bell, Joseph Hudson, William Gaddis, Mathew Loudon, James McCurdy, Thomas Donaldson, William Marshal, William Brooks, Joseph McClure, Nathaniel Wilson, Samuel Lam and James McCormick say that the defendant Moses Kirkpatrick is guilty, fined 10 shillings.

The King vs Joseph Kirkpatrick
Assault and battery on William Armstrong. January 1773 defendant retracts his plea, submits to the Court protesting his innocence, fined 2 shillings and six pence, pay costs of prosecution.

Page 4 April Sessions 1772
The King vs John McCrea
Fornication and bastardy with Mary Quillan.

The King vs Mary Quillan
Fornication & bastardy with John McCrea.

The King vs Joseph Kirkpatrick
Assault and battery on William Faith.

Page 5
The King vs Joseph Kirkpatrick
Assault and battery on Joseph Patterson.

The King vs Margt Glap
Assault and battery

The King vs George Anderson et al
Forcible entry and detainer.

The King vs Joseph Kirkpatrick
Assault and battery on Elenor Farrel.

The same vs the same
Assault and battery on John Hambright..

The King vs John Hambright
Assault and battery on Joseph Kirkpatrick.

The King vs David Sample
Assault and battery on Thos Hardley.

Page 6
The King vs Rebecca Wallace
David Wallace of Fanet Township £40, conditioned for the appearance of Rebecca Wallace at the next Court then and there to answer such things as shall be objected against her on his Majesties behalf and not depart the Court without license.

The King vs Hugh McCurdy
Hugh McCurdy £40, Hugh Cook £20, conditioned for the appearance of Hugh McCurdy at the next General Court of Quarter Sessions to be held at Carlisle for the County of Cumberland then and there to answer such things as shall be objected against him on his Majesties behalf and not depart the Court without license.

The King vs Michael Coleman
Michael Coleman £40
Andrew Jones of Tyrone Township £20, conditioned for the appearance of Michael Coleman at the next Court then and there to answer such things as shall be objected against him on his Majesties behalf and not depart the Court without license.

The King vs Philip Hutchinson
William Gamble of Fannet Township £40, conditioned for the appearance of Philip Hutchinson at the next Court then and there to answer such things as shall be objected against him on his Majesties behalf and not depart the Court without license.

Page 7 April Sessions 1772
The King vs William Hunter and Thomas Miller
Samuel Irwin £20, conditioned for the appearance at the next Court then and there to testify on his Majesties behalf and depart the Court without license.

The King vs William Gamble
William Gamble £40, Nathaniel Paul of Fanet Town £20, conditioned for the appearance of William Gamble at the next Court then and there to answer such things as shall be objected against him on his Majesties behalf and not depart the Court without licence and in the mean time keep the peace and be of good behaviour to all his Majesties l__ subjects and especially to Arthur McMichael then this Re__ to be void otherwise to be and remain in full force and virtue.

The King vs Philip Hutchinson
Hugh Johnston £20, conditioned for the appearance of Jane Johnston at the next Court then and there to testify on his Majesties behalf and not depart the Court without license.

The King vs Joseph Kirkpatrick and Moses Kirkpatrick
Joseph Kirkpatrick £40, Moses Kirkpatrick £40, James Lee £20, conditioned for the appearance of Joseph Kirkpatrick and Moses Kirkpatrick at the next Court then and there to answer such things as shall be objected against them on his Majesties behalf and not depart the Court without license.

Page 8 April Sessions 1772
The King vs Joseph Kirkpatrick & Moses Kirkpatrick
George Sanderson £40. William Faith £40, conditioned for their appearance at the next Court then and there to testify on his Majesties behalf and depart the Court without license.

The King vs Elizabeth McLucas
Recognizance of her self and Archibald Ros for her bail filed and forfeited.

The King vs Nicholas Young
Recognizance of him and Jacob Cart his bail filed and forfeited.

The King vs Thomas Martin
Recognizance filed and forfeited.

Upon application of Robert Guthrie Senr to the Court his is discharged from his bail.

Upon Motion to the Court, the Court order that all the proceedings in regard to roads petitioned for by John Lush and James Smith be quashed.

Page 9
Petition of sundry of the inhabitants of Westpennsboro township to the Court Setting forth that they labor under many inconveniences for want of a road leading from James Smiths Mill to Fall in the Walnut Bottom Road where the old road and new to Carlisle meet. Praying the Court to appoint men to view and lay out a publick road, appointed John Mitchel, Jonathan Homes, Robert Urie, James Parker, Thomas Craighead and Richard Parker to view the premises and if they or any one of them do see cause to lay out the same that they lay out the same by courses and distances the nighest and best way in a manner the least injurious to private property and most conducive to the publick good and make report of their proceedings to next Court.

Upon the petition of sundry of the inhabitants of Eastpennsborough and Middleton Townships in the Court of Cumberland to the Court setting forth that they labor under many inconveniences for want of a publick road leading from Carlisle to Harris's Ferry by William Chamber's, Justice Hogis, Ephramin Blain Esquires and Tobias Hendricks some part of the road now used by the aforesaid inhabitants not being laid out by order of Court. Praying the Court to appoint proper men to view and lay out a publick road as aforesaid. Court do appoint James Galbraith, David Hoge. Edward Morton, Robert Callender, John Sample. and William Chesney to view the premises and if they or any four see cause to lay out the same, that they lay out the same by courses and distances the nighest and best way in a manner the least injurious to private property and most conducive to the publick utility and make report of their proceedings to next Court.

Upon the petition of the inhabitants of Middleton Township the town of
Carlisle and Shermans valley to the Court setting forth that they labor under
many inconveniences for want of a publick road from Carlisle to the Forty
Shilling Gap there being no tolerable way of passing or repassing to Shermans
Valley without going by Crohans which is found to be very impracticable. And
praying the Court to appoint proper men to view and lay out a Great road the
nearest and best way from the north end of Hanvover Street in the Town of
Carlisle to

Page 10
the alley between James Pollock and James Stackpoles lots, from thence to the
Cove and Ford and from thence the nearest and best way to the Forty Shilling
Gap. The Court do appoint William Miller, James Pollock, John Davis Junior,
John Dinsmore, John Mitchel and John Pollock to view the premises and if
they or any four of them see cause to lay out the same that they lay out the
same by courses and distances the nighest and best way, in a manner the least
injurious to private property and most conducive to publick utility and make
report of their proceedings to next court.

Upon the petition of the inhabitants of Peters township in this county of
Cumberland, setting forth that they labor under difficulties for want of a road
leading from the house of John Work to Archibald Irwin's Mill, and from the
said mill to the great road leading to Baltimore, such a road would be of great
convenience to the inhabitants of said township, carrying their produce to
market. Appointed William Smith, James Maxwell, William Dunwoody,
Robert McFarland, John McClellan and William Houston to view the premises
and if they see cause, lay out a road.

Upon the petition of the inhabitants of Guilford and Hamilton townships in the
county of Cumberland, setting forth that they are much aggrieved about a road
leading from Falling Spring Meeting House to Rocky Spring Meeting House
which answers no public end, and laid out on such bad ground that it would be
attended with great expense to uphold, and as a road leading from Falling
Spring to Robert Dukson's mill is now opened which answers the same end,
and as it is laid out on much better ground, praying the Court to grant them a
review of the premises. Appointed James Eaton, William Swan, Thomas Baird,
Patrick Vance, James McCammon and Robert Duckson to review the premises,
and if they see necessary, to lay out a road as aforesaid, that they lay out the
same by courses and distances the nearest and best way and make report of
their proceedings to the next Court.

Page 11 April Sessions 1772
The persons appointed at Last January Court to view and if they should see
cause lay out a road leading from Canidogu Creek along the line running
between Capt. William Thompsons land and the lands of Alexander Parker and
John McClure into the Road laid out from Carlisle Town to John Schoolers

Mill Returned to the Court the said road is viewed and laid out by them according to the following courses and distances viz, begging at Conadoquet Creek north 3 ½ degrees west 197 perches along the line as aforesaid north 45 degrees west 80 perches to the road from Carlisle to Schoolers Mill Which road viewed and laid out as aforesaid the said persons viz William Thompson, John McClure, John Davis, William Clark, John Forbes.

Upon the petition of sundry of the inhabitants of Antrim township in the county of Cumberland, setting forth that they labor under disadvantage for want of an established public road from the Rev. Mr. James Long's to the meeting house at William Rankin's, apprehend the same would not be hurtful to any farm through which it passes, also engage to keep it in repair at their private expense, such a road laid out would be of great utility to many individuals as a road leading to Matthews Ferry on Potomac as a place of public worship, and pray the Court to appoint viewers. Appointed George Brown, James Pollock, Samuel Lindsay, Matthew Wilson, John Vance, and William Ranklin to view, and if they see cause, lay out the road and make report to the next Court.

Page 12
Cockran now returned to this Court as a publick road highly necessary and of public utility, laid out in a manner the least injurious to private property and most conducive to the publick good which said return being now taken into consideration is approved of by the Court. Ordered the road laid out be cut cleared and bridged if necessary by the several supervisors of the respective townships through which the said road runs forthwith the breadth of thirty feet.

The persons appointed at last January Court to view and lay out a road from Capt. Robert Callinders Mill at the mouth of Letart Spring the nearest and best road leading past the Iron works thro' Mehaffy's Gap in the South Mountain to the York County line. Returned that the road laid out by them according to the following courses, beginning at Letort Spring south 48 degrees east 118 perches south 34 degrees east 106 perches south 2 ½ degrees west 1432 perches south 53 degrees east 49 perches south 34 degrees east 76 perches south 29 degrees west 40 perches south 22 degrees east 74 perches south 12 degrees east 48 perches south 22 degrees west 109 perches south 20 degrees west 460 perches south 43 ½ degrees west 111 perches south 15 degrees west 33 perches through Mahaftys Gap in the South Mountain to the York County line being eight miles one quarter and sixteen perches. Road viewed and laid out as aforesaid the said persons, John Pollock, Jonathan Homes, Samuel Hay, William Lamb and William Miller now returned to the court as a publick road highly necessary and of publick utility and is laid out in a manner the least injurious to private property and most conducive to the publick interest which said __ being taken into consideration is accordingly approved of and confirmed by the Court. Ordered the road laid out as aforesaid be cut cleared and bridged if necessary by the several supervisors of the respective townships through which the said runs forth with of the breadth of 33 feet wide.

Page 13 April Sessions 1772

The persons appointed at last October Sessions to view and lay out a road from Logans Gap in Armagh township to the road already laid out and from thence to William Millers in the township aforesaid, Returned to the Court the said road as viewed and laid out by them according to the following courses and distances viz beginning at t popular in the East end of Keshocaquillas Valley near Logans Gap and from thence by Courses and distances as follows viz south 10 degrees west 170 perches to white pine south 7 degrees east 64 perches to white pine south 17 degrees west 64 perches to hickory south 36 degrees west 216 perches to hickory south 20 degrees wet 130 perches to black oak south thirty nine degrees west 92 perches to white pine south 25 degrees west 174 perches to white oak south 45 degrees west 168 perches to hickory crossed a branch of water 106 perches south 60 degrees west 40 perches to white oak south 20 degrees 96 perches to white oak south 13 degrees west 81 perches to hickory south 20 degrees west 130 perches to black oak south 27 degrees west 360 perches to white oak south 39 degrees west 92 perches to white south 56 degrees west 200 perches to black oak south 40 degrees west 60 perches to white oak south 49 degrees west 98 perches to black oak south 31 degrees west 36 perches to Elm south 19 degrees east 24 perches to Walnut south 38 degrees west 28 perches to White Oak south 2 degrees west 20 perches to white oak that stands between William Brown Esqr and James Read north 67 degrees west 14 perches to ___ tree north 40 degrees west 21 perches to black oak north 45 degrees west 92 perches to white oak at ten perches Crosses the middle branch of the Shacoquillis South 58 degrees west 404 perches to post south 52 degrees west 58 perches to Elm south 55 degrees west 104 perches to white oak at 80 perches cross Teafs Branch south 40 degrees west 265 perches to hickory south 45 degrees west 72 perches to white oak south 40 west 76 perches to walnut south 47 west 150 perches to walnut south 43 degrees west 86 perches to spanish oak south 60 degrees west 832 perches

Page 14

to black oak at 274 perches cross the Ledar Spring south 20 degrees west 312 perches to white oak north 88 degrees west 61 perches to hickory south 64 degrees wet 86 perches to post at 23 perches crosses Greenwood Spring South 69 degrees west forty perches to white oak south 60 degrees west 100 perches to white oak south 20 degrees west 98 perches to white oak south 39 degrees west 218 perches to hickory south 53 degrees west 318 perches to white oak south 40 degrees west 1098 perches to white oak in the west end of the proprietors survey which road viewed and laid out as aforesaid the said persons viz, Henry Taylor, Joseph Makibben, William McNott, and James Reed now returned to the Court as a publick road highly necessary and of publick utility and is laid out in a manner the least injurious to private property. most conducive to the publick interest. approved by the Court. Ordered the road laid out as aforesaid be cut cleared, bridged if necessary by the several supervisors of the respective townships through which the said road runs forthwith of the breadth of thirty three feet wide.

The persons appointed at last January Court to view and lay out a road from the late dwelling house of John McClure to James Weakleys Mill and from thence to Trents Gap and returned to the Court the said road was viewed and laid out by them according to the following courses, beginning at a white oak at John McClures road on the lands of John Davidson thence south 31 degrees west 227 perches thence south 60 degrees east 282 perches thence south 45 degrees east 440 perches thence south 30 degrees east 420 perches to the Mill thence south 25 degrees east 520 perches to the Baltimore Road near Trents Gap which road viewed and laid out as aforesaid the said persons viz James Byers, Wm Clark,

Page 15
William Caruthers and John McClure now returned to the Court as a publick road highly necessary and of publick utility and is laid out in manner the least injurious to private property and the most conducive to the publick interest which said return being taken into consideration is accordingly approved of and confirmed by the Court upon this condition only that Weakley his heirs or assigns agreeable to his own proposal do make or cause to be made a sufficient Bridge over Yellow Britches Creek fit for carriages and keep the same in good repair during the continuance of said road and also at all time hereafter keep in repair the road leading from said Mill to the Walnut Bottom road at his or their own expense And it is further ordered that the said road laid out as aforesaid be cut cleared and bridged if necessary (saving the Bridge as aforesaid over Yellow Britches Creek) by the several supervisors of the respective townships through which the said road runs forth with of the breath of 33 feet wide.

The persons appointed at last January Court to view and lay out a road from Hugh Torrance's to John Scoullers Mills from __ John Dennie's Ford on Canedogwinet creek and from thence to Carlisle and returned to this Court the said road as viewed and laid out by them according to the following courses and distances, beginning at a new schoolhouse at Hugh Torrance's, south 53 and ½ degrees east 120 perches south 62 degrees east 40 perches south 49 degrees east 60 perches south 55 degrees east 110 perches south 60 degrees east 110 perches south 21 degrees east 46 perches south 40 degrees east 106 perches south 74 degrees east 26 perches south 56 degrees east 104 perches south 25 degrees east 40 perches south 2 degrees east 80 perches south 83 degrees east 72 perches north 8 degrees east 500 perches south 60 degrees east 68 perches north 85 degrees east 26 perches north 59 degrees east 24 perches north 53 degrees east 132 perches north 38 degrees east 42 perches south 60 degrees east 88 perches south 89 east 586 perches north 81 and 1/4 east 149 perches north 84

Page 16
128 perches south 86 east 136 perches south 75 degrees east 64 perches south 83 degrees east 84 perches south 78 degrees east 90 perches north 86 degrees east 292 perches south 67 ½ degrees east 30 perches north 65 degrees east 80

perches south 38 degrees east 34 perches south 87 degrees east 36 perches
south 85 degrees east 80 perches south 24 east 102 perches south 88 ½ east 286
perches south 81 ½ east 380 perches to Carlisle which road viewed and laid out
as aforesaid the said persons viz James Laughlin, Andrew McFarlane, John
Bowman, and Ezikeil Dunning now returned to the Court as a publick road
highly necessary and of publick utility and is laid out in a manner the least
injurious to private property and the most conducive to the publick interest
which said return being taken into consideration is accordingly approved of ad
confirmed by the Court and it is further ordered that the said road laid out as
aforesaid be cut cleared and bridged if necessary by the several supervisors of
the respective townships through which the said road runs forthwith of the
breadth of 33 feet wide.

The King vs John McCrea

The Same vs Charles McCormick

The Same vs William Hunter & Thos Miller

The Same vs Isaac Winn

The Same vs James Moore

Page 17
At Carlisle, 2 July 1772.
The sheriff, Ephraim Blain, returns the following panel of grand jurors; Samuel
Naylor, Stephen Duncan, James Pollock, John Pollock, Joseph Spear, Charles
McClure, Robert McKinzie, William Blair, John Boyd, John Kinkead, John
Wilkins, Joseph Wallace, Samuel Porter, John Pollock (carpenter), Ephraim
Steel, John Glen, William Brown, Ralph Naylor, Robert Gibson, William
Denny, Andrew Colhoone, John Grier, Charles Cooper, James Shannon.

Page 18 July Session 1772
The King vs Michael Brandon
Misdemeanor. Jury; John Creigh, James Davis, John Gray, Michael Finlay,
John Johnston, John Murdock, Anthony Harwick, George Hamilton, George
Loge, John Norris, James McClintock, and John Dickson do say that the
prisoner Michale Brandon is guilty. Ordered that he receive 39 lashes on his
bare back tomorrow between the hours of 12 and 4 of the clock, on Saturday
the first day of August next stand in the pillory two hours between the hours of
12 and 2 of the clock, stand committed until the whole be complied with.

The King vs Joseph Challerlon
Felony. Ordered that the defendant restore the goods stolen to the owner if not
already done that he pay the like value of the goods stolen to the Governor for
support of Government pay the costs of prosecution that he receive 21 lashes

on his bare back at the publick whipping post tomorrow between the hours of 12 and 2 of the clock find two sureties in the sum of 100 pounds for one year and stand committed till the whole be performed.

Page 19
The King vs Enoch Rose
Felony.

The Same vs William Kelso
Assault and battery. October 1772 the defendant By George Ross his attorney submits to the Court protesting his innocence. Judgement that the defendant William Kelso be fined 7 shillings ad six pence pay the costs of prosecution and stand in the custody of the Sheriff until the whole be complied with.

The Same vs James Huey
Assault and battery. October 1772, jury; William Carrothers, William Gettiz, Alexander McBridge, James Irwine, David Blaine, James Wilson, James Gordon, Alexander __ine, John Gregg, Alexander McGeeghan, John Campbell and Andrew Miller say that James Huey is guilty, fined 1 shilling pay costs of prosecution.

Page 20 July Sessions 1772
The King vs James McCabe
Assault and battery.

The Same vs John Cogdon
Felony.

The Same vs William Hunter
William Hunter £50, Robert Cannon of Allan Town £25, conditioned for the appearance of William Hunter at the next Court then and there to answer such things as shall be objected against him on his Majesties behalf and not depart the Court without licence.

The Same vs Hugh McCurdy
Elizabeth Potts £40, Samuel Kearsley £20, conditioned for the appearance of Elizabeth Potts at the next Court then and there to testify on his Majesties behalf and not depart the Court without license.

The Same vs William Kelso
Robert Russell £20, conditioned for his appearance at the next Court then and there to testify on his Majesties behalf and not depart the Court without license.

Page 21
The King vs Moses Kirkpatrick
Joseph Kirkpatrick £40, Andrew Irwin £40

The Same vs Joseph Kirkpatrick
Conditioned for the appearance of Joseph Kirkpatrick and Moses Kirkpatrick at
the next Court then and there to answer such things as shall be objected against
them on this Majesties behalf and not depart the Court without licence.

The Same vs Moses Kirkpatrick
William Armstrong £20, Thomas Moore £10, conditioned for the appearance
of William Armstrong at the next Court then and there to testify on his
Majesties behalf and not depart the Court without licence.

The Same vs Morgan McIwine
George Loge of Carlisle £100, conditioned for the appearance of Morgan
McIwine at the next Court then and there to answer all such things as shall be
objected against them on his Majesties behalf, not depart the Court without
licence.

The Same vs James Huey
James Huey £40, James McCall £20, conditioned for the appearance of James
Huey at the next Court to answer such things as shall be objected against him
on his Majesties Behalf and not depart the Court without licence.

Page 22 July Sessions 1772
Hugh McCurdy being three times solemnly called to appear appeareth not
forfeits his recognizance.

Hugh Cook being three times solemnly called to bring forth the body of Hugh
McCurdy bringth not forth forfeits his recognizance.

Hugh Johston being three times solemnly called to bring forth the body of Jane
Johnston bringeth not forth forfeits his recognizance.

William Gamble being three times called to bring forth the body of Philip
Hutchison bringeth not forth and forfeits his recognizance.

James Forsyth being three times solemnly called to appear appeareth not
forfeits his recognizance.

Henry Coyle being three times called to bring forth the body of James Forsyth
bringeth not forth and forfeits his recognizance.

Alexander Culbertson and John Hamilton being three time solemnly and
separately called to appear to testify on his Majesties against a Certain James
Forsyth appeared not forfeited their recognizance.

Page 23

John Pollock, John Gray, Tobas Kendericks, John Miller, Christopher Van Lear, James David, Ralph Nailer, Robert Jack, William Peoples, Duncan McDonald, William Kelso, James Pollock, William McCune, Henry Gordon, Robert Hamill, John Miller Blacks Gap, Nicholas Young, Arthur Buchanan, Mary McCormick, John Johnston having petitioned the Court to be recommended to his Honour the Governour for his licence to keep publick houses of entertainment. The Court taking the same petitions under consideration the said John Pollock, John Gray, Tobias Hendericks, John Miller, Christopher Vanlear, James Daves, Ralph Nailer, Robert Jack, William Peoples, Robert Galbraith, William Smith, John McCardy, George Menser, Duncan McDonald, William Kelso, James Pollock, William McCune, Henry Gordon, Robert Harnel, John Miller, Nicholas Young, Arthur Buchanan, Mary McCormick, John Johnston were accordingly recommended and allowed. Jacob Sailer, William Chambers, William Morrow, William Keppy allowed also Conrad Beamer beer licence. The following petitioned at Jan Sessions 1773 William Niels and John Calvert.

Petition of sundry subscribers to the Court setting forth that they are greatly Interrupted in their way to Carlisle on account of the many clearings of out lots by the Inhabitants thereof who year after year fence up the accustomed road and also stop the alleys by means whereof they are held to many great difficulties they having had a review three times and yet not road granted them and praying the Court to appoint proper men to review a road from Carlisle to the House of Andrew Holmes. The Court do appoint William Miller, Robert McKinzie, James Pollock, Mathew Laird, and James Henry to review the Premises and if they or any four of them to see necessary to lay out a road as aforesaid that they lay out the same by courses and distances the nearest and best way the least Injurious to private property and most conducive to the publick good and make report to next Court.

Page 24 July Sessions 1772

Petition of sundry inhabitants of Shermans Valley to the Court saying that a Waggon Road from Mr. Wests Mill to Baskins Ferry on Susquehana would be of the great Benefit and utility to the said inhabitants and praying the Court to appoint proper men to view and lay out a wagon road as aforesaid. Appointed William Power, Robert Magaghy, Frederick Watt, Finley McCoune. Thomas Bernet and Richard Coller to view the premises and if they or any 4 of them see necessary to lay out a road as aforesaid that they lay out the same by courses and distances the nearest and best way the least injurious to private property and most conducive to publick utility and make report to next Court.

Upon the petition of a number of the inhabitants of the Town of Carlisle and Middleton Township to the Court setting forth that a wagon road is much wanted from the north end of Bedford street of the said Town leading to Robert Robbs Fording on Condequinne Creek and from thence to Cranes Gap of the

North Mountain and praying the Court to appoint proper men to view the premises and layout a wagon road as aforesaid. Appointed James Pollock, John Pollock, James Davis, John Davis, Junr, Robert Sanderson and David Drennan to view the premises and if they or any four of them see cause they lay out the same by courses and distances the nighest and best way the least injurious to private property and most conducive to the publick utility and make report to next Court.

Page 25
Petition of sundry of the inhabitants of Newtown and Westpennsborrough Townships to the Court setting forth that a wagon road from the three Square hollow above Robert McCombs in the North Mountain the greatest and best way to Chamber's Mill and from thence to John Piper Mill and to James Smiths gap in the South Mountain is much wanted and praying the Court to appoint proper men to view and lay out a wagon road as aforesaid. Appointed James Task, Robert McComb, John Piper, John Siven, Robert Bell, and James Carnahan to view the premises and if they or any four of them see necessary to lay out a wagon road as aforesaid that they lay out the same by courses and distances the nighest and best way the least injurious to private property and most conducive to publick utility and make report to next Court.

Petition of several of the inhabitants of Middleton Township to the Court setting forth that they labor under many inconveniences for want of a great road leading from the Town of Carlisle to Hurly's Gap to begin at the north end of Pitt Street from thence the nighest and best way to the dwelling house of John Mitchell from thence to Cross Canedogwenet Creek at David Williamsons Fording and from thence the nighest and best way to the said Gaps keeping as nigh as possible to the old bridle road from Carlisle to said Gap, praying the Court to appoint proper men to view and lay out the same as aforesaid. Appointed Andrew Holmes, Mathew Miller, Samuel Laird, James Sharron, Richard Parker, and Mathew Gregg to view the premises, if they or any four of them see cause to lay out a road as aforesaid they lay out the same by courses and distances the least injurious to private property and most conducive to publick utility and make report to next Court.

Page 26 July Sessions 1772
Petition of sundry of the inhabitants of Middleton and West pennsborrough Township to the Court setting forth that there is a necessary for a publick road from the Town of Carlisle to the Mills of John Holmes, Esquire to begin at the Town of Carlisle of the nearest and best way to the Mills aforesaid by the house of Captain William Thompson, praying the Court appoint proper men to view and lay out a publick road as aforesaid the Court do appoint John McClure, William Clark, William Cockran, John Davis Junr, James Pollock and Christopher Vanlear to view the premises and if they or any four of them see cause to layout the same by courses and distances the nighest and best way the least injurious to private property and most conducive to publick utility.

The persons appointed at last April Sessions by the Court to view and lay out a road from the Forty Shillings Gap in the North Mountain to Carlisle returned to the Court the said road as viewed and laid out by them according to the following courses and distances, beginning at a white oak in the Forty Shilling Gap thence south 38 degrees east 190 perches thence south 32 degrees east 120 perches, south 54 degrees east 38 perches south 25 degrees east 30 perches, south 50 degrees east 18 perches south 65 degrees east 27 perches, south 41 degrees east 81 perches, south 55 degrees, east 54 perches, south 67 degrees, east 46 perches south 33 degrees east 90 perches, south 63 degrees east 52 perches, south 38 degrees east 18 perches south 29 degrees east 68 perches south 50 degrees east 34 perches south 35 degrees east 160 perches, south 25 degrees east 40 perches, south 5 degrees east 58 perches, south 53 degrees east 64 perches, south 35 degrees, east 45 perches south 22 degrees east 54 perches south 80 degrees east 32 perches to Connedegqinet Creek and across the same, thence south 47 degrees East 32 perches, south 28 degrees east 80 perches south 25 degrees west 16 perches and south 8 degrees

Page 27
west 37 perches to an out lot belonging Duncan McDonald and from thence to the Court house of Carlisle 368 perches being 5 miles and a half and 64 perches which road viewed and laid out as aforesaid the said persons viz John Pollock, John Davis Junr, John Dinsmore, William Miller, James Pollock and John Mitchel now returned to this Court as a publick road highly necessary and of publick utility and by them laid out in a manner the least injurious to private property, most conducive to the publick good which said return being now taken into consideration is accordingly approved of and confirmed by the Court and it is further ordered that the same road laid out as aforesaid be to all intents purposes a publick road and highway and the same as such be forth with opened of the breadth of 32 feet wide and cut cleared and bridged if necessary and the supervisors of the respective townships through which the said road runs are to take notice.

The King vs Hugh Fall

The Same vs John McCrea

The same vs Barthw Davis et al

The Same vs Isaac Wyne

The Same vs Charles McCormick

The Same vs James Moore

the Same vs Enoch Rose

Page 28 October Session 1772
At Carlisle, 26 October 1772, before John Armstrong and his associates.
The Sheriff, Ephraim Blain, returns the following grand jurors; William
McFarland, Thomas Butler, James Chambers, Ezekiel Dunning, James Love,
John Piper, James Brown, David King, Adam Hays, John Lusk, Charles
Leaper, David Herron, William Woods, James Carothers, John Aspy, James
Jack, James Smith, John McFarland, John Dunning, James Graham, James
Brown, Robert Walker, James Weakley, David Ralston.

Page 29
The following gentlemen having been duly impaneled by Ephram Blain, high
Sheriff of the County of Cumberland, to serve on the grand inquest; Thomas
Butler, William McFarland, James Chambers, Ezekiel Dunning, James Love,
John Piper, James Brown, David King, Adam Hays, John Lusk, Charles
Leaper, David Herron, William Woods, James Carrothers, John Espy, James
Jack, James Smith, John McFarland, John Denny, James Gr__, James Brown,
James Weakley and David Ralston having been solemnly called to appear to
serve on the inquest aforesaid and appearing not the Court order and direct that
the said Thomas Butler, William McFarland, James Chambers, Ezekiel
Dunning, James Love, John Peper, James Brown, David King, Adam Hays,
John Lusk, Charles Leaper, David Herron, William Woods, James Carrothers,
John Espy, James Jack, James Smith, John McFarland, John Denny, James
Graham, James Brown, James Weakley and David Ralston be fined in the sum
of 40 shillings each for default in not appearing first day of the Session unless
they can show sufficient cause at next January Session.

The following gentlemen having been duly impaneled and returned to try the
several causes, by Ephraim Blaine Esqr, high Sheriff of the County of
Cumberland; James Carnahan, William Carrothers, William Gaddis, Alexander
McBride, William Walk, James Wilson, Robert Hawthron, James Irwin, David
Blaine, James Gordon, John Robison, Alexander Irwin, John Gregg, Robert
Gillespie, Alexander McGeeghan, John Campbell, Andrew McCallister,
William Hodge, Thomas Wilson, __, James Denniston, Joseph Connelly,
Andrew Miller, John McClure having been solemnly called to appear and
appearing not the Court order that the said gentlemen above named be fined in
the sum of 40 shillings each for default unless they can show sufficient cause at
next January Session.

Page 30 October Sessions 1772
The King vs Enoch Nash als Bow Nash
Felony. Jury; William Carrothers, William Gillis, Alexander McBride, James
Irwin, David Blaine, James Wilson, James Gordon, Alexander Irwin, John
Gregg, Alexander McGeeghan, John Campbell and Andrew Miller say that the
defendant Enoch Nash otherwise called Bow Nash is guilty. Judgement of the
Court is that the prisoner, Enoch Nash otherwise called Bow Nash restore the
horse so stolen to the owner if not already done or pay the value thereof (viz 20

pounds) pay the costs of prosecution, pay the like value of the horse so stolen to his Honor the Governor for support of Government, stand in the pillory on the 19 day of January next the space of one hour, be publickly whipped at the publick whipping post on his bare back with 39 lashes well laid on between the hours of 10 and 4 of the clock in the afternoon, be imprisoned 1 month, stand committed until the whole be complied with.

The King vs John Griffith
Assault and battery. Defendant being charged submits to the Court protesting his innocence. Ordered John Griffith be fined 5 shillings pay the costs of prosecution and stand committed until the whole be complied with.

Page 31
The King vs John Hannah
Assault and battery on Isabella Whenie. Jury; William Carrothers, William Gettis, Alexander McBride, James Irwin, David Blaine, James Wilson, James Gordon, Alexander Irwin, John Gregg, Alexander McGeeghan, John Campbell, and Andrew Miller say that the defendant John Hannah is guilty. John Hannah be fined 2 shilling and six pence pay the costs of prosecution, find security for his good behaviour to all his Majesties subjects and in particular to Issabella Whinie for one year, stand committed until the whole be complied with.

The King vs Lawrance Sullivan
Assault on William Thomas. Defendant submits to the Court pleading his innocence, ordered that the defendant Lawrance Sullivan be fined of 6 pence, pay the costs of prosecution, stand committed until the whole be complied with.

Page 32
The King vs Jacob Hyselgeser
Felony. January 1773, jury; David Bell, Joseph Hudson, William Gaddis, Mathew Loudon, James McCurdy, Thomas Donaldson, William Marshal, William Brooks, Joseph McClure, Nathaniel Meson, Samuel Lamb and James McCormick say that the defendant is not guilty.

The King vs Thomas Pallan
Assault and battery. January Sessions 1773, defendant retracts his plea and submits to the Court protesting his Innocence. Thomas Pallan is fined 20 shillings and pay costs of prosecution.

Page 33
The Kings vs John Williamson
Assault and battery.

The King vs William McCune
Assault and battery on Francis Drake. April 1773, jury; William Duncan,
William Linn, David Sterrat, Thomas Knox, James Knox, William Thompson,
James Clark, John Stewart, Alexander McBride, William Sharp, John Dickey
and Samuel Culbertson say the defendant William McCune in guilty. Fined 10
shilling pay costs of prosecution stand committed in the custody of the Sheriff
until the whole be complied with.

Page 34 October Sessions 1772
The King vs William McCune
Assault and battery on __ Drake. April 1773, jury ; William Duncan, William
Linn, David Sterrat, Thomas Knox, James Hnose, William Thompson, James
Clark, John Stewart, Alexander McBride, William Sharp, John Duckey &
Samuel Culbertson say that the defendant William McCune is guilty. William
McCune is fined 10 shillings pay the costs of prosecution and committed in the
custody of the Sheriff until he the whole be complied with.

The King vs William McCune
Assault and battery on James Armstrong. April 1773, jury; William Duncan,
William Linn, David Sterrat, Thomas Knox, James Knox, William Thompson,
James Clark, John Stewart, Alexander McBride, William Sharp, John Dickey,
and Samuel Culbertson say that the defendant William McCune is guilty of the
assault but not of the battery whereof he stands indicted. Fined ten [nothing
indicated], pay costs of prosecution, stand committed until the whole be
complied with.

Page 35
The King vs Morgan McSwine
Assault and battery on Wm Cochran. Defendant retracts his plea submits to the
Court protesting his innocence. Fined 6 pence, costs of prosecution, stand
committed until fine and fees are paid.

The King vs Enoch Nash als Bow Nash
Felony.

The King vs Mary Myer
Assault and battery.

The King vs John Glen
Assault and battery.

The King vs Lawrance Sullivan
Felony.

Page 36 October Session 1772
The King vs John McCurdy
Tippling house.

The King vs Duncan McDonald
Tippling house.

The King vs John Johnston
Tippling house.

The King vs William Rippy
Tippling house.

The King vs James Davis
Tippling house.

The King vs Ralph Nailer
Tippling house.

The King vs Nicholas Young
Tippling house.

The King vs Sarah Montgomery
James McClintock £40, conditioned for the appearance of Sarah Montgomery
at the next Court then and there to answer such things as shall be objected
against her on his Majesties behalf and not depart the Court without licence.

Page 37 October Sessions 1772
The King vs William McCune
Thomas Drake £20, John Jack £20, conditioned for their appearance at the
next Court then and there to testify on his Majesties behalf and not depart the
Court without licence.

The King vs Joseph Kirkpatrick & Moses Kirkpatrick
Joseph Kirkpatrick£40, Moses Kirpatrick £40, James Lee £40, conditioned for
the appearance of Joseph Kirkpatrick and Moses Kirkpatrick at the next Court
then and there to answer all such things as shall be objected against them on his
Majesties behalf and not depart the Court without license.

The King vs the Same
William Faith £40, William Armstrong £40, George Sanderson £20, David
Deennan £20, conditioned for the appearance of William Faith, William
Armstrong and George Sanderson at the next Court then and there to testify on
his Majesties behalf and not depart the Court without licence.

Page 38 October Sessions 1772
The King vs Thomas Pallan
John English £40, conditioned for the appearance of Thomas Pallan at next Court then and there to answer such things as shall be objected against him on his Majesties behalf, not depart the Court without licence.

The King vs Jacob Heyselgeser
Thomas Wilson £20, Edward Owens £20, William Kinny £20, John Hamilton £20, conditioned for their respective appearance at the Court then and there to testify on his Majesties behalf, not depart the Court without licence.

The King vs William Hunter
William Hunter £40, Robert Cannon £20, conditioned for the appearance of William Hunter at the next Court then and there to answer all such things as shall be objected against him, not depart the Court without licence.

The King vs Jacob Heyselgezer
Jacob Heyselgezer £100, Robert Campbell £50, conditioned for the appearance of Jacob Heyselgezer at the next Court__ and good behaviour toward Thos Wilson.

Page 39
On motion of Mr. Stevenson the Court order that the horses taken from Bow Nash by John Moore late Constable of Westpennsburgh Township be advertised in the Pennsylvania Gazette 1 month and other publick places of the County, and if no owner appears within that time that they be then publickly sold and the price disposed as the Court shall hereafter direct.

Upon the petition of sundry of the inhabitants of Peters township to the Court, setting forth that they labor under an embarrassment for want of a road, confirmed by authority of these common places of worship, praying the Court to take their case under consideration, order proper men to view and lay out a road between William McDowell to the Meeting House now occupied by Mr. King and from thence to Robert May's to be cleared and kept in repair at the sole expense of the subscribers. The Court appointed James Campbell, William M. Ellhatton, Adam Holiday, Andrew White, Archibald Erwin, and William Scott to review the premises and if they see cause to lay out a road and make return to the next Court.

Petition of sundry inhabitants of East Pennsburgh and Middleton Townships to the Court setting forth that there is great need of a publick road from the house of Andrew Armstrong to Captain Callenders Mills in Middleton Township, praying the Court to appoint men to view and lay out a road from said Andrew Armstrong to Captain Callenders Mills aforesaid. The Court appoint Robert Callender, James Irwin, Andrew McBeath, David Bell, James McCormick and John Sample to view the premises and if they or any four of them

Page 40
see cause to lay out a road as aforesaid they lay out the same by courses and
distances the nighest and best way the least injurious to private property and
most conducive to publick utility and make report to next Court.

Petition of Williams Parks with sundry other subscribers to the Court setting
forth the great inconvenience that the said William Parks labors under for want
of a road from the edge of Yellow Britches Creek to the road leading past
Andrew Millers towards Lisburn Town to intersect that road near to James
Beatty's field upon the west side of said Beatty's House upon the side of said
Creek and also setting forth that he lyes under great hardships by reason of said
Beatty's stopping up at the passage from the Creek to that road so that he
cannot pass either to Mill or Marked and that the length of the whole road that
is wanted doth not exceed 15 perches. The Court appoint Robert Galbraith,
Henry Quigley, John Trindle, James Gregory and Hugh Laurd and William
Abernathy to view the premises ad if they or any four of them see cause to lay
out a road as aforesaid they lay out the same by courses and distances the last
injurious to private property and most conducive to publick utility and make
report to next Court.

Upon the petition of divers of the inhabitants of Letterkenny township to the
Court, setting forth that they labor under great inconvenience for want of a
public road through the said township from the back part thereof to mill and
market, and apprehending that a road from McCommons Gap on the north, the
nighest and best way to Black's Gap in the south mountain would be a benefit
to the public in general, as such a road would answer to three Merchant Mills
on the Canegogigne Creek, all of which is near to a straight course between
these two gaps and consequently each of them to Black Gap opened, and to
Baltimore, and praying the Court to appoint viewers to lay out said road.
Appointed Samuel Culbertson, (fourth), Robert Stogdill, John Mahn, John
Baird, William Lindsay, Sr., and William Long to view, and if they see cause,
to lay out a road and make report to the next Court.

Page 41 October Sessions 1772
Upon the petition of sundry inhabitants of Middletown Township to the Court
setting forth that they labor under great difficulties for want of a Great Road
leading from Carlisle to Hurley's gap beginning at the end of pit street from
thence the nighest and best way to John Mitchels from thence to David
Williamsons Fording from thence the nighest and best way to said Gap to keep
as nigh the old bridle road as possible and praying the Court to appoint proper
men to view and lay out the same as aforesaid. The Court appoint Andrew
Holmes, Samuel Laird, James Sharron, Richard Parker, Mathew Gregg, and
John Davis Junr to view the premises and if they or any four of them see cause
they lay out the same by courses and distances the least injurious to private
property and the most conducive to public utility and make report to next court.

A petition of sundry of the inhabitants of Guilford and Hamilton townships in the County of Cumberland, to the Court, setting forth that they labor under many inconveniences for want of a road leading from the Rocky springs meeting house to the Falling Springs meeting house, and pray the Court to appoint proper persons to view, and if they see cause, lay out a road aforesaid. The Court appointed John Miller, Samuel Thompson, John Kerr, Benjamin Gass, Moses Barnet, and Thomas Baird to view, and is they see cause, lay out a road as aforesaid, and make report to the next Court.

Page 42
The persons appointed at last April Court to view and lay out a road from the Walnut Bottom Road to James Smith Mill returned to the Court the said road as viewed and laid out by them according to the following courses and distances, beginning at the Walnut Bottom road aforesaid thence south 54 degrees west 87 perches, south 37 degrees west 22 perches, south 33 degrees west 186 perches, south 1 degrees east 40 perches, south 15 degrees, west 90 perches, south 35 degrees, west 90 perches, south 46 perches, south 25 degrees east 52 perches, south 76 degrees west 12 perches, to James Smiths Mill the whole being 1 ½ mile and 65 perches which road viewed and laid out as aforesaid the said persons viz Jonathan Homes, James Parker, Thomas Craighead, John Mitchel, Richard Park, Robert Urie having viewed and now returned to the Court as a publick road highly necessary and of Publick Utility and is laid out in a manner the least injurious to private property and the most conducive to the publick interest which said road being taken into consideration is confirmed by the Court. And it is further ordered by the Court that the said road laid out as aforesaid be cut and cleared and bridged if necessary by the several supervisors of the respective townships through which the said road runs forth with the breadth of 33 feet wide.

Page 43 October Sessions 1772
The persons appointed as last July Court to review and if they should see cause, lay out a road from the Three Square Hollow above Robert McCombs in the North Mountain, the nighest and best way to Chambers Mill and from thence to John Pipers mill, and to John Smith's Gap in the south Mountain, and return to the Court said road was viewed, and laid out by them according to the following courses and distances, beginning at Three Square Hollow, thence south 5 degrees, east 113 perches, south nine degrees, west 360 perches, south 330 perches, south 25 degrees, east 111 perches, thence by various courses and distances to Big Spring thence south 38 perches to John Peper's mill, thence by various courses and distances to the Walnut Bottom nearly 4890 perches, amounting to 15 miles and 90 perches, which road reviewed and laid out as aforesaid make report as necessary.

Page 44

The persons appointed at last July Term to view and layout a road leading from the North end of Bedford street of the Town of Carlisle to Robert Robbs Fording on Consdogwainet Creek and from thence to Craines Gap of the North Mountain the nearest and best way returned the said road as viewed and laid out by the, according to the following courses and distances, beginning at Bedford Street north 16 ½ degrees east 148 perches north 25 degrees west 112 perches north 4 degrees east 73 perches, north 10 degrees west 46 perches, north 33 degrees east 56 perches north 59 degrees east 68 perches north 51 ½ degrees east 18 perches north 210 perches north 18 degrees west 22 perches to Robert Robbs house north 30 degrees east 44 perches, north 35 degrees west 14 perches to Conedog Creek 2 miles and 157 perches north 2 degrees and an half west 134 perches north 56 ½ degrees west 102 perches north 15 degrees east 6 perches north 50 degrees west 34 perches north 23 degrees west 64 perches schoolhouse north 7 ½ degrees and 118

Page 45

perches north 25 degrees west 76 perches north 38 degrees east 43 perches north 6 degrees west 28 perches north 20 degrees west 20 perches north 4 degrees and ½ east 58 perches north 11 degrees west 28 perches north 5 degrees east 111 perches to Craines Gap of the North Mountain 751 perches amounting to five miles and 151 perches which road viewed and laid out as aforesaid the said persons viz James Pollock, John Polock, James Davis, David Drennan, John Davis Junior and Robert Sanderson Now returned to the Court as a publick road highly necessary and of publick utility and is laid out in manner the best Injurious to private property and most conducive to the publick interest which said road being taken into consideration is accordingly approved of by the Court and confirmed and it is further ordered by the Court that the said road laid out as aforesaid by cut cleared and bridged if necessary by the several supervisors of the respective townships through which the said road runs forth with of the breadth of 33 feet wide except where __ with the town lots already laid out.

Upon the petition of divers inhabitants of Newton and Hopewell Townships to the Court setting forth that a road leading from Carlisle to James McCallisters near the house of Robert Meeky thence to go by the house of Robert Meekey the younger the nighest and best way to Shippensburgh, praying the Court to order and appoint six sufficient housekeepers of the neighbourhood inhabiting over where the road is wanted to view the said place. The Court appoint James Chambers, Patrick McFarland, John McKune, Robert Clarke, John Jack and Hugh Torrance to view the premises aforesaid and if they or any four of them see cause to lay out a road as aforesaid they lay out the same by courses and distances the least injurious to private property and the most conducive to publick utility and make report to next Court.

Page 46

At a Court of Private sessions, held at Carlisle, 20 Nov 1772, before Robert Miller. John Holmes and John Agnew. Adjudged by the Court that Honor Sullivan indented servant to Allan Brown do serve the said Allen Brown his said master or his assigns the further time of 2 years over and above the time specified in her said indenture in compensation of run-away time and expenses.

At a Court of Private Sessions, 20 Mar 1773, before James Maxwell, Henry Prather and John Allison. Adjudged by the Court that Sampson Barry indented servant to John Shelby do serve the said John Shelby his said master or assigns the further time of 10 months over and above the time specified in his said indenture for compensation of run away time and expenses.

Page 47

At a Court of Private Sessions held at Carlisle 7 Nov 1772, before John Armstrong, William Lyon and John Agnew. Adjudged that Patrick Leaden indented servant to Samuel McCall do serve the said Samuel McCall his said master or assigns the further time of 2 years over and above the time specified in his indenture also over and above the term of 1 year adjudged before Martin Schelberger, Robert McPhuson and Michael Swoope Esquires at an adjour of the County Court of Common Pleas held at York for the County of York 26 Mar 1771 for compensation of runaway time and expenses.

Page 48

At Carlisle, 19 January 1773. The Sheriff, Ephraim Blain, returns the following list of grand jurors; Francis Silver, Tobias Hendricks, Robert Whitehill, Samuel Adams, John Sample, Edward Morton, William Chambers, Abram Adams, John McCombs, Isaac Hendricks, John Carson. William Kelson, John Kimbel, John Wormley, George Rupley, Samuel Caddis, John Sample, John Galbraith, Richard Rogers, Jeremiah Talbutt, John Quigley, Conrad Monusmith, Robert Gilfillin, Andrew Ervin.

Page 49 January Sessions 1773

The King vs Andrew Herron & Randle McDonald

Felony. Jury; David Bell, Joseph Hudson, William Gaddis, Mathew Loudon, Thomas Donaldson, James McCurdy, William Marshal, William Brooks, Joseph McCure, Nathaniel Wilson, Samuel Lamb and James McCormick say the Prisoner Andrew Herron and Randle McDonald are guilty. Judgment that the prisoners Andrew Herron and Randle McDonald Restore the goods stolen to the owner if not already done or pay the sum of 3 pounds the value thereof also pay the like sum of 3 pounds each to the Governor for support of Government, pay the costs of prosecution with all such sums of money as shall be allowed to the owner for his trouble and expense in the prosecution, taken to the common whipping post on Thursday the 21 inst and their receive 21 lashes each on their bare backs well laid on between the hours of 11 and 4 of the clock, stand committed until the whole be complied with.

Page 50
The King vs Michael Gillispie
Felony in stealing one bay horse the property of James Armstrong.
July 1773, jury; Jonathan Kearsley, Robert Gibson, John McKee, James
Ramsey, John Gray, John Kerr, John Dukson, James McClinlock, John Jordon,
William Armore, John Holmes, and George Loge say that the prisoner Michael
Gillispie is not guilty.

The King vs George Hall
Felony.

Page 51
The King vs Henry Carr
Fornication and bastardy.

The King vs Judith O'Brien
Fornication and bastardy.

Page 52 January Sessions 1773
The King vs William Musgrove
Assault and battery. Oct 1773, defendant submits to the Court protesting his
innocence, fined sixpence, pay costs of prosecution, stand committed until fine
and costs are paid.

The King vs Robert Duggan
Assault and battery. Defendant submits to the Court protesting his innocence,
fined 10 shillings, pay costs of prosecution, stand committed until complied.

Page 53
The King vs Daniel Mickey
Felony.

The King vs Andrew Herron and Randle McDonald
Felony.

The King vs William Kelso
Assault and battery.

The King vs Michael Gillispie
Samuel Colhoone £20, James Armstrong £20, Robert Little £20, Robert
McClelland £20, conditioned for their appearances at next General then and
there to testify on his Majesties behalf and not depart the Court without license.

The King vs Sarah Montogomery
James McClintock £20, conditioned for the appearance of Sarah Montgomery
to testify on his Majesties behalf and not depart the Court without license.

Page 54
The King vs Moggan McSwine
William Cochran £20, conditioned for his appearance at next Court then and there to testify on his Majesties behalf and not depart the Court with license.

The King vs William McCune
John Jack for his own appearance and the appearance of Francis Drake £40, James Armstrong £20, William Duffield £20, conditioned for their appearance at next Court then and there to testify on his Majesties behalf and not depart the Court without license.

The King vs Judith Obrien
Samuel Irwin £20, conditioned for the appearance of Judith Obrien at the next of Court then and there to testify on his Majesties behalf and not depart the Court without license.

Page 55 January Sessions 1773
Petition of inhabitants of Newtown and Hopewell Townships to the last Sessions persons were appointed by this Court to view and lay out a road to begin at the road leading from Carlisle to James McCallisters near the house of Robert Meekey thence to by the house of Robert Meekey the younger the nearest and best way to Shippensburgh in case they conceived the same road necessary and of publick utility, the persons appointed have viewed the same road, made a report which said report so made, Court hath ruled to be informal and in sufficient on motion in behalf of the petitioners for the said road, appointed George Brown, William Clark, Andrew McFarland, William Duncan, William Slarret and Alexander Laughlin to view the said road, if they or any four of them do see cause to lay out the same as a publick road that they lay out the same by courses the least injurious to private property & most conducive to the publick good & they make report to next session.

Whereas upon the petition of divers inhabitants of the township of Letterkenny to the Court, persons were appointed at last October Sessions to view and lay out a road McAmmons Gap in the north, the nighest and best way to Black's Gap in the South Mountain, in case they conceive the same road necessary, and of public utility, and the persons so appointed have viewed the same road and made a report to this Court which said report so made was ruled to be informal and in sufficient for motion on behalf of the petitioners of said road. The Court appointed Thomas Baird, James McConnel, John McKibben, Thomas Grier, John Johnson, and James Mcannon to view the said road, and if they see cause lay out the same and make report to the next Court.

Page 56
Upon the petition of divers inhabitants of Middleton Township to the Court
setting forth that they labor under many inconveniences for want of a road from
Jonathan Holmes's House to James Wilsons Mill and praying the Court to
appoint proper men to view and lay out the same from the dwelling house of
Jonathan Homes the nearest and best way to James Wilsons Mill to be opened
and kept in repair by the subscribers viz Jonathan Homes, John Holmes, Junr.
Wm Fleming, James Irwin, Paul Martin, Mathew Miller, Saml Lamb, and John
Armstrong. The court appoint Robert Urie, William Chambers, Ralph Slarrel,
James Bell, Hugh McCormick and Robert Robb to view the premises and if
they or any four of them see cause to lay out a road as aforesaid they lay out the
same by courses and distances the nighest and best road the least injurious to
private property and the most conducive to the public good and make report of
their proceedings to the next Sessions.

Petition of divers inhabitants of Hamilton and Guilford townships setting forth
that they labor under great difficulty for want of a road from Patrick Jack's mill
to the road leading through Black's and praying the Court to appoint men to
view and lay out the same. The Court appointed John Howe, William Holiday,
William Rennels, Jacob Cook, George Brown, and James Campbell to view,
and if they see cause, to lay out the same and make report to the next Court.

Page 57 January Session 1773
Upon the petition of divers Inhabitants of Shermans Valley to the Court setting
forth that a publick highway from Hunters Ferry to intersect the Great road
leading through said Valley near the Widow Smilie's would be of the greatest
utility to said inhabitants by opening a shorter communication with the
Philadelphia and other Markets and also to avoid crossing the mountain and
praying the Court to appoint men to view and lay out a road from Hunters Ferry
to intersect the Great Road leading through said Valley near the Widow
Smylies. The Court appoint William Richardson, Frederick Watt, Andrew
Irwin, Thomas Barnet, James Gaeley and Samuel Goudy to view the premises
and if they or any four of them see cause to lay out a road as aforesaid they lay
out the same by courses and distances the nearest and best way the least
injurious to private property and most conducive to publick utility, make report
of their proceedings to next sessions.

Persons appointed at the last Court to review and lay out a road from the Rocky
Spring Meeting House to Falling Spring Meeting House return to the Court the
said road as viewed and laid out by them aforesaid, according to the following
courses and distances returned to Court at April Sessions last by former
viewers. Beginning north 10 ½ degrees, west 255 perches, thence by various
courses and distances into the new cut road from Fulton's to Rocky Spring
Meeting House, thence 260 perches. Length of the road in all 3 miles and 50
perches, which road viewed and laid out the said persons report of public
utility. Approved and ordered that the same be laid out.

Page 58

The persons appointed last April Sessions to view and layout a road from the Revd Mr. James Longs to the Meeting House at William Renkins returned to the Court the said road as viewed and laid out by them according to the following courses and distances, beginning at Mr. Longs thence south 65 ½ degrees west 426 perches thence south 42 degrees west 520 perches thence north 69 degrees west 30 perches, which road viewed and laid out as aforesaid the said persons viz James Potter, George Brown, Mathew Wilson, James Lindsay, John Vance and William Ranken now returned to the Court as a publick road highly necessary and of publick utility and is laid out in a manner the least injurious to private property and the most conducive to publick interest which said road being taken into consideration is accordingly approved of and confirmed by the Court. And it is further ordered by the Court that the said road laid out as aforesaid be cut cleared and bridged if necessary by the several supervisors of te respective townships through which the said road runs forthwith of the breadth of 30 feet wide to be kept up and repaired at the private expense of the petitioners.

Page 59 January Sessions 1773

The persons appointed at last Court to view and lay out a road from Carlisle to Husley's Gap in the North Mountain returned to the Court the said road as viewed and laid out by them according to the following courses and distances viz Beginning at the north end of Pitt Street north 51 ½ degrees west 87 perches, north 50 degrees west 146 perches north 50 degrees west 83 perches north 13 ½ degrees west 62 perches north 10 degrees east 58 perches north 41 degrees west 20 perches north 4 ½ degrees west 27 perches north 41 degrees west 46 perches north 7 ½ degrees west 54 perches north 51 ½ degrees west 48 perches north 32 degrees west 20 perches north 88 perches north 52 degrees west 74 perches north 84 ½ degrees west 16 perches south 75 degrees and ½ west 32 perches north 60 degrees west 62 perches north 32 1/4 west 77 perches north 55 degrees west 48 perches north 35 degrees west 32 perches north 46 degrees west 18 perches north 71 3/4 degrees west 26 perches south 69 3/4 degrees west 10 perches north 21 degrees west 14 perches north 25 ½ degrees west 6 perches north 34 ½ degrees west 37 perches north 45 ½ west 14 perches north 18 ½ degrees west 83 perches north 36 ½ degrees west 37 perches north 5_ degrees west 28 perches north 34 1/4 degrees west 32 perches north 21 degrees west 21 perches, north 41 degrees west 12 perches north 63 degrees west 52 perches north 68 degrees west 56 perches north 63 ½ degrees west 48 perches north 22 ½ degrees west 62 perches north 4 degrees east 14 perches north 25 degrees west 75 perches north 43 degrees west 46 perches north 20 1/4 degrees west 110 perches

Page 60
north 34 degrees west 90 perches amounting in the whole to 2025 perches
equal to 61/4 miles and 25 perches which road viewed and laid out as aforesaid
the said persons viz John Davis, Junr, James Sharron, Samuel Laird, Mathew
Gregg, Richard Parker and Andrew Holmes now returned to the Court as a
publick road highly necessary and of publick utility and is laid out in a manner
the least injurious to private property and the most conducive to publick
interest which said road being taken into consideration is accordingly approved
of by the Court and confirmed. And it is further ordered by the Court that the
said road laid out as aforesaid be cut cleared and bridged if necessary by the
several supervisors of the respective townships through which the said road
runs forthwith of the breadth of 33 feet wide.

Persons appointed at last Court to view and lay out a road from William
McDowell's Mill to Mr. King's meeting house, thence to Robert McCay, return
said road as viewed and laid out by them according to courses and distances,
beginning at William McDonnell, south 14 degrees, east 71 perches, south 25
degrees, west 68 perches, thence by various courses and distances to Robert
McCay's which road viewed and laid out cut, cleared and bridged.

Page 61
The persons appointed at Last Court to view and lay out a road from the House
of Andrew Armstrong to Capt. Robert Callenders Mills returned to the Court
the said road as viewed and laid out by them according to the following courses
and distances; beginning at Andrew Armstrongs South 59 degrees west 170
perches south 68 degrees west 231 perches south 27 degrees west 75 perches
south 61 degrees west 160 perches south 42 degrees west 82 perches west 20
perches south 55 degrees west 47 perches north 65 degrees west 44 perches
being all 2 miles 4 furlongs and 29 perches which road viewed and laid out as
aforesaid the said persons viz Robert Callender, James Irwin, Andrew
McBeath, James McCormick, David Bell, and John Semple now returned to
the Court as a publick road highly necessary, of publick utility and is laid out in
a manner the least injurious to private property, the most conducive to publick
interest which said road being taken into consideration is accordingly approved
of and confirmed by the Court. And it is farther ordered by the Court that the
said road laid out as aforesaid be cut cleared and bridged if necessary by the
several supervisors of the respective townships through which the said road
runs forth with of the breadth of 33 feet wife.

Page 62 January Sessions 1773
The persons appointed at Last Court to view and lay out a private road from
Yellow Britches Creek to intersect the road leading from Andrew Millers to
Lisburn Returned to the Court the said road as viewed and laid out by them
according to the following courses and distances, beginning at the edge of
Yellow Britches Creek to the west of James Beatty's House at an old Fording
place to the west of an island in said creek running thence north 28 degrees

west 15 perches to the Lisburn Road which road viewed and laid out as aforesaid the said persons viz Henry Quigley, John Trindle, William Abernathy, Hugh Laird and James Gregory Now returned to the Court as a private road highly necessary and of public utility and is laid out in a manner the least injurious to private property which said road being taken into consideration is accordingly approved of and confirmed by the Court and it is further ordered by the Court that the said road be cut cleared and kept in repair at the expense of the said William Parks the petitioner for said road and opened the breadth of 20 feet wide.

page 63- blank

Page 64
At a court of private sessions held at Carlisle, 25 March, 1773, for the following officers were appointed.
Antrim Township. Simon Eaker, constable; John Culbertson, Roger Hart, supervisors of roads; John Irwin, Adam Robinson, overseers of the poor; John Johnson, William Stover, viewers of fences.
Hamilton Township. John Burns, constable; Joseph Swan, John Roack, supervisors of roads; William Rannells, John Taylor, overseers of poor; James McFarland, William Dakson, viewers of fences.
Lurgan Township. John Fustis, constable; Francis Graham, Archibald Mahn, supervisors of roads; William Ervin, William McDonnell, overseers of poor; John Cummins, Oliver Culbertson, viewers of fences.
Letterkenny township. Martin Weir, constable; William Baird. (Mount), William Lindsey, supervisors of roads; John Stuart, James Robinson, overseers of poor; John Stephenson, John Nielson, viewers of fences.
Peters township. William Dickey, constable; Archibald Erwin, James Campbell, supervisors of roads; William Campbell, Kern Sterritt, overseers of poor; John Welsh, Archibald Scott, viewers of fences.
Guilford township. Peter Gooshead, constable; John Keer, Samuel Rannicks, supervisors or roads; John Vance, William Glass overseers of poor; John Andrew, John Harmony, viewers of fences.

Page 66
At Carlisle, 20 April 1773, before John Armstrong. Esq., and his associates. The Sheriff of the county, Ephraim Blain, returns the following grand jurors; Thomas Baird, John McClay, Walter Denny, John Mahn, Francis Graham. Isaac Martin, William Mitchell, Adam McCormick, James McCall, Charles McClay, Thomas Craighead, Samuel McCune, Samuel Smith, James Caldwell, Robert Culbertson, William Sterritt, John Kilpatrick, William Lamb, Richard Steel, John Cunningham, John McClaine, Thomas Montgomery, Adam Turner, George Cunningham.

Page 67 April Sessions 1773
The King vs John Pollock
Felony in stealing goods the property of James Bill. Jury; William Duncan, William Linn, David Sterrat, Thomas Knox, James Knox, William Thompson, James Clark, John Stewart, Alexander McBride, William Sharp, Robert Sanderson and John Dickey say that the prisoner John Pollock is guilty.

Judgment that the prisoner restore the goods to the owner or the value thereof if not already done the like value thereof to the Governor for support of Government be taken on Saturday the 24th inst between the hours of 10 and 4 of the clock to the common whipping post, there receive 21 lashes on his bare back well laid on, pay costs of prosecution and stand committed in the custody of the Sheriff until the whole be complied with.

The King vs Jacob Grove
Assault and battery on Roger McGonnegal. Jury; William Duncan, William Linn, David Sterrat, Thomas Knox, James Knox, William Thompson, James Clark, John Stewart, Alexander McBride, William Sharp, Samuel Culbertson and John Dickey say that the defendant is not guilty.

Page 68
The King vs Michael Gillespie
Michael Gillespie £200, Jacob Grove £100, conditioned for the appearance of Michael Gillespie at the next Court then and there to answer such things as shall be objected against him and not depart the Court without licence.

James Armstrong £20, Robert Little £20, Daniel McClelland £20, John Clark £20, John White £20, Jacob Grove £20, conditioned for their respective appearance at the next Court then and there to testify on his Majesties behalf against a certain Michael Gillespie and not depart the Court without license.

The King vs Morgan McSwine
Morgan McSwine £40, Alexander Sutton £20, conditioned for the appearance of Morgan McSwine at the next court then and there to answer to a certain bill of Ind__ for assault and battery and not depart the Court without licence.

Page 69
Upon the application of James Wilson, Esq., to the Court praying that Mr. John Riley be admitted an attorney of this Court, and upon his taking the oath, he was admitted.

Upon the petition of Robert McGan, Esq., praying that Mr. John Steel be admitted as an attorney of this Court, upon taking the oath, he was admitted.

The King vs Sarah Montgomery
James McClintock £20, conditioned for the appearance of Sarah Montgomery at the next court, there to answer and not depart the Court without licence.

William Cochran being three times solemnly called to appear but appeared not forfeits his recognizance.

Returned by Ephm Blaine Esquire high Sheriff to serve on the jury being solemnly called to have their fines but appearing not the Court order them viz; David Simeral, William Irwine, James Kelly, Joseph Eatton, John Baird, Abraham Wier, William Montgomery, Archibald Mahan, Samuel Leeh, David Herron, Robert Quigley, Robert Scot, to be each of them fined in the sum of 40 shillings unless they can show sufficient cause at next July Court.

Page 70 April Sessions 1773
Petition of John Armstrong Esquire to the Court setting forth that he is under several inconveniences for want of a private road from his meadow and plantation in West Penns borrough Township to the Town of Carlisle. Praying the Court to appoint proper men of the neighbourhood to view and if they see cause lay out a private road the nearest and best way from that part of his plantation aforesaid where he is now about building and dwelling house. To the Town of Carlisle. The Court appoint John Montgomery Esqr, John Agnew Esqr, William Lyon Esquire, James Wilson Esquire, Doctr William Irwin and Robert Magaw Esquire to view the premises and if they or any four of them see necessary to lay out a road as aforesaid they lay out the same by courses and distances the nighest and best way the least Injurious to private property and most conducive to publick utility and make report to next court.

Petition of John Byers Esqr and William Miller to the Court Setting forth that they want a private road from the house of John Byers Esqr to Carlisle to be laid out and confirmed through the lane between Col. John Armstrongs Meadow and William Millers Meadow and along the road that is to fall into the great Road near __ Montogomerys new field and praying the Court to appoint proper persons to view the premises and lay out a road as aforesaid. The Court appoint James Pollock, John McKee, John Davis, Junr, John McClure, William Brown and Andrew McCallister to view the premises as aforesaid and if they or any four of them see cause they lay out the same by courses and distances the least injurious to private property and most conducive to publick utility and make report to next court.

Page 71 April Sessions 1773
Petition of William Park to the Court persons were appointed at last October Sessions to view and lay out a great road beginning at an old fording in Yellow Britches Creek to the West of James Beatty's House thence to the road leading from Lisburn to Carlisle the length of the whole road is but fifteen perches, in case they conceived the same road necessary and of public utility. And whereas the persons so appointed have viewed the same road and made report to this court which said report to made this court hath ruled to be informal and insufficient. On motion in behalf of the petitioner for said road the Court here appoint John Clark, Samuel Cunningham, John Work, John Trindle, Alexander

Trindle, and Hugh Cook to view the said road and if they or any four of them see cause to lay out the same as a publick road that they lay out the same by courses and distances in a manner the least injurious to private property and most conducive to publick utility and make report to next court.

Whereas upon the petition of Jonathan Holmes and John Holmes inhabitants of Middleton Township in Cumberland County to the Court persons were appointed at Last January Sessions to view and lay out a road the nearest and best way from the dwelling house of Jonathan Holmes to James Wilsons Mill in case they conceived the same road necessary and of publick utility. And whereas the persons so appointed have viewed the same road and made report to this Court hath ruled to be informal and insufficient. On motion in behalf of the petitioners for said road the Court here appoint James Irwin, Andrew Armstrong, William Fleming, Andrew McBeath, Mathew Miller and James Davis to view the said road and premises and if they or any four of them see cause to lay out a road as aforesaid they lay out the same by courses and distances in a manner the least injurious to private property and most conducive to publick utility and make report to next court.

Page 72
Upon the petition of sundry of the inhabitants of Armagh Township to the Court setting forth that they labor under many inconveniences for want of a publick road leading from the Bedford line above Jacks Narrows the nighest and best way untill it falls into the road near James Alexanders Senior. And praying the court to appoint proper men to view and if they see cause lay out a great road the nearest and best way as aforesaid. The Court appoint Samuel Holliday, William Brallan, Mathew Wakefield, William Miller, Robert McClelland and James Alexander to view the premises as aforesaid and if they or any four of them see cause to lay out a publick road as aforesaid that they lay out the same by courses and distances the nighest and best way the least injurious to private property and most conducive to publick utility and make report next Court.

Upon the petition of Samuel Harper of Middleton Township in the County of Cumberland to the Court setting forth that he labors under great difficulty for want of a road from his plantation to the great road leading from Carlisle to the Forty shilling Gap. And praying the Court to appoint proper men to view and if they see cause lay out a private road as aforesaid and he will __ the expense that may attend the same. The Court order and appoint William Davison, William Watson, George Sanderson, Junr, Robert Sanderson, John Pollock, Malster and Charles McClure to view the premises and if they or any four of them see cause to lay out a private road as aforesaid they lay out the same by courses and distances the nighest and best way the least injurious to private property and most conducive to the publick interest and make report to next court.

Page 73 April Sessions 1773

The persons appointed at Last January Sessions to review and lay out a publick road from Robert Meeky the Elder to Robert Meeky Junior from thence the nighest and best road to Shippensburgh. Returned to the Court the said road as viewed and Laid out by them according to the Following Courses and distances; beginning at the road leading from Carlisle to James McCallisters near the house of Robert Meeky thence south 21 degrees east 28 perches south 41 degrees east 28 perches south 19 degrees east 44 perches through James Kilgores field east 30 perches a __ and a line between James Scroggs and Widow Kilgore south 39 degrees east 134 perches south 27 degrees east 150 perches south 3 degrees west 180 perches to the house of Robert Meeky the younger south 39 degrees west 209 perches south 20 degrees west 412 perches to George Clarks south 38 degrees west 164 perches south 44 degrees west 338 perches south 33 degrees west 190 perches south __ west 148 perches south 36 degrees west 308 perches south 47 degrees west 136 perches to the north east end of Kings Street Shippensburgh in all 7 miles and 259 perches which road viewed and laid out as aforesaid the said persons viz George Brown, William Clark. Andrew McFarlin, William Slarrel, Alexander Laughlin and William Duncan now returned to the Court as a publick road highly necessary and of publick utility and is laid out in a manner the least Injurious to private property and most conducive to publick interest which said road being taken into consideration is accordingly approved of and confirmed by the Court. And it is further ordered by the Court that the said road laid out as aforesaid be cut cleared and bridged if necessary by the several supervisors of the respective townships through which the said road runs forthwith of the breadth of 33 feet wide.

Page 74 April Sessions 1773

Petition of sundry inhabitants of Lack and Fermanagh Townships saying they labor under many inconveniences for want of a publick road leading from William Wiselys House near the Head of Tuscarora Creek and from thence to William Patterson Esqr old Plantation on Juniata River, to enable them and the other Inhabitants to carry their produce to a landing place on said plantation from whence it may be cheaply transported to Middleton. The Court appoint William Arbuckle, Robert Hoge. Wm Graham, John Keer, Hugh Quigly and James Armstrong to view the premises and if they or any four of them see cause to lay out a publick road as aforesaid they lay out the same by courses and distances the nighest and best way the least injurious to private property and most conducive to publick utility and make report to next Court.

The persons appointed at last Court the view and if they should see cause lay out a publick road from Hunters Ferry to intersect the Great Road leading from Carlisle through Shermans Valley returned to the Court the said road viewed and Laid out by them according to the following courses and distances, beginning at the River Susquehanna south 85 degrees west 320 perches thence south 50 degrees west 98 perches thence south 80 degrees west 240 perches thence north 25 degrees east 248 perches, thence south 24 degrees west 554 perches, thence north 78 degrees east 635 perches thence south 70 degrees west 60 perches thence north 81 degrees east 146 perches thence south 85 west 20 perches thence south 20 degrees east 34 perches thence south 54 degrees west 36 perches thence north 81 degrees east 22 perches, thence east 46 perches thence south 55 degrees west 28 perches

Page 75
Thence north 76 degrees east 76 perches thence south 22 degrees west 66 perches thence south 87 degrees west 48 perches thence north 21 degrees west 32 perches thence north 42 degrees east 30 perches thence north 60 degrees east 22 perches thence south 72 degrees west 45 perches thence east 34 perches thence __ 79 west 134 perches thence north 85 west 152 perches thence south 50 degrees west 50 perches to the intersection containing in all 10 miles and 36 perches to the place of beginning which road viewed and laid out as aforesaid the said persons; William Richardson, Frederick Watts, James Gaily, Thomas Barnet, and Samuel Gowdy now returned to the Court as a publick road highly necessary and of publick utility and is laid out in a manner the least injurious to private property and the most conducive to publick interest which said road being taken into consideration is approved. Ordered by the Court that the said road laid out as aforesaid be cut cleared and bridged if necessary by the several supervisors of the respective townships through which the said road funs forth with of the breadth of 33 feet wide.

The persons appointed at last Court to view and if they should see cause lay out a Road from McCammons Gap in the North Mountain to Blacks Gap in the South Mountain returned to the Court the said road viewed and laid out by them according to the following courses, beginning at the North Mountain Shippensburgh Road north 45 degrees west 324 perches James McCammons, north 48 degrees west 212 perches Adam Sim and John Mahan's north 30 degrees west 148 perches Robert Calwells North 48 degrees west 486 perches Widow Boyd and Jermiah Gelvin North 25 degrees west 115 perches north 76 degrees west 142 perches north 48 degrees west 500 perches

Page 76
north 86 degrees west 140 perches John Hummels north 60 degrees west 104 perches Thomas Lindsay north 81 degrees west 42 perches William Nickelson north 41 degrees west 34 perches Valentine Berrik north 14 degrees west 60 perches north 66 degrees west 42 perches Hugh Torrence north 31 degrees west 160 perches Robert Thompson John Ferguson. Halbert Torrence north 38 Degrees west 983 perches north 41 degrees west 640 perches __ of the Mountain north 55 degrees west 80 perches north 82 degrees west 120 ½ perches north 76 degrees west 80 perches north 71 degrees west 96 perches Conegocheage old road in the South Mountain which road viewed and laid out as aforesaid the said persons; Thomas Beard. Thomas Grier, John Johnston, James McConnell, John McCubence, James McCammon now returned to the

Court as a publick road highly necessary and of public utility and is laid out in a manner the least injurious to private property and the most conducive to publick good which said road being taken into consideration is accordingly approved of and confirmed by the Court. And it is further ordered by the Court that the said road laid out as aforesaid be cut cleared and bridged if necessary by the several supervisors of the respective townships through which the said road runs forth with of the breadth of 33 feet wide.

Page 77- blank

Page 78
At Carlisle, 20 July 1773. The Sheriff Ephraim Blain, returned following list of grand jurors; William Denny, William Blain, John Pollock, James Pollock, John Wilkins, Ralph Naylor, Charles McCune, Andrew Colhoone, Henry McKinla, John Weigh, William Brown, Christopher Van Lear, John McCurdy, John Pollock, Alexander Blain, John Henry, John Hunter, Charles Cooper, Nehall Finley, John Forbes, James Davis, John Green, Anthony Warwick, Jacob Sailer.

Page 79 July Sessions 1773
The King vs Daniel McClelland
Felony in stealing the goods of James Briseland viz cash. Jury; Jonathan Kearsley, Robert Gibson, John McKee, James Ramsey, John Gray, John Keer, John Dikson, James McClintock, John Jordon, William Armor, John Holmes and George Loge say that the Prisoner Daniel McClelland is not guilty. The Court order the prisoner to be discharged upon payment of his fees.

The King vs Martha Barclay
Indictment keeping a disorderly House. Judgment that the defendant be taken to the public stocks and be therein confined the space of 2 hours on Monday the 26th instant between the hours of 10 and 4 of the clock, pay a fine of 20 shillings, stand committed until the whole be complied with.

The King vs Samuel Royer
Assault and battery on Henry Coyle. Defendant submits to the Court protesting his innocence. The Court fines him in sixpence and costs of suit.

Page 80 July Sessions 1773
The King vs John Robinson
Indictment felony in stealing the goods and chattels of Henry McBride
The judgment of the Court is that the prisoner John Robinson restore the goods so stolen to the owner if not already done. The like value thereof viz 2 pounds, 18 shillings and six pence to the Governor for support of Government be taken to the publick whipping post this afternoon and there receive 21 lashes on his bare back well laid on stand committed until the whole be complied with.

The Same vs the Same
Felony in stealing the goods of Peter Mosser. Judgment that the prisoner John Robinson restore the goods so stolen to the owner if not already done the like value thereof viz one pound 15 shillings to the Governor for support of Government be taken to the public whipping post on the __ instant and there receive 21 lashes on his bare back well laid on stand committed until the whole be complied with.

Page 81
The King vs John Robinson
Felony in stealing on bay gelding of the price of £15 the property of Martin Long. Judgment that the prisoner John Robinson restore the horse so stolen or the value thereof if not already done the like value thereof to his Honour the Governor (viz 15 pounds) for support of Government, pay the costs of prosecution with all such sums of money as shall be allowed by the Court to the owner for his trouble and expense in the prosecution that he be taken to the common whipping post on Saturday the 31st instant, receive between the hours of 10 and 4 of the clock in the afternoon 39 lashes on his bare back well laid on stand in the pillory one hour, be imprisoned on month stand committed in the custody of the Sheriff until the whole be complied with.

The King vs James Smiley
Assault and battery on William Livingston. October 1773 the defendant retracts his plea and submits to the Court protesting his innocence. Judgment that the defendant is fined sixpence pay costs of prosecution, stand committed until fine and costs are paid.

Page 82 July Sessions 1773
The King vs Thomas Murray
Felony in stealing 2 pair silk mitts the property of Wm. Holmes.

The Same vs the Same
Felony in stealing two deer skins the property of Simon Clouser.

Page 83
The King vs Thomas Galbreath
Fornication.

The King vs Sarah Montgomery
Fornication.

Page 84
The King vs William Livingston
Assault and battery on James Nensley. October 1773 the defendant submits to the Court protesting his innocence. Fined sixpence, pay costs of prosecution and stand committed until fine and costs are paid.

The King vs Jane Dougan
Assault and battery on Mary Lewis. October 1774. Defendant submits to the
Court protesting her innocence. Defendant fined 2 shillings and six pence and
pay costs of Prosecution stand committed until the fine and costs are paid.

Page 85
The King vs Moses Kilpatrick
Assault and battery on Samuel Wallace.

The King vs Sarah Eule
Assault and battery on Abraham Trump.

James Cunningham being three times solemnly called to appear appeareth not
forfeits his recognizance.

Abraham Smith being three times solemnly called to bring forth the body of
Jas. Cunningham brings not forth for recognizance.

George Kelman being three times solemnly called to appear to testify appeareth
not forfeits his recognizance.

James McLardy being three times solemnly called to appear appeareth not
forfeits his recognizance.

James Baskins being three times solemnly called to bring forth the body of
James McLardy brings not forth forfeits his recognizance.

James Craig being three times solemnly called to appear to testify appeareth not
forfeits his recognizance.

Thomas Murray Junr being three times solemnly called to appear appeareth not
forfeits his recognizance.

Thomas Murray being three times solemnly called to bring forth the body of
Thomas Murray Junr brings not forth forfeits his recognizance.

Page 86 July Term 1773
The King vs Timothy Keif
William Stewart £20, James Moore £10, conditioned for the appearance of
William Stewart at next Court then and there to testify on his Majesties behalf
and not depart the Court without licence.

The King vs Thomas Murray Junr
Simon Clouser £10, conditioned for his appearance at next Court then and
there to testify on his Majesties behalf and not depart the Court without licence.

The King vs William Livingston
William Livingston £40, James Carrothers £20, conditioned for the appearance of William Livingston at next Court then and there to answer to such things as shall be objected against him on his Majesties behalf and not depart the Court without licence.

The King vs James Smiley
James Smiley £40, Samuel Rule £20, conditioned for the appearance of James Smiley at next Court then and there to answer all such things as shall be objected against him on his Majesties behalf and not depart the court without licence.

Page 87
The King vs John Dougherty
John Dougherty £20, James Pattan £10, conditioned for appearance of John Dougherty at next Court then and there to answer to all such things as shall be objected against him on his Majesties behalf and in the mean time to keep the Peace and be of good behaviour to all his Majesties subjects and in particular to Isiah Reese and not depart the Court without licence.

John Pollock, John Gray, James Pollock, Tobias Hendericks, Robt Galbraith, John Jack, John Forbes, Jacob Irwin, Benjamin Gas, George Sommerville, George Minser, William Smith, William Rippy, William Peoples, William Nielson, Mathew Scot, William Morrow, Robert Hamill, Robert Darlington, James McCall, Mary McCormick, George Gibson, William Crawford, Isaac Simmis, Conrod Beamer, John Hamilton, Henry Gordon, Jacob Sailer, Christopher Vanlear, John Johnson, William Chambers, Arthur Buchannan, Duncan McDonald, James Davis, James Davis, Tyrone Township John Reed Fermanagh township James Galloher

Upon motion of Mr. McGaw on behalf of Mr. Robert Buchanan praying he may be admitted as an attorney of this Court, the Court upon consideration of the same, and being sworn, he was admitted.

Page 88   July Sessions 1773
The persons appointed at Last April Sessions to view and lay out a private road from the house of John Byers Esqr to Carlisle Returned to the Court the said road as viewed and laid out by them according to the following courses and distances, beginning at a post on the edge of the Great Road near John Montogomery Esqr new field, thence south 62 degrees west 226 perches thence south 36 degrees west 120 perches thence south 62 degrees west 62 perches thence south 20 degrees west 46 perches thence south 60 degrees 408 perches thence south 85 degrees west 100 perches to the road leading from John Byers's to Andw McCallisters now returned to the Court as a Private Road by John McClure, Andrew McCallister, Samuel Pollock, John McKee and William Brown 5 of the persons in said order mentioned the 6 having viewed

highly necessary and the least injurious to private property and now conducive to the utility of the petitioners which said road being taken into consideration is accordingly approved of and confirmed by the Court. And it is further ordered by the Court that the said road laid out as aforesaid be cut cleared and bridged if necessary by the persons using the same to and from their respective dwellings and opened the breadth of 35 feet wide.

Page 89
Upon the petition of sundry of the inhabitants of Antrim township saying they labor under inconveniences for want of a road from George Mercer's mill into the road leading from Ft. Loudon above Nicholas's Gap to Baltimore, pray the Court to appoint men to view and if they see cause, lay out a road. Appointed John Jack, Samuel Royer, Gasper Hanley, Abram Slifer, Robert Erwin, and Jacob Warts to view and lay out road, make return to the next Court.

Upon the petition of sundry of the inhabitants of East Pennsbr and Middleton Townships to the Court setting forth that they labor under great inconvenience for want of a publick road leading from Carlisle to Harris's Ferry, by William Chambers, Justice Hoges, George Gibsons and Tobias Hendericks that some part of the road now used by the aforesaid places is not laid out by order of Court. And praying the court to appoint proper persons to view and if they see cause to lay out the road as aforesaid. Appointed David Hoge, Edward Morton, Andrew Armstrong, Robert Gibson, Jonathan Holmes and Mathus Louden to view the premises and if they or any four of them see cause to lay out a road as aforesaid they lay out the same by courses and distances the nearest and best way the least injurious to private property and most conducive to publick utility and make report of their proceedings to next court.

Page 90
Upon the petition of Samuel Gay of Middleton Township to the Court setting forth one Samuel Harper the last April Court obtained an order or grant for a road from his the said Harper's House into the main road Middletown Township, That said Samuel Harper has greatly annoyed him and saith that if said road is let to stand and not all__ed he will be injured and damaged about 20 acres of his Tellable land and praying the Court to appoint proper men to review the premises ad lay out a private road that will least injurious to his Plantation. The Court appoint William Fleming, Hugh McCormick, Andrew McBreath, James Irwin, William Seneth, Richard Crain to review the premises aforesd. and if they or any four of them see necessary to lay out a road from said Harpers into the Great Road, laid out the same by courses the least injurious to private property and make report of their proceedings to next court.

Upon the petition of James Beatty of Allen Township to the Court setting forth that in pursuance of an order of last sessions a road has been viewed and laid out from Yellow Britches Creek to the West of James Beallys House at an old Fording to the Lisburn road. That the said road is very inconvenient and will be a useless burden on the inhabitants if the Court should confirm it as there is another road near which answers very necessary purpose. Praying the Court to appoint proper persons to review said road. The Court appoint Robert Urie, James Parker, Samuel Lamb, James Silver, Mathias Sailer, and Robert Roseburgh to review the premises and if they or any four of them see cause to lay out a road from said Park's to the Lisburn road that they lay out the same as a private road the least injurious to private property and make report of their proceedings to next court.

Page 91
Petition of Jonathan Holmes of Middleton Township, setting forth that he has labored under many inconveniences for want of a road leading the best way from his dwelling house to James Wilsons to be opened and kept in repair at his costs and charges and praying the Court to appoint proper men to view and if they see proper to lay out a road as aforesd. Appointed James Pollock, William Blair, Stephen Duncan, John Murdock, John McCurdy and Charles McClure and if they or any four of them see necessary to lay out a private road as aforesaid they lay out the same by courses and distances the least injurious to private property the nearest and best road and make report to next Court.

The persons appointed at October Sessions 1770 to view and lay out a road from Croghans Gap on the side the North Mountain from thence to run the nighest and best way to the Great Road leading from Carlisle to Baltimore past McDills Tavern returned to the Court the said road as viewed and laid out by them according to the following courses and distances viz [nothing written]

Page 92- blank

Page 93
At Carlisle, 9 September 1773, before Robert Miller, William Lyon and John Agnew Justices of the Peace. Adjudged that Rose Keer indented servant to John Kennor do serve the said John Kennor her said master or his assigns the further time of 6 months over and above the time specified on her indenture in compensation of run away time and expenses.

Page 94
At Carlisle, 19 October 1773. The Sheriff Ephriam Blain returns the following grand jurors; James Johnson, Samuel Lindsey, Andrew Boyd, Elias Davison, Robert Peoples, William Long, John Andrew, Robert Jack, Samuel Mitchell, Peter Dickey, John Immell, Edward Crawford, John Bowman, John Dunning, William Sharp, James Patten, John Vance, Patrick Jack, Joseph Cook, Andrew McFarland, John Flack, David Williamson, John Welsh, Henry Gordon.

Page 95 October Sessions 1773
The King vs George Johnston
Indictment keeping a tippling house. The defendant submits to the Court,
ordered that he pay a fine of 5 pounds for support of Government, that he pay
the costs of prosecution and stand committed till performed.

The King vs Thomas McMurray
Indictment tippling house. The defendant submits to the Court, ordered that he
pay a fine of 5 pounds for support of Government that he pay the costs of
prosecution and stand committed till performed.

The King vs James Cunningham
Assault and battery. Defendant submits to the Court protesting his innocence,
ordered that he pay a fine of six pence and that he pay costs of prosecution.

Page 96 October Sessions 1773
The King vs Katherine McPherson
Felony in stealing the goods of James Gibbons. The prisoner being charged
pleads not guilty, Jury; Robert Patterson, William Vanlear, William Thompson,
John Thorne, Samuel Henry, Robert Meekey, Joseph McKenney, John
Moorhead, Samuel Rennox, Thomas McClelland, William Peoples and
Andrew Reed who say that the prisoner Katherine McPherson is guilty.
Ordered that she receive 15 lashes on her bare back at the publick whipping
post tomorrow the 22nd inst. that she pay a fine of 5 pounds 3 shillings and 9
pence for the support of Government, that she make restitution of the goods
stolen if not already done to the owner, that she pay the costs of prosecution
and stand committed performed.

Page 97
The King vs Hugh Quigley
Assault & battery. April 1774, jury; Robert Sanderson, Robert Patterson,
Robert McComb, Andrew McBeath, William Watson, Abram Wier, William
Clark, George Sanderson, Thomas McComb, Samuel McCall, William
McFarland, and Thomas Croughead who say that the defendant Hugh Quigley
is not guilty.

The King vs John Dunning, Margery Dunning and John Knox.
Indictment forcible entry and detainer. January Term 1774, jury; James
McCormick, Samuel Goudy, John Buchanan, John Scot, John Black, Robert
Hunter, Thomas Elliot, William Sanderson, Thomas Fisher, Andrew Simison,
Jeremiah Reese and John Orr who say that John Dunning Margery Dunning
and Robert Dunning are guilty and that John Knox is not guilty. Judgment that
John Dunning is fined 10 shillings, Margery Dunning and Robert Dunning is
fined two shilling and six pence each pay costs of prosecution and that they be
severely committed until fine and fees are paid and the Court further __ that a
writ of restitution do your forth with John Knox is discharged paying costs.

Page 98
The King vs Timothy Keiff
Assault & battery. October 1775, defendant retracts his plea and pleads guilty. The Court fines defendant is six pence, pay costs of prosecution, stand committed until the whole be complied with.

The King vs William Kelso
Indictment keeping a tippling house. January 1774, defendant submits to the Court, judgment that the defendant William Kelso pay 5 pounds as a fine to the Governor, pay costs of prosecution.

Page 99
The King vs Timothy Keiff
William Stewart £20, William Moore £10, conditioned for the appearance of William Stewart at the next Court then and there to testify on his majesties behalf and not depart the Court without license.

The King vs Hugh Quigley
James Stone £20, James Heddleston £20, conditioned for their respective appearance at the next court then and there to testify on his Majesties behalf and not depart the Court without license.

The King vs John Dunning, Margery Dunning, and John Knox
Mark Brady £20, Ephraim Blaine £20, conditioned for the appearance of Mark Brady and Jacob Work at the next Court then and there to testify on his Majesties behalf and not depart the court without license.

On Motion of Mr. Yeates on behalf of Mr. George Ross Junr. To the Court Praying he may be admitted an attorney of this Court and Court of Common Pleas. The Court upon considering the same his is accordingly admitted.

Page 100 October Sessions 1773
Upon the petition of John Montgomery to the Court setting forth that he labores under much difficulty for want of a road to market and meeting and cannot get it conveniently without going about 20 perches through William Kelso's land, praying the Court to appoint proper men to view and lay out a road beginning at John Montgomery's House in the Township of East Pennsburgh and from that into the Great Road leading from Carlisle to Harri's Ferry the nighest and best way. Appointed John Nailer, John Quigley, Creek, John Carrothers, William Gaddis, Samuel Gaddis and John Orr Junior to view the premises and if they or any four of them see cause to lay out a road as aforesaid they lay out the same by courses ad distances the nighest and best way the least injurious to private property and make report to next court.

Page 101

Upon the petition of several of the inhabitants of Antrim township saying that they labor under great inconvenience for want of a road to George Mencer's Mill in the township aforesaid, leading through the lands of Gasper Hanley, John Coughrin, and others into the great road leading near Ft. Loudon above Nicholas' Gap, praying the Court to appoint viewers.

The Court appointed James Mauk, Joseph Nicholson, William Finley, Frederick Foreman, Jr., John Crooks, and Samuel Bohel to view, and if they see cause lay out a road and make report to the next Court.

Upon the petition of sundry inhabitants of Middleton township to the Court setting forth that there is a necessity for a publick road beginning where John McClure's Road intersects the great road leading from Carlisle to Shippensburg and from thence the nearest and best way to Ephraim Blaines Mill at the Coves. Praying the Court to appoint proper persons to view the premises and if they see cause to lay out a road as aforesaid. The Court appoint Jonathan Holmes, James Pollick, Samuel Laird, Stephen Duncan, James Davis and Richard Coulter Junior to view the premises and if they or any 4 see cause to lay out a road as aforesaid they lay out the same by courses and distances the nearest and best way the least injurious to property and most conducive to public utility and make report to next court

Page 102 October 1773

Upon the petition of a number of the inhabitants of Middleton Township and the town of Carlisle to the Court setting forth that they labor under great inconveniences for want of a publick road leading from Carlisle to Mathew Lairds Mill and from which there is a road laid out to Baltimore and praying the court to appoint a competent number of men to view and if they see cause to lay out the aforesaid road. The Court appoint William Fleming, John Davis Junior, John McClure, Robert Gibson, James Wakely and Samuel Hay to view the premises and if they or any four of them see cause to layout a road as aforesaid they lay out the same by courses and distances the nighest and best way the least injurious to private property and make report to next court.

The persons appointed at last October Sessions to view and layout a private road from the house of Jonathan Homes to James Wilsons Mill returned to this Court the said road as viewed and laid out by them according to the following courses and distances, James Pollock, William Blair, Stephen Duncan, John Murdock, John McCurdy and Charles McClure Beginning at Jonathan Holmes's dwelling house north 63 degrees east 6 perches north 8 degrees east 13 perches north 41 degrees west 29 perches north 15 degrees west 14 perches south 66 degrees west 46 perches in all 120 perches and ½ to James Wilsons Mill which road viewed and laid out as aforesaid they now return to the Court as a private road highly necessary and the least injurious to private to private property and most conducive to the utility of the petitioners which said being taken into consideration by the Court is approved. Further ordered that said road laid out as aforesaid be cut cleared and opened at the expense of the petitioner also to make and keep up the fence on the west side of the road from Jonathan Holmes's Barn across the Letart Spring and no farther.

Page 103 October Sessions 1773
The persons appointed at last April Court and continued same appointment last July Sessions, to view and lay out a private road from the meadow of John Armstrong Esqr in West Pennsborrow Township to the Town of Carlisle. Returned to this Court the said road as viewed and laid out by them according to the following courses and distances, beginning at the south end of Pitt Street of the Town of Carlisle south 53 ½ degrees west 395 perches south 26 ½ degrees west 330 perches south 59 degrees west 244 perches south 26 ½ degrees west 194 perches south 57 degrees west 152 perches to the Meadow of John Armstrong Esqr equal to 4 miles and 35 perches now returned to this Court as a private road by James Wilson, Robert Magaw, William Lyon, John Agnew, William Irvine, and John Montgomery highly necessary and is laid out in a manner the least injurious to private property which said road being taken into consideration is accordingly approved of and confirmed by the Court.

Upon the petition of James Beatty of Allen Township to the Court at last July Sessions setting forth to the Court that a road had been viewed and laid out from Yellow Britches Creek to the west of his house __ an old Fording to the Lisburn Road which if confirmed would be useless and burdensome as a nearer road could be got, praying the Court to appoint men to review the same upon which the Court did appoint men to review the same and to make return to this Court but if appearing that the said petitioner hath and prosecuted his said order for a review the Court order that the said Road as viewed and returned at Last January Sessions by the following persons viz Henry Quigley, John Trindle, William Abernathy, Hugh Laird and James Gregory and according to the following courses and distances, beginning at the edge of Yellow Britches Creek to the West of James

Page 104
Beattys House at old Fording place to the west of an island in said creek running thence north 28 degrees west 15 perches to the Lisburn Road be confirmed and be to all intents and purposes a private road as viewed and laid out by the aforesaid persons and it is further ordered by the Court that the said road by cut cleared and bridged if necessary at the expense and charges of the petitioner. William Parks.

Page 105
Process to January Sessions 1774

The King vs Jane Dougan

Page 106

At Carlisle, 18 January 1774. The Sheriff. Ephraim Blain. returns the following list of grand jurors; Henry Cunningham, John Byers, Hugh Alexander, George Wood, James Blain, William Richardson. Samuel Ramsey, Andrew Holmes, Alexander Roddy, John Carothers, John Hamilton. William McClure, John Orr, Alexander Murray, Robert Pollock, Jonathan Ross, John Clark. William Paterson, David Carson, Robert Robinson. John Alexander. William McLintock, John Irvine, John Darlington.

Page 107 January Sessions 1774
The King vs Mary Cowan
Felony. Jury; James McCormick, Samuel Goudy, John Buchanan, John Scot, John Black, Robert Hunter, Thomas Elliot, William Sanderson, Thomas Fisher. Andrew Simison, Jeremiah Reese, and John Orr say the prisoner Mary Cowan is guilty of stealing the bracelets but not guilty with respect to the other artikles laid in the indictment. Judgment that the prisoner Mary Cowan is fined 15 shillings, pay costs of prosecution, stand committed until fine and fees are paid.

The King vs Thomas Mathews
Forgery. Prisoner pleads guilty. Judgment the prisoner Thomas Mathews be taken to the common whipping post on Friday next between the hours of 11 and 4 of the clock and there receive 21 lashes on his bare back well laid on, stand in the pillory one hour pay costs of prosecution, stand committed until the whole be complied with.

Page 108
The King vs William Gullighan
Felony. Prisoner pleads guilty. Judgment the Prisoner William Gullighan return the goods stolen to the owner if not already done or the value thereof, like value thereof to the Governor (being 20 shillings), be taken to the common whipping post on Thursday next between 10 and 2 and there receive 21 lashes on his bare back, pay costs of prosecution, stand committed until the whole be complied with.

The King vs John Dunning, Robert Dunning, Margery Dunning and John Knox
Entered at October Sessions 1773.

The King vs James Eekles
Tippling house. April Sessions 1774, Defendant by Mr. Ross his attorney retracts his pleas submits to the Court protesting his innocence. The defendant is fined 5 pounds, costs of prosecution, stand committed until the whole be complied with.

Page 109 January Sessions 1774
The King vs John Lawrance
Tippling house.

The King vs William McManus

Felony. April 1774, Jury; Robert Sanderson, Robert Patterson, Robert McComb, Andrew McBeath, William Watson, Abram Wier, William Clark, George Sanderson, Samuel McCall, Thomas McComb, William McFarland and Thomas Craighead say that the prisoner William McManus is guilty. Judgment is that he restore the goods stolen to the owner if not already done or the value thereof pay the like value to the Governor, pay costs of prosecution, on Friday 22nd receive on his bare back 15 lashes well laid on, stand committed until the whole be complied with.

Page 110

The King vs Ezekiel Chambers

Assault and battery. Defendant retracts his plea and submits to the Court. Judgment that the defendant Ezekiel Chambers is fined 5 shillings, pay costs of prosecution.

The same vs the same

Assault and battery. Defendant retracts his pleas submits to the Court. Judgment Ezekial Chambers is fined 5 shillings, pay costs of prosecution.

The same vs George Long

Assault and battery. The Defendant submits to the Court protesting his innocence. Judgment, George Long is fined 6 pence, pay costs of prosecution.

Page 111

The King vs James Pindy

Assault and battery. April 1774, defendant pleads guilty, fined half a crown, costs of prosecution.

The King vs Katharin Long

Assault and battery.

The King vs John Leap

Assault and battery.

The King vs Hugh Quigley

Hugh Quigley £40, William Bell £20, conditioned for the appearance of Hugh Quigly at the next Court then and there to answer to a certain bill of indictment found against him for assault and battery and not depart the Court without license.

Page 112 January Sessions 1774

The King vs Hugh Quigley

James Hiddleston £20, conditioned for his appearance at next Court then and there to testify on his Majesties behalf and not depart the Court without license.

The King vs William McManus
John Magill £20, John __ £10, conditioned for the appearance of John Magill at next Court then and there to testify on his Majesties behalf and not depart the Court without licence.

The King vs James Eekles
James Eckles £40, James Thomas £20, conditioned for the appearance of James Edkles at the Court there to answer to a bill of indictment found against him for keeping a tippling house & not depart the Court without licence.

Page 113
The King vs Timothy Huff
William Stewart £20, Robert Walker £10, conditioned for the appearance of William Stewart at the next Court then and there to testify on his Majesties behalf and depart the Court without licence.

The King vs Barny Naham
Barny Naham £40, John Glen £20, conditioned for the appearance of Barny Naham at the next Court to answer to such things as shall be objected against him on his Majesties behalf and not depart the Court without licence.

The King vs the same
William Kirk £20, conditioned for his appearance at the next Court then and there to testify on his Majesties behalf and not depart the Court without licence.

Page 114
The King vs James Sample
James Samle £200, Robert Sample £100, conditioned for the appearance of James Sample at the next Court then and there to answer to all such things as shall be objected against him on his Majesties behalf and not depart the Court without licence.

James Foley on Motion is discharged from his recognizance paying costs
James Stone being 3 times called to appear but appears not forfeits his recognizance.

On motion of Mr. Wilson on behalf Samuel Wilson that Laughlin McAfee indented servant to the said Samuel leave him the __ of his said indenture. The judgment of the Court is that said Laughlin McAfee serve the said Samuel Wilson or his assigns the further term of 2 years and 6 months or pay the sum of 14 pounds.

Page 115 January Sessions 1774
Persons appointed at last January Session to view and lay out a road from Patrick Jack's mill into the great road leading through Black's Gap at Charles McCormick's, return to the Court that the said road was laid out by them

according to the following courses and distances, beginning at the post at above mentioned road, thence through Hamilton township, south 30 degrees, east 320 perches to a black, thence south 8 degrees, west 20 perches to a white oak. Thence by various courses and distances to Conococheague creek, thence through Guilford township, south 60 degrees, east 170 perches, to a white oak, south 76 degrees, east 85 perches to Charles McCormick's, which road viewed and laid out as aforesaid the viewers report as of public utility, and is accordingly approved by the Court and ordered to be laid out.

Page 116
Petition of inhabitants of East Pennsborrough Township, to the Court setting forth that they labor under many inconveniences for want of a road to carry their produce to market the old road being stopped by sundry new improvements. Praying the Court to appoint men to view & if they see cause to lay out a road to begin at the fork of the road on the east side of James Elliots run from thence through the Fording at John Carrothers's the nearest and best way into the Great Road leading to Carlisle at or near the Rodge above James Bells House. Appointed David Hoge, George Wood, James McCormick, John Sample, Thomas Donaldson, Mathew Loudon to view the premises aforesaid and if they or any four of them see cause to lay out a road as they layout the same by courses and distances the least injurious to private property and most conducive for the utility of the petitioners and make report to next Court.

Upon the petition of sundry of the inhabitants of Letterkenny and Lurgan townships, setting forth that they are put to great inconvenience for want of a road from Joseph Clark's near a gap formerly called by the name of Cisney's Gap in Letterkenny township to William McKnight's mill and from thence to Herron's Ford in Lurgan township, pray the Court to appoint viewers to lay out said road. The Court appointed Samuel Culbertson, (fourth) Thomas McComb, Alexander Sterritt, William Kilpatrick, John Baird, and Charles Cummins to view, and if they see cause, to lay out said road and make report to next Court.

Page 117 January Sessions 1774
Petition of sundry of the inhabitants of Antrim and Peters townships setting forth that they stand in need of a road through both of said townships leading toward Hagerstown in Maryland, and as there is a road laid now and confirmed by order of the Court from Mr. King's meeting house to Robert McCoy's, likewise a road from Hagerstown to the provincial line laid out and confirmed by order of Frederick County Court, and that a road leading from said Robert McCoy's leading by Peter Wister's mill to intersect said Maryland road at the line near Dr. Henry Snibley's would be of great advantage to the public, and praying the Court to appoint proper persons to view and lay out the same. The Court appointed Andrew Miller, Robert Crunkleton, James Cross, James McCullough, James Ervine, and Robert McClellan to view, and if they see cause, lay out a road and make report to the next Court.

Upon the petition of sundry of the inhabitants of Antrim township, setting forth that a petition was preferred last session and an order obtained for men to view and lay out the old road near George Mencer's mill to John Wallace spring on the great road that leads to Baltimore and the said road be through John McLenahan's Meadow already fenced, and through clear land of Thomas McLenahan will be of great detriment to both if confirmed, they apprehend there can be a better and straighter road got from said Mencer's mill to the great road without real injury to any persons, and praying the Court to appoint viewers. The Court appointed James McLane, John Erwin, Abram Smith, William Rankin, James Johnson, and Simon Aire to view the premises and if they see fit lay out the road.

Page 118 January Sessions 1774
Petition of William Kelso to the Court setting forth that a road has been laid out through his lands greatly to his prejudice in consequence of the application of John Montgomery for a road from his house into the Great Road leading from Carlisle to Harris's Ferry. That the said road as laid out runs through his garden and otherwise much injures his plantation, and that a more convenient & less injurious road can be there laid out. Praying the Court to appoint proper me to review the said road and make such alterations as they may deem necessary. The Court appoint John Semple James McCormick, John Beard Junior, John McCormick Junior, John Trindle, Alexander Trindle to review the aforesaid premises and if they or any 4 of them see cause to lay out the same or make any necessary alterations therein they lay out the same by courses and distances the least injurious to private property and make report to next court.

The persons appointed at last Court to view and lay out a road from the Forks of the Great Road leading from Carlisle to Shippensburgh and the road leading from said road to John McClures from said Forks to Ephraim Blains Mill Have returned to this court the said road as viewed and laid out by them according to the following courses and distances, beginning at the road from Carlisle to Shippensburgh N41 degrees E220 perches N20 degrees E78 perches N13 degrees W54 perches N87 2/3 of a degrees E112 perches N2 degrees and 1/3 W26 perches N87 degrees and ½ E198 perches N80 degrees E17

Page 119
perches N25 degrees E16 perches N28 degrees W80 perches containing in the whole 801 perches to Blains Mill being 2 ½ miles and one perch. Which road viewed and laid out as aforesaid the said Persons viz Jonathan Holmes, Richard Coulter, Stephen Duncan, James Pollock, Samuel Laird and James Davis returned the road highly necessary, of publick utility and is laid out in manner the least injurious to private property. Which said road being taken into consideration by the court is accordingly approved. Ordered that the said road laid out as aforesaid be cut cleared and bridged if necessary by the several supervisors of the respective townships through which the said road passes forth with of the breadth of 32 feet wide.

The persons appointed at last Court to view and lay out a road the nearest and best way from Carlisle to Mathew Laird Mill, thence to Thomas Craidheads Mill. Have returned to this Court the said road as viewed and laid out by them according to the following courses and distances, beginning at the south end of Hanover Street S80 degrees W244 perches S15 degrees W160 perches s26 degrees W32 perches S82 degrees E94 perches S67 degrees E24 perches S53 degrees E18 perches S18 degrees E12 perches S5 ½ degrees E14 perches S46 degrees E92 perches S30 degrees E36 perches S14 degrees EE122 perches S25 degrees E226 perches S32 degrees E104 perches S8 degrees 1/3 E119 perches S33 degrees E12 perches S74 ½ degrees E20 perches to Craigheads

Page 120
Mill being in the whole _ miles and 29 perches which road viewed and laid out as aforesaid the said persons viz William Fleming, John Davis Junr, John McClure, Robert Gibson, Samuel Hay & James Weakley now returned to the Court as a road highly necessary and of publick utility and the least injurious to private property which road being taken into consideration is accordingly approved of and confirmed by the court. And it is further ordered by the Court that the said road laid out as aforesaid by cut cleared and bridged if necessary forthwith by the several townships through which the said road passes of the breadth of 33 feet wide.

The persons appointed at last July Sessions (and continued in force by the Court at last October Sessions) to review a private road lately laid out from Samuel Harpers House to the Main Road (of the Road from the Forty Shilling Gap to Carlisle Town). Have returned to this court the said road as reviewed and laid out by them according to the following courses and distances, beginning at Samuel Harpers House in Middleton Township thence S16 degrees E200 perches to a marked white oak S36 degrees W9 perches to a marked white oak N87 degrees W12 perches to a marked hickory S40 degrees W22 perches to a marked white oak S15 degrees S44 degrees W38 perches to a marked Hickory S38 degrees W46 perches to a marked hickory, and S20 degrees W52 perches to the main road aforesaid in all 403 perches or 1 1/4 mile and 3 perches. Which road viewed and laid out as aforesaid the said persons; Andrew McBeath, Richard Crain and William Smith now returned to the Court as a road very necessary for the said Samuel Harper to go to church meeting and market and is

Page 121
laid out in a manner the least injurious to private property which road being taken into consideration is accordingly approved of and confirmed by the Court. And it is further ordered that the said road laid out as aforesaid be cut cleared and bridged if necessary by the said Samuel Harper.

Page 122-123 - blank

Page 124

At a court of private sessions, in Carlisle, 25 Mar 1774

Township: Allen; constable Rowland Chambers; supr of roads Alexander Work
    & Alexander Hamilton; overseer poor, William Hammeny & John
    Sands

Township: Antrim; constable John Wallace; supr of roads Elias Dowison &
    James Coyle; overseers of poor; Andrew Roberson & John Irwin

Township: Armagh; constable James Reed, supr roads Edmond Richson &
    William Miller; overseerer poor William Dickson & Saml Beard

Township: Carlisle, constable John Wilkins; supr roads John Crugh & John
    McCurdy; overseer of poor John Jordon & Jacob Cart

Township: Derry; constable Thomas Hold; supr of roads Jonas Balm & John
    Carmichael; overseerer of poor Edward Johnston & Joseph
    Westbrook

Township: East Pennsburgh: constable Samuel Fisher; supr roads George
    Rupely & Jeremiah Reec; overseer poor John Carrothers & Samuel
    Gaddis

Township: Fermanagh; constable David Martin; supr roads James Purdy &
    John Tennis, overseer poor Abraham Lukens & Hugh Sharron

Township: Fannet; constable Robert Anderson, supr roads Robert Lawther &
    Alexr McConnell, overseer poor John Holliday & Francis Elliot

Township: Greenwood; constable James Fenton, supr roads Leonard Foutz &
    George Albright; oversee poor Hoppel Long & Graft Coaz

Township: Hamilton; constable Mathew McDowell; supr roads Robert Dickson
    & Paul Barnet; overseer poor James McFarlane & William Dickson

Township: Hopewell; constable Andrew Boyd; supr roads David Mahan &
    Wm Trinble; overseer poor William Duncan & Joseph Brady

Page 125

Township: Lurgan; constable John Justice; supr roads David Porter &James
    McKebben; overseer poor William Irwin & William McConnell

Township: Lack; constable Wm Campbell; supr roads Adams Hay & David
    Wallace; overseer poor John Stewart & Jno Harvey

Township: Letterkinny; constable James Clark, supr of roads John Beard & T
    hos Lindsay; overseer poor John Stuart & James Robertson

Township: Newtown; constable Samuel Weir; supr roads Samuel Murray &
    Gawin Mitchel; overseer poor Richard Nicholson & Wm Thompson

Township: Middletown, constable Samuel Ramsey; supr roads William
    Chambers & John Dinsmor; overseer poor Walter Denny & John
    Gregg

Township: Milford; constable William Runeston; supr roads Thomas Baale &
    John Lyon; overseer poor Samuel Irwin & Robert Campble

Township: Peter; constable William Shannon; supr roads James Pattan &
    Dougl Campble; overseer poor Mc McIllhattan & John Rae

Township: Rye; constable John McCoy Senr; supr roads Andrew Steen & Joel
    McCallister; overseer poor Wm Richardson & John Ramsey

Township: Teboyne; constable William Townsly; supr roads Robert Hunter &
    James Wilson; overseer poor Joseph McClintock & John Neepher
Township: Tyrone: constable Samuel Fisher Senr; supr roads John Sharp &
    Obed Gariwood; overseer poor John McCallister & Hance Ferguson
Township: Guilford; constable Ezekl Chambers; supr roads Robert Jack &
    Edward Crawford; overseer roads John Vance & Peter Fray
Township: Westpennsburg; constable John Whitten; supr roads James Smith &
    John Davidson; overseer poor William Clark & George Davidson

Page 126 April Sessions 1774
At Carlisle, 19 April 1774. The Sheriff Ephraim Blain returns the following list
of grand jurors; Joseph Erwin, Adam Holloday, William Moore, William
Waddle, Patrick Jack, Samuel McCune, James Caldwell, John McCune, Robert
Montgomery, James Finley, Hugh Wiley, William Kirkpatrick, John Nielson,
Samuel Walker, John McKnight, Ralph Steritt, John Mahn, William Duncan,
John Barr, Thomas Pomeroy, Richard Parker, Thomas Parker, David English,
James Rippeth.

Page 127 April Sessions 1774
The King vs John Deloghry & John Brown & John Cook
Felony. Jury; Robert Sanderson, Robert Patterson, Robert McComb, Andrew
McBeath, William Watson, Abn Wier, William Clark, George Sanderson,
Samuel McCall, Thomas McComb, William McFarland and Thos Craighead
say that John Deloghrey is guilty. John Brown also ___ John Cook is not guilty.
Judgment the prisoner John Deloghrey restore the goods stolen to the owner if
not already done pay the like value to the Governor be taken to the common
whipping post on Friday the 22 inst and there receive 15 lashes on his bare
back between the hours of 7 & 4 of the oclock, pay costs of prosecution &
stand committed until the whole be complied with.

Page 128
The King vs John Brown & John Cook
Felony. Jury; Robert Sanderson, Robert Patterson, Robert McComb, Andw
McBeath, William Wilson, Abran Wier, William Clark, George Sanderson,
Samuel McCall, Thomas McComb, William McFarland and Thomas Craighead
say that the prisoner John Brown otherwise Cook is guilty. Judgement restore
the goods stolen to the owner if not already done pay the like value to the
Governor that he be taken to the common whipping post between the hours of
11 & 4 of the clock on Friday the 22 instant and there receive 21 lashes on his
bare back well laid on, pay the costs of prosecution, stand committed until the
whole be complied with.

Adjudged by the Court that Sarah Montgomery indented servant to James
Galbraith Esq or is assigns do serve her said master the further term or time of
15 months over and above the time specified in her indenture for bearing a
bastard child and expenses.

Page 129

The King vs Barney Naham

Felony. October 1774, jury; James Brown, William Thompson, Alexander
__ier, Robert McClure, Patrick Wallace, James Wilson, John McDowell,
William Hoage, George Hudson, Charles Farguher, Hugh McCormick and
James McGuhoge (?) say that Barney Naham is not guilty.

The King vs John Deloghrey & John Brown Als John Cook
Felony.

The King vs John Foutz Senr
Battery.

Page 130

James Hunter being solemnly called to appear but appearth not forfeits his
recognizance.

Robert Hunter being solemnly called to bring forth the body of James __ but
brings not forth forfeits his recognizance.

The King vs Barny Naham
William Kirk £ 40, John McIntyre £40, conditioned for the __ appearance and
the appearance of James McConnell at the next Court then & there to testify on
his Majesties behalf against a certain Barney Naham & not depart the court
without license.

The King vs Barny Naham
Barny Naham £40, John Glen £40, conditioned for the appearance of Barney
Naham at the next Court to answer to a certain __ of indictment found against
for felony and not depart the Court without license.

Page 131 April Sessions 1774

Upon the petition of sundry inhabitants living in Peters Township and Great
Cove to the Court setting forth that they labor under much inconvenience for
the want of an established road leading from Patrick Campbells to Wm Kings
Meeting House as Patrick Campble is under much hardship for want of away of
communication between his two Farms. Praying the Court to appoint men to
view and lay out a road from John Irvins house where Robert Bell now lives to
Patrick Campbles to the Great Cove said road to be cleared and kept in repair at
the soul expense of Patrick Campbell. The Court appointing Laimes Starrel,
John Work, Archibald Scot, James Irwin, John McClelland & Robert
McFarland to view the premises aforesaid and if they or any 4 of them see
cause to lay out a road they as aforesaid may layout the same by courses and
distances the nearest and best way the least injurious to private property and
make report to next court.

Upon the petition of sundry inhabitants of Rye and Greenwood Townships and others in said County to the Court setting forth that since the County of Northcumberland has been erected and the Courts of Justice in the same have been held at Fort Augusta & Sunberry the Communication between them and other Inhabitants of Cumberland County with __ those of Northumberland County has been of considerable advantage to both That a publick road has been confirmed by the Court of some years ago & opened from the Town of Carlisle to the River Juniata nearly opposite to the Mouth of Cockolamus Creek And that a road has been lately opened from the Town of Sunberry to the line dividing the said Counties near the Mouth of Mahantongo And also that from Juniata where the road from Carlisle terminates to the end of the Sunberry Road at Mahanlongo aforesaid there is no laid out Road. Praying the Court to appoint proper persons to view and if they see cause lay out a road from Juniata where the Carlisle Roads strikes the same the nearest and best way to Mahantongo Creek aforesaid where the Sunberry Road intersects the same. The Court appoint James Galloher, Robert Lorrimore, James Mitcheltree, John Martin, Robert McIntyre,

Page 132
and John Tinnis to view the premises aforesaid and if they or any 4 of them see cause to lay out a road aforesaid they lay out the same by courses and distances the nearest and best way to least injurious to private property and most conducive to publick utility and make report to next court.

Upon the petition of sundry inhabitants of Rye & Tyrone Townships in the County aforesaid to the Court setting forth that they labor under many inconveniences for want of a great road leading from George Robinsons Esqr. The nighest and best way to Samuel Fishers from thence to Finley McCowns and from there to Baskens Ferry and praying the court to appoint proper persons to view and if they see proper to lay out a road according to the above mentioned courses. The Court appoint Henry Cunningham, John Black, William McClure, Robert Robeson, George Douglass and John Hamilton to view if they or any four of them see cause to lay out a road as aforesaid they lay out the same by courses and distances the nearest and best way the least injurious to private property and most conducive to publick utility and make report to next Court.

Upon the petition Charles McClure to the Court setting that he is in much want of a private road from the great road leading from Carlisle to Trents Gap the nighest and best way from said road to his house and praying the court to appoint men to view the said road and lay out the same. The Court appoint James Pollock, John Creigh, Stephen Duncan, Christopher Vanlear, and John McCurdy to view the premises and if they or any four of them see cause to lay out a road as aforesaid they lay out the same by courses and distances the nearest and best way and least injurious to private property and make report to next Court.

Page 133

Petition of a number of the inhabitants of Carlisle Middleton and Allen Townships, setting forth that a considerable trade is carried on at Carlisle Iron Works and that they labor under great inconveniences for want of a publick road leading from the town of Carlisle to said Works, praying the Court to appoint men to view the ground and if they see proper lay out the road as aforesaid. Appointed Andrew Holmes, John Holmes, William Lamb, Charles McClure, Samuel Laird and John Miller to view the premises and if they or any four of them see cause to lay out a road as aforesaid. They lay out the same by courses and distances the nighest and best way the least injurious to private property, most conducive to the publick interest and make report to next Court.

The petition of sundry of the inhabitants of Antrim township setting forth that they labor under inconveniences for want of a road leading from Lawrence Tar's mill up or across the county to John Forehiller's near Conocheague Creek, and praying the Court to appoint viewers.

The Court appointed William Rankin, Henry Sights, James Brotherton, Charles Snively, and William Hanna, and James Poe to view and if they see cause lay out a road and make report to the next Court.

Page 134 April Sessions 1774

Upon the petition of sundry inhabitants of East Pennsbro Township in said County to the Court setting forth that they labor under great inconvenience for a road from the land of Samuel Fisher at the mountain foot or from any other part thereof that may be thought most convenient to answer the lower end of said township to William Kelso's Ferry on Susquehanna amongst the banks of said river from Bogs's to said Kelso's Ferry. Praying the Court to appoint men of said township to view the premises where said road might be made. The Court appoint John Quigly, John Orr Senr, John Semple, William Gaddis, James McCormick the younger and Samuel Gaddis and if they or any four of them see cause to lay out a road as aforesaid they lay out the same by courses and distances the nearest and best way the least injurious to private property and most conducive to the publick utility and make report to next Court.

The persons appointed at last January Sessions to review and lay out a private road from George Mercer's mill to the great road that leads to Baltimore, and return to this Court the said road as reviewed and laid out by them according to the following courses and distances. Beginning at said Mencer's mill, from thence to John Seachrist's land, up said land and through his cleared fields, passing Gasper Hamlin's two small fields, and on the west side of the pine hill to the run about fifty yards above John McLenahan's land, and thence north of John Coughoung at a pond of water, and so on to the great road at the upper end of John Wallace's lane, which road reviewed and laid out the said viewers return which being taken into consideration by the Court is accordingly approved and it is ordered that the said road be laid out.

Page 135
The Persons appointed to view and lay out a road from the fork of the road on the east side of James Elliots Run into the Great Road leading from Carlisle to Harris's Ferry at or near the ridge above James Bells have returned to this Court the said road as viewed and laid out by them according to the following courses and distance; beginning at the east side of James Elliots Run S30 W13 perches thence S24 degrees W22 perches thence S55 degrees E20 perches thence S45 degrees W23 perches thence S59 degrees W28 perches thence S40 degrees W24 perches thence N89 degrees W126 perches, thence S40 degrees W154 perches thence S27 ½ degrees W91 perches thence S53 degrees W539 perches to intersect the Great Road at James Bells which road viewed and laid out as aforesaid the said persons; David Hoge, George Wood, James McCormick, John Sample, Thomas Donaldson, & Mathew Loudon now returned to the Court as a road highly necessary __ in manner the least injurious to private property which said road being taken into consideration by the Court is accordingly approved and confirmed __ the said road laid out as aforesaid be cut cleated and bridged if necessary by the several subscribers __ thirty _ feet wide

Page 136 April Sessions 1774
The persons appointed at last January Sessions to view and lay out a road leading from John Flemmings to Wm Patterson's now Kepplers on Juniata have returned to this Court the said road as viewed and laid out by them according to the following courses and distances viz beginning Flemings N12 ½ degrees E20 perches thence N40 degrees E25 perches thence N34 degrees E32 perches N54 degrees E17 ½ perches N46 degrees E84 perches thence N52 degrees E40 perches thence 38 degrees E28 perches thence N36 degrees E45 perches thence N32 degrees E51 perches thence __ 35 degrees E30 perches thence N25 ½ degrees E58 perches thence N23 degrees E33 12 perches thence N30 degrees E18 perches thence N34 degrees E63 perches to Pyals thence N12 degrees E40 perches thence N1 degree E21 and ½ perches thence N38 degrees E58 perches thence N29 degrees E59 perches to John Arbuckles thence N31 degrees E42 perches thence N42 and ½ degrees E46 perches thence N36 degrees E78 perches N34 degrees E37 perches thence n35 degrees E35 perches thence N48 degrees E134 perches thence N57 degrees E30 perches thence N50 degrees E51 perches __ 35 degrees E46 perches to __ McConnells thence N53 degrees E3_ perches N40 degrees E24 ½ perches thence N37 degrees E28 perches thence _34 degrees E28 perches thence n44 degrees E51 ½ perches thence 60 degrees E

Page 137
45 perches thence N51 degrees E45 perches N42 degrees E36 perchres thence N59 degrees E33 perches thence 42 degrees E26 perches to John McIntire's field thence N47 ½ egrees E19 perches thence N40 degrees E26 perches thence N28 degrees E22 perches thence N28 degrees E22 perches thence N37 degrees E31 perches thence N35 degrees E32 perches thence N51 ½ degrees E53

perches N41 degrees E25 perches N44 degrees E46 perches N40 degrees E39
perches N67 degrees E42 perches n57 degrees E41 perches N65 degrees E8
perches N37 degrees E39 perches N54 degrees E20 perches N63 degrees E29
perches N43 ½ degrees E23 Perches N6 degrees W28 perches to Jas Stones
thence N19 ½ degrees E36 perches N14 degrees E16 perches N30 degrees E39
perches N48 degrees E166 perches N39 degrees E36 perches N58 degrees
E119 perches N51 degrees E60 perches N49 ½ E 42 perches N53 ½ degrees
E38 perches to William Morrisons thence N84 degrees E35 perches N59
degrees E32 perches N48 ½ degrees E50 perches N46 ½ E20 perches N65
degrees E20 perches N62 degrees E66 perches N78 degrees E50 perches N67
degrees E12 perches N64 degrees East 28 perches N46 ½ degrees E28 perches
N49 degrees E52 perches N34 ½ degrees E35 perches N34 ½ degrees E35
perches N43 degrees E23 perches N40 degrees

Page 138
32 perches N47 ½ degrees E79 perches N53 ½ degrees E44 perches N53
degrees E10 perches N36 degrees E74 perches to David Beale's Mill thence
N39 ½ degrees E91 perches N46 degrees E32 perches N47 degrees E45
perches N46 degrees E32 perches N47 degrees E45 perches N52 degrees E27
perches N51 degrees E27 perches N33 degrees E30 perches N38 ½ degrees
E75 perches N49 ½ degrees E50 perches N47 ½ degrees E18 perches N60
degrees E38 perches N48 degrees E53 perches N40 degrees E36 perches N46
degrees E36 perches N42 degrees E41 perches N39 degrees E66 perches N37
degrees E40 perches N39 degrees E66 perches N37 degrees E40 perches N35
degrees E84 perches N40 degrees 70 perches N53 perches E18 perches N55
degrees E23 perches N61 ½ E39 perches N63 degrees E52 perches to
Millegans N57 degrees E197 perches N55 degrees E23 perches N48 degrees
E29 perches N48 degrees E44 degrees N57 degrees E48 perches N53 ½
degrees E232 perches N53 ½ perches E232 perches N61 ½ degrees E18
perches n49 degrees E25 perches n46 ½ degrees E42 perches N50 degrees E34
perches N51 degrees E29 perches N61 degrees E30 perches N56 degrees E27
perches to John Hear's Run N76 degrees E66 perches N60 degrees E24
perches N56 ½ degrees E38 perches N53 degrees E31 perches N40 degrees
E31 perches to James Chrities run, N34 degrees E54 perches N41 degrees E68
perches

Page 139
N43 degrees E42 perches N52 degrees E38 perches to Croziers Run N49
degrees E80 perches N57 degrees E33 perches N71 degrees E38 perches N76
degrees E78 perches to Rennesons N70 degrees E25 perches N69 degrees 51
perches N59 ½ degrees E39 perches N65 degrees E218 perches N65 degrees
E50 perches N51 degrees E46 perches N˙_ E125 perches N69 degrees E104
perches N74 perches N69 degrees E104 perches N74 degrees E36 perches N52
degrees E35 ½ degrees E42 perches to Solmon Brice's field N69 E32 perches
N61 degrees E63 perches N49 degrees E52 perches N39 degrees E27 perches
N44 degrees E13 perches N49 degrees E49 perches N35 degrees E36 perches

N69 degrees E42 perches N65 degrees E35 perches N51 degrees E14 perches N41 degrees E74 perches N27 ½ degrees E40 perches N25 degrees E45 perches N41 degrees E41 perches N28 degrees E74 perches N55 degrees E21 perches N58 degrees ½ E32 perches N56 degrees E80 perches N68 degrees E49 perches N40 degrees E12 perches N36 degrees E35 perches N55 degrees E46 perches N74 degrees E53 perches to Wm Pattersons or Kepplers which road viewed and laid out as aforesaid the said persons; William Arbuckle, John Kerr, William Graham, Robert Hogg, David Beale and Hugh Quigley now returned to the Court as a road highly necessary and of publick utility and is laid out in a manner the least injurious to private property which said road being taken into consideration is accordingly approved and ordered that the said road laid out as aforesaid be cut cleared and bridged if necessary by the several supervisors of the townships through which the said road passes of the breadth of 33 feet wide.

Page 140
The persons appointed at last January Sessions to view and lay out a road through part of Antrim and Peters township leading towards Hagerstown to intersect the Maryland road at the line near Dr. Snively have laid out the said road and viewed the same according to the following courses and distances. Beginning at Robert McCoils, thence, south 48 degrees, east 106 perches, south 38 degrees, east 200 perches, and thence by various courses and distances to the Maryland line, which road viewed and laid out as aforesaid is returned and approved by the Court, and it is ordered that the said road be laid out.

Page 141 April Sessions 1774
The persons appointed at October Term Last to view and lay out a road from the house of John Montgomery in East Pennsburgh Township to the Great Road leading from Carlisle to Harris's Ferry Returned to this Court that they had viewed and laid out the same according to the following courses and distances; beginning at the house of John Montgomery thence south 43 degrees east 44 perches south 38 Degrees E88 perches south 48 degrees east 10 perches south 38 degrees east 15 perches to the Great Road leading from Carlisle to Harris's Ferry which Road viewed and laid out as aforesaid the said persons; John Quigley, John Caruthers, William Geddis (?), Samuel Geddis and John Orr returned to the Court as a private road highly necessary and is laid out in a manner the least injurious to private property and being taken into consideration is accordingly approved by the Court.

Court of Private Sessions, at Carlisle 16 June 1774, before Robert Miller, William Lyon and John Agnew Esqrs, Justices of the Peace for the County of Cumberland. Adjudged that Robert Pelan indented servant to Samuel Brice do serve the said Samuel Brice his said master or his assigns the further time of 6 months over and above the time specified in his said indenture in compensation of runaway time expenses.

Page 142
At a Court of Private Sessions, adjudge the within indented servant woman Margaret Martin the property of John Allison Esqr __ing her bearing a bastard child since she became the property of said Allison adjudge the said Margaret Martin to serve her said master or his assigns the full term of one year after the expiration of her within indenture as a satisfaction to her said master for the loss of time and expense during her inability.

Adjudge the within indented servant (Patrick Fleming the property of John Allison Esqr) in regard to his running away sundry times as also the several expenses in taking up the said servant do adjudge that the said servant do serve his said master or his assigns the full term of 1 year, 3 months exclusive of the term mentioned in the within indenture.

Page 143 October Sessions 1774
The King vs Thomas Galbraith
To Westmoreland County

The Same vs Robert Crawford

The Same vs the Same

The Same vs David Wilson Junr

The Same vs John Anderson

The Same vs Robert Graham

The Same vs Timothy __

The Same vs Morgan McSwine

The Same vs Jane Dougan

The Same vs Tho Murray Junr

The Same vs the Same

Page 144
The King vs Henry Carr

The Same vs Enoch Rose (?)

The Same vs George Hall

The Same vs John McCrea

The Same vs Samuel Guen

The Same vs Bartholomew Davis

The King vs Charles McCormick

The King vs Hugh __

Page 145
At Carlisle, 19 July 1774. The sheriff Ephraim Blain returns the following
grand jurors; Samuel Perry, Daniel Duncan, James Pollock, John Pollock,
William Denny, William Blain, Ephraim Steel, Jeremiah Talbot, Charles
Cooper, Andrew Colhoone, Robert Sample, William Campbell, John Blythe,
Thomas Gibson, John Campbell, John Maclay, James Ramsey, William
Peoples, Joseph Wallace, Matthew Scott, James Colhoon, James Chambers,
William Morrow, Matthew Wilson.

Page 146 July Sessions 1774
The King vs Margaret Henezey (?) and Ann Brown.
Felony. Jury; David Duncan, Ralph Starret, Albert Torrance, John McKee,
Michael Finlay, William Morrow, James McCall, John Jordon, Joseph
Wallace, John Murdock, David __, and Thomas Baird say that Margaret
Henezey is guilty. Judgment that she restore the goods stolen to the owner if
not already done or the value thereof pay the value of the goods stolen to the
Governor for support of Government that she be taken to the common
whipping post on Saturday the 23rd instant between the hours of 10 and 4, there
receive 21 lashes on her bare back well laid on, pay costs of prosecution, stand
committed until complied.

Page 147
The King vs Robert Graham, James Forsyth, and Benjamin Phillips
Felony. Jury; David Duncan, Ralph Starret, Albert Torrance, John McKee,
Michael Finlay, William Morrow, James McCall, John Jordon, Joseph
Wallace, John Murdock, David Rowan and Thomas Baird say that James
Forsyth is not guilty.

Page 148
The King vs Robert Fulhy (?), John Denniston and James Forsyth
Felony. Robert Fulhy pleads guilty, submits to the Court. Jury; David Duncan,
Ralph Starret, Albert Torrance, John McKee, Michael Finlay, William Morrow,
James McCall, John Jordon, Joseph Wallace, John Murdock, David Rowan,
and Thomas Baird say that the prisoners John Denniston and James Forsyth are
guilty. Judgment that James Forsyth pay the value of the money stolen to the
Governor for support of Government be taken to the common whipping post on
Saturday the 27th instant between the hours of 10 and 4 be publickly whipped
on the bare back 21 lashes well laid on and that he be bound in 200 pounds and

2 sureties in 100 pounds each for his good behaviour for one year, pay costs of prosecution. That John Denniston be taken to the common whipping post on Saturday the 23rd instant between the hours of 10 and 4 of the clock be publickly whipped 20 lashes on his bare back well laid on, restore the goods stolen or the value to the owner if not already done pay the like value to the Governor pay costs of prosecution. That Robert Futhy restore the foods stolen if not already done or the value thereof pay the Like value to the Governor be taken to the common whipping post on Saturday the 24th day of __ next between the hours of 10 and 4 of the Clock be publickly whipped 21 lashes on his bare back well laid on, pay costs of prosecution, stand committed.

Page 149 July Sessions 1774
The King vs Edward Wilson
Felony. Jury; David Duncan, Ralph Starret, Albert Torrance, John McKee, Michael Finlay, William Morrow, James McCall, John Jordon, Joseph Wallace, John Murdock, David Rowan, and Thomas Baird say that Edward Wilson is guilty. Judgement that Edward Wilson restore the goods stolen or the value thereof to the owner pay the like value thereof to the Governor that he be taken to the common whipping post on Saturday the 23rd instant between the hours of 10 and 4 of the clock, there be publickly whipped 39 lashes on his bare back well laid on, stand in the pillory one hour, be imprisoned one month be bound in 50 pounds each for his good behaviour for one year, pay costs of prosecution and stand committed until the whole be complied with.

Page 150
The King vs Mary Simonton
Indictment disorderly house. Defendant retracts her plea, pleads guilty. Fined of 20 shillings, be committed to the stocks one hour on Friday the 22th, between the hours of 10 and 4, pay costs of prosecution.

The King vs Francis Nichols
Assault and battery. Defendant not willing to contend with the King, submits to Court protesting his innocence, fined 5 shillings and pay costs of prosecution.

The King vs William Starret
Assault and battery. Defendant submits to the Court protesting his innocence, fined defendant in 6 pence.

Page 151
The King vs David Wilson Junr
Fornication.

The King vs Jane Hunter
Fornication.

Page 152
The King vs Michael Gillespie
Assault and battery on Thomas Shortes (?). Defendant by Mr. Johnston his Attorney pleads not guilty. October 1774 defendant retracts his plea and by Mr. Johnston his attorney submits to the Court. Fined 3 shillings and 9 pence, pay costs of prosecution, stand committed until the whole be complied with.

The King vs the same
Assault & battery on William Starrel. Pleads not guilty. October 1774 the Defendant retracts his pleas and by Wm Johnston his attorney submits to the Court, fined 3 shillings and 9 pence, pay costs of prosecution, stand committed until the whole be complied with.

Page 153
The King vs William McCune
Assault & battery. Defendant submits to the Court, fined 5 shillings, costs of prosecution.

The King v John Anderson
Assault & battery. October 1774, submits to the Court protesting his innocence, fined 6 pence, costs of prosecution, stand committed until fine & costs are paid.

Page 154   July sessions 1774
The King vs Robert Crawford
Assault & battery on George Sommerville.

The King vs The Same
Assault & battery on William Nimmens.

Page 155
The King vs Richard Thompson
Assault & battery.

The King vs William Thompson
Assault & battery.

Page 156
The King vs Robert Crawford
Assault & battery on Jane Kennedy.

The King vs Richard Baird, Adam Capler, Joseph Allinder
Assault & battery on John Reddick.

The King vs Robert Peoples
Assault & battery.

Page 157
The King vs Barney Naham
Barney Naham £40, John Glen £20, conditioned for the appearance of Barney Naham at the next Court then and there to answer a certain bill of indictment and not depart the Court without license.

The same vs the same
William Kirk £40, John McIntyre £40, James McConnell £40, conditioned for their appearance the one for the other at the next Court then and there to testify on his Majesties behalf and not depart the Court without license.

The Same vs Michael Gillispie
Jacob Groves £40, conditioned on the appearance of Michael Gillepie at the next Court then and there to answer to a certain indictment found against him and depart the Court without license.

The same vs the same
Thomas Shortes £20, Thomas Reed £20, Ralph Starret £20, conditioned for the appearance of Thomas Reed, Thomas Shortes and William Starrel at the next Court to testify on his Majesties behalf, not depart Court without license.

Page 158 July Sessions 1774
The King vs John Anderson
Samuel David £40, conditioned for his appearance at next Court then and there to testify on his Majesties behalf and not depart the Court without license.

The Same vs David Wilson Junr
Jane Hunter £40, conditioned for her appearance at next Court then and there to testify on his Majesties behalf and not depart the Court without license.

The same vs Edward Worthington
Christopher Brandon £40, Stephan Duncan £20, conditioned for the appearance of Christopher Brandon at next Court then and there to testify on his Majesties behalf and not depart the Court without license.

The same vs the same
Edward Worthington £40, Stephen Duncan £20, conditioned for the appearance of Edward Worthington at the next Court then and there to testify and also to answer to all such things as shall be objected against him on his Majesties behalf and not depart the Court without license.

Page 159
The King vs Richard Thompson
Richard Thompson £40, John Boyd £20, conditioned for the appearance of Richard Thompson at the next Court then and there to answer to a certain bill of indiction and found against him and not depart the Court without license.

The King vs Robert Crawford
George Sommervill £40, Thomas Baird £20, conditioned for the appearance of George Sommervill at the next Court then and there to testify on his Majesties Behalf and not depart the Court without license.

The same vs the same
Jane Kennedy £40, George Sommervill £20, conditioned for the appearance of Jane Kennedy at the next Court then and there to testify on his Majesties behalf and depart the Court without license.

The same vs the same
William Nimmins £40, John Houston £20, conditioned for the appearance of William Nimmins at the next Court then and there to testify on his Majesties behalf and not depart the Court without license.

Page 160 July Session 1774
John Anderson being three times solemnly called to appear to answer Samuel David appeareth not forfeits his recognizance.
William Cambell being three time solemnly called to bring forth the body of John Anderson brings not forth the body of said John Anderson forfeits his recognizance.
Robert Crawford being three times Solemnly called to appear to answer George Sommervill appearth not forfeits his recognizance.
Patrick Jack being three times solemnly called to bring forth the body of Robert Crawford brings forth the body of said Robert Crawford forfeits his recognizance.
Charles McCormick being three times solemnly called to bring forth the body of Robert Crawford brings not forth the Body of said Robert Crawford forfeits his recognizance.
Robert Crawford being three times solemnly called to appear to answer Jane Kennedy and appeareth not forfeits his recognizance.
Patrick Jack being three times solemnly called to bring forth the body of Robert Crawford beings not forth the body of said Robert Crawford forfeits his recognizance.
Charles McCormick being three times solemnly called to bring forth the body of Robert Crawford beings not forth the Body of said Robert Crawford forfeits his recognizance.
Robert Crawford being three times solemnly called to bring forth the body of Robert Crawford brings not forth the body of said Robert Crawford forfeits his recognizance.
Charles McCormick being three times solemnly called to bring forth the body of Robert Crawford brings not forth the body of said Robert Crawford forfeits his recognizance.

Page 161

Elizabeth Lee being three times solemnly called to appear appeareth forfeits her recognizance.

David Nielson being three times called to appear appeareth not forfeits his recognizance.

James Jamison being three times solemnly called to bring forth the body of David Nielson brings not forth the body of the said David Nielson forfeits his recognizance.

John Gray, John Pollock, Carpr, James David, William Peoples, Thomas Wilson, James Colhoone, Bartholomew Segrist, Nicholas Schnider, William Kelso, Isaac Sammis, John McCurdy, Robert Jacks, Tobias Hendericks, Thomas Welsh, Frederick Beamer, Henry Sets, Robert Galbraith, Mathew Scot, Robert Hammil, Conrad Beamer, William Smith, Ralph Harret, William Nielson, John Pollock Malster, Jacob Swem, Owen Aston, George McCleave, Jacob Sailer, James McCall, George Sommervill, John Forbes, James Pollock, Christopher Vanlear, Mary McCormick.

Page 162 July Session 1774

The persons appointed at last April Sessions to view and if they see cause lay out a road from Lawrence Tar's mill up or across the country to John Foreheller's at Conocheague Creek, have returned to the Court that they viewed and laid out the same according to the following courses and distances, beginning at Lawrence Tarr's mill south 62 degrees, west 17 perches, north 29 degrees, west 19 perches, north 49 degrees, west 19 perches, and thence by various courses and distances to Conococheague near Foreheller's which said road was returned, and the Court accordingly confirmed the same and ordered that the said road by laid out.

Page 163

The persons appointed to view and if they should see cause to lay out a private road from the Great Road leading from Carlisle to Trents Gap to Charles McClures House on the east side of Letach Spring have returned to this Court that they had viewed and laid out the same according to the following courses and distances viz beginning at the road from Carlisle to Trents Gap south 81 degrees east 60 perches to a post north 29 degrees east 21 perches to a post on the east side of Letarts Spring south 34 degrees east 20 perches to Charles McClune house in all 101 perches or one quarter of a mile and 20 perches which road viewed and laid as aforesaid the said persons; James Pollock, John Pollock, John Creigh, Stephen Duncan, Christr Vanlear and John McCurdy returned to the Court as a private road which being taken into consideration by the Court is accordingly approved of and confirmed and it is further ordered by the Court that the said road be cut, cleared and kept in repair at the expense of the aforesaid Charles McClure and that it be of the breadth of 25 feet.

The persons appointed at last April Sessions to view and if they should see cause to lay out a road from Carlisle Iron Works to Carlisle Town have returned to this Court that they had viewed and laid out the same according to the following courses and distances, beginning at Carlisle Iron Works north 51 degrees west 51 degrees south 85 degrees west 15 perches north 59 degrees west 24 perches north 81 degrees west 35 perches north 20 degrees west 1152 perches north 55 and a half degrees west 60 perches to Letort Spring in all five miles and 55 perches which road viewed and laid out as aforesaid the said persons, William Lamb, John Miller, Andrew Holmes, John Holmes, Samuel Lourd and Charles McClure returned to the Court as a road highly necessary and of publick utility and laid out in a manner the

Page 164
least injurious to private property. The road is approved is ordered that the said road laid out as aforesaid by cut cleared and bridged if necessary by the several supervisors of the respective townships through which the said road passes forth with of the breadth of 33 feet wide.

Petition of Albert Torrence of Letterkenny township setting forth to the Court that he labors under many inconveniences for want of a private road from the plantation he now lives on through unimproved apart of the tract of land, the property of Benjamin Chambers, and praying the Court to appoint viewers to lay out a road the nearest and best way. Appointed Samuel Culbertson, Thomas Baird, Robert Culberston, James Finley, Joseph Culberston, and John Miller to view and if they see cause to lay out a road and make report to the next Court.

Petition of sundry of the inhabitants of Armagh town setting forth to the Court that they labor under many inconveniences for want of a road from William Browns Esqrs Mill extending through said township, the nighest and best ground to the Bedford Line. Praying the Court to appoint men to view the premises and if they should see cause to lay out a road as aforesaid the Court appoint Capt William Armstrong, Samuel Holliday, William Meane, William Junkin, Samuel Brown Sen, and Thomas Hunter and if they or any four of them see cause to lay out a road as aforesaid they lay out the same by courses and distances the nighest and the way the least injurious to private property and most conducive to the publick utility and make report to next Court.

Page 165
At a Court of Private Sessions, at Carlisle, 23 August 1774, before Robert Miller, William Lyon, and John Agnew. Adjudged that Thomas Connor indented servant to William Lamb to serve the said William Lamb his said master or assigns the further time of six months over and above the time specified in his indenture in compensation of runaway time expenses.

At a Court of Private Sessions, at Carlisle 30 August 1774, before Robert Miller, William Lyon, and John Agnew. Adjudged that William Allegim indented servant to William Brown do serve his said Master William Brown or his assigns the further time of six months over and above the time specified in his indenture in consideration of runaway time expenses.

At a Court of Private Sessions held at Carlisle, 11 October 1774, before Robert Miller, William Lyon, and John Agnew. Adjudged that George Cook indented servant to John Armstrong Esqr do serve his said master John Armstrong or his assigns the further time of six months over and above the time specified in his indenture in consideration of run away time expenses.

At a Court of Private Sessions, held at Conecheage in Cumberland County, 6 September 1774 before John Rannells, Henry Prather, John Allison. Adjudged that a certain Elizabeth Malory indented servant to James McClenahen serve her master or his assigns the further time of two years exclusive of her old indenture in consideration of her bearing a bastard child and other expenses.

Page 166
At a Court of Private Sessions held at Carlisle, 11 October 1774, before John Armstrong, William Lyon and John Holmes. Adjudged that Hannah Harding indented servant to James Moore to serve her said master James Moore or his assigns the further time of 14 months over and above the time in her indenture specified in consideration of run away time expenses.

Page 167
At Carlisle, 18 October 1774. The Sheriff, Robert Semple, made return of the following grand jurors; Edward Morton, James Smith, Charles McClure, John Davison, Samuel Finley, David Blain, John Piper, David English, John Carson, Allen Scroggs, David Ralston, Robert Mahn, William Hudson, Albert Torrence, Thomas Welsh, John Trindel, Alexander Blain, Hugh McCormick, Joseph Hudson, William Laughlin, William Potter, James Graham, Thomas Armstrong, John Kearsly.

Page 168-169 blank

Page 170 October Sessions 1774
The King vs William Barclay
Felony in stealing one bay mare the property of Jacob Seyler. Judgment the Prisoner William Barclay restore the mare to the owner if not already done pay the value thereof pay the like value thereof viz, to his Honor the Governor for support of Government, pay the costs of prosecution, that he be taken to the common whipping post on Friday next the 23rd instant between the hours of 10 and 4 of the clock and there be whipped with 39 lashes on his bare back well laid on stand in the pillory one hour also be committed to prison for the space of 1 month, remain in the custody of the Sheriff until complied.

The King vs John Lin
Felony in stealing good the property of William Beads. Judgment that he restore the goods stolen to the owner if not already done pay the like value thereof viz; three pounds and 7 shillings and six pence to the Govr for support of Govt pay costs of prosecution be taken to the common whipping post on Thursday the 20th inst between the hours of 10 and 4 of the clock and there be whipped with 21 lashes on his bare back well laid on stand committed under the whole be complied with.

Page 171
The King vs James Campbell also James McDonald, also James Morrison
Felony in stealing sundry goods the property of John Gray. Prisoner pleads guilty as to the feloniously stealing of the Half Johanes but not guilty as to stealing the two bills of credit said in the indictment and of this he puts himself on the Country the Attorney General in like manner. Jury; James Brown, Alexander Officer, Robt McClure, Patrick Wallace, James Wilson, John McDowell, William Hodge, George Hudson, Charles Fargher, James McGuppage (?), Arthur Foster and Hugh McCormick say that the prisoner is guilty. Judgement that the prisoner James Campbell also James McDonald, also Jas Morrison restore the goods stolen to the owner if not already done pay the like value thereof (viz) 3 pounds 17 shilling, and 6 pence to the Govenor for support of Government, pay costs of prosecution, be taken to the whipping post on Thursday the 20th inst between the hours of 10 and 4, be whipped with 21 lashes in his bare back well laid on, stand committed until the whole be complied with.

Page 172 October Sessions 1774
The King vs James Mitchel
Assault and battery on Daniel Loughry. Defendant submits to the Court protesting his innocence, fined 2 shillings and 6 pence, costs of prosecution.

The King vs Ross Mitchel
Assault and battery on Daniel Loughey. Defendant submits to the Court protesting his innocence, fined six pence and prosecution.

Page 173
The King vs Edward Worthington
Assault and battery on William Thompson.

The King vs John Lamberton
Nuisance. Defendant pleads guilty, fined 5 pounds to be paid to the Supervisors of the Roads of Middletown Township and costs of prosecution and further adjudges that the nuisance be atal.

Page 174
The King vs James Patton
Tippling House. Defendant pleads guilty. Jan 1775, fined 5 pounds, costs of prosecution, stand committed until fine and costs are paid.

The King vs James Basken
Tippling house.

Page 175 October Sessions 1774
The King vs John Lawrence
Tippling house.

The King vs Daniel Loughry
Assault & battery.

The King vs Daniel Cummins
Felony.

The King vs Rodgers
Nuisance.

Page 176 October Sessions 1774
The King vs David Shavey
Tippling house.

The King vs James Patton
John McCoy Senr £20, conditioned for his appearance at next Court then and there to testify on his Majesty's behalf, not depart the Court without licence.

The King vs Edward Worthington
Edwd Worthington £40, William Campbell £20, conditioned for the appearance of Edward Worthington at next Court then and there to testify on his Majesty's behalf and not depart the Court without license.

The King vs Charles McCormick
Charles McCormick £50, Patrick Jack £25, conditioned for the appearance of Charles McCormick at next Court then and there to answer and not depart the Court without license.

Page 177
Richard Thompson being three times solemnly called to appear, appeareth not forfeits his recognizance.
John Boyd being three time solemnly called to bring forth the body of Richard Thompson but brings forth forfeits his recognizance.

On motion of Jasper Yates Esquire Praying the Court that Jasper Ewing may be admitted as an Attorney of the Court, he is accordingly admitted.

Page 178
Petition of sundry inhabitants of Tuskorara Valley to the Court setting forth that they labor under many inconveniences for want of a publick road from David Beales's Mill to George Sharps in Sherman's Valley, praying the Court to appoint men to view and if they should see cause to lay out a road. Appointed George Sharp, William Townsley, William Arbuckle, John Stewart, William Logan and William Williams to view the premises and if they or any four of them see cause to lay out a road as aforesaid, they lay out the same by courses the nighest and best way the least injurious to private property and most conducive to publick utility and make report to next Court.

Upon the petition of sundry inhabitants of Teboyne Township to the Court setting forth that they labor under many inconveniences for want of a publick road leading from Alexander Smith's near the Head of Sherman's Creek and from thence to Thomas Clark's from which a road has already been laid out to intersect the road leading from Logan's to Chambers's Mill, praying the Court to appoint proper men to view and if they see cause to lay out a road as aforesaid the nearest and best way. The Court appoint George Kinkead, Wilm McCoard, Alexander Murray, John Watts, Robert Adams Junr and Anthony Morrison to view the premises and if they or any four of them see cause to lay out a road as aforesaid they lay out the same by courses and distances the nighest and best way the least injurious to private property and most conducive to publick utility and make report to next Court.

Page 179 October Sessions 1774
Upon the petition of Andrew Holmes, Charles McClure and John Glenn to the Court setting forth that they labor under many inconveniences for want of a private road leading from Carlisle to the place where John Glenn now lives and from thence to Andrew Holmes's and from there to the road leading from Carlisle to Greaghead mill, praying the Court to appoint proper persons to view and if they see cause to lay out a road as aforesaid the nearest and best way. The Court appoint Saml Hay, Matthew Laird, William Moore, John Pollock, John Creigh and John McCurdy to view the premises and if they or any four of them see cause to lay out a road as aforesaid the lay out the same by courses and distances the nighest and best way the least injurious to private property and make report to next court.

Upon the petition of sundry inhabitants of Armagh Township to the Court setting forth that they labor under many inconveniences for want of a publick road from the Ford of the Creadon Spring at James Alexander's to William Brown's Mill the nearest and best way, praying the Court to appoint proper men to view and if they see cause to lay out a road as aforesaid. The Court appoint James Adams, Wm Wilson, James McClure, Abraham Stanford, John

Galloway and Henry McElroy to view the premises and if they or any four of them see cause to lay out a road as aforesaid they lay out the same by courses and distances the nighest and best way the least injurious to private property and most conducive to publick utility and make report to next Court.

Page 180
Upon the petition of sundry inhabitants of Middleton in East Pennsborough Township in the County of Cumberland to the court, setting forth that they labor under great inconveniences for want of a pulick road or highway from the Town of Carlisle to the River Susqehannah at William Kelso's Ferry (formerly called Harris's ferry) and tho a road has been heretofore used from the said Town, to the said ferry as the same has not then laid out and confirmed by legal authority it has not been nor cannot be kept in proper repair , praying the Court to appoint six proper men to view and if they see cause to lay out a road as aforesaid. The Court appoint David Hoge, Esqr, Edward Morton, James McCormick, Andrew Armstrong, Samuel Laird, Willm Chambers to view the Premises and if they or any four of them see cause to lay out a road as aforesaid they lay out the same by courses and distances the nighest and best way the least injurious to private property and most conducive to publick utility and make report to next Court.

The persons appointed at the last July Sessions to view and lay out a private road from the plantation of Albert Torrence in Letterkenny township through an unimproved tract of land the property of Benjamin Chambers to another plantation of the said Torrence, have returned to this Court that they did view and lay out the same according to the following courses and distances. Beginning at a hickory on the west side of Conococheague creek east 55 degrees, north 236 perches. to a pine in said Torrence's land which road viewed and laid out the said persons make return. The Court accordingly approved and confirmed and ordered that the said road be cut, cleared and kept in repair.

Page 181
At Carlisle, 24 January 1775. The Sheriff, Robert Semple, returns the following list of grand jurors; Francis Silver. Samuel Adams, Abram Adams. Ralph Naylor, Francis Nicholas, William Miller, William Hendricks, John Quigley, Alexander McDonald, Thomas Fisher, Matthew Loudon, Samuel Gaddis, William Gaddis. John Carothers, George Woods, Joseph Semple. David Hege, Thomas Armstrong, David Reddick. John Boggs, Robert Galbraith, John Carson. William Kelso.

The King vs Joseph Armstrong
Felony.

The King vs Samuel Dodds
Felony.

Upon the petition of the inhabitants of Lurgan township setting forth that they are shut up from carrying their produce to market except by going around by Loudon which is at least thirty or forty miles round, and find from ocular demonstration that there can be a wagon road from James McCarrolls through the Gap of the North Mountain commonly called McAllaster's, with a great deal less trouble than is or was imagined, for ten men in one day hath already cut and cleared out one and one half miles of road sufficiently side for a wagon to carry 2000 weight in as bad a part as there is to cut, and that a wagon road at said gap would be of great benefit to them, and to the county in general, and praying the Court to appoint proper men to view and if they see cause to lay out a wagon road from McCarrolls mill into Amberson's Valley and down said valley into the Path Valley. The Court appointed John Macclay, Sr., Samuel Colter, Francis Graham, Hugh McCurdy, James McKibben, and Thomas Askey to view the premises and if they see cause to lay out the road.

Page 182 January Sessions 1775
The King vs Hugh Smith
Felony. April 1775, Jury; Walter Denny, Thomas Guy, John McClelland, Robert Stewart, Robt Polk, Joseph Shields, Samuel Williamson, John Hall, William Sanderson, John Samrock, William Townsly, Alexander Irwin say that Hugh Smith is guilty. Judgment that he restore the goods or value thereof, the like value to the Governor, be whipped on the 17th July, 12 lashes on his bare back, well laid on, stand committed until the whole be complied with.

The King vs Joseph Gordon and James Gordon
Assault and battery on John Henderson. Defendants submits to the Court by protesting their innocense. Fines defendant in 2 shillings and six pence each, costs of prosecution.

The King vs James Gordon
Assault and battery on Robert Wilson. Defendant submits to the Court protesting his innocence, fined 2 shillings and 6 pence, costs of prosecution.

Page 183
The King vs Robert Gordon and James Gordon
Assault and battery on Elizabeth Henderson. James Gordon being charged submits to the Court protesting his innocence. Robert Gordon retracts his plea and submits to the Court protesting his innocence. Fines defendants in 2 shillings and 6 pence each, costs of prosecution.

The King vs John Henderson
Assault and battery on Robert Gordon. The defendant retracts his plea being unwilling to contend with the King and submits to the Court with protestations of his innocence. Fines defendant 12 shillings and 6 pence and costs of prosecution.

Page 184

The King vs James Campbell alias McDonald

Felony. Prisoner pleads guilty. Judgment that the prisoner restore the goods to the owner if not already done or the value thereof, pay a fine of the like value to the Governor for support of Government, to taken to the whipping post this day (26th instant) between the hours of 2 and 4 of the clock in the afternoon, receive 21 lashes on his bare back well laid on, stand committed until the whole be complied with.

The King vs James Patton and John Allen

Nuisance. January Sessions 1776, jury; William Giddes, David Bell, James McCormick, William McLere, Mathew Louden, John __ Junr, Thomas Donaldson, Andrew Gap, David Riddick, Richard Coulter, Thomas Craighead and Alexander Work who say that the defendants James Patton and John Allen are guilty. Judgment that the defendants fined 50 pounds each, order that the nuisance be abated, pay costs of prosecution, stand committed till the whole be complied with.

Page 185 January Sessions 1775

The King vs Elizabeth Henderson

Assault and battery on Robt Gordon.

Joseph Armstrong being three times solemnly called to appear appeareth not forfeits his recognizance.

John Armstrong being three times solemnly called to being froth the body of Joseph Armstrong brings not forth the body forfeits his recognizance.

Felix Doyle being three times solemnly called to appear appeareth not forfeits his recognizance.

Incas McMullan being three times solemnly called to bring forth the body of Felix Doyle brings not forth the body forfeits his recognizance.

John Daugherty being three times solemnly called to appear appeareth not forfeits his recognizance.

Neil Dougherty being three times solemnly called to bring forth the body of John Doughterly brings not forth the body forfeits his recognizance.

Charles McCormick being three times solemnly called to appear appeareth not forfeits his recognizance.

Patrick Jack being three times solemnly called to bring forth the body of Charles McCormick brings not forth the body forfeits his recognizance.

Page 186 January Sessions 1775
The King vs Saml Dodds
Samuel Dodds £100, James Elliot £50, conditioned for the appearance of
Samuel Dodds at the next Court then and there to answer and not depart the
Court without licence.

William Gilston £40, Edward Long £40, conditioned for their several
appearances at Next Court then and there to testify on his Majesties behalf and
not depart the Court without licence.

James Roddy £40, Edward West £40, conditioned for their several appearances
at Next Court then and there to testify on his Majesty's behalf and not depart
the Court without licence.

Page 187 January Sessions 1775
Robert Dickey £40, James Elliot £40, conditioned for their several appearances
at Next Court then and there to testify on his Majesties Behalf and not depart
the Court without licence.

James Pattan £100, James Baskens £60, Saml Goudy £60, conditioned for the
appearance of James Pattan at next Court then and there to answer and not
depart the Court without licence.

John Allen £100, James Baskins £60, Samuel Goudy £60, conditioned for the
appearance of John Allen at Next Court then and there to answer and not depart
the Court without licence.

Page 188
Samuel McCord £40, conditioned for the appearance of Samuel McCord at
Next Court then and there to testify on his Majesty's Behalf and not depart the
Court without licence.

John Pollock Carpr. £20, conditioned for his appearance next Court then and
there to testify on his Majesties behalf, and not depart the Court without
licence.

The following gentlemen summoned to serve on the General Inquest; George
Woods, John Simple, Joseph Simple, David Hoge, Thomas Armstrong, David
Reddick, John Boggs, Robert Galbraith, John Carson, and William Kelso
appeared not fined in 20 shilling unless they show cause at next sessions.
David Reddick excused by the Court.

Page 189
Petition of sundry inhabitants of Milford Townshipsetting forth that they labor
under many inconveniences for want of a publick road leading from the great
road already laid out at or near Thomas Kerrs and from thence to Juniata River

at or Near John McClellands, praying the Court to appoint proper persons to view and lay out the same and if they see cause layout a road as aforesaid. The Court appoint John Hardy, Alexander Robinson, Joseph McCoy, John Beale, David Beale, and John Stuart to view the premises and if they or any four of them see cause to lay out a road as aforesaid the layout the same by courses and distances the least injurious to private property and most conducive to publick utility and make report to next Court.

Petition of sundry inhabitants of Lurgan Township setting forth to the Court that they are shut up from carrying their produce to market except going round by Louden which is at least 30 or 40 miles round, and finding from occular demonstration that there can be a wagon road from James McCarrol's Mill through the Gap of the North Mountain commonly known McCallesters with a great deal less trouble than is or was imagined, for ten men in one day hath already cut and cleared a mile and an half of a road sufficient for a wagon to carry 20 hundred weight in as bad a part as is to but and a wagon road at said Gap would be of great benefit to them and to the county in general, praying the Court to appoint proper men to view and if they see cause to lay out a wagon road From McCarrol's Mill into Ambersons Valley and down said Valley into Path Valley. The Court appointing John McClay Senr, Samuel Cutler, Francis Graham, Hugh McCurdy, James McKibbin and Thomas Askey to view the

Page 190 January Sessions 1775
premises and if they or any four of them see cause to lay out a road as aforesaid they lay out the same by distances the least injurious to private property and most conducive to publick utility and make report to next Court.

Petition inhabitants of Peters township setting forth that they labor under difficulties for want of a bridge over the branch of the Conochocheague creek at or near the line between the lands of Samuel Finley, and Thomas Dunwoody, which would be of great utility on account of its situation and likewise would be of public advantage to east side of said creek and praying the Court to appoint men to view and lay out a wagon road the nearest and best way from Meeting House of the Rev. John King's to the branch proposed for the bridge, and from thence the nearest and best way to the house of Dugal Campbell on the great road leading from the Great Cove to Baltimore.

The Court appointed William McDowell, James McDowell, Patrick Maxwell, James Campbell, John Work, and William Houston to view the premises and if they see cause to lay out a road and make report to the next Court.

Page 191
Petition of Ephraim Blaine of Middletown Township setting forth that in Pursuance of an order of the last session a road has been laid out from Andrew Holmes's to Carlisle that said road will be very Injurious to him if the same should be confirmed as there are many other ways Andrew Holmes and people

in that neighbourhood can have a road that will answer every purpose and praying the Court to appoint proper persons to review said road. Appointed James Irwin, John McClure, William Brown, James Mitchel, William Rainey and Walter Denny to review the said road and if they or any four of them see cause to lay out a road as aforesaid they lay out the same by courses and distances, the least injurious to private property and make report to next Court.

Page 192   April Sessions 1775
The King vs John McCrea

The King vs George Hall

The King vs David Wilson Junr.

The King vs Timothy Huff

The King vs Enoch Rose

The King vs Henry Carr

The King vs John Lawrence

The King vs John Williamson

The King vs Morgan McSwine

The King vs Joseph Armstrong

The King vs Robert Graham

Page 193
The King vs Hugh Toaffe

The King vs Bartholomew Davis

The King vs Samuel Quin

The King vs Charles McCormick

Page 194
At a Court of private Sessions held at Carlisle, 25 March 1775, for the appointment of officers, etc.
Antrim township; William McClellan, constable; John Coughrin, Bartholomew Seacrist, supervisors of roads; Henry Gordon, Andrew Miller, overseers of poor.

Fannett township; John Noble, constable; James Elder, Robert McGuire, supervisors of roads; Nathan Paul, Thomas Armstrong, overseers of poor.

Hamilton township; Joseph Thorn, constable; John Wilkinson, William McCune, supervisors of roads; John McClane, George Matthews, overseers of poor.

Lurgan township; John Justice, constable; James McKibben, David Porter, supervisors of roads; Francis Grimes, William Montgomery, overseers of poor.

Letterkenny township; William Nicholson, constable; James Henry, Hugh Wiley, supervisors of roads; John Stevenson, Alexander Thompson, overseer of poor.

Guilford township; John Kerr, constable; Edward Crawford, Jr., Jacob Cook, supervisors of roads; John Vance, George Smith, overseer of poor.

Peters township; Johnson Elliott, constable; Kearne Sterritt, Thomas McDowell, supervisors of roads; John Welsh, Robert Taggart, overseer of poor.

Page 196- blank

Page 197
At Carlisle, 18 April 1775, before John Armstrong and his associates. The Sheriff, Robert Semple, returns the following list of grand jurors; John Harris, William Chambers, William Moore, Robert Darlington, James Ramsey, Alexander Parker, Samuel Rippey, John Holmes, Jr., Ross Mitchell, David Lusk, George Smiley, James Sharron,. Patrick Vance, Andrew Kinkead, James Caldwell, William Gass, Nathaniel Wilson, Robert Patten, David McNair, Hugh Wiley, James Brotherton, Ralph Steritt, William McClure, Andrew Boyd.

Page 198 April Sessions 1775
The King vs William McKibben
Assault and battery on David McNeil. Defendant submits to the Court protesting his innocence, fined 6 pence and costs of prosecution.

The King vs the Same
Assault and battery on Mary McNeil. Defendant being submits to the Court protesting his innocence. Fined 6 pence and costs of prosecution.

The King vs William Gallagher, James McFeathers, James Cochran also James Currin
Assault and battery on Andrew Ferrio (?). April Sessions 1778, Jury; John Carrothers, John Welsh, Alexander Erwin, James Carnahan, Andrew Walker, William Steen, Nathan McDowell, Samuel Findly, Robert Rogers, Gabriel Glenn, David Elder and Robert Anderson say that Wm Gallagher is guilty , fined 10 pounds, stand committed until fine and fees are paid.

Page 199
The King vs Samuel McCord
Felony. Defendant pleads not guilty, jury; Walter Denny, Thomas Craighead, Thomas Guy, John McClelland, Robert Polk, William Townsby, Joseph Shields, Saml Williamson, Robert Stewart, William Sanderson, John Lamrock and John Hall, who say that the prisoner Samuel McCord is guilty. Judgment, pay the value of the ax stolen, restore the goods stolen to the owner if not already done or the value thereof be taken to the publick whipping post tomorrow the 20th instant and there receive 12 lashes on his bare back well laid on, between 9 and 4, stand committed until the whole be complied with.

The King vs John Brown
Felony. Prisoner pleads not guilty. Jury; Walter Denny, Thomas Craighead, Thomas Guy, John McClelland, Robert Polk, William Townsby, Joseph Sheilds, Samuel Williamson, Robert Stewart, William Saunderson, John Lamrock and John Hall, say that the prisoner John Brown is guilty. Judgment that the prisoner restore the goods stolen to the owner if not already done or the value thereof, pay the like value to the Governor, pay costs of prosecution, tomorrow the 20th inst receive on his bare back 12 lashes well laid on, stand committed till the whole be complied with.

Page 200 April Sessions 1775
The King vs Stephen Terry
Felony. Prisoner pleads not guilty as to the three pounds, but guilty as to the two dollars said in the indictment, and of this he puts himself on the County the Attorney General in like manner. Jury; Walter Denny, Thomas Craighead, Thomas Guy, John McClelland, Robert Polk, William Townsby, Joseph Shields, Samuel Williamson, Robert Stewart, William Sanderson, John Lamrock and John Hall say that the prisoner is guilty. Judgment that Stephen Terry, restore the goods stolen to the owner if not already done, pay costs of prosecution be taken to the common whipping post on Thursday the 20th instance between 9 and 4, be whipped with 21 lashes on his bare back well laid on stand committed until the whole be complied with.

The King vs William Elliot
Assault and Battery. Defendant submits to the Court protesting his innocence, fined 6 pence and costs of prosecution.

Page 201
The King vs James Feagan
Assault and battery.

The King vs Robert Collins
Tippling house. July Term 1775, defendant pleads guilty. Fined 5 pounds, pay costs of prosecution, stand committed till the whole be complied with.

The King vs John Irwin, James Irwin Senr, James Irwin Jur, Joseph Sommerville and Richama Sommerville.
Forceable Detainer. January Sessions 1776, jury; William Gaddis, David Bell, James McCormick, Wm McLeer, Mattw L__, John Orr, Thomas Donaldson, Andrew Capp, David Reddick, Richd Coulter, Thomas Craighead and Alexander Work, say that John Irwin is guilty, fined 5 shillings, writ of restitution to issue, pay costs of prosecution, stand committed until the whole be complied with.

Page 202 April Sessions 1775
The King vs Edward Hagan
Felony. Jury; Walter Denny, Thomas Guy, John McClelland, Thomas Craighead, Robert Stewart, Robert Polk, Joseph Shields, Samuel Williamson, John Hall, William Sanderson, John Lamrock and William Townsley, say that Edwd. Heagen is not guilty, prisoner discharged paying costs.

Edward West £20, James Reddy £20, conditioned for the appearance ___ at next Court then and there to Testify on his Majesties behalf, and not depart the Court without licence.

The King vs John Irwin
John Irwin £200, Richd. Irwin £100, conditioned for the appearance of John Irwin at next Court, in the mean time to behave himself to his Majesties subjects, keep the peace in particular to John Buyers and not depart the Court without Licence.

Page 203
James Patten being three times called to appear but appeareth not forfeits his recognizance.

James Baskins being three times solemnly called to bring forth the body of James Patten, brings not forth the body forfeits his recognizance.

Samuel Goudy being three times solemnly called to bring forth the body of James Patten, brings not forth the body forfeits his recognizance.

John Allen being three times called to appear, appeareth not forfeits his recognizance.

James Baskins being three times solemnly called to bring forth the body of John Allen brings not forth the body forfeits his recognizance.

Samuel Goudy being three times solemnly called to bring forth the body of John Allen, brings not forth the body forfeits his recognizance.

John Robinson being three times solemnly called to appear, appeareth not forfeits his recognizance.

John Dougherty being three times solemnly called to appear appears not forfeits his recognizance.

Thomas Dougherty being three times solemnly called to bring forth the body of John Dougherty, brings not forth the body forfeits his recognizance.

James Goudy being three times solemnly called to appear, appeareth not forfeits his recognizance.

Joseph Armstrong being three times called to appear, appeareth not forfeits his recognizance.

John Armstrong being three times solemnly called to bring forth the body of Joseph Armstrong, brings not forth the body forfeits his recognizance.

Page 204 April Sessions 1775
Mary Gordon being three times called to appear, appeareth not forfeits her recognizance.

James Goudy being three times called to appear, appeareth not forfeits his recognizance.

William Gallagher £100, Thomas Askey £50, conditioned for the appearance of William Gallaugher at next Court then and there to answer and not depart the Court without licence.

Andrus Ferrier £20, conditioned for his appearance at next Court then and there to testify on his Majesties behalf and not depart the Court without licence.

John Lockrey £20, James Nisbit £10, conditioned for the appearance of John Lochrey at next Court then and there to testify on his Majesties behalf and not depart the Court without licence.

The King vs Robert Collens
James Calhoon £40, conditioned for the appearance of Robert Collens at next Court then there to testify on his Majesties behalf, not depart the Court without licence.

Page 205
Upon the petition of sundry inhabitants of Millford Township to the Court setting forth that they labor under many inconveniences for want of a publick road leading from the summit of the Tusinora Mountain at or near the head of the Run gap, from thence to Robert Gorrells on Juniata at the lower end of the

Long Narrows, praying Court to appoint men to view the same, if they see cause to lay out a road, the Court appointed William Graham, John Hamilton, James Rodman, William Irwin, Thomas Hardy, and John Elliot to view the premises and if they or any four of them see cause they lay out the same by courses and distances, the nearest and best way the least injurious to private property and most conducive to publick utility and make report to next Court.

Upon the petition of sundry inhabitants of Teboyne Township to the Court setting forth that they labor under many Inconveniences for want of a publick road leading from John Sheavers to Thomas Clark's from which there has been a road already laid out to Chamber's Mill, praying the Court to appoint proper persons to view the same, if they see cause to lay out a road as aforesaid. Court appointed John __, Robert Adams Junr, Alexander Murry Wheelwright, Anthony Morrison, William McCord, and George Kinkead, to view the premises and if they or any four of them see cause they lay out the same by courses and distances the nearest and best way the least injurious to private property, and most conducive to publick utility, make report the next Court.

Page 206 (it also continues on page 207 and part of 208) April Sessions 1775
Upon the petition of sundry of the inhabitants of Guilford and Hamilton townships to the Court setting forth that they labor under any inconveniences for want of a public road leading from Chambersburg to the forks of Back Creek and from thence to Capt. Armstrongs near the foot of the North Mountain, and praying the Court to appoint viewers. Court appointed Joseph Armstrong, Samuel Lindsay, James Chambers, Robert Jack, Samuel Patten and John Jack to view and lay out a road and make report to the next Court.

The persons appointed at January Sessions to view and if they should see cause, to lay out a road near Thomas Kerr's on the Juniata river at or near John McClellan's, return to this Court that they have viewed and laid out the same according to the following courses and distances; beginning at a post at the Great Road from the Path Valley to the Juniata, thence north 7 degrees, east 173 perches, thence north 18 degrees, west 40 perches, thence north 30 degrees, west 147 perches, and thence by various courses and distances to a post at Juniata river, which road viewed and laid out as aforesaid the said persons report as highly necessary and of public utility, which being considered by the Court is approved and confirmed, and is ordered that the said road by laid out as aforesaid.

Page 208
The persons appointed at last January Sessions to view and lay out a private road from Carlisle to John Glenn's from thence to Andrew Holmes's and from thence to the road laid out from Craighead's Mill, have returned to the Court the said road as viewed and laid out by them according to the following courses and distances, beginning at the end of Hanover street, 8 degrees and a half west 248 perches thence S81 degrees East 60 perches, thence N79 degrees E 60

perches thence N79 degrees E21 perches to Letort Spring, thence S34 degrees E20 perches to Charles McClure's, thence S21 degrees W31 perches, thence S 5 degrees E 84 perches, to John Glenn's thence south 68 degrees E 52 perches, thence N 79 degrees E52 perches, thence N79 degrees E22 perches thence S21 degrees

Page 209
E50 perches, thence S32 degrees and ½ E65 perches to Andrew Holmes's, thence S68 degrees E26 perches, thence S23 degrees E14 perches, thence S61 degrees and ½ W106 perches, thence S64 degrees W40 perches to Craigheads Road. Now returned to the Court as a private road by James Irwin, John McClure, William Brown, James Mitchel, William Rainey and Walter Denny, the persons in said order mentioned highly necessary and the least injurious to private property and most conducive to the utility of the petitioners. Which said road being taken into consideration is accordingly approved of and confirmed by the Court,it is further ordered that the road laid be cut, cleared and kept in repair at the expense and costs of the petitioners, opened the breadth of 25 feet.

The persons appointed at April Sessions 1771 to view and lay out a publick Road from James Badsken's Ferry on Susquihannah to James Gallagher's on Juniata returned to the Court the road as viewed and laid out by them according to the following courses; beginning at James Baskins thence north 68 degrees W68 perches thence N17 degrees W274 perches, thence N40 W100 perches thence N 27 degrees west 56 perches to a pine, thence N20 degrees east 160 perches to a pine, thence N57 degrees west 200 perches thence N 32 degrees west 120 perches, thence N 17 degrees West 340

Page 210
perches to a locust tree, thence N70 degrees west 180 perches, thence south 75 degrees W144 perches thence N 21 degrees W34 perches, thence W40 perhces, thence N35 degrees W168 perches to a white oak, thence N53 degrees W166 perches to a white oak thence N80 degrees W124 perches, thence N78 degrees W90 perches thence N78 degrees W90 perches to a white oak, thence N45 degrees W74 perches to a white oake, thence N70 degrees W320 perches to a black oak, thence N14 degrees E134 perches thence N274 perches thence N25 degrees W440 perches thence N274 perches thence N25 degrees W440 perches to a white oak, thence N30 degrees W360 perches to James Gallagher's on Juniata which road viewed and laid out as aforesaid by William Richardson, Fredrick Watts, James Watts, Joseph Martin, James Carson and David English returned to this Court as a road highly necessary and of publick utility which road was then (to wit, April 1771) taken under consideration by the Court, and ordered to be kept under advisement, and now April Sessions 1775, upon petition of sundry inhabitants of Rye Township praying the Court to confirm the road, ordered by the court, and it is further ordered the said road laid be cut, cleared and bridged if necessary forthwith by the inhabitants of the several townships through which the same passes. & be of the breadth of 33 feet wide.

Page 211 July Sessions 1775
The King vs James McFaters & James Cochran also James Currin
Renewed to October Session 1775.

The King vs James Feagan
To October 1775.

At a Court of Private Sessions,at Carlisle, 21 April 1775 before Jonathan
Hoge, William Thompson. and James Oliphant Justices of the Peace.

Adjudged by the Court that Joan Liddane (?) indented servant of Ralph Nailer
do serve her said master Ralph Nailer or his assigns the further time of one year
over and above the time specified in her said Indenture in consideration of
runaway time expenses.

At a Court of Private Sessions, at Carlisle, 6 June 1775, before Robert Miller,
William Lyon and John Holmes. Adjudged by the Court that John Doyl
indented servant to Thomas Stewart to serve his said master Thomas Stewart or
his assigns the further time of one year over and above the time specified in
said indenture in consideration of runaway time, expenses.

Page 212
At a Court of Private sessions, at Carlisle, 7 June 1775 before Robert Miller,
John Holmes and John Agnew. Adjudged that Peter Jennet indented servant to
Joseph Alexander do serve his said master Joseph Alexander or his assigns the
further time of one year over and above the time specified in his indenture in
consideration of runaway time, expenses.

At a Court of Private Sessions, at Carlisle __ July 1775 before Robert Miller,
William Lyon and John Holmes. Adjudged that Mary Beamond late indented
servant to John Agnew do serve him the said late master or his assigns the
space of one year in compensation of bearing a bastard child in the time of her
late servitude and other expenses.

At a Court of Private Sessions, at Carlisle 1 August 1775 Before Robert Miller,
William Lyon and John Holmes. Adjudged that Catherine Lindon indented
servant to Hugh Wiley so serve her said master Hugh Wiley or his assigns the
further time of 1 year and 11 months over and above the time specified in her
said indenture in consideration of runaway time, expenses.

Adjudged that Daniel Nation indented servant to James Dunbarr do serve his
said master James Dunbarr or assigns the further time of seven months over
and above the time specified in said indenture in consideration of runaway
time, expenses.

Page 213
At Carlisle, 18 July 1775, before John Armstrong and his associates. Sheriff, Robert Semple, Esq., returns the following list of grand jurors; Joseph Laird, John Boyd, Andrew Colhoone, Robert White, Ephraim Steel, William Holmes, James Ramsey, John Henry, Matthew Scott, Charles Cooper, John Heap, Jacob Herwick, William Diven, Thomas Gibson, Frederick Beemer, Robert Jack, Christopher Naylor, William Holmes, merchant, William Morrow, Andrew Boyd, Samuel Lindsay, John Hughes, John Pollock, James Davis.

Page 214 July Sessions 1775
The King vs William Lidy
Felony in stealing cash the property of James Wilson. Jury; John Creigh, James McClintock, James Gregg, William Blair, John Forbes, Peter Smith, John McKee, Andrus McKee, John Robinson, Robert Mahan, George Logue, and Joseph Wallace, say that the prisoner William Lidy is guilty. Judgment to restore the cash stolen to the owner if not already done, pay the like sum to the Governor for support of government, pay costs of prosecution, be taken to the common whipping post this afternoon the 19th, between 5 and 6, whipped with 21 lashes on his bare back, stand committed till the whole be complied.

The King vs The Same
Felony stealing goods, property of George McGormigle. Jury; Jno. Cregh, James McClintock, James Cregg, Wm Blair, John Forbes, Jon. McKee, Andw McKee, Jon. Robinson, Robt Mahan, Geo. Logue and Joseph Wallace, who say he is guilty. Judgement William Lidy restore the goods stolen to the owner if not already done, pay the like value to the Governor for support of government pay costs of prosecution, be taken to the common whipping post on Friday next, 21st, between 5 and 6, be whipped 15 lashes on his bare back, well laid on, stand committed until the whole be complied with.

Page 215
The King vs Thos. Fitzgerald & James McGraw
Felony in stealing cash the property of Fredrick Bramer. Prisoners pleads guilty. Judgment that they return the money stolen to the owner if not already done, pay the like sum to the Governor for support of Government, be taken to the common whipping post on Friday next the 21st, between 4 and 6, there receive 15 lashes each on their bare backs well laid on pay costs of prosecution, stand committed until the whole be complied with.

The King vs William Stuart
Felony. The prisoner pleads guilty. Judgment prisoner return the goods to the owner if not already done, pay the like value thereof to the Governor for support of Government, be taken to the common whipping post on Friday next the 21st, between 5 and 6, there receive 15 lashes on his bare back well laid on, pay costs of prosecution, stand committed until the whole be complied with.

The King vs Andw. Galheath
Assault and battery. Jan Sessions 1776, Jury; Wm. Gaddis, David Bell, James McCormick, William McLeer, Mathw. Loudon, John Orr Junr. Thomas Donaldson Andr. Capp, David Reddick, Richard Coulter, Thomas Craighead and Alexander Work, who say that the defendant is not guilty.

Page 216 July Sessions 1775
The King v John Glenn, Hugh Glenn, Robt. Philips & John Fury
Trespass. January 1776, Jury; Wm. Gaddis, David Bell, Jas. McCormick, William M__, Matw. Saunder, Jno. Orr Junr, Thos. Donaldson, Andw. Capp, David Reddick, Richd. Coulter, Thomas Craighead and Alexr. Work, who say that John Glenn is guilty, Hugh Glenn is not guilty, Robert Phillips is not guilty, John Fury is not guilty. John Glenn fined in 7 shillings, six pence, pay costs of prosecution.

The King vs Jemina Brown
Petty Treason. Ordered discharged on payment of fees.

The King vs Richard White
Burglary. Ordered discharged on payment of fees.

The same vs the same
Felony. Ordered discharged from his confinement on payment of fees.

The King vs Mathias Kepler
Felony in sundries from Willm. McFarson. William McFarson £20. conditioned for his appearance at next Court then & there to testify on his Majesties behalf and not depart the Court without licence.

Page 217
The King vs Abraham Keplan
Felony in sundries from John Martin. October Sessions 1775, jury; John Bowman, William Smith, Samuel McCormick, Ralph Starret, Robert Saunderson, Robert Campbell, Archibald Hanna, Thomas Menzus. Samuel Ra_meeks, David, Nevens, James Mitchel and John Flack, who say that the prisoner at the Barr is not guilty.

The King vs Margatet Isset
Felony.

Mathias Skiplan being three times solemnly called to appear appeareth not forfeits his recognizance.

Robert Campbell being three times solemnly called to bring forth the body of Mathias Skiplar brings not forth the body forfeits is recognizance.

James Caldwell being three times solemnly called to appear appeareth not forfeits his recognizance.

William Reynolds being three times solemnly called to bring forth the body of James Caldwell brings not forth the body forfeits his recognizance.

James Stewart being three times solemnly called to appear appeareth not forfeits his recognizance.

Page 218 July Sessions 1775
Joseph Sommerville being three times solemnly called to appear appeareth not forfeits his recognizance.

Joseph Wallace being three times solemnly called to bring forth the body of Joseph Sommerville brings not forth the body forfeits his recognizance.

Andrew Farrier £20, William Campbell £20, James McCutchen £20, conditioned for their several appearances at next Court, then and there to testify on his Majesties behalf, and not depart the Court without licence.

William Gallagher £100, James Askey £50, conditioned o the appearance of William Gallagher at next Court, then and there to answer, not depart the Court without licence.

Abraham Kepler £200, John Keplar £100, conditioned for the appearance of Abraham Kepler at Next Court, then and there to answer and not depart the Court without licence.

John Martin £20, William Lewis £20, conditioned for their appearances at next Court then and there to testify on his Majesties behalf and not depart the Court without license.

Page 219
Margaret Dyer £50, conditioned for her appearance at next Court then and there to testify on his Majesties behalf and not depart the Court without license.

Francis West £20, conditioned for his appearance at next Court, then and there to testify against Jas. Pattan and John Allen, on his Majesties behalf and not depart the Court without license.

John Irwin £200. George Robinson £100. conditioned for the appearance of John Irwin at next Court, then and there to answer and not depart the Court without licence.

John Allen £100, James Pattan £100, John Gray £100, conditioned for the appearance of John Allen and James Pattan at next Court then and there to answer and not depart the Court without licence.

John Justis Constable of Lurgan fined 20 shillings, William Campbell Junr. Constable of Lack, fined 20 shillings.

William McPherson £20, conditioned for his appearance at next Court then and there to testify on his Majesties behalf.

Page 220
The persons appointed at last January Sessions to view and lay out a road from William Logan's to David Beale's Mill, have returned to the Court the said road as viewed and laid out by them according to the following distances, beginning at William Logan's thence N 70 degrees W 80 perches N37 degrees W 54 perches, N55 degrees and ½ W 30 perches N 42 degrees W 30 perches N 82 degrees west 30 perches N 61 degrees W 30 perches N 48 perches N87 degrees W 34 perches N 39 degrees W 32 perches N 10 degrees W 40 perches W 32 perches, N 43 degrees W 72 perches, N 60 degrees, W 102 perches, W 30 perches , S 64 degrees W 88 perches, S 71 degrees, W66 perches, S 64 degrees, W 68 perches, N 54 degrees W44 perches, N 70 degrees, W 22 perches, S 52 degrees, W 74 perches, S 75 degrees, W 52 perches, S 58 degrees, W82 perches, S84 degrees, W 104 perches, N 82 degrees, W 46 perches, S 74 degrees, W 64 perches, S22 degrees, W 30 perches, S 82 degrees, W 116 perches, S 80 degrees, W46 perches, S 64 degrees, W108 perches, S 82 degrees, W 54 perches, S 51 degrees, W 52 perches, S 42 degrees, W 58 perches, S 61 degrees, W 12 perches, S 68 degrees, W 54 perches south

Page 221
51 degrees, W 76 perches, S 75 degrees, W 29 perches, N 18 degrees, W 20 perches, S 58 degrees, W 75 perches, S 32 degrees, W 20 perches, S 65 degrees, W 76 perches, S 56 degrees, W 172 perches, N 87 degrees, W 64 perches, N 43 degrees, W 28 perches, N 15 degrees, E 30 perches, N 53 degrees, E 38 perches, N 43 degrees, E 17 perches, N 38 degrees, E 20 perches, N 48 degrees, E 31 perches, N 40 degrees, E 49 perches, N 20 degrees, E 38 perches, N 32 degrees, W 20 perches, N 96 perches, to David Beale's Mill, which road viewed and laid out as aforesaid the said persons, John Stuart, William Arbuckle, William Williams, William Logan, George Sharp and William Trinsloy returned to this Court as a road highly necessary and of publick utility, which road was, last April Sessions taken under consideration by the Court, ordered to be kept under advisement till July term, and was July Sessions the Court do confirm the said road, and is laid out in a manner the least injurious to private property and most conducive to the publick interest, ordered by the Court that the said road laid out aforesaid be cut, cleared, bridged if necessary forthwith by the inhabitants of the respective townships through which the said road passes, that it be of the breadth of 33 feet wide.

Page 222
At a Court of Private Sessions, at Carlisle 17 Aug 1775 before Robert Miller, William Lyon and John Holmes. Adjudged that Patrick Crosby indented servant to Robert Callender do serve his said master or his assigns the further time of two years over and above the time specified in his indenture in consideration of run away time expense.

John Gray, Samuel Coulter, Conrod Beamer, Robert White, Mathew Wilson, Owen Aston, John Heatherington, James Marvol, Henry Gordon, William Peoples, John McCusdy, Frederick Beamer, Mathew Scot, James Colhoune, Jacob Swem, James Cosby, Daniel Nevens, Robert Cullens, William Holmes, William Nielson, John Renkin, James Davis, John Forbes, James Pollock, Tobias Hendericks, Isaac Samonis, William Kelso, John Pollock, Thomas Wilson, Robert Galbraith, Christopher Vanlear.

The King vs Ann Galbraith

The King v Mathias Keplan

The King vs James McFiataro (?), James Cochran, James Currin

Page 223
At a Court of General Quarter Session, at Carlisle, 24 October 1775, before John Armstrong and his associates. Sheriff, Robert Semple returns the following list of grand jurors; William Peoples, Robert Culbertson, William McClure, Obadiah Garwood, Arthur Buchanan, David McCurdy, David McNair, Abram Stamford, Hugh Miller, William Baird, Henry Gordon, Joseph Armstrong, James Campbell, Hugh Wiley, Thomas Menzers, James Jamison, James Love, Patrick Vance, William Shaw, Thomas Baird, Robert Allison, William Rippey, James Johnson, William McFarland.

Page 224 October Sessions 1775
The King vs John Ward
Felony in stealing sundry goods the property of Thomas Johnston. Prisoner pleads guilty. Judgment the prisoner restore the goods stolen to the owner if not already done, pay a like fine to the Governor for support of Government, costs of prosecution be taken to the common whipping cost tomorrow the 26th, between 10 and 2, there receive 21 lashes on his bare back well laid on, stand committed till the whole be complied with.

The King vs William Shaw
Indictment felony in stealing sundry goods the property of James Bratton. Jury; John Bowman, William Smith, Samuel McCormick, Ralph Starret, Robert Sanderson, Robert Campbell, Archibald Hanna, Thomas Minzes, Samuel Remick, Daniel Nevin, James Mitchel and John Flack who say that William Shaw is guilty. Judgment that he restore the goods stolen to the owner if not

Quarter Session Docket 5 1772-1776 279

already done pay the like value to the Governor for support of Government pay costs of prosecution, be taken to the common whipping post on Friday the 27th between 10 and 2, there receive 21 lashes on his bare back well laid on, stand committed till the whole be complied with.

Page 225 October sessions 1775
The King vs Timothy Keiff
Felony in sundry stolen from Andrew Oughtpson (?). Jury; John Bowman, William Smith, Samuel McCormick, Ralph Starret, Robert Sanderson, Robert Campbell, Archibald Hanna, Thomas Menzias, Samuel Rarmicks, Daniel Nevins, James Mitchel, and John Flack, who say that he is guilty. Judgment he restore the goods stolen to the owner if not already done, pay the like value to the Governor for support of Government, pay costs of prosecution, be taken to the common whipping post on Friday, the 27th, between 10 and 2 o'clock, receive 21 lashes on his bare back well laid on stand committed till the whole be complied with.

The King vs George Haberling
Felony. Jury; John Bowman, William Smith, Samuel McCormick, Ralph Starret, Robert Sanderson, Robert Campbell, Archibald Hanna, Thomas Menzey, Samuel Rammicks, Daniel Nevin, James Mitchel, and John Flack who say that George Haberling is not guilty.

Page 226
The King vs Ann Welch
Indictment fornication. April Sessions 1776, pleads guilty. Fined 10 pounds, pay costs of prosecution stand committed until the whole be complied with.

The King vs Hugh Cook
Indictment fornication. April Sessions 1776. Mr. Wilson his Attny. retracts his plea and submits to the Court. Fined 10 pounds, and that he pay the sum of 15 pounds to Ann Welch besides what he had already paid for her trouble and expenses in lying in nursing and give security to indemnify the township, pay costs of prosecution stand committed until the whole be complied with.

Page 227
The King vs John Brown
Indictment felony.

The King vs George Keitz
Indictment trespass, pleads not guilty.

The King vs Robert Smith
Indictment fornication.

Page 228
The King vs Ann Holmes
Indictment fornication.

The King vs Daniel Sullahan
Indictment assault & battery.

The Same vs the Same
Assault & battery.

The Same ve William McKibben, Hannah McKibben, Daniel Sullahan
Indictment riot.

The King vs Henry McKewn
Assault & battery.

The same vs James Cole
Assault & battery.

Page 229 October Sessions 1775
The same vs Andrew McKeag
Assault & battery.

The Same vs Andrew McKeag & James Cole
Indictment trespass.

The King vs Hugh Cook
Hugh Cook £100, George Hudoon £50, conditioned for the appearance of
Hugh Cook at next Court then and there to answer and not depart the Court
without license.

The King vs Ann Welsh
Ann Welch £20, conditioned for her appearance at next court of court, then and
there to testify on his Majesties behalf, and not depart the Court without
license.

William McTherson £20, conditioned for his appearance at next Court then and
there to testify on his Majesties behalf and not depart the Court without license.

Page 230
George Keitz £100, Adam Cook £50, conditioned for the appearance of George
Keitz at next Court then and there to answer and not depart the Court without
license.

John Glenn £100, John Steel £50, conditioned for the several appearances of John Glenn, Hugh Glen, Robert Philips and John Fury at next Court then and there to answer and not depart the Court without license.

John Allen £100, Andrew Steer £100, conditioned for the appearance of John Allen at next Court, there to answer and not depart the Court without license.

John Quin £200, William McCune £100, Aaron Terraise (?) £100, conditioned for the several appearances of John Irwin, James Irwin Senr, James Irwin Junr, Joseph Simmwills and Richard Ironville (?) at next Court then and there to answer and that John Irwin keep the peace and be of good behaviour and in particular to John Byers, Esq and not depart the Court without license.

Page 231 October Sessions 1775
James McCutchen £20, John Stoner £20, conditioned for their appearances at next Court, then and there to testify on his Majesties behalf and not depart the Court without license.

Andrew Ferviere £40, conditioned for his appearance at next Court, then and there to testify on his Majesties behalf and not depart the Court without licence.

James Pattan £100, John Gray £100, conditioned for the appearances of James Pattan at sext Court, there to answer and not depart the Court without license.

John Irwin being three times solemnly called to appear, appeareth not forfeits his recognizance.

George Robinson Esquire being three times solemnly called to bring forth the body of John Irwin, brings not forth the body forfeits his recognizance.

William Gallaugher being three times solemnly called to appear appeareth not forfeits his recognizance.

James Askey being three times solemnly called to bring forth the body of William Gallaugher brings not forth the body forfeits his recognizance.

Upon the petition of Elizabeth Clements the wife of Benjamin Clements of Teboyne Township setting forth that her brother John White served Adam Hays a number of years, and being weak in judgment is not capable to act for himself as other men do, and prayed that upon giving sufficient security to indemnify the county or township where he resides from his being chargeable thereto she may be allowed to take him home and provide for him. They considering the same are of opinion that upon the said Elizabeth Clements giving sufficient security to the overseers of West Pennsborough township for the time being she ought to have her said brother John White.

Upon the petition of Hannah Shaw indented servant to Thomas Wilson, setting forth to the Court that she served her said master four years who refuses to give freedom dues agreeable to an act of assembly of this province in such case made and provided. Ordered that the said Thomas Wilson do give the said servant sufficient freedoms or the value thereof in cash.

Page 232 October Sessions 1775
On complaint of William Clark, one of the overseers of the poor of West Pennsborough township, on behalf of John White, for freedom due from Adams Hays, his late master, agreeable to indenture between them. Ordered that Adam Hays do provide and give said John White one new coat, one new hat, and one heifer of three years old, the sufficiency of the said heifer to be adjudged by Ezekiel Dunning and George Brown in ten days.

Page 233
Upon the petition Charles McClean indented servant to Thomas Wilson setting forth, that he served his said master 4 years, and that his said master refuses to give him freedom dues agreeable to an act of assembly of this province in such case made and provided. Ordered that the said Thomas Wilson do give the said servant sufficient freedoms, or the value thereof in cash.

Upon the petition of Veronica Coyne indented servant to Hugh McCormick setting forth to the Court that she served her said master four years, and refuses to give her freedom dues agreeable to an act of assembly of this province in such case made and provided. Ordered that the said Hugh McCormick do give the said servant sufficient freedoms, of the value thereof in cash.

Upon the petition of sundry inhabitants of Rye Township to the Court setting forth that they labor under many inconveniences for want of a public road leading from Croghan's Gap to Baskins ferry on Junitata. And praying the Court to appoint proper persons to view the same, and if they see cause to lay out a road as aforesaid. Appointed Samuel Goudy, Frederick Watt, Thomas Watson, Robert Taylor, Duncan Walker and Albert Maxwell to view the premises and if they or any four of them see cause they lay out the same by distances the nearest and best way the least injurious to private property and most conducive to publick utility and make report to next court.

Page 234
Upon the petition of sundry inhabitants of Tyrone and Rye Townships to the Court setting forth that James Sharon one of the petitioners at a great expense hath cleared a good road over the mountain about a mile above Crane's Gap, which road would be very beneficial to the inhabitants of Sherman's Valley, if there was a road laid out from the foot of the mountain where the road that James Sharron hath made ended, to fall into the Great Road leading from Carlisle to Crane's Gap about a 1/4 of a mile south of Richard Crane's plantation. And praying the Court to appoint proper persons to view the same,

and if they see cause to lay out a road as aforesaid. The Court do appoint Samuel __, George Witzel, Hugh McCormick, Henry Gass, Hugh Kilgore and Alexander Roddy to view the premises, and if they or any four of them see cause they lay out the same by courses and distances the nearest and best way the least injurious to private property and most conducive to publick utility and make report to next Court.

Page 235
At Carlisle, 3 January 1776. Sheriff, Robert Semple, returns the following grand jurors; David Hoge, James Johnson. John Semple, James Laird, David Dummings, John McDonald, Francis Silver, John Hoge, Alexander Trindle, John Trindle, John Naylor, Joseph Hudson, John Johnson, Joseph McDonald, John Walker, Edward Morton, John McCurdy, John Quigley, Joseph McClure, Andrew Erwin, William Houston, William Mackey, John Trimbel.

Page 236 January Sessions 1776
The King vs Anthony Morning Dollar
Felony. Jury; William Giddis, David Bell, James McCormick, William McLeer, Matthew Louden, John Orr, Thomas Donaldson, Andrew Cap, David Reddick, Richard Coulter, Thomas Craighead and Alexander Work, who say that Anthony Morning Dollar is guilty. Judgment that the prisoner Anthony Morning Dollar restore the horse stolen to the owner if not already done of the value thereof (to wit 33 pounds) pay the like value to the Governor for support of Government, be taken to the common whipping post on Friday next the 26th between 10 and 4 o'clock, be whipped with 39 lashes well laid on, stand in the pillory one hour, be committed to prison one month, pay costs of prosecution stand committed until the whole be complied with.

The King vs John Armstrong
Indictment assault and battery. Retracts his plea, submits to the Court. Fined 10 shillings pay costs of prosecution, stand committed.

Page 237
The King vs William Tarecoat and Elizabeth Tarecoat
Felony, William Tarecoat pleads guilty, Elizabeth Tarecoat pleads non Cul __. Judgment that William Tarecoat restore the goods stolen to the owner if not already done or the value thereof (to wit 11 pounds, 4 shillings and 7 pence) pay the like value to the Governor for support of Government, be taken to the common whipping post on the 26th, between 10 and 4, be whipped with 21 lashes on his bare back, pay costs of prosecution stand committed. As to Elizabeth Tarecoat, jury; William Geddis, David Bell, James McCormick, William McTeer, Matthew Louden, John Orr, Thomas Donaldson, Andrew Cap, David Reddick, Richard Coulter, Thomas Craighead and Alexr. Work, who say that Elizabeth Tarecoat is not guilty.

The King vs Patrick Sheehan
Indictment felony. Prisoner pleads guilty. Judgment that the prisoner restore the goods stolen if not already done or the value thereof (to wit 1 pound, 5 shillings and 2 pence) pay the like value to the Governor for support of Government be taken to the common whipping post on Friday the 26th, be whipped with 21 lashes, between 10 and 4, on his bare back well laid on, pay fine & costs of prosecution, stand committed until the whole be complied with.

Page 238 January Sessions 1776
The King vs Jonathan Coates and Richard Harden
Forgery. Richard Harden not willing to contend with the King, protesting his innocense submits to the Court. Judgment that Richd. Harden is fined 6 pence, be taken to the common whipping post on Monday the 22 April next, between 10 and 4, receive 21 lashes on his bare back, stand in the pillory one hour, pay costs of prosecution, stand committed till the whole be complied with.

The King vs John Hardner
Assault and battery.

Page 239
The King vs George McCleave
Tippling house. April Sessions 1776, defendant submits to the Court. Fined 5 pounds, pay costs of prosecution, stand committed til complied with.

The King vs George Keitz

Page 240
The King vs James Gardner
Assault and battery. April Sessions 1776, submits to the Court. Fined 6 pence, pay costs of prosecution, stand committed until the whole be complied with.

The King vs Thomas Gardner
Assault and battery.

Page 241
The King vs Robert Fausset
Defendant discharged on payment of fees.

The King vs Thomas Roberts
Felony.

The King vs Andrew Stern, Alexander Stern, Duncan Campbell and Joseph Martin.
Felony.

The King vs Rose Keer
Rose Keer £40, John McKendry £20, conditioned for the appearance of Rose
Keer at next court, then and there to answer, not depart the Court without
license.

The King vs Margaret Whitackre
Samuel Whitackre £40, conditioned for the appearance of Margaret Whitackre
at next Court then and there to answer and not depart the Court without license.

Page 242 January Sessions 1776
The King vs John Armstrong
John Armstrong £20, John Glenn £10, conditioned for the appearance of John
Armstrong at next Court, then and there to answer and in the mean time to keep
the peace, and be of good behaviour to all his Majesty's subjects, and in
particular to William Carhart and not depart the Court without liccence.

The King vs George McClave
William Neiloon £20, conditioned for this appearance at next Court, then and
there to testify on his Majesty's behalf, not depart the Court without liccence.

The King vs George Keitz
Henry Kyle £20, Martin Cook £20, John Jacob Houke £20, conditioned for
their several appearances at next Court, then and there to testify on his
Majesty's behalf, and not depart the Court without liccence.

The King vs George Keitz
George Keitz £50, George Adam Cook £25, conditioned for the appearance of
George Keitz at next Court, then and there to answer and not depart the Court
without licence.

Page 243
The King vs George Keitz
George Keitz £100, George Adam Cook £50, conditioned for the appearance of
George Keitz at next Court then and there to answer and not depart the Court
without licence.

The King vs Thomas Garner, John Garner Junr, James Garner
Robert McClintock £40, John McClintock £40, conditioned for their several
appearances at next Court then and there to testify on his Majesty's behalf, and
not eepart the court without licence.

The King vs Mathusalah Griffey
Mathusalah Griffey £100, William Long £50, conditioned for the appearance of
Mathusalah Griffy at next Court then and there to answer and not depart the
Court without licence.

The King vs Ann Welch
Ann Welch £20, conditioned for her appearance at next Court, then and there to testify on his Majesties behalf and not depart the Court without licence.

Page 244
Hugh Cook being 3 times solemnly called to appear, appearth not forfeits his recognizance.

George Hudson being 3 times solemnly called to bring forth the body of Hugh Cook, brings not forth the body forfeits his recognizance.

John Irwin being 3 times solemnly called to bring forth the bodies of John Irwin, James Irwin Senr, James Irwin Junr, Joseph Sommerville and Richana Sommerville, brings not forth the bodies, forfeits his recognizance.

William McCune being 3 times solemnly called to bring forth the bodies of John Irwin, James Irwin Senr, James Irwin Junr, Joseph Sommerville and Richana Sommerville, being not for the bodies, forfeits his recognizance.

Aaron Torrance being 3 times solemnly called to bring forth the bodies of John Irwin, James Irwin Senr, James Irwin Junr, Joseph Sommerville and Richana Sommerville brings not forth the bodies forfeits his recognizance.

On application of Samuel Johnson Esquire to the Court praying Mr. Lewis Bush be admitted an Attorney of this Court and County Court of Common Pleas. He is admitted an attorney.

Page 244 ½ January Sessions 1776
Upon the petition of sundry inhabitants of Armagh Township to the Court setting forth that they Labor under many Inconveniences for want of a publick road, laid out the nearest and best way from Esquire Brown's Mill, unto the Bedford County line, and praying the Court to appoint proper persons to view the same, and if they see cause to lay out a road as aforesaid. The Court appoint James Burns, Robert Chambers, Thomas Alexander, Arthur Buckanan, Matthew Kelly, and Ulrick Stealey to view the premises and if they or any four of them see cause they lay out by distances the nearest and best way the least injurious to private property and most conducive to publick utility and make report to next Court.

Upon the petition of sundry inhabitants of Tyrone and Rye townships to the Court setting forth that they labor under a great many disadvantages for want of a publick road leading from Juniata River, from about the mouth of Racoon Creek fm James Gallagher's and to proceed up Racoon Valley, and through the Buffalo Creek Settlement, the nighest and best way to intersect the road leading from Croghans Gap to Logans, and they do apprehend that said road would be publick utility both for the people of Juniata and Sherman Valley, and praying the Court to appoint proper persons to view the same and if they see cause to lay out a road as aforesaid. The Court do appoint John Black, John Fergy, Edward Elliot Snr, Thos. Elliot, James Louden and George Logan to view the premises and if they or any four of them see cause, they lay out the same by courses and distances, the nearest and best way the least injurious to private property and most conducive to publick utility and make report to next Court.

Page 245 January Sessions 1776
The persons appointed at last October sessions to view and lay out a road from the foot of the mountain where the road that James Sharron hath made ended, to fall into the great road leading from Carlisle to Crane's Gap, about a quarter of a mile south of Richard Crane's Plantation, have returned to the Court the said road as viewed and laid out by them according to the following courses, beginning at a post in Martin Bower's Land on the great road leading from Carlisle to Crane's Gap north 51 degrees and a half west 69 perches, thence north 15 degrees West 159 perches on the line between William Davison and Richard Crane, thence from a white oak tree north 55 degrees west 24 perches, thence from a hickory post north 23 degrees west 51 perches, thence from a white oak north 47 degrees west 34 perches to a Chestnut tree on Sharron's Road, and there ends, which road viewed and laid out as aforesaid the said persons; Samuel Harper, George Witzel, Hugh McCormick, Henry Gass, Hugh Kilgore and Alexander Roddy, returned to this Court as a road highly necessary, and of publick and is laid out in a manner the least injurious to private property, and most conducive to the publick interest, which said road being taken into consideration by the court is accordingly approved and confirmed. Ordered by the Court that the road laid out as aforesaid be cut, cleared, and kept in repair by the several supervisors of the respective townships through which the said road passes, and that it be of the breadth of 30 feet wide.

Page 245 ½
At a Court of Private Sessions, at Carlisle, 25 January 1776, before John Allison, James Dunlap, and William Elliot.
Adjudged that Isaac Parks indented servant to Andrew Boyd and William Pillars do serve his said master or their assigns the further time of 6 months over and above the time specified in his indenture, in consideration of run away time, expenses.

Processes to April Sessions 1776
The King vs Mathias Keplan
The King vs James McFeaters, James Cochran, James Currin
The King vs James Fagan
The King vs John Gardner
The King vs George McCleave

Page 247- blank

Page 248 - 249
At a Court of Private Sessions, at Carlisle, 25 March 1777, for the appointment of officers before Robert Miller, Esq., and his associates.

Antrim township. Hoppell Dull, Sr., constable; John Nigh, William Shover, Sr., supervisors of roads; Henry Gordon, Andrew Miller, overseers of poor.

Fannett township. Felix Doyle, constable; James Michael, Samuel Gamble, supervisors of roads; Patrick Davis, Andrew Douglas, overseer of poor.

Hamilton township. Joseph Eaton, constable; John Buzzard, James Anderson, supervisors of roads; Robert Dickson, James Moore, overseer of poor.

Lurgan township. James Randles, constable; John Cummins, John White, supervisors of roads; John McComb, Joseph Ross, overseers of poor.

Letterkenny township. James Gibson, constable; James Clark, James Finley, supervisors of roads; John Imbill, William Kirkpatrick, overseer of poor.

Guiford township. Peter Snider, constable; Edward Crawford, Jacob Dock, supervisors of roads; John Vance, George Smith, overseers of poor.

Peters township. William Duffield, constable; Joseph Rankin, William Dickey, supervisors of roads; David Humphreys, Robert Campbell, overseer of poor.

Page 250
At a Court of special and private sessions, at Carlisle, 8 April 1776, before Robert Miller, William Lyon and John Holmes. On motion of George Stevenson, that an indented servant of William Thompson of Middleton Township, named Edmund Carmiddy, who ran away the 11th day of Sept last, was taken up and committed to the prison of this County the 3rd day of February last may be adjudged for his runaway time and expenses of bringing him from Blosenburg in the Province of Maryland to Carlisle 39 shillings, __ __ and 12 shillings the __ of this adjudgication and amounting in the whole to 7 pounds and 1 shilling. Adjudged the said servant Edmund Carmaddy do serve his said master or his assigns 2 years over the time mentioned in his indenture.

Page 251
At Carlisle, 26 April 1776, before John Rennells Esquire and his associate justices.
Adjudged that George Pattison indented servant to Samuel Moore do serve his said master or his assigns the further time of ten months over and above the time specified in his indenture, in consideration of runaway time. expenses.

Adjudged that Hannah Standing indented servant to James Moore do serve her said master or his assigns the further time of 12 months over and above the time specified in her indenture, in consideration of runaway time, expenses.

Page 252

At Carlisle, 23 April 1776, before John Rennells, and his associates. The sheriff, Robert Semple, returns the following list of grand jurors; William Clark, John McClure, Andrew Homes, Thomas Guy, Robert Darlington, Charles Leeper, William Chambers, Thomas Butler, William McFarland, Ezekiel Dunning, Robert McFarland, Samuel Davison, John Davison, James Byers, Daniel Duncan, John Piper, John Young, James Carothers, Abram Sanford.

Page 253 April Sessions 1776

The King vs Thomas Dougherty

Felony in stealing 1 black mare the property of John McClelland. Jury; William Flemming, Saml Williamson, Saml Lamb, Saml McCall, Alex McGreeghan, John Rannells, Robert Pattan, John Miller, Mattw Laird, Wm Swancey, Danl Duncan, and Geo. Robinson who say that Thos. Dougherty is guilty. Judgement the prisoner restore the mare stolen to the owner if not already done or the value thereof (15 pounds) pay the like value to the Governor for support of Government, be taken to the common whipping post on Monday the 22nd of July next between 10 and 4 o'clock, be whipped with 39 lashes on his bare back well laid, stand in the pillory one hour, be imprisoned 1 month, pay costs of prosecution, stand committed till the whole be complied with.

The same vs the same

Felony in stealing one dun gelding the property of James Evans. Jury; Wm Flemming, Saml Williamson, Saml Lamb, Saml McCall, Alexr McGreighan, Jno Rannells, Robt Patton, Jno Miller, Mattw Laird, Wm Swaney, Danl Duncan and Geo. Robinson who say that Thomas Dougherty is guilty. Ordered that the prisoner restore the horse stolen to the owner if not already done of the value thereof (19 pounds) pay the like value to the Govenor for support of Government, be taken to the common whipping post on Monday the 22rd of July next between 10 and 4 o'clock, there be whipped with 39 lashes on his bare back well laid on, stand in the pillory one hour, be imprisoned one month, pay costs of the prosecution, stand committed till the whole be complied with.

Page 254

The King vs Richard Taylor

Assault and battery.

The King vs James Armstrong, Alexander McHatten, John Fisher, George Colhoon, Samuel Wyborne, Howard Marshal, Marshal Stanley and John Scot.

Assault and battery.

Page 255

The King vs Henry McKewn and Thomas McKewn

Assault and battery.

The King vs Andrew McKing
Assault and battery.

Page 256 April Sessions 1776
The King vs Thomas Martin, Andrew McKeag and James Coale
Assault and battery on Henry McKewn.

The Same vs the Same
Assault and battery on William McKewn.

Page 257
The King vs James Porter
Felony in stealing cash and the property of Paul Taylor the younger.

The King vs Thomas Fisher
Tippling house.

Page 258
The King vs William Gowdey
Fornication.

The King vs Rose Kerr
Fornication.

Page 259
The King vs James Dickey
Tippling house.

The King vs William McKewn
Assault and battery.

The King vs Paul Taylor
Felony. Paul Taylor £20, conditioned for the appearance of Paul Taylor Junr at next Court then and there to answer and not depart the Court without licence.

The King vs William Gowdry
Fornication. William Gowdey £60, Charles Luper £40, conditioned for the appearance of William Gowdey at next Court then and there to answer and not depart the Court without license.

The King vs Rose Kerr
Fornication. Rose Kerr £20, conditioned for her appearance at next Court then and there to testify on his Majesty's behalf and not depart the court without license.

Page 260 April Sessions 1776
The King vs Methusalah Griffey
Fornication. Mathusalah Griffy £40, William Gass £20, conditioned for the appearance of Mathusalah Griffey at next Court then and there to answer and not depart the Court without licence.

The King vs William McCracken
Tippling House. William McCracken £20, conditioned for his appearance at next Court then and there to testify on his Majesty's behalf and not depart the Court without licence.

The King vs George Keitz
Trespass. George Keitz £50, George Adam Cook £25, conditioned for the appearance of George Keitz at next Court then and there to answer and not depart the Court without licence.

The King vs John Carrothers
Fornication. John Steel £50, conditioned for the appearance of Agnes at next Court then and there to testify on his Majesty's behalf and not depart the Court.

Page 261
The King vs George Keitz
Henry Coyle £20, Jacob Hick £20, Martin Cook £20, John Maybries £20, conditioned for their several appearances at next Court then and there to testify on his Majesty's behalf and not depart the Court without licence.

The King vs Robert Cua Junr
Robert Cuaj £40, Robert Cua Senr £20, conditioned for the appearance of Robert Cua Junr at next Court then and there to answer and not depart the Court without licence.

The King vs Robert McPherson
Assault and battery. Robert McPherson £20, conditioned for his appearance at next Court then and there to testify on his Majesty's behalf and not depart the Court.

The King vs Michael Gillaspie
Assault and battery. Michael Gillaspie £20, conditioned for his appearance at next Court then and there to answer and not depart the Court without licence.

Page 262
The King vs Thomas Martin, Andrew McKeag and James Cole
Assault and battery. Thomas Martin £50, James Sharron £50, conditioned for the several appearances of Thomas Martin, Andrew McKeag and James Cole, at next Court then and there to answer and not depart the Court without licence.

The King vs Henry McKewn, William McKewn and Francis McKewn
Assault and battery. Henry McKewn £60, Samuel Williamson £30, conditioned
for the appearance of Henry McKewn and Francis McKewn at next Court then
and there to answer and also for the appearance of the said Henry McKewn,
William McKewn and Francis McKewn at next Court then and there to testify
on his Majesty's behalf and not depart the Court without licence.

The King vs James Porter
Felony. Robert Denny £100, conditioned for the appearance of James Porter at
next Court then and there to answer and not depart the Court.

Page 263 April Sessions 1776
Upon the application of William Elliott, Esq., on behalf of the inhabitants of
Fannett township, in the county of Cumberland, setting forth that there is
considerable space between the townships of Fannett, Letterkenny and Lurgan
within the boundaries, the boundaries are not ascertained, and praying the
Court to appoint proper persons to view and fix the boundaries.

The Court appointed Alexander Laughlin, James Glenn, and William Gass to
ascertain and fix the boundaries between Lurgan and Letterkenny townships
where no already fixed, and likewise between the said townships and Fannett,
and make report to the next Court.

Upon the petition of sundry of the inhabitants of Hamilton and Guilford
townships to the Court, setting forth that they labor under disadvantage for
want of a road from the Great Road leading near James Campbell's to
Chambersburg, to be laid outstruck off from said road about John Andrews
Mill at the head of the Falling Spring. From thence the straightest and best
course to the Gap of the Mountain formerly called Black's Gap, and praying
the Court to appoint viewers, and if they see cause lay out a road as aforesaid.

The Court appointed Matthew Wilson, James Poe, George Brown, James
Armstrong, Col. Leonard Stans, and Peter Snider to view the premises and lay
out the same by courses and distances and make report to the next Court.

Upon the petition of sundry inhabitants of Tyrone Township to the Court
setting forth that they labor under many Inconveniences for want of a road
leading from that part of the wagon road leading from Croghan's Gap in the
North Mountains up Sherman's Valley where George McClure lives to the Top
of the said Mountain at Hurley's Gap, would be of great use to the publick as
well as to your petitioners in particular. And praying the Court to appoint
proper persons to view the same, and if they see cause, to lay out a road as
aforesaid. The Court do appoint Thomas Roso, John Hamilton, William
McClure, John Dunbar, James Davis and Robert Scott to view the premises and
if they any four of them see cause they lay out the same by courses upon the
petition of sundry inhabitants of Tyrone Township to the Court setting forth

that they labor under many inconveniences for want of a road leading from that part of the wagon road leading from Croghan's Gap in the North Mountains up Sherman's Valley where George McClure lives to the Top of the said Mountain at Hurley's Gap, would be of great use to the publick as well as to your petitioners in particular, praying the Court to appoint proper persons to view the same, and if they see cause, to lay out a road as aforesaid. Appointed Thomas Roso, John Hamilton, William McClure, John Dunbar, James Davis and Robert Scott to view the premises and if they any four of them see cause they lay out the same by courses

Page 264
distances, the nearest and best way, the least injurious to private property and most conducive to publick utility and make report to next Court.

Upon the petition of sundry inhabitants of Armagh Township to the Court setting forth that by an order of last January Sessions there was a road laid out leading from Squire Brown's Mill unto the Bedford County line which road is confirmed as laid out would aggrieve several inhabitants of said township. Praying the Court to appoint proper persons to review the same and if they see cause lay out a road as aforesaid. The court appoint James Hustion, John Robison, George Mitchel, Jonas Bamm, John Ceaver and Abraham Stanford to review the premises, and if they or any four of them see cause, they lay out a road by courses and distances the nearest and best way the least injurious to private property, most conducive to publick utility, make report to next Court.

Page 265
Upon the petition of the inhabitants of Aire and Hamilton townships, setting forth that they labor under hardships for want of a road to their common place of public worship, the nearest and best way from William McCoy's, and from thence to the Rev. Mr. King's meeting house, praying the Court to appoint viewers and if they see cause to lay out a road as aforesaid.

The Court appointed John McClellan, Robert McCoy, Jr., James Irvine, Patrick Jack, and Adam Holiday, to view the premises and if they see cause lay out a road by courses and distances and make return to the next Court.

Upon the petition of sundry inhabitants of Greenwood Township to the Court setting forth that they labor under great necessary

Page 266 April Sessions 1776
for want of a road or cart way through said township to begin at the Bridge that Crossth the Branch that comes out of Susquihannah into Juaniata at Huling's Plantation and from thence thorough said Township the nearest and best way towards Sunbury and to intersect with the road that leads from a Mahontongo to said Borough, praying the Court to appoint proper persons to view the same and if they see cause to lay out a road as aforesaid. The Court do appoint James

Gallagher, Charles Barger, David Moody, Henry Gillaspie, David Mathias, and Marcus Hullinger to view the premises and if they or any four of them see cause they lay out the same by distances the nearest and best way the least Injurious to private property and most conducive to publick utility and make report to next Court.

Processes to July Session 1776
The King vs Mathias Keplan
The same vs James McDatersctal
The same vs James Feagan
The same vs John Gardner
The same vs Thomas Gardner
The same vs Richard Taylor
The same vs Jas. Armstrong
The same vs Thomas Fisher

Page 267
The King vs James Porter
Felony. Robert Derry £100, 31 August 1776 Robert Derry the bail delivered James Porter to the Sheriff, Sheriff acknowledges to have him in custody. And now on the petition of the said James Porter to Robert Miller, Stephen Duncan and John Homes in pursuance of an ordinance of the Honorable __ Convention of this State, the said James Porter in hereby en__ged on payment of fees.

John Shaw, a languishing prisoner in the jail of this county committed by the Court in October Sessions last, in pursuance of a verdict of a jury whereby he was found guilty of felony, on application to us the subscribers, is hereby enlarged in pursuance on an ordinance of the Honorable Convention of this state of Pennsylvania, as he appears to __ want of clothing, has one of his feet burned, and hath, it is said, the convulsion fits.

Page 268
At a Court of Private Sessions, at Carlisle, 19 November 1777, before John Creigh, Hugh Laird and Alexander Laughlin.
Adjudging that Ann Bean indented servant to Robert McClean do serve the said Robert McClean or his assigns the further term or time of ten months over and above the time specified in her indenture for runaway time and expenses.

Page 269- blank

Page 270 - 271
At a Court of Private Sessions, at Carlisle, 25 March 1778, for the appointment of officers, before John Rennells, and his associates.
Antrim Township. James Crooks, constable; George Brown, James McLenahan, supervisors of roads; John Cunkleton, Michael McNulty, overseers of poor.

Fannett Township. Samuel Gambel, constable; William McKibben, Andrew
Miller, supervisors of roads; James Walker, James Orday, overseers
of poor.
Hamilton township. James Ferguson, constable; Samuel McClure, Leonard
Harts, supervisors of roads; John Russell, Thomas Knox, overseers of
poor.
Lurgan township. James McKibben, constable; John McClay, Sr., Alexander
Starrett, supervisors of roads; James Ross, John McComb, overseers
of poor.
Letterkenny township. John Baird, constable.
Guilford township. Jacob Cook, constable; Edward Crawford, John Bard,
supervisors of roads; Abram Snyder, Capt. William Long, overseers
of poor.
Peters township. John McClellan, constable; William Dickey, James Rankin,
supervisors of roads; William Marshal, Hugh Donaldson, overseers
of poor.

Page 272
Process to April Sessions 1778
Pennsylvania vs James Lee
Tippling house.

The same vs Thomas Jackson
Tippling house.

The same vs Cath. Kelly also Cath. Grier
Felony.

The same vs James Gutherie
Tippling house.

The same vs Henry Brooks
Trespass and felony.

The same vs Robert Fossel

The same vs Geo. Greesorger
Tippling house.

Page 273
Process to July Sessions 1778
Pennsylvania vs Alex Grahams
Assault and battery.

The same vs Jas. Armstrong
Assault and battery.

The same

The same vs Jacob Groave
Assault and battery.

The same vs Jacob Crow
Assault and battery.

The same vs Isaac Sammis
Tippling house.

The same vs Geo. Lockridge
Felony.

The same vs David Miller
Tippling house.

The same vs Benjamin Newgent
Assault and battery.

Pennsylvania vs Thomas Lemmon
Tippling house.

The same vs Daniel Davidson

Page 274
Process to October Sessions 1778
Pennsylvania vs Edward Donnall
Assault.

The same vs Patrick Grant
Assault.

The same vs Thomas Jackson
Tippling house.

The same vs Danl Davidson
Assault.

The same vs Benjamin Huges
Assault.

The same vs Thomas Lemon
Tippling house.

The same vs Alexandr Grahams
Assault.

The same vs Isaac Jarris
Tippling house.

The same vs James Reynolds
Nuisance.

The same vs John Irwin

[written by John G. Orr 1925]
During the years 1777, 1778, and 1779, the business of the Court seems to have been practically suspended. The records show the issuing of processes but no trial of cases and only show that at private Quarter Sessions held, sentences were passed upon indentured servants for absenting themselves from the services of their masters. In fact very little seems to have been done as shown by the records filed during the period of the Revolution, except the appointment of officers of the respective townships.

Page 275
Processes to January Sep 1779
Pennsylvania vs Edwd. O'Donall
Assault.
.
The same vs Patrick Grant
Assault.

The same vs Daniel Davidson
Assault.

The same vs Benjamin Nugent

The same vs Alexandr Graham

The same vs William Richardson
Assault.

The same vs James Renkin
Assault.

The same vs the same

Page 276
At a Court of Private Sessions, at Carlisle, 10 February 1779, before James Oliver, John Creigh, and Andrew McBeth.
Adjudged that Mary Mattimore indented servant to John Agnew do serve her said master or his assigns the further time of two years over and above the time specified in her indenture in consideration for the loss and damage he sustained by reason of her bearing a bastard child in the time of her servitude.

Page 277
Processes to April Sessions 1779
Pennsylvania vs James McDowell
The same vs James Clark
The same vs John Rhea et at
The same vs John Rhea
The same vs James McCann
The same vs William Richardson
The same vs Edwd. O'Donnall
The same vs Michl Gillis et at
The same vs the same
The same vs Daniel Davidson
The same vs Benj. Nugent
The same vs Alexander Graham
The same vs Michl Gillispy

Page 278 - 279
At a Court of Private Sessions, 25 March 1779, for the appointment of officers, before John Rannells and his associates.
Antrim township. Joseph Snively, constable; Richard Gabriel, John Crunkleton, overseers of poor.
Fannett township. Joseph Mitchell, constable; David Elder, Jr., William Elliott, supervisors of roads; John Elder, Thomas Armstrong, overseers of poor.
Hamilton township. Robert Hutchinson, constable; Robert Peoples, John Taylor, supervisors of roads; Simon _couler, Joseph Finton, overseers of poor.
Washington township. George Adams Cook, constable; William Irvine, David Stover, supervisors of roads; James Moorehead, Frederick Foreman, overseers of poor.
Lurgan township. Theophilus Cessna, constable; Benjamin Allswith, John Herron, supervisors of roads; Robert Scott, Abram Weir, overseers of poor.
Letterkenny township. Paul Reed, constable; Alexander Thompson, Robert Stogton, supervisors of roads; Hugh Torrence, William Baird, overseers of poor.

Guilford township. David Wineman, constable; William Long, (road), John Lindsey, supervisors of roads; William Long, Anthony Schynder, overseers of poor.

[written by John G. Orr 1925]
There does not appear to have been any appointment of officers until at a private sessions held on the 25th day of March, 1785, and in that appointment there does not appear any of the townships hereto were mentioned within the confines of Franklin County.

Page 280
At a Court of Private Session, at Carlisle, 20 April 1779, before Hugh Laird, Mathew Wilson and Samuel Laird.
Adjudged that Barbara Campbell an indented servant to David Hoge do serve her said master or his assigns the further term or time of two years over and above the time specified in her Indenture in consideration of the loss he sustained by reason of bearing a bastard child in the time of her servitude.

At a Court of Private Sessions, at Carlisle, 20 April 1779, before Hugh Laird, Mathew Wilson and Samuel Laird Justices.
Adjudged that Barbara Campbell an indented servant to David Hoge do serve her said master or his assigns the further term or time of two years over and above the time specified in her Indenture in consideration of the loss he sustained by reason of bearing a bastard child in the time of her servitude.

Page 281
Process to July Sessions 1779
Pennsylvania vs David Christy
The same vs David Wallace
The same vs James Armstrong
The same vs Daniel Davidson
The same vs John McCurdy et al

Process to October Sessions 1779
Pennsylvania vs Michael Gillespie
The same vs the same
The same vs Edmd. Kean
The same vs Robert Topet
The same vs Daniel Davidson
The same vs Hugh Duffy

Page 282
Process to January Sessions 1780
Pennsylvania vs John Williams
The same vs Daniel Davidson

Process to April 1780
The same vs John Irwin
The same vs George Shade
The same vs John Koutz Junr
The same vs Michael Gillespie
The same vs the same
The same vs John Williams
The same vs Daniel Davidson
The same vs Alexr. Grahams
The same vs John Murphy

Process to July sessions 1780
The same vs Robert Gulherie Junr
The same vs John McNeal
The same vs Michl. Gillispie
The same vs the same

Page 283
Process to October Sessions 1780
Pennsylvania vs Jacob Thrush
The same vs William Irwin and Hugh Gibb Supr of Lurgan Township
The same vs William Sleer and Saml. Adams Supr.__ of E. Pennsboro
The same vs Robert Clark & Wm. Whary supr. __ of Hopewell
The same vs James Graham supr. __ of W. Penns
The same vs Michl. Gillispie
The same vs the same
Pennsylvania vs Edwd. O'Donall

Page 284
At a Court of Private Sessions, at Carlisle, 25 March 1780, for the appointment
of officers, before John Trindle, Samuel Laird and John Agnew.
Allen Township; Constables- Alexr. Hamilton
Antrim Township; Constables- Joseph Cook; supervisors of roads- Richd.
          Gabriel, Geo. Hover; Overseers of Poor- Humphry Fullerton, James
          Watson
Armagh   Township; Constables- John McDowall; supervisors of roads-
          William McKnit, Robt. Campbell; Overseers of Poor- Mathew
          Kinny, David Nelly
Carlisle Township; Constables- Alexr. McDowell; Overseers of Poor- Andrew
          Colhoon, John Henry
Derry Township; Constables- Hugh Magill; supervisors of roads- Allerick
          Heely, William Robinson; Overseers of Poor- James Lyon, Abm.
          Sandford
Eastpennsboro Township; Constables- Abm. Adams; supervisors of roads-
          William Steer, Saml. Adams

Fermanagh Township; Constables- Robt. Nielson; supervisors of roads- John
Hamilton, James Blaine; Overseers of Poor - William McCallister,
William Riddle
Fannet Township; Constables- Barnabas Doyle; supervisors of roads- Nathl.
Paul, David McConashey; Overseers of Poor- Robert Elder, William
Elliot
Greenwood Township; Constables- John Kelpar; Overseers of Poor- John
Clain, Henry Gillispie
Guilford Township; Constables- Richard Benson; supervisors of roads-
William Thompson, John McClean; Overseers of Poor- William
Wier, James Moore
Hopewell Township; Constables- John Wilson; supervisors of roads- Robert
Clark, William Sherry

Page 285
Lurgan Township; Constables- William Campbell; supervisors of roads-
William Irwin, Hugh Gibbs; Overseers of Poor- Robert Scol, Charles
Maclay
Lack Township- Constables- James Divers; supervisors of roads- William
Williams, Andrew Lerrier; Overseers of Poor- Edward Thalcher,
David Bales
Letterkenny Township; Constables- Rob. Brotherlon; supervisors of roads-
John Immille, Mathew Shields; Overseers of Poor- James Mitchel,
Saml. Rea
Millford Township; Constables- Thomas Hardy; supervisors of roads- John
Hamilton, Thomas Harris; Overseers of Poor- James Rodman, Chrisr.
Irwin
Middleton Township; Constables- Casper Foster; supervisors of roads- John
Glenn Senr, Joseph Semple; Overseers of Poor- Mathew Laird, James
Irwin
Newtown Township; [blank]
Peters Township; Constables- Rowland Harris; supervisors of roads- John
McCoy, Robt Taggart; Overseers of Poor- Thomas McDowell,
Alexr. Wilson
Rye Township; Constables- John Black Junr.; supervisors of roads- William
Robinson, Richd. Colter; Overseers of Poor- Michael Marshal,
Robert Johnston
Teboyne Township; Constables- Samuel Glas; supervisors of roads- Robert
Adams, Samuel Lemon; Overseers of Poor- James Miller, William
Anderson
Tyrone Township; Constables- John Dunbar; supervisors of roads- Geo.
Hamilton, James Devin; Overseers of Poor- Robert Irwin, Benjamin
Junken
Westpennb Township; Constables- Patrick Wallace; supervisors of roads- __
Grahams, Michl Kiner; Overseers of Poor- John Denny, James
Carrothers

Washington Township; Constables- Roger Hart; supervisors of roads- David Stoner, William Irwin; Overseers of Poor- Frederick Foreman, James Moorhead

Page 286
Process to July Session 1780
Daniel Davidson, Alexr. Graham, Michl. Gillispie, Michl. Gillispie, John Rhea et al. John Rhea & McCann, Jno. Immel & Math Skeel, Edwd. O'Donnal

April Sessions 1781
Danl. Davidson, Michl. Gillipsie, John Rhea et al, Jno. Rhea & McCann, Ricd. Gabriel & George Slover, Irwin & Gill, Alex. Graham

Process to July Sessions 1781
Alexr. Graham, John Rhea, Rhea & McCann, Archd. Keminy, Stephen Winslow, Corn. Murphy, Michael Gillispie,

Process to October Sessions 1781
Alexr. Graham, John Rhea, Rhea & McCann, James Lamb, Sam. Paxton & __ Blair, Martin Doyle, Corn. Murphy, James Burns, William Kennedy, Jno. Stuart & Jno. Ferguson, Danl. Neven & Alexr. Starret, Paul Martin & David Starret, Nathan Wyland & Joseph Vance, John Brownfield & Benj. Dysert, Thos. Henderson, Richr. Gabriel & Hoover, William Irwin & Gibbs, Hugh Duff

Page 287
Process to January Sessions 1782
Brown & Taylor, Gibson & Gordon, Jacob Harsberg, James Lamb, Jas. Paxton & Jas Blair, Cornl. Murphy, Martin Doyle, Atkinson & Gutherie, Negro Jack

Process to April 1782
Samuel Dukey, The same, Murry Brown, Robert Taylor, Charles Cohan, James Baskens, Jas. Paxton & James Blair, James Lamb, Cornilius Murphy, Matthew Atkinson

Process to July 1782
Robert Taylor, Ezekiel Sample, John Rhea, Rhea & McCann, Alexr. Grahams

Page 288
At a Court of Private Sessions, at Carlisle, 26 March 1781, before James Oliver, Samuel Laird, John Trindle and Thomas Kennedy.
Antrim township; constable- Michael McAnulty; overseers of road- Thos. Johnston, Christ. Widener; overseers of poor- Wm. Rankin, Henry Snivly

Armagh township; constable- John McArnet (?); overseers of road- John
Campbel, Mathew Taylor; overseers of poor- James Class, James
Huston
Allen township; constable- William Brooks; overseers of road- Frederick
Swiser, John Greer; overseers of poor- Jacob Holeman, Jacob Knoop
Carlisle township; constable- James Ramsey; overseers of poor- Andw.
Colhoon, John Henry
Derry township; constalbe- Hugh Magill; overseers of road- Colus Gonsalus,
Geo. Rotherick; overseers of poor- Matthew Kelly, Alexr.
McKinstry
East Pennsbro township; constable- Henry Clayton; overseers of road- Simon
Crouse, Joseph McClure; overseers of poor- Jno. Carrothers, Martin
Longstaff
Fannet township; constable- Saml. Walker; overseers of road- John Ward, John
Noble; overseers of poor- Wm. Query, Rob. Elder
Fermanagh township; constable- Christ. Lintner; overseers of road- David
Martin, Will. Thompson; overseers of poor- Wm. McCoy, Rot.
Thompson

Page 289

Greenwood township; constables- John Houtz; overseers of roads- Acquhla (?)
Burchfield, Marcus Hulan; overseers of poor- Saml. Reed, Joshua
North
Guilford township; constable- George Greeinker; overseers of roads- Wm.
Brotherston, David Adams; overseers of poor- John Thorn, Edw.
Crawford Junr
Hamilton township; constable- Thoms. Knox; overseers of roads- Nath.
Highland, Joseph Vance; overseers of poor- David Shields, Wm.
Thompson
Hopewell township; constable- Robert Hamil, overseers of roads- John
Brownfield, Benj. Dyert; overseeers of poor- Jams. Cummin, Jas.
McCune
Lurgan township; constable- Samuel Cox; overseers of roads- Danl Neiven,
Alexr. Starret; overseers of poor- Thos. McComb, Thos. Montgomery
Letterkenny township; constable- Hugh Torrence; overseer of roads- John
Ferguson, John Stuart; overseers of poor- Hugh Wiley Senr., Hugh
Wiley Junr
Lack township; constable- Edwe. Thatcher; overseers of roads- John Arbuckle,
David Beales; overseers of poor- Jno McConnell, William Work
Middleton township; constable- Dasper Diller, Frederick Dowey, dept;
overseers of roads- Thos. Henderson, Adam Ritchey; overseers of
poor- Chas. McClure, Nathan Wilson
Millford township; constable- John Boner; overseers of roads- John Hamilton,
John Williams; overseers of poor- Thos. Harris, Alexr. Robinson
Newtown township; constable- Samuel Morrow; overseers of roads- Paul
Martin, Wm. Starret; overseers of poor- William Walker, John
Schooler

Peters township; constable- Richard Beard; overseers of roads- Joseph Irwin,
Hugh Gibson; overseers of poor- John Welch, Wm. Hays
Rye township; constable- Isaac Jones; overseers of roads- Saml. Gowdey, Wm.
Graham; overseers of poor- Henry Bull, John Curry
Tyrone township; constable- Peter Stone; overseers of roads- Chas. Stuart,
Arch. Kinkead; overseers of poor Jno. Buchanan, John Linsson (?)
West pennsbro township; constable- David Murdy; overseers of roads- Robt.
Semple, Wm. Simons; overseers of poor- Wm. Galbraith, Robt.
Patterson
Teboyne township; constable- John Gardiner; overseers of roads- James
Armstrong, James Blaine; overseers of poor- William Gardiner, Thos.
Blaine
Washington township; constable- Henry Thomas
Montgomery township; constable- Jno. Cunningham; overseers of roads- John
Rea, Wm. Loring; overseers of poor- Jas. Cross, John Kennedy

Page 290 - 291- blank

Page 292
At a Court of Private Sessions, at Carlisle, 25 March 1782, before James Oliver,
John Trindle, Samuel Laird, Thomas Kennedy
Antrim township; constable- Andw. Gibson Senr; overseers of road- Samuel
McCulloch, Henry Stall; overseers of poor- William Ranken, Henry
Snively
Allen township; constable- Joseph McMeen; overseers of roads- John Fleming,
John Mateer; overseers of poor- William Mateer, William Hartnes
Armagh township; constable- Joseph McKibben; overseers of roads- John
Davis, James Scot; overseers of poor- James Glass, Jams. Hurton
East pennsburgh township; constable- John Montgomery; overseers of roads-
James Bell, Thomas Fisher; overseers of poor- Jas. McCormick,
Michael Cunkle
Derry township; constable- Francis Pierce; overseers of roads- George Seigler,
Jo. Westbrook; overseers of poor- John Means. John Glasgow
Carlisle township; constable- Abm. Loughridge; overseers of roads; Abram
McGeehan, James Davis; overseers of poor- John Hunter, Thoms.
Forster
Fermanagh township; constable- Sylvanus Moss; overseers of roads- David
Martin, William Thompson; overseers of poor- William McCoy,
Robt. Thompson
Fannet township; constable- Randle Alexander; overseers of roads- Thos.
Armstrong, John McClure; overseers of poor- Andrew Miller,
William McKibben

Page 305

At a court of private Sessions, at Carlisle, 25 Mar 1785, appointment officers.
Allen Township; constable- Adam Weaver; supervisors roads- Abraham Hide,
James McDonell; overseers poor- James McCurdy, John Wolf
Armagh Township; constable- James Gold; supervisors roads- Neal
McMonegal, Hugh McClelland; overseers poor- Alexander Cochran,
Joseph Harlet
Carlisle Township; constable- James Rowney; John Holmes, John
Montgomery; overseers poor- Robert Semple, Jacob Creaber
Derry Township; constable- Christr. Martin; supervisors roads- John Mc_eaver,
Wm. Frampton; overseers poor- George Seigler, Daniel _
East Penns. Township; constable- David Hoge; supervisors roads- Joseph
Junken, Michael Dell; overseers poor- James McKinsty, Thomas
Fisher
Fermanagh Township; constable- John Tennis; supervisors roads- Saml. Mc__,
Christ. Snider; overseers poor- James Marklen, Edward McConnell
Hopewell Township; constable- William Piper; supervisors roads- James
Young, Adam McCormick; overseers poor- James Sharp, Andrew
Thompson
Lack Township; constable- John McIntyre; supervisors roads- John Fleming,
Neal McCoy; overseers poor- Daniel McCohheon, John Stone
Middleton Township; constable- Jacob Wagoner; supervisors roads- Michael
Ege, John Templeton; overseers poor- David Williamson, Jeremiah
Wolf
Millford Township; constable- John Williams; supervisors roads- Hugh Hardy,
James Harrell; overseers poor- Joseph McCoy, James Perman
Newtown Township; constable- James McCowen; supervisors roads- Alexr.
Thompson, Andrew Denniston; overseers poor- Joseph McIllwain,
Nathan Gillespie
Rye Township; constable- Saml Gowdy; supervisors roads- Francis McCowen,
Isaac Jones; overseers poor- William Robinson, Archibald Homes
Shippensburgh Township; constable- Jacob Millison; supervisors roads-
William Rippy, Robert Doweway; overseers poor- Francis Campbell,
Alexander Pubbs
Tyrone Township; constable- Hance Ferguson; supervisors roads- James
Sharron, George Douglas; overseers poor- Alexr. Sanderson, John
Davidson
Teboyne Township; constable- Andrew Everhart; supervisors roads- Robert
Hunter, Robert Clark; overseers poor- Robert Pollock, Jams.
Armstrong
West Pennsburgh Township; constable- Thomas Greer; supervisors roads-
Hugh Pallon, Saml. Weakley; overseers poor- John Davidson,
Edward Hickley
Wayne Township   [blank]

Page 307

"Accounting of public and private roads petitioned for, commencing 1772"
Beginning at James Smith's mill to fall into the Walnut Bottom road.
Beginning at Carlisle, from thence to Harris' Ferry.
Beginning at Carlisle, from thence to Forty Shillings Gap.
Beginning at John Work's in Peters Township, from thence to Archibald Irwins.
Beginning at Falling Spring Meeting House, to Rocky Spring Meeting House.
Beginning at the Rev. John Lang's to meetinghouse at William Rankin's.
Beginning at Conoguinet Creek to Schooler's Mill, confirmed.
Beginning at Capt. Calendat's Mill by the Iron works to Mahaffy's Gap.
Beginning at Logan's Gap in Armagh township to William Miller's confirmed.
Beginning at the late dwelling of John McClure to Joseph Weakley and Trent's Gap, confirmed.
Beginning at Hugh Torrens to Schooler, and from thence to Carlisle, confirmed July Sessions, 1772.
Beginning at the house of Andrew Holmes, to Carlisle.
Beginning at Wort's Mill to Baskins Ferry on the Susquehanna.
Beginning at the North end of Bedford street in Carlisle to Crane's Gap.
Beginning at Three Square Hollow to Roler's mill, from thence to Smith's Gap.
Beginning at Carlistle to the mill of John Holmes, Esq., by Capt. Thompson's.
Beginning at John McClure's gap road to the Baltimore Gap in Trent's Gap.
Beginning at Fort Shillings Gap to Carlisle.
Beginning near Logan's Gap to William Miller's.
Beginning at William McDowells to the Rev. William King's meeting house.
Beginning at Andrew Armstrong's to Capt. Callender's mill.
Beginning at William Parks, past Beatty's, to Andrew Mullen's road.
Beginning at McCommon's Gap to Black's Gap.
Beginning at Pitt Street, to Hurley's Gap by David Williamson's fording.
Beginning at the walnut Bottom road, to Smith's mill, confirmed.
Beginning at Three Square Hollow, to Smith's Gap, confirmed.
Beginning at Bedford Street, in Carlisle, to Crane's Gap, confirmed.
Beginning at Robert Mickey's to Shippensburg.

Account of roads confirmed commencing January 7, 1773
Beginning at Falling Spring Meeting House to Rocky Spring.
Beginning at Rev. Lang's to the Meeting House at Rankin's.
Beginning at Pitt Street to hurley's Gap.
Beginning at McDowell's mill to William King's meeting house.
Beginning at Andrew Armstrong's to Callender's mill.
Beginning at Yellowbreeches west of James Beatty's House.

April Sessions 1773
Beginning at the road leading near Carlisle to McAllaster's, (Roxbury), by Mickey's.
Beginning at Susquehanna to intersect the road leading from Carlisle.

Beginning at North Mountain, Shippensburg, road to Black's Gap.

July Sessions 1773
Beginning at post near Mr. Montgomery's field to the road from Byers to McAllasters.

October Sessions 1773
Beginning at Jonathan Holmes to Wilson's mill.
Beginning at Pitt Street to the meadow of John Armstrong, Esq.

January Sessions 1774
Beginning at Patrick Jack's mill to the road leading through Black's Gap.
Beginning at a road leading from Carlisle to Shippensburg to Blain's mill.
Beginning at south end of Hanover Street to Mr. Laird's mill and Craigheads.
Beginning at Samuel Harper's to main road from Fort Shillings gap to Carlisle.

April Sessions 1774
Beginning at Mercer's mill to great road leading to Baltimore.
Beginning at Elliott's run to the great road at James Bell's.
Beginning at Fleming's and from thence to Kepler's.
Beginning at Robert McCord's and from thence to Maryland line.
Beginning at John Montgomery's East Pennsborough, to the road leading from Carlisle to Harri's Ferry.

July Session 1774
Beginning at the road from Carlisle to Trent's Gap, from thence to Charles McClure's.
Beginning at Tarr's mill to Conococheague creek near Foreheller's.
Beginning at Carlisle Iron Works to Letort Spring.

October 1774
Beginning at Albert Torrence's in Letterkenny township.
Beginning at the great road to Juniata river, thence to McClellan's.
Beginning at the end of Hanover street, to Craighead's road.
Beginning at Joseph Raskin's to James Gallagher's on Juniata.

July 1775
Beginning at William Logan's to David Beales' Mill.

January Session 1776
Beginning at a gap in Martin Bowers land to the road leading to Crane's Gap.

309

Index

Abbreviated given names are indexed under the full given name spelling; "Benj." is indexed under "Benjamin," "Wm." under "William," "Jas." under "James," etc. Surnames are grouped together under the most frequently used spelling, for example; Abernethy includes Abernethy, Aberthany, Abethenathy. Be sure to check all variant spellings.

Ranken, Thomas, 146,
147
William, 217, 304
Rankin, 306
James, 64, 134, 136,
295
Joseph, 288
Richard, 2, 22, 32, 58,
84, 85, 87, 99, 100,
123-126, 136, 137
Robert, 34
Thomas, 5, 7, 12, 23,
39, 45
William, 4, 51, 58, 74,
106, 155, 161, 196,
239, 245, 302, 306
Ranklin, William, 196
Rannells, John, 54, 164,
257, 289, 298
William, 219
Rannicks, Samuel, 219
Ransey, James, 69, 89,
109
Rarmicks, Samuel, 279
Rarron, Joseph, 12
Raskin, Joseph, 307
Raugh, William, 122
Ray, William, 81
Rea, John, 304
Saml, 301
Read, James, 8, 13, 15,
26, 27, 197
John, 13, 23, 171, 172
John, Jr., 13, 23
William, 13, 15
Reads, Joseph, 113
Reaney, William, 44, 110
Rearty (?), James, 10
Red Rock, 132
Red Stone Creek, 142
Reddick, David, 261, 264,
269, 275, 283
John, 252
Reddy, Alex, 189
James, 269
Redmon, William, 156
Reec, Jeremiah, 241
Reed, Andrew, 231
Casper, 98
Daniel, 42
David, 110, 113
James, 14, 65, 177, 188,
197, 241
John, 39, 188, 228

John, Jr., 22
Paul, 298
Robert, 49
Saml, 303
Thomas, 253
William, 14
Reeds, James, 105, 143
Rees, Abiah, 109
Jeremiah, 95
Reese, Isiah, 228
Jeremiah, 60, 117, 231,
235
Remick, Samuel, 278
Reney, William, 89, 90
Renken, James, 144
Thomas, 149
Renkin, James, 297
John, 278
Renkins, William, 217
Rennell, John, 133
Rennells, James, 122, 135,
145
John, 9, 140, 156, 288,
289, 294
William, 101, 112, 216
Rennels, Joseph, 9
Rennox, Samuel, 231
Reock, Saml, 60
Reppey, William, 112
Rerces, Paul, 163
Reynolds, James, 26, 27,
297
John, 1, 6, 48, 106, 133,
151, 173
Mary, 11
Robert, 15
Sarah, 60
Thomas, 151, 182
William, 26, 27, 61, 66,
71, 276
Rhea, 302
John, 98, 298, 302
Rhoades, John, 131
Richardson, William, 98,
153, 216, 224, 235,
241, 272, 297, 298
Richson, Edmond, 241
Rickenbough, John, 179
John, Jr., 179
John, Sr., 179
Riddick, David, 263
Riddle, William, 9, 19,
31, 47-50, 147, 301
Ride, William, 34

Ridle, William, 26, 34
Rie township, 98, 123
Riley, John, 220
William, 91
Rio (?), Benjamin, 49
Rippeth, James, 242
Rippey, Samuel, 13, 36,
41, 52, 57, 61, 112,
113, 155, 267
William, 112, 155,
167, 278
Ripply, William, 80
Rippy, Samuel, 10
William, 113, 208,
228, 305
Ritchey, Adam, 303
Roack, John, 219
Road, Wm, 21
Roades, John, 131
Rob, Robert, 123
Robb, James, 21, 42, 58,
78, 90
John, 8, 9, 14, 131
Robert, 19, 36, 41, 45,
58, 66, 72, 77-78,
115, 130, 151, 191,
216
Robbard, Robert, 39
Robbs, Robert, 152, 202,
212
Robbs Fording, 176
Roberson, Andrew, 241
Robert, James, 89
Roberts, Thomas, 284
Robertson, James, 241
Robeson, James, 10
Robert, 244
Robins, Patrick, 22
Robinson, Adam, 74, 219
Alexander, 32, 33, 123,
189, 265, 303
George, 33, 38, 52, 74,
86, 98, 140, 276,
281, 289
James, 136, 219
John, 26, 27, 62, 93,
225, 226, 270, 274
Jon, 274
Patrick, 22, 23
Robert, 86, 153, 235
Samuel, 85
Stewart, 139
Thomas, 89
Will, 156